THE *Idiot* GARDENER'S HANDBOOK

Dedication

To John and his patience,
which only once or twice
wore a little thin!

THE *Idiot* GARDENER'S HANDBOOK

Daphne Ledward

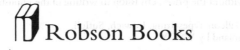
Robson Books

This revised edition first published in 1995

First published in Great Britain in hardback in 1985 by Robson
Books Ltd, Bolsover House, 5–6 Clipstone Street, London W1P 8LE,
as *Simply Gardening*. Robson paperback edition first published in 1987.

Copyright © 1985, 1995 Daphne Ledward

British Library Cataloguing in Publication Data
A catalogue record for this title is available from the British Library

ISBN 0 86051 899 X

Typeset by Galleon Typesetting, Ipswich, Suffolk
Printed in Finland by WSOY

CONTENTS

ACKNOWLEDGEMENTS

Over the years I have received a great deal of advice and information from firms, organizations and enthusiasts, too numerous to mention, who have helped me to sort out my ideas and put this book together, so my grateful thanks to you if you are among these. I would like to express my appreciation to my husband, John, for his help with the photographic material, and also those who were kind enough to allow us to photograph the gardens featured in the colour plates, especially Bridgemere™ Nurseries, Mr and Mrs Swarbrick, Mr and Mrs Head, Colgrave's Seeds and Mr and Mrs Ferguson. Thanks must also go to Anglian Water Services for allowing me to reproduce the plan for the Water Conservation Garden on pages 366–7. Last, but not least, my gratitude to my publishers, who have managed to sort out my ramblings and hieroglyphics so efficiently.

INTRODUCTION

I am a self-taught gardener, and proud of it. The advice I give is that which has been learned through trial and error, and while it may not always coincide with that found in horticultural textbooks, through experience I have found it has worked for me.

There is no such thing as 'green fingers' – of that I am sure. Being a successful gardener is not a gift possessed only by a chosen few. All that is needed is a keen interest in living plants, the ability to see how much they can do in the right hands to brighten our lives, and an enquiring mind. Good gardening skills are not hereditary. Neither of my parents ever knew much about growing things, though they had the capability to appreciate a beautiful plant or a pretty garden. Yet my love of gardening began at three years old, at the moment when a packet of sown lettuce seeds (admittedly with a little help!) emerged as a straight row of tiny green plants.

When I became well and truly bitten by the gardening bug, in my late teens, there was not the huge selection of gardening books around that there is today, in the wake of the burgeoning interest in gardening as a leisure activity. The ones that did exist were fairly weighty, and though they got me started, most of them assumed some basic knowledge of, for instance, biology, geology and geography, to say nothing of garden tools and simple horticultural techniques. They were also fairly unattractive at first glance – certainly not designed to awaken an almost unconscious curiosity about the subject.

Today, these useful but stodgy all-in-one manuals have largely given way to coffee-table photographic masterpieces – lovely to flip through but generally not much use for getting you started when faced for the first time with a piece of land and the feeling that you simply do not know where to begin.

When I started writing *Simply Gardening* (later reprinted as *The Idiot Gardener's Handbook*) over a decade ago, it was my intention to bridge this gap between heavy reading and pictures without information. Ten years on, although my original approach remains the same, methods have moved on, attitudes towards the environment have undergone a revolution and the general outlook is very different, so it has become necessary to rewrite this book substantially for a new generation of gardeners-in-the-making.

But perhaps the most obvious change since this book was first published is that now, more than ever, people *want* to garden. The feeling that it has to be done as a necessary evil is becoming very much a thing of the past. You have only to visit a garden centre on a Sunday afternoon to see how more and more people are choosing to spend their spare time. So many of these are self-confessed idiots where gardening is concerned, easy prey to those ready to sell them unsuitable plants, inappropriate accessories, unnecessary chemicals or inessential tools.

So if you feel you need leading by the hand through what appears to be the potential 'minefield' of gardening, this book is written especially for you.

Daphne Ledward

1

SOME GARDENING TERMS

The problem with many gardening books and programmes is that they tend to *assume* that you understand all the terms associated with the subject, whereas in truth even the most experienced gardener sometimes has to check on definitions. You should find most words and expressions you are likely to encounter in the following glossary. (*Words in small capitals in the text are defined in more detail elsewhere in this section under their own headings.*)

ACID, ACIDITY Most substances are either acid, alkaline or neutral. Acidity is measured on the pH scale, the term pH referring to the percentage of hydrogen ions in the material. Things are neutral at pH7; numbers above 7 indicate that a substance is alkaline, figures below mean it is acid. The right quantity of an alkaline compound can neutralize an acid one, and vice versa. It is important to know if a SOIL, potting COMPOST, or even WATER is acid, alkaline or neutral, as the pH value can affect the type of plant intended to be grown.

Some plants will only thrive in an acid soil and cannot tolerate the alkaline conditions found in the presence of LIME. These are known as CALCIFUGES and examples are heathers and rhododendrons. Other plants (e.g. cabbages) are CALCICOLES – that is, they prefer an alkaline soil – and there are plants which will do well in either. The pH of a soil can be checked by means of a chemical soil-testing kit or meter; if the soil is found to be unsuitable to grow a particular type of plant, substances can be added to it to adjust the pH.

AERATION   Introducing air between the particles of a SOIL by digging, forking, spiking, etc., to encourage healthy growth of the ROOTS and allow beneficial BACTERIA to break down decaying materials into plant foods.

AEROBIC   *See* BACTERIA.

ALGAE   Primitive plants usually seen in the garden in the form of green slime on paths and clay pots, green water and blanket weed in ponds.

ALKALINE   *See* ACID.

ALPINE   Technically a plant whose natural habitat is a mountainous region, but the term has become used to describe many more types of plant suitable for planting in a ROCKERY. *See also* ROCK PLANTS.

ANAEROBIC   *See* BACTERIA.

ANNUAL   A plant which completes the cycle of GERMINATION, maturing, flowering, seeding and finally dying in the period of one year. Many PERENNIAL plants, such as antirrhinums and fibrous-rooted begonias, are treated as annuals as they are at their best in their first year. Bedding geraniums now fit into this category as good plants of new VARIETIES can be easily grown from SEED using nothing more elaborate than the kitchen windowsill.

   HARDY annuals (HA) originate in temperate climates such as our own so they are not damaged by cold weather and can be sown direct into their flowering positions outside. They can therefore spend the whole of their lifespan in the open garden (e.g. Virginian stock, candytuft). HALF-HARDY annuals (HHA) come from warmer climates than that of the United Kingdom. They are damaged or killed by FROST and the SEED needs a higher temperature for GERMINATION. They therefore have to be raised in a heated GREENHOUSE or similar and kept there until all chance of frost has passed (e.g. lobelia, salvia).

ANTHER   The part of a FLOWER producing POLLEN grains

which in turn produce the male cells for FERTILIZATION; these fuse with the female cells, ultimately to develop into a SEED.
AQUATIC PLANTS   Those growing in water.

BACTERIA   These are microscopic primitive organisms existing in their countless millions everywhere. SOIL contains vast numbers of them, mostly beneficial to plants. *Aerobic* bacteria require air to exist and break down decaying matter in the soil into soluble foods which can be taken up for healthy plant growth by the ROOTS. *Anaerobic* bacteria can live without air, generally thrive in soggy SOUR SOIL and conditions of poor CULTIVATION, and sometimes do more harm to plants than good. Other less desirable members of the bacterial fraternity can cause DISEASES in plants, but, in general, bacteria are some of a gardener's best friends.
BARE ROOT   plants dug out of the ground during the DORMANT season (usually late autumn to early spring) to TRANSPLANT them are known as *bare root plants*. Because the plants run a risk of their growth being checked by this method, many commercial growers now use CONTAINERS, or offer plants with a protected ROOTBALL.
BARK   The outer protective layer of the mature STEMS of woody plants, usually brown, but sometimes other quite spectacular colours and often of interesting textures, for which two reasons alone many ORNAMENTAL plants are grown.

Bark from stripped timber is now being shredded or pulverized and compressed and sold for MULCHING purposes, or as a substitute for PEAT.
BED   Usually an island area of SOIL in a garden, for stocking with ORNAMENTAL plants, or sometimes edible crops. It can be surrounded by LAWN, paving, gravel, or other decorative surfacing and can be edged with a dwarf HEDGE, or with bricks, tiles, or similar.
BEDDING PLANTS   Those usually raised in SEED TRAYS under GLASS or in NURSERY beds and planted out in a mass for temporary display – this is known as a *bedding scheme*. Bedding plants are usually planted out in the autumn for a spring display (e.g. wallflowers, forget-me-nots) or in late spring and early summer for the summer and early autumn period (e.g., French marigolds, stocks, petunias). A winter bedding scheme of HARDY winter-flowering pansies has become very popular.

BERRY Technically, this is a SEED or seeds enclosed in a juicy pulp (e.g., tomato). Just to confuse the issue, the fruits we call berries (raspberries, blackberries and the like) are correctly known as *drupes*, but by regular usage the term 'berry' has become applied to many SOFT FRUITS that are botanically not berries at all.

BIENNIAL A plant which in one year undergoes GERMI-NATION and develops LEAVES; FLOWERS and SEEDS in its second year and then dies (e.g., foxgloves, carrots, cabbages). Many PERENNIALS are best treated as biennials (e.g., wallflowers and sweet williams). These are sown one year and encouraged to make sturdy unflowered plants that season, for replanting in BEDDING schemes to flower the following year, after which they are replaced. Left to their own devices they will continue to grow and flower every year but will gradually get more and more straggly and unmanageable, hence it is better to pull them up after their first year's flowering and start again.

BLANCHING If a green plant is put into darkness by covering it with some light-excluding material or soil, it loses its green colour and turns white. This is often done to certain VEGETABLES (e.g., leeks, chicory, celery) to make them sweeter and more tender.

BLEEDING The leaking of SAP from a wound when a plant is cut or damaged. It often occurs when PRUNING is done if a plant is not fully DORMANT and the sap is rising. It is not usually harmful, unless it is excessive; and can be stopped by applying cigarette ash to a small cut, or a sealing compound (or even oil-based paint) to a large one.

BLIND A plant is said to be 'blind' when it stops growing at the GROWING TIP. This usually occurs after an injury of some sort. ORNAMENTAL plants will usually bush out from BUDS lower down the STEM, VEGETABLES should be scrapped. This term is also applied to flowering plants which fail to flower for some reason.

BLOOM Another term for BLOSSOM, or FLOWER. It can also refer to a waxy or powdery coating on some FRUIT (e.g., grapes and plums).

BLOSSOM A FLOWER or a collection of flowers.

BOLTING This occurs when a VEGETABLE produces its FLOWER prematurely, and, in doing so, becomes unusable. It generally follows a check in growth, caused by something

14

such as drought or ROOT rot, and should not happen under conditions of good CULTIVATION.

BORDER An area of planted-up ground running around the *edge* of a feature such as a LAWN or paving.

BOTTOM HEAT The application of warmth to SOIL or potting COMPOST from below, these days usually by means of soil-warming cables such as those incorporated into heated PROPAGATORS. The warm soil encourages the GERMINATION of certain SEEDS, and the speeding up of the formation of the ROOTS in CUTTINGS.

BRANCH Woody SHOOTS of a TREE or SHRUB not forming a single TRUNK in the case of a shrub, and usually growing from the upper part of the trunk in the case of a tree.

BRASSICA A member of the cabbage family (e.g., Brussels sprout, cauliflower, wallflower stock).

BREAK The formation of side-SHOOTS in a plant. Also a BUD at the moment of its opening is said to be *breaking*.

BROADCASTING Scattering SEED all over an area (for example, when seeding a LAWN), instead of SOWing in straight lines.

BROAD-LEAVED A term used to describe plants with broad, flattish LEAVES, instead of spike or sword-like ones (e.g., GRASSES) or needles (like some CONIFERS).

BUD The part of a plant containing embryo LEAVES, FLOWERS and/or STEMS.

BUDDING The implanting of a growth BUD in the BARK or outer layer of STEM of another plant. The resultant plant will have the characteristic FLOWERS and LEAVES of the plant from which the bud was removed, but the growth habit or vigour of the ROOTSTOCK. This is still the most widely used method of PROPAGATING roses.

BULB This is strictly speaking a swollen, modified leaf base which acts as a food storage organ for the plant during its DORMANT period (e.g., daffodil). Like the term BERRY, the definition of the word *bulb* has been widened to refer to any fleshy modified STEMS such as those produced by gladioli and crocuses (which are really CORMS), and ROOTS, like those of the dahlia and some begonias (which are actually TUBERS).

BUSH A woody plant with a group of STEMS, as opposed to a TREE, which usually has only one STEM, or TRUNK. In gardening terms, the word *bush* is generally used in connection with roses and fruit, the word SHRUB being applied to the remainder.

BUSH FRUITS These are produced on low BUSHES (e.g., currants).

CALCICOLE A plant that thrives on an alkaline soil. *See also* ACID *and* LIME.

CALCIFUGE A plant that needs an ACID soil.

CALYX A whorl of modified leaves forming the outer case of bud or envelope of flower.

CANE A thin STAKE, usually made of bamboo, used to steady or TRAIN plants. Also a long, cane-like STEM produced by certain plants (e.g., blackberry).

CANE FRUITS Types of fruit bushes producing CANE-like STEMS (e.g., blackberry, raspberry).

CHITTING The practice of letting certain plants (e.g., potatoes) SPROUT before being planted.

CHLOROPHYLL The green pigment in most plants which combines WATER (in SAP) and carbon dioxide from the air in the presence of sunlight to produce sugars to feed the plant, during which process oxygen is given off as a waste product. If a plant loses its natural green colour and begins to turn yellow, it is said to be *chlorotic*. This condition is often caused by a lack of available iron and magnesium in the SOIL, and frequently happens with CALCIFUGES, as these minerals are 'locked up' in a soil with a high pH in a form which the plants cannot absorb.

CLAY A soil made up of minute particles of mineral rock.

CLOCHE A portable structure of glass or other transparent material (e.g., PVC, polythene), used to protect early crops against bad weather and to encourage earlier maturing.

COCOA SHELL The outer husk of the chocolate bean, which makes an excellent mulch.

COIR The outer covering of the coconut. Originally used as matting, it is now composted as a substitute for PEAT, or woven into hanging basket liners.

COLD FRAME *See* FRAME.

COMPOST This word has two totally different meanings which are often confused. It can refer to garden or kitchen refuse which has been rotted down in a *heap* or *bin* and is dug in as a useful SOIL improver. It can also mean a mixture based on PEAT or PEAT SUBSTITUTE sometimes containing good quality LOAM) into which SEEDS are sown, CUTTINGS struck (*see* STRIKE) and plants potted (*see* POTTING).

CONIFER A type of EVERGREEN, which usually (though not always) produces its SEED in structures called *cones*. They generally have specially-shaped LEAVES, often needle-like.

CONTAINER A receptacle in which a plant or plants are grown independent of the open ground. A container can be almost anything from an antique stone urn to an old bucket. In recent years 'containerization' has become a popular way of growing NURSERY STOCK for replanting and resale. By this method, until they are ready for planting in their permanent positions, plants are grown from the SEED or CUTTING stage in a series of containers of increasing size, POTTING ON into larger ones as they grow bigger, instead of being raised in the OPEN GROUND and dug up for replanting. In this way, when the plants are eventually ready to PLANT OUT, they suffer the minimum of disturbance and consequently re-establish themselves more quickly.

CORDON A method of TRAINING a plant, usually a fruit BUSH or TREE. Instead of allowing it to branch naturally, growth is usually restricted to one, though sometimes to two or three STEMS supported by CANES and/or wires. The main purpose is to enable more than one VARIETY to be grown in a small space.

CORM A swollen modified STEM base with a similar function to that of a BULB (e.g., crocus).

CROWN The top part of the ROOTS, from which SHOOTS emerge. Also the mass of BRANCHES at the top of the TRUNK of a TREE.

CULTIVAR See VARIETY.

CULTIVATION Working land or soil for the purpose of growing plants on it; also giving active attention to the growth of plants or crops.

CUTTING A piece of a plant removed from the parent and prepared in some way, which will eventually grow ROOTS and SHOOTS of its own and develop into a new independent plant.

DEAD-HEADING The practice of removing dead FLOWER heads. This serves two purposes – to tidy up the plant and to encourage the production of further flowers.

DECIDUOUS Plants that lose all their LEAVES once a year, usually in winter.

DISEASE   A plant illness not directly caused by PESTS. Usual causes of disease amongst plants are FUNGI, BACTERIA and VIRUSES.

DISORDER   A plant malfunction not caused by PESTS or DISEASE. Unsuitable growing conditions, bad CULTIVATION and SOIL deficiencies are all responsible for plant disorders.

DIVIDE   To split a plant into several sections, each having its own portion of ROOTS, for PROPAGATION purposes.

DORMANT   When a plant is in a state of rest. In plants, growth and other functions are much reduced and in a DECIDUOUS plant the LEAVES fall off. Dormancy usually occurs in winter and is the best time to TRANSPLANT as a plant is less likely to sustain a shock to the system while at its least active.

DRESSING   A substance supplying plant foods applied dry to a SOIL. *Top dressings* are added to the surface, *base dressings* are incorporated into the soil when digging.

DRILL   A channel made in SOIL into which SEEDS are SOWN, and then covered up. Also an appliance for sowing seeds.

DUST   A PEST or DISEASE control applied to a plant or the SOIL as a fine, dry dust as opposed to a liquid SPRAY.

DWARF   A plant of naturally small and slow-growing habit.

ERICACEOUS PLANTS   Plants belonging to the heather FAMILY, including rhododendrons, which are CALCIFUGES and therefore require special growing conditions in an ACID SOIL, preferably one containing some PEAT.

ESPALIER   A method of TRAINING plants, mainly apples and pears, which are then themselves known as 'espaliers' where the BRANCHES are trained out horizontally at approximately 15-inch (400 mm) intervals, usually along wires for support. Espalier-trained trees are ideal for planting against walls, as the warmth from the wall helps make the fruit, and also the wood, RIPE, so making the wood more FROST resistant. Espaliers also make a useful division or screen between different parts of a garden.

EVERGREEN   Plants which do not shed all their LEAVES at once at a certain time of the year. They do lose leaves, but gradually, a few, usually the oldest, at a time – so the plant never becomes totally bare as DECIDUOUS plants do.

EYE   A growth BUD, usually DORMANT, from which new growth is capable of arising.

F1 HYBRIDS   The first generation from a cross between two plants. This expression has come to refer to plants raised in this way by plant breeders from specially selected parents. SEED so obtained is usually expensive because of the amount of effort which has gone into its production, but the resultant plants are very strong and healthy (this is known as *hybrid vigour*), with special characteristics purposely bred into them. Seed from F1 hybrids will not breed true to the parent plants; the resulting SEEDLINGS are known as *F2 hybrids* and usually turn out to be a pretty motley crew, though not, in many cases, without their own merits.

FAMILY   A group of several genera (*see* GENUS) of plants. For example the rose family (Rosaceae) contains many smaller groups (genera) such as *malus* (apples), *pyracantha* (firethorn) and *cotoneaster*, all with basically similar characteristics.

FAMILY TREE   One where more than one VARIETY has been GRAFTED on to one ROOTSTOCK. This is often done with apples and pears, to enable several sorts to be grown on one tree when space is limited.

FAN   A method of shaping certain plants, often plums, peaches and figs, in which branches are TRAINED into a flat fan-shape and supported by a fence, wall or similar means.

FARMYARD MANURE   Animal excreta and straw or other bedding materials, partially rotted down, which is a rich source of HUMUS and plant foods when incorporated into SOIL.

FASTIGIATE   A TREE with an erect growth habit, such as the Lombardy poplar.

FEATHERED   You will sometimes encounter this expression in NURSERY catalogues. It means a young TREE with BRANCHES growing right down the STEM, instead of having a clear TRUNK.

FERN   A rather primitive group of green plants which do not flower, and reproduce themselves by spores instead of SEEDS.

FERTILE   A plant is fertile if it is capable of producing SEED. SOIL is fertile if it is of good texture, rich in HUMUS, beneficial organisms and plant nutrients, and thus able to support strong, healthy plants.

FERTILIZATION   The fusion of a male and female cell. In the case of plants, this happy event ultimately produces a SEED.

19

FERTILIZER　A compound providing plant foods, usually in a concentrated form.

FILAMENT　The part of the male organ of a FLOWER supporting the ANTHER.

FLESHY-ROOTED　Plants with thick, fleshy ROOTS.

FLOWER　The sex organs of a plant, usually surrounded by a protective ring of often eye-catching PETALS and SEPALS which attract creatures for POLLINATION, so that a SEED or seeds can be formed.

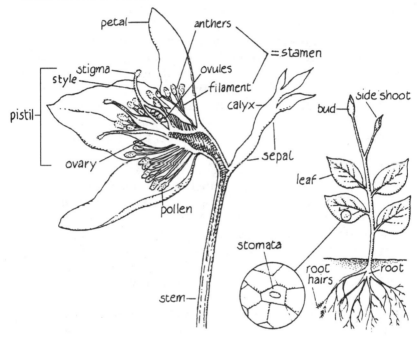

FOLIAGE　The LEAVES of a plant.

FRAME (COLD FRAME)　A protective structure, made of glass or other transparent material, similar to, but generally lower and smaller than, a GREENHOUSE. It can be used in a similar way to a CLOCHE, and also for HARDENING OFF young plants raised in heat to prepare them for PLANTING OUT. Frames are usually placed horizontally, although narrow, vertical frames are also available for attaching to a wall.

FROST　This arises when the temperature falls below 32°F (0°C) and can be damaging to TENDER plants not suited to low temperatures, unless protection is given in some way.

FRUIT   Any SEED-bearing organ: a POD, a BERRY and a NUT are all technically 'fruit'.

FUNGICIDE   A chemical formulated specifically for controlling FUNGUS DISEASES on plants.

FUNGUS   A type of plant which contains no CHLOROPHYLL and therefore, unlike green plants, cannot make its own food. A fungus derives sustenance from other living things, when it is known as a PARASITE, or dead ones, when it is a SAPROPHYTE. Saprophytic fungi can be very beneficial in that they help to break down dead matter into food for other plants as well as themselves, but some parasitic ones cause DISEASE on plants, and have to be controlled with FUNGICIDES.

GARDEN   To tend or cultivate an area of ground; the piece of ground receiving this attention.

GARDEN CENTRE   A retail outlet for plants, sundries and other gardening accessories.

GARDEN TOOLS AND APPLIANCES   See Chapter 3.

GENUS (plural *genera*)   A group of plants all very similar in characteristics to each other, e.g., members of the genus *sorbus* (mountain ash and whitebeam) are all recognizably alike in many details. The generic name (in this case *sorbus*) is like a person's surname, the specific name (see SPECIES) being akin to a first name.

GERMINATION   The stage at which a SEED begins to grow ROOTS and SHOOTS to become a plant.

GLASS   In gardening parlance, a collective term referring to all structures made entirely or partly of glass or other light-transmitting material and designed for the protection of plants.

GRAFT   A process in which one plant is artificially combined with another. The main reason for doing this is to 'borrow' some of the characteristics from the ROOTSTOCK (the part receiving the graft) for the SCION (the piece being grafted on). For example, an apple tree may grow far too large on its own ROOTS. If a piece of it is grafted on to a 'dwarfing rootstock' it will inherit the slower growth habit of the STOCK, while retaining its own fruiting characteristics.

GRASS   Plants which are members of the Graminaceae family, having strap-, spike- or sword-like LEAVES and usually feathery flower-heads. Grass is also the term used to describe thin, grass-like leaves produced by young BULBS and sometimes bulbs suffering from certain DISORDERS.

GREENHOUSE A structure of glass or other transparent material on a wooden or metal framework for the CULTIVATION and protection of plants, mainly ones which through some or all of their lives could not survive out of doors in a particular environment. Greenhouses are generally used to protect plants from low temperatures, but can also be used to protect them from excessive moisture. An example of this is the alpine house, which is not heated, but is used to house collections of ALPINES, plants whose normal habitat is crisp, dry localities and that take exception to our cold, damp winters if permanently planted outside.

GREEN VEGETABLES Ones grown primarily for their leaves, e.g., cabbage, spinach, etc.

GROUND COVER PLANTS Ones suitable for close planting which will eventually cover the ground completely and so exclude WEEDS.

GROWING BAG A long, flattish, heavy-duty plastic sack filled with potting COMPOST which is used as a temporary CONTAINER in which to grow plants, especially VEGETABLES.

GROWING TIP The tip of a SHOOT, from which growth is made.

HALF-HARDY Plants that in our climate will live outside only in summer, and are killed by FROST.

HARDENING OFF Gradually accustoming plants raised in warmth to cooler conditions. *See* FRAME.

HARDY A plant that should be capable of thriving outside all the year round.

HAULM The STEM of a plant, usually applied to VEGETABLES, e.g., pea, bean, potato.

HEAD A cluster of FLOWERS, collection of BRANCHES at the top of the TRUNK of a TREE, or the hearted part of a green VEGETABLE, e.g., cabbage.

HEDGE Shrubby plants grown in a continuous row as a boundary or division.

HEEL A small side-SHOOT torn from the parent plant with a piece of bark attached at the base, often used as a CUTTING.

HEELING IN The practice of planting BARE ROOT stock temporarily if the permanent site is not ready, in order to prevent the ROOTS from drying out.

HERB This word is now generally taken to mean plants, often aromatic, grown for seasoning food, medicinal purposes, or for the fragrance of their leaves or seeds.

HERBACEOUS   Herbaceous plants are those with soft, not permanently woody, upper growth. An herbaceous BORDER contains a collection of such plants.

HERBICIDE   A chemical which will kill plants, often referred to also as a WEEDKILLER.

HOUSE PLANTS   Are usually of a TENDER nature and have been grown for indoor decoration.

HUMIDITY   Moisture in the atmosphere.

HUMUS   Organic matter in SOIL.

HYBRID   A cross between two SPECIES of plant. *Hybridization* is the deliberate crossing of parent plants, and is usually performed by plant breeders to produce a new VARIETY.

INORGANIC   This word really refers to the fact that a substance does not contain carbon. Over the years it has come to refer to a method of CULTIVATION where inorganic FERTILIZERS ('artificials') are used as a supplement to (or instead of) ORGANIC ones (the organic in this context intended to mean those derived from natural sources) and chemicals having a synthetic method of manufacture, instead of those of natural origin, are used to control PESTS and DISEASES. Exponents of 'organic growing' methods contend that 'inorganics' are unnatural or harmful in some way. However, plant foods in such substances are often obtained from minerals occurring naturally, and many organic compounds (that is, those containing carbon) can be produced synthetically. Most synthetic INSECTICIDES and FUNGICIDES contain carbon, and can be anything but harmless if used incorrectly, although technically 'organic'. At best, many so-called 'natural' organic fertilizers are produced from slurry or poultry manure from intensively farmed animals, so the concept of 'natural' and 'unnatural' can become somewhat confused.

INSECTICIDE   A chemical that will kill insects and often other small garden pests such as mites as well, though the latter is more correctly known as an *acaricide*.

INTERNODE   A piece of STEM between two LEAF joints.

LATERAL   The term used to describe side growths on the main stems of a TREE or SHRUB.

LAWN   A specially cultivated piece of grassland, for ORNAMENTAL or recreational purposes.

23

LAYERING   Pegging down a young BRANCH or STEM into the SOIL, so that the point which touches the soil produces ROOTS and will eventually form a new plant. This occurs naturally sometimes if a stem touches the ground somewhere along its length.

LEAF-MOULD   The dark brown, broken-down remains of LEAVES, very good as a SOIL-improving material. True leaf-mould differs from COMPOST in that the latter is mainly broken down by BACTERIA, whereas in leaf-mould the materials are broken down by the action of FUNGI.

LEAVES   The part of a green plant containing most CHLOROPHYLL and therefore the main food-manufacturing part.

LEGUME   A member of the pea and bean family.

LIFT   To dig up a plant from the ground.

LIME   A blanket term used by gardeners to cover several compounds containing calcium which can be added to SOIL to improve the texture, sweeten it, and increase its alkalinity (*see* ACID).

LOAM   Another word for SOIL, especially that of good quality.

MAIDEN   A young TREE or BUSH in its first year, after GRAFTING or BUDDING before any PRUNING or TRAINING has taken place to begin the formation of its eventual shape.

MANURE   A substance, often bulky, containing and capable of supplying ORGANIC plant foods when added to SOIL. *Green manure* is a quick-growing leaf crop, capable of decaying to produce plant foods, which is dug in on maturity to rot down, e.g., mustard.

MARKET GARDEN   An enterprise, usually commercial, for the raising of mainly food-producing plants (FRUIT and VEGETABLES).

MICROCLIMATE   An environment in a limited area differing in some respect from that surrounding it. It can refer to an area outside, such as one sheltered by trees and shrubs, or to the inside of a GREENHOUSE, or even to the practice of surrounding the POT of a HOUSE PLANT with an outer container of moist absorbent material to raise the HUMIDITY in the immediate vicinity through evaporation.

MICROPROPAGATION   A method of PROPAGATION in which tiny pieces of plants are reproduced rapidly in a series of

24

nutrient solutions. This produces vast quantities of propagation material and consequently new plants, very fast. As yet the method is mainly used by professional nurserymen because laboratory conditions are essential.

MISTING Spraying the leaves of plants with a fine mist of water to prevent them from becoming dehydrated in hot, dry conditions.

MULCHING The application of a thick layer of a substance to the surface of the SOIL. Mulches are usually of bulky, naturally occurring materials such as BARK, COIR, COMPOST, COCOA SHELL, FARMYARD MANURE, shredded garden waste, grass clippings, etc. The main function is to retain moisture in the soil by preventing excessive evaporation, but mulches have the additional benefit of adding plant foods to the soil and keeping ROOTS cooler in hot weather. A well-applied mulch will also smother WEEDS. Black polythene is sometimes used as a mulch, though mainly in VEGETABLE gardens as amongst ORNAMENTAL plants it tends to look rather untidy. Woven fibre mulches, which are laid as a sheet and allow rainwater to permeate, are becoming more popular.

NATURALIZING A form of gardening where plants are positioned informally and left more or less to 'do their own thing'. Daffodils are suitable for this kind of semi-wild CULTIVATION.

NEMATODE A tiny organism often living off animals or plants. Nematodes can be beneficial or harmful to plants according to their way of life.

NEUTRAL *See* ACID.

NODE Positions on a STEM where LEAVES or leafbuds are capable of appearing.

NURSERY A place where young plants, known as *nursery stock*, are raised. *Nursery beds* are beds in which young plants are grown and tended until well-developed enough to be transferred to their permanent positions.

NUT A SEED with an outer shell, usually hard, and an inner skin.

OPEN GROUND Ground for CULTIVATION not protected by a covered structure.

ORGANIC Literally, an organic compound is one containing carbon. Many organic compounds are produced from the

breaking down of plant or animal remains, especially substances in rotting MANURE, COMPOST and the like which in
turn become plant foods. *See* INORGANIC.

ORNAMENTAL A plant grown mainly for decorative
effect.

OVARY The part of the female organ of the FLOWER containing the OVULES.

OVULES Female cells contained in the OVARY of a
FLOWER.

PANNING An undesirable condition of the surface of a
SOIL, usually a heavy one, which has become smooth and
hard. The problem is usually caused either by too much
walking on a particular area, or by breaking the soil down too
finely during CULTIVATION. Heavy rain then settles down the
surface into a crust, which eventually dries out to a rock-hard
finish. The GERMINATION of SEED is difficult under such
conditions and young plants cannot thrive. A pan should
be broken up by thorough digging and steps taken to improve the soil's texture by adding HUMUS-forming materials to
prevent it happening again.

PARASITE A plant or animal obtaining nourishment
directly from the body structure of another living organism.

PEAT Like COMPOST, peat is formed from vegetable
remains, but occurs in wet, ACID places where AEROBIC
BACTERIA have not been able to rot it down properly. It is
used for horticultural purposes mainly as an ingredient of
soil-less composts.

PEAT SUBSTITUTES Substances derived from non-PEAT
sources (COIR, wood waste, etc.) used in COMPOST, MULCHES
or for SOIL conditioning.

PERENNIAL Strictly speaking, this means any plant with
a life cycle longer than two years (often indefinite). The
expression has come to refer mainly to HERBACEOUS perennials, although TREES, SHRUBS, BULBS, and many other types of
plant should correctly be placed in this category.

PERLITE Expanded volcanic rock in granules used as an
additive to SOILS and COMPOSTS to improve the texture, retain
WATER and let in air. It is very lightweight and therefore easier
to handle – both on its own, and in combination with PEAT or
PEAT SUBSTITUTES for soil-less composts – than SAND.

PERPETUAL FLOWERING A plant with a prolonged or

indefinite flowering period, as opposed to one which only has a single flush.

PEST   A living creature which can cause damage to plants.

PESTICIDE   A chemical for killing or controlling PESTS.

PETALS   The parts of a FLOWER, often eye-catching, surrounding the male and/or female reproductive organs.

PHOTOSYNTHESIS   The process in which the CHLOROPHYLL in plants combines WATER in SAP and carbon dioxide from the air in the presence of sunlight to make sugar from which are created many more complex food compounds for the support of the plant during its lifetime.

PINCH   To remove the growing SHOOT of a plant in order to make it bush out. (*See* STOPPING.)

PISTIL   The female organ of a FLOWER.

PLANT FOODS   Chemicals in solution in SOIL, capable of being absorbed by a plant for feeding purposes. Plants also make certain energy-giving foods by PHOTOSYNTHESIS.

PLANTLETS   Baby plants produced by certain species as a means of VEGETATIVE PROPAGATION.

PLANT OUT   To place a SEEDLING or other young plant in its permanent position after its time in a SEED TRAY or NURSERY bed.

PLUNGE   To submerge a POT-GROWN PLANT up to its rim in SOIL outside or in a specially made 'plunge bed'. Many HOUSE PLANTS may be treated like this during the warmer summer months and pots of BULBS required for indoor decoration can be plunged several inches deep after planting to encourage the production of strong, healthy ROOTS before the top growth develops.

POD   A dry SEED container capable of splitting into two halves down its length and enclosing many SEEDS, e.g. peapod.

POLLEN   Dust-like grains producing male reproductive cells found in the ANTHERS of most flowering plants. *Pollination* occurs when these male grains alight on the female STIGMA after which FERTILIZATION takes place if the male and female cells (known as *gametes*) successfully fuse. Pollination is brought about naturally by wind, animals, insects or in self-pollination by the pollen falling on to the stigma in the same flower and can be done artificially by dusting the appropriate parts with a soft paintbrush or similar.

POT   A receptacle usually, but not always, having drainage holes in the bottom, and intended for containing a growing plant.

POT-BOUND A state reached by a plant when its ROOTS have entirely filled its container. Some plants flower better in this condition, as they are placed under stress, but generally speaking a pot-bound plant will start to deteriorate if its roots are restricted too much, and it should be replanted in a bigger pot.

POT-GROWN A plant grown in a container. The term is often used to describe the method of raising new stock in a series of containers until it is finally planted in its permanent site in the OPEN GROUND.

POTTING The transference of a plant from a SEED TRAY into an individual POT, or the replanting from a small pot into a bigger one. (Also known as 'potting on'.)

PRICKING OUT The planting out of SEEDLINGS from the container in which they reached GERMINATION into another CONTAINER or BED where they can be spaced further apart to allow more room for development.

PROPAGATION Increasing a stock of plants. Naturally, this occurs through SEED production, and also by producing PLANTLETS, RUNNERS, STOLONS, or similar. In addition to these methods gardeners can increase their stock through CUTTINGS, LAYERING and the like, and also by the comparatively new method of *tissue culture*. A *propagator* or *propagating case* is a container with a transparent lid fitting over a tray base which may contain or be attached to some form of heating appliance, and is filled with COMPOST or other growing medium. The purpose is to create a beneficial MICROCLIMATE with increased warmth and HUMIDITY for the GERMINATION of seeds, and to raise SEEDLINGS and STRIKE CUTTINGS.

PRUNING The cutting back of woody plants to encourage the formation of a healthy, well shaped specimen and improve or control flower production.

RESPIRATION In this process, plants absorb oxygen from the air to turn the sugars formed during PHOTOSYNTHESIS into energy for growth, carbon dioxide being given off as a waste product.

RHIZOME This is an underground STEM, producing ROOTS along its length and one or more SHOOTS at the end.

Many are fleshy and are used as food storage organs for the dormant period (e.g., bearded irises) but some, like those of couch grass, are long and thin.

RIPE   A state of maturity, in FRUITS, usually encouraged by warmth, sunlight and chemicals in the SOIL. Young growths on TREES and SHRUBS are ripe when they turn woody.

ROCKERY, ROCK GARDEN   An area where ALPINE and ROCK PLANTS are grown, and which usually, but not necessarily, contains rocks or large stones arranged as if in a natural outcrop.

ROCK PLANTS   Technically, a rock plant is not the same as an ALPINE, which should come from a mountainous region to qualify as such, but in practice the terms have come to be accepted as the same, i.e. DWARF, slow and low-growing plants which are suitable for growing on a ROCKERY.

ROOTBALL (BALL)   This is the term used to describe a mass of SOIL and ROOTS either occurring naturally with some plants having fine fibrous roots, or more often it is what is found when a POT-GROWN plant is removed from its CONTAINER. Generally speaking, when replanting or repotting this ball must not be damaged, and whenever possible it should be kept intact.

Sometimes plants are offered for sale with a ball of soil around their roots kept in place with sacking or netting. This prevents the roots from drying out before they are replanted and the plant usually stands a higher chance of survival.

ROOTS   The parts of a plant which anchor it to the SOIL or growing medium, and absorb moisture and PLANT FOODS in solution through *root hairs* at the tips.

ROOTSTOCK, STOCK   A plant into which a GRAFT is inserted, or which provides the ROOTS when BUDDING is done.

ROOT VEGETABLES   Those grown primarily for their edible ROOTS such as carrots, parsnips, etc. In some cases other parts can also be eaten (e.g., the tops of turnips).

ROTATION   A method of growing crops so that no two similar ones are grown in succession in the same plot. This is done mainly to prevent the build-up of PESTS and DISEASES affecting a certain crop and also so that MANURE and FERTILIZER can be applied to best possible effect and any special benefits of certain groups of plants (e.g. peas and beans) can be maximized. (See pages 284–5 for a suggested 3-year rotation for the vegetable garden.)

29

RUNNER A STEM running along the surface of the SOIL which produces new PLANTLETS at intervals from the NODES. This is a good method of PROPAGATION in certain cases, e.g., strawberries.

SALAD VEGETABLES Those intended to be eaten raw in salads, e.g., lettuces, radishes and spring onions.

SAND A substance consisting of small particles of broken mineral rock.

SAP The liquid in plants (rather like plant's blood) containing WATER, PLANT FOODS and substances such as hormones, which control the plant's growth and development.

SAPROPHYTE A plant or animal living directly on dead and decaying matter for feeding purposes, such as some FUNGI.

SCION The part joined on to the ROOTSTOCK when a GRAFT is made.

SEED A structure designed for sexual reproduction. A SEED is formed when a male cell in POLLEN combines with a female OVULE. A seed is really an embryo plant capsule with enough stored food for nourishment during GERMINATION until the resultant SEEDLING is capable of absorbing food itself through its ROOTS.

SEED BED A finely cultivated area of ground into which SEED may be sown.

SEED COMPOST A fine grade of COMPOST suitable for sowing SEED into.

SEED DRESSING A coating of chemicals designed to control any PEST or DISEASE which might affect the SEED or the resultant young SEEDLINGS.

SEEDLING A baby plant grown from a SEED.

SEED TRAY A flattish receptacle in which SEED can be sown in COMPOST, sometimes referred to as a seed pan.

SEPALS The leaf-like outermost parts of a FLOWER, collectively known as the CALYX.

SET Specially selected or treated parts of a plant, capable of being grown on into a crop, e.g., onion sets. A FLOWER which is beginning to develop FRUIT or SEED after FERTILIZATION is also said to have 'set'.

SHADING Providing means of partially obscuring sunlight, often under GLASS.

SHOOTS New vertical growths in plants.

SILT A soil comprised of very tiny particles of broken mineral rock.

SOIL The upper layer of earth which supports higher plant life. This consists of disintegrated rock, organic matter and beneficial organisms including BACTERIA.

SOUR SOIL An ACID soil in which the balance between plant remains and organisms has become out of order.

SOW To scatter or otherwise introduce SEED into the earth or purpose-made COMPOST in order to raise plants.

SPECIES A group of plants resembling each other in all but minor details and which can interbreed easily and successfully.

SPECIMEN A plant specially selected for individual display.

SPHAGNUM A type of coarse MOSS which when it decays in a certain way under wet conditions forms sphagnum moss PEAT.

SPIKING To introduce air into compacted SOIL with a sharp, spiked tool such as a fork or other gadget with spikes on it.

SPIT The depth of a standard spade or fork in SOIL.

SPRAY Several FLOWERS grouped on a single stem. This word is also used to denote the spreading of fine droplets of a liquid over the surface of a plant by means of a device known as a *sprayer*.

SPROUT A new SHOOT, or the production of this shoot.

SPUR A cluster of buds on a FRUIT TREE which will open to form FLOWERS.

STAKE A straight support introduced at the side of a plant to keep it straight and prevent it from falling or blowing over.

STALK A STEM-like growth supporting LEAVES or FLOWERS.

STAMENS The male organs of a FLOWER.

STANDARD PLANT One TRAINED to grow on a single STEM for a certain height, and then PRUNED to form a head of STEMS or BRANCHES.

STEM The part of a plant which has BUDS from which can grow FLOWERS, side-SHOOTS or LEAVES.

STIGMA The part of the female organ of a FLOWER that collects the POLLEN.

STOCK *See* ROOTSTOCK.

STOCK PLANT One kept to provide material for the PROPAGATION of new plants.

STOLON A STEM that can produce new ROOTS and SHOOTS at its tip, as, e.g., the blackberry does.

31

STOMATES The pores through which a plant breathes, usually found on LEAVES, mainly on the underside, but occasionally on the STEM as well.

STONE FRUITS Those like plums, which contain a hard stone (the technical term for these fruits is *drupe*).

STOOL The term for both the CROWN of plants (e.g., chrysanthemum) lifted annually and used for PROPAGATION, and for SHRUBS or TREES PRUNED down to ground level every year and so kept as a cluster of young STEMS. In the latter case, stooling is done either to provide young stems for propagation, or because the young stems (and perhaps their LEAVES) are the decorative feature for which the plant is grown.

STOPPING The removal of a GROWING TIP to encourage the production of side-SHOOTS.

STRIKE To take a CUTTING of a plant, which is said to have *struck* when it has started to produce ROOTS.

STYLE The part of the female organ of a FLOWER which conducts the male cells in POLLEN to the OVARY.

SUBSOIL The infertile layer of SOIL below the TOPSOIL, lacking in HUMUS and plant nutrients.

SUCKER A SHOOT arising from the ROOTSTOCK of a BUDDED or GRAFTED plant, which must be removed to preserve the desired habit. A sucker is also a secondary growth developing from an underground BUD, by which many plants produce natural thickets.

SYSTEMIC A substance capable of being absorbed into a plant's tissue.

TAP ROOT A strong, straight ROOT growing downwards into the SOIL.

TENDER Plants which cannot grow outside permanently in a climate likely to experience FROST.

TENDRIL The twining part of certain climbing plants, by which they can support themselves.

THERMOMETER A gauge for measuring temperature.

THINNING OUT The removal of certain overcrowded plants, SHOOTS, or STEMS to enable better development of the remainder.

TILTH A SOIL in CULTIVATION, broken down to a fine texture, and suitable to SOW SEED in.

TOLERANT Plants which will tolerate certain substances or conditions without adverse effect.

TOP FRUIT   FRUIT which is produced on a TREE or tree-like BUSH, as opposed to BUSH FRUIT (e.g., blackcurrants) which are produced on low bushes.

TOPSOIL   The top layer of a SOIL which is usually FERTILE and capable of supporting healthy plant life.

TRAINING   By manipulating, PRUNING or general CULTI-VATION a plant is 'trained'; i.e. persuaded to grow in a specific form, e.g., ESPALIER.

TRANSPIRATION   The giving-off of water through the STOMATES as a part of the process of PHOTOSYNTHESIS.

TRANSPLANT   To move a plant from one location to another.

TREAD   To firm down SOIL gently with the feet.

TREE   A woody plant growing on one main STEM or TRUNK, and of fairly mature age, as opposed to a SHRUB or BUSH, with many stems.

TRUNK   A hard, woody, main STEM of a TREE.

TUBER   A swollen STEM or ROOT used by certain plants for food storage in the DORMANT period. Potatoes are stem tubers, dahlias are tuberous roots.

TURF   A piece of GRASS, ROOTS and SOIL cut from mature grassland for re-establishing elsewhere usually as a LAWN. The expression *turf* is also used to denote the actual grassland itself.

UNION   The point at which a SCION is combined with a ROOTSTOCK.

VARIEGATED   Plants whose LEAVES and sometimes STEMS have two or more colours; e.g., some hollies have green and cream or gold leaves, and these are described as *variegated*. Variegation is often caused by lack of chlorophyll in certain parts of the leaf or by a virus and so a variegated plant can often be weaker in growth than the plant from which it originated.

VARIETY   A group of plants in a SPECIES similar to each other but different from other groups in the species in some respects, e.g., *Chamaecyparis lawsoniana* 'Allumii' is a variety of *Chamaecyparis lawsoniana*, the Lawson's cypress. Varieties which have occurred in CULTIVATION either by deliberate breeding or by accident are called *cultivars* (short for cultivated variety).

VEGETABLE   In common usage, a vegetable is a plant grown primarily for the edible qualities of one or more of its parts.

VEGETATIVE PROPAGATION   To increase the stock of a plant by any method other than by growing from SEED.

VENTILATION   To provide fresh air in an enclosed structure (e.g., a GREENHOUSE).

VERMICULITE   A lightweight substance formed by heating certain minerals such as mica. It can be added to PEAT, or PEAT SUBSTITUTE, to form a POTTING COMPOST, or used on its own to provide a soil–less growing medium.

VIRUS   A minute organism about which comparatively little is known at present, capable of producing DISEASE and DISORDER in any plant or animal it invades.

WALL PLANTS   Those suitable for growing up or TRAINING on walls.

WATER   A naturally occurring compound of hydrogen and oxygen, and liquid at normal temperatures, water is essential for the life of a plant. *Watering* is the artificial application of water to plants by one means or another.

WEEDKILLER   A HERBICIDE used for the killing or control of WEEDS.

WEED   'Something growing where it is not wanted!' Weeds are the most successful of plants, being vigorous, invasive and persistent.

WHIP   A young TREE with a single thin STEM or TRUNK.

WILT   A term used to describe the turning limp and subsequent collapse of a plant, which can be due to lack of WATER, injury, or DISEASE.

WINDBREAK   A living or constructed shelter to prevent the full force of a wind from damaging plants growing behind it. It should not be a solid structure, which encourages harmful draughts, but should filter the wind as does a HEDGE.

WINDFALL   A fruit which has fallen off the tree on to the ground; it should be eaten immediately as it will quickly start to rot.

WINDROCK   An effect of wind on plants which causes damage to ROOTS. It can result in death unless a WINDBREAK is constructed, or a CANE or STAKE supplied.

WORKED   A BUDDING or GRAFTING term. The expression 'top-' or 'bottom-worked' is often encountered in connection with a GRAFTED TREE. This refers to whether the SCION has been introduced at the top or bottom of the TRUNK.

34

2

TAKING STOCK

When you take over a garden or prospective garden, it's bound to fall into a certain category, and your plan of action will largely depend on what you've already got.

The brand-new garden

This usually comes with the brand-new house. New gardens vary in size, of course, but these days they tend to be smaller than 30 or 40 years ago and plots of 30 ft by 50 ft (9 m by 15 m) are quite common. This looks a lot when everything has to be done to it, but once you start planting things you can soon find you have a space problem, so the smaller the area, the greater the need for careful planning.

New gardens come in 'front' and 'back' varieties. The front garden is the part that the prospective buyer sees first, even before viewing the house, so it is generally tidy. It may even look as though it has been cultivated. It is often weed-free and the soil appears good. At least you won't have to put a lot of effort into *that*, you think. Don't, however, be fooled. It is a popular ruse to cover up a multitude of sins with a bit of topsoil frequently bearing no resemblance to the local soil because it has been 'borrowed' from the garden of the poor person who is having a house built in the next village. Underneath may be a hard layer, compacted by months of workmen's feet and heavy equipment, seasoned with the washings-out of the concrete mixer, burnt polythene, and enough timber, wall-tiles and broken bricks to start your own business. There is no point in trying to take a short-cut. All this will have to be got out and the crusty layer broken up before you do anything permanent, or buying plants and grass seed will be a waste of money.

A variation of the 'quick clean up' approach is the landscaped front garden beloved of the speculator's advertising brochure. This is the condition already described, but it goes one step further by having a layer of turf – usually scruffy stuff full of weeds and coarse grasses – slapped down over the top of the thinly disguised rubbish tip. Somewhere in the middle of this a young tree has been planted. Look at this tree closely – it is often a sapling of something which will eventually be more at home in a primeval forest than the front garden of number 2 Lilac Close. If you find this is the case, it is better to remove it now and replace it before it becomes a light-obliterating menace. But take a good look at where the builders have actually *put* the thing. If it is going to restrict your view of the road in four years' time, when you back the car out of the garage with your eyes still half-shut at 8 a.m., forget about that position altogether and choose another place. Unfortunately, it may have been a planning condition that this totally unsuitable tree was planted. Technically it cannot be removed without incurring the wrath of the local authority. It can, however, be encouraged to die!

Of course, this is not always the case. Some front gardens have been done with care, using good turf properly laid by an experienced contractor, and a conscientious builder will have taken advice on suitable trees for a particular place. See if you can find another site the builder is engaged upon and watch how he's going about that one. If he is levelling the ground with a vibrating roller and filling all the holes which refuse to disappear with sand – and this really happens – then you could be in for problems.

The back garden is a different thing entirely. Here you can

often judge just how careful the builder has been, both inside and out, from the remains that litter the plot. You can also see whether he has left you any topsoil (you can insist on this) or whether it has been given to the chap down the road to replace his – which was given to the chap down to the road to replace his, and so on. The one advantage is you can at least *see* how much rubbish you're going to have to tackle.

The derelict garden

This is like the brand-new garden, only worse. It is usually found attached to old properties which have remained empty for a long time and then possibly been renovated. What has not been squashed rock-hard during the alterations will be a jungle of neglected and overgrown trees and shrubs, grass and weeds, briars and brambles. It has probably also been the secret neighbourhood dumping ground for a quarter of a century, so lurking in the bushes could be a wealth of bedsteads and broken crockery. These gardens are often larger as they belong to properties built when land was more plentiful. They are usually very fertile, nature having taken its course, and so everything, including all the stuff you want to be rid of, grows very strong and healthy. A slight improvement on this sort of plot is one which has originally been an orchard, or similar. Orchard sites are now becoming popular building plots and if they have not been neglected for too long can form the basis of a decent garden, as they often have passable grass and trees on them which can give you a head start.

The established garden

The established garden can be the easiest type of garden to inherit, or the hardest. If you take over a property which has been occupied up to the moment you move in, it is more than likely that someone, possibly several previous occupants, will have had a go at planting up. You could be fortunate enough to take over from a knowledgeable gardener or plantsman, or you could inherit the mistakes of a dozen previous residents. Unfortunately, until you become more experienced, it could be difficult to tell the difference between a potential paradise and a prospective disaster. And however inexperienced you are, you nearly always know what you *like*, and your predecessor's ideas of Eden might not be yours.

This type of garden is a difficult one, because it is unlikely that *nothing* will be worth keeping, and it is far easier to clear the lot than to remove certain things and retain others. On the other hand, inheriting an established garden is more often an asset than a drawback because, assuming that some of the stock is worth keeping, the mature plants can give you a head start. It might mean that a bit more thought has to be given to the planning, but providing what you save is *really worthwhile*, i.e. suitable, healthy and a useful inclusion in a garden, you will get the benefit of not having everything small and new at once.

No garden at all

This is virtually impossible because even though you may have no garden in the accepted sense, that is, an area of soil capable of being cultivated, if you want to grow things badly enough, there are many ways in which you can achieve an outside growing area.

For a start, unless you live in a hole in the ground, you are almost certain to have walls and providing these are sound, and, if you are in rented or leasehold accommodation, there are no restrictions on what you are allowed to do to them, there are scores of receptacles which can be used as planting containers if attached firmly to the wall. Flat roofs can be used as sites for troughs and tubs if they aren't too weighty or too numerous. The dankest concrete backyard can be a green oasis with very little effort using shade-loving subjects in large containers. Most councils would not object to the odd plant trough on the pavement against your house, provided it is not a hazard to passers-by. Many street footpaths are already inadequately narrow, so if there is any possibility that you might cause inconvenience (especially to the blind and partially-sighted, who may have used that route unobstructed all their lives and so consider they are familiar with every hazard – until they fall headlong into an over-enthusiastic new resident's pot of petunias), it is better to confine that type of planting to, say, first-floor window boxes (fixed so they do not fall off and kill an unsuspecting passer-by, of course; some heavily planted boxes in full bearing can be quite weighty and unbalanced!) well out of the way of pedestrians – or vandals.

Perhaps the biggest challenge is the balcony as found on so many high-rise flats. This can often provide quite a large growing area if properly planned, and although there can be certain cultural problems with windy sites half-way to Heaven, there is a certain satisfaction in sitting surrounded by greenery with a bird's-eye view of the hustle and bustle below. If every multi-storey balcony were cultivated, the Hanging Gardens of Babylon would be eclipsed by our tower blocks!

3

THE TOOLS FOR THE JOB

It is no good trying to start a garden with poor tools. Cheap second-hand items are a false economy. I am not going to try to tell you that gardening isn't a tiring occupation – some of it can be extremely hard work, especially if you are not used to it, but having the right sort of tools to suit *you* can cut your effort down by half.

You do not need a lot of equipment to start a garden, or keep it in shape. You can, of course, spend a great deal of money on gimmicks and gadgets. Some work reasonably well, some do not, but most of them you can manage quite well without.

Here are a few tips to bear in mind when shopping for your tools:

1. Always go to a reputable shop. It does not have to be one specializing in garden products, as most DIY chains sell reliable brands, although specialist tool shops will probably have staff more capable of giving expert advice. The shop to

avoid is the cheap discount place selling inferior and badly made products. One can frequently be 'caught' this way with small hand tools – trowels, secateurs and the like. Often they do not function well, and break easily after a few weeks' use.

2. Look for well-known brand names, which on the whole, produce tools of a quality you can rely on.

3. Get the best that money can buy. All gardening tools are pricey items these days but, generally speaking, the more expensive the tool, the more dependable it will be, although there are some inexpensive imports from the Far East around which are of reasonable quality and quite adequate for average use. Some manufacturers produce a variety of ranges, priced accordingly, designed with the occasional gardener, regular user, and professional contractor respectively in mind.

4. Take your time handling the items before you buy. See if you feel happy holding them. The problem here is that you probably do not have the experience to know whether a particular tool feels 'right' for you. You will, however, know whether it seems too heavy, or too long, or too short, or whatever. Don't buy until you've had a look at a *lot*.

5. Don't automatically accept other people's cast-offs. Do not put yourself off for ever before you have even started by using something badly maintained, broken or poorly designed. However, if it looks as though it has been well looked after and has been used for the job for which it was originally intended, it's worth giving it a try. Car boot sales are often outlets for redundant tools and occasionally you can find a good one.

What to buy

Gardening tools can be divided into two basic categories, hand tools and mechanical ones. The owner of a small garden can manage quite well with a minimum of mechanization if funds are limited. Even a larger plot, say up to an acre, can be maintained adequately with no other mechanized tools than a power-driven mower and hedge trimmer, if appropriate.

These are the *hand* tools you will need to get started:

SPADE. A spade is used for turning over soil, lifting plants, and digging holes. It can also be used to trim the edges of the lawn where it adjoins a bed or border. It is *not* designed for lifting manhole covers, hammering in stakes, and mixing concrete!

A spade is essentially a rectangular, slightly curved steel

41

blade on the end of a wooden handle, usually ash. The blade is attached to the handle (shaft) by means of a metal socket – the longer the socket, the stronger the handle. The handle should be riveted to the socket with steel rivets. The spade is provided with a hand-grip at the end of the handle. This is either made in the shape of a T formed out of the wood, or a D, nowadays mainly of plastic. It is a matter of preference which hand-grip to buy. (At one time, the D-grip used to be preferred by people living in the south of Britain and the T-grip by those living in the north – but this has largely gone by the board.)

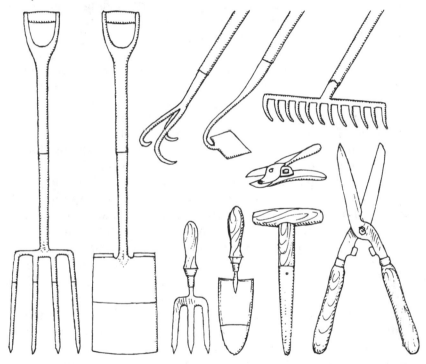

To use a spade, you insert the blade into the ground by pressing down on the top of it where the socket starts, either on the left-hand side if you are left-footed, or the right-hand side if you tend to use the right leg more for such operations. It should enter the ground as nearly vertical as possible and soil is brought up on the blade by levering the handle. The secret of easy digging is not to take too much soil up on the blade at once, then you don't tire so quickly. Sometimes earth will stick to the back of the spade; this should be scraped off regularly. If you want to treat yourself, a stainless steel spade is wonderful as no matter how sticky the soil, it comes off easily. It will be expensive but the backache it saves could be worth it.

Spades come in several sizes, both in relation to the blade and the handle. Blades usually range in size from about 12 by 8 in. (300 by 200 mm) for a 'digging spade', to 10 by 6½ in. (250 by 165 mm) for a 'medium', down to 9 by 5½ in. (225 by 140 mm) for a 'border spade', often referred to as a 'ladies' spade'. Naturally, the bigger the blade, the heavier it is, both empty and with a load of soil on it, when it can become quite unmanageable for many people. It is not always the best policy to buy the largest blade available as it can become exhausting to use after a short time, especially for the unaccustomed or weekend gardener. It is not 'cissy' to plump for the smaller blade – I know many men who are happier and work faster using a border spade.

Handles also vary in length, and a tall person would be wise to choose a spade with a longer one to avoid unnecessary strain on the back.

FORK. A garden fork is not quite as essential as a spade, but nevertheless a very useful acquisition. Forks usually have four narrow, square or round tines and come in sizes of head and handle similar to the spade. Forks are mainly used for lifting plants and root vegetables by inserting under and around them in the same way as a spade. Because four tines are easier to push into the ground than one long blade, a fork is often also used for digging, especially on heavy or stony ground. In this case a digging fork, otherwise known as a 'spading' or 'potato' fork, which has flat tines, is often the best one to acquire. It is lighter to use than a spade, and if the ground is sticky it does not require the compacted earth to be scraped off all the time in the same way that a spade does.

A border fork is used for finer work in between plants and in restricted spaces. Again, stainless steel is a good investment.

Wherever possible, forks should always be given equal stress on all tines and should not be used for levering or prising with one prong. Even though reputable manufacturers submit their tools to stress tests far in advance of the type of abuse they are likely to encounter in normal usage, there is no point in bending or breaking them through faulty handling.

A useful addition to a collection of garden tools, though not imperative, is the *long-handled weed fork*. This is like a small hand fork, sometimes with only three tines, on a long handle. It is an ideal implement for tickling-up soil and removing odd weeds between plants. The long handle obviates bending and cuts down walking on the soil to a minimum.

HOE. The primary functions of this implement are to cut off weeds at soil level, and to draw soil into drills and ridges. The hoe has appeared in several different forms over the centuries but is now found mainly as two types, the Dutch hoe and the draw hoe. The Dutch hoe is a sharp blade on the end of a long ash, hardwood or aluminium handle which sometimes has a plastic grip on the end of it, although I find that this is not really necessary. It is used by pushing it backwards and forwards over the surface of the soil to sever the weeds from their roots. This is best done during hot, dry weather so that any weeds which have come out of the soil with some roots still attached, as often happens in light soils, will wither and die before they can re-root themselves. Hoeing is mainly used as an annual weed control as perennial weeds will usually shoot again from where they have been cut off, although in time they will become progressively weakened by this treatment.

The draw hoe is also a blade on a long handle, but here the blade is attached at right angles to the shaft by a metal swan-neck. Weeds are cut off with a chopping action or by scraping them off when the tool is pulled towards its user. The draw hoe can also be used to pull earth over plants to blanch them, and by pulling one corner along a finely tilled soil a shallow drill can be formed into which seeds and similar can be placed, the soil being drawn back into the drill using the same tool.

I find the Dutch hoe an important inclusion in a set of basic gardening tools, but because the draw hoe takes a little skill to operate satisfactorily, and because its functions can usually be performed by other more essential tools, it is not essential. Some manufacturers offer a 'hybrid' of the two, which works equally well either when pushed or pulled.

RAKE. A garden rake is a very necessary piece of equipment. It consists of short metal teeth, usually 11 or 12, projecting from a metal cross-piece and socket, into which is fitted an ash, hardwood or aluminium shaft. In some the teeth are an integral part of the crosspiece ('tanged and ferruled'), in some they project through it like nails (these are known as 'bolstered' teeth and because of its appearance the rake is sometimes referred to as a 'nail rake'), but provided the tool has been properly manufactured, neither method of construction should affect the rake's performance.

Garden rakes are used for the final levelling of soil and the like, and for working the top layer of soil into a fine tilth suitable for seed sowing. They can also be used for drawing lightweight rubbish such as prunings and fallen leaves into piles. They are not designed for breaking up solid clods of earth by bashing them with the head turned sideways-on – unless you want to bend both the crosspiece and the end tines! A rake is one piece of equipment, which, through heavy work, is all too easy to damage, especially when using it on a new site. If your garden falls into this category and you intend to buy a rake, go to a supplier who specializes in tools not only for the amateur but for the professional gardener as well. Many manufacturers produce a heavy-duty tool range, including rakes, designed with this type of purchaser in mind and these are well worth the extra money.

If you have inherited a lawn, or intend to lay one, then you might find a spring-tined rake helpful. This has about 20 spring-steel tines attached to a long handle as before, and is designed to 'comb' and scrape up 'thatch' and moss often found around the base of grass. Another useful acquisition is the plastic, flat-tined version of this which is used for raking up leaves and grass mowings from the surface of the lawn gently, without tearing all the grass out, as happens if you use a garden rake or spring-tined rake on it too often. If cash is limited, however, a similar job can be done with a *soft* sweeping brush.

CULTIVATOR. A long-handled cultivator is a sort of cross between a rake and a hoe, and consists of 3 (occasionally 5) tines on a long handle. Although not imperative, it is a handy tool for working the surface of soil up to a depth of about 3 in. (15 cm), to loosen it and let in air. It can be useful for cultivating between plants where some loosening of settled soil is required and digging would be unsuitable because of the risk of damage to roots.

TROWEL. This has a scooped blade and a short wooden handle,

inserted into a metal socket attached to the blade. It is used for making small planting holes and doing cultivation jobs of an intricate nature. Trowels vary in quality from very good to really shoddy, so if you do not want one that bends in half in no time, stick to good names.

HAND OR WEED FORK. This is a small fork with a short plastic, or wooden handle, useful for intricate work among closely planted subjects.

SHEARS. Most gardeners will require a pair of shears for trimming long grass and clipping soft growths on hedges and certain shrubs. Shears look like large, strong scissors and although one-handed models are available, generally they are designed to be held, one handle (usually made of beechwood but modern versions are available in moulded plastic) in each hand, and operated with a chopping motion. Good-quality shears are manufactured in a range of sizes, lengths of blade, weights and strengths, and if only one pair is being bought it should be chosen for the job it is intended to do – e.g., if you intend to use them to cut fifty feet of beech hedge, a light-weight ladies' pair would soon need attention, but if you only need them to trim a bit of grass now and again, there is no need to wear yourself out with a heavy-duty model designed for really tough stuff. Some shears are now fitted with an adjusting device which alters the shearing force to suit the type of material being clipped. If the only clipping work you need to do is on the lawn, shears with long handles take a lot of the ups and downs out of the job. These are either designed to operate on a horizontal plane, such as when trimming long grass round trees, and are really just the same as hand shears with long handles attached at right angles, or are designed to work in the vertical plane for trimming edges round borders, etc. Not surprisingly, these are usually known as edging shears.

SECATEURS (sometimes referred to as pruners). A good pair of secateurs is an essential acquisition once you have plants in the garden. They are used for trimming back soft growth, and woody stems up to about ⅜ in. (10 mm) thick. Most secateurs nowadays consist of one sharp blade and an anvil, either positioned underneath the blade or to the side of it when the tool is closed up, a centre pivot, and two handles which open up by means of a spring when the secateurs are being used.

46

The cut is made by the blade against the side or bottom anvil, and this blade should always be kept sharp or the tool will chew the stem and bruising will occur against the anvil, causing possible damage and subsequent disease to the remaining stem. Cheap secateurs are not usually a good buy and, like shears, if you anticipate they are going to get a lot of use, or the things you're going to use them on are tough, it is best to aim for a 'professional' pair.

Secateurs are precision tools and must be looked after. They must not be forced into cutting something which is too thick or strong for them or the blade will become unaligned. They must always be cleaned and oiled and properly stored in a dry place after use and shouldn't be dropped if it can be avoided as they can be irreparably damaged by such treatment. Secateurs are tools for the specialist pruning of plants, sometimes very expensive or cherished ones. They are *not* gadgets for prising open paint tins, nor makeshift screwdrivers, nor wire cutters, though some heavy-duty models have a notch at the base of the blade designed for cutting thin wire, such as that used in training plants. This is the only part of the implement which should be used for this purpose; if the pair you buy does not have such a notch it is advisable to obtain a cheap pair of wire-cutters as well and keep them near your secateurs.

Some secateurs have stronger springs than others. Before buying a pair, try them first. If you have a very small hand, or a weak grip, you might need to try several pairs before you find one which suits you. ('Ladies' ' secateurs are smaller and easier for gripping, but they are not usually suitable for any but the lightest pruning jobs round the garden.) A long-handled pruner is useful if there are large trees in the garden as it saves much ladder work.

LOPPERS. Loppers are a two-handed, heavy-duty version of pruners and are used for removing branches thicker than secateurs can cope with. Loppers are made in various strengths and lengths of handles up to about 28 in. (700 mm), and so they are useful for cutting out inaccessible branches, such as those in the centre of prickly shrubs. Loppers are not usually necessary in the brand-new garden, but can be very useful if you are reclaiming an overgrown one.

SAW. A saw, like loppers, is another piece of equipment which may or may not be an essential depending on whether your garden

47

is established or not, but as any garden matures, the necessity of a saw for heavy pruning and major surgery jobs becomes ever greater. Possibly the best purchase is the true *pruning saw* which has a tapering blade to get in easily between close branches and teeth down both edges, fine on one side and coarse on the other. Many manufacturers give their saws a non-stick coating to prevent friction; while this is not absolutely essential if you keep your saw dry and properly greased when not in use, it does make life easier. A small, folding pruning saw is handy, as you can keep it with you all the time, in a pocket, when not in use.

Some tool companies offer a range of detachable heads which clip into various lengths of handles. This is an ideal way of building up a tool collection which can be stored in a very little space.

In addition to the above tools, it is not a bad idea to make up a kit of small things you may need once you start maintaining your garden. Suggested items would be a strong screwdriver, a hammer, a brace and bit, screws and nails, plastic-covered wire, a hand drill, a pair of pliers and a pocket-knife. If you intend to do a lot of tree planting you may also think the purchase of a *lump hammer* worthwhile. This is a heavy, large-headed hammer rather like a sledge hammer, only with a short handle. It is primarily useful for driving wooden stakes firmly into the ground, but can also be employed in connection with many other projects around the garden. A length of nylon string makes a good guideline, attached to a pointed stick at either end, and canes cut to 12, 24 and 36 in. (250, 500, 750 mm and 1 m) lengths are handy to keep by you for marking planting distances. A lightweight pair of aluminium steps can be an asset.

TOOL CARE. If you have ever witnessed the amount of sweat, toil, care and expertise that has gone into the design and production of a first-class garden tool, even one as mundane as, say, an ordinary spade, apart from the fact that it has just set you back a good few pounds, you'll want to look after it correctly, if only because it will be easier to use, to say nothing of showing respect for the effort that went into its creation. A few minutes spent at the end of each working session will ensure that tools are kept in tip-top form. First, clean off all mud and other debris thoroughly, and dry metal parts if they are wet. Then wipe them with an oily cloth, ensuring that every bit has been covered with a thin film. Silicone aerosols, such as WD40, are a useful substitute for oil; they are actually water repellent so a quick spray all over with one of these should keep rust away until you next want to use it. Check wooden handles to make sure they have not been damaged and will not stick splinters into the fleshy part of your hand when you least expect it.

It is not doing your tools a kindness to keep them too warm. Storing them in, say, a heated garage where the air is too dry could cause the wooden handles to split and shrink. An unheated garage or tool shed is more suitable as the wood won't dry out as much. Some people recommend wiping the handles over with linseed oil or similar to 'feed' the wood – I find that if you use them a lot, the natural oil out of your hands is enough.

I like to hang my tools on the wall. There are several good tool hangers on the market, or you can use 'terry clips' or even pairs of nails. Each tool has its own named place – in this way it is easier to see if you have inadvertently left one outside. I do not like to stand tools, especially sharp-bladed ones, for very long periods on the floor unless I am sure it is absolutely dry. Sometimes old sheds, especially brick and stone ones, have very damp floors and the sharp edge of a spade or hoe can rust away quickly under such conditions.

Mechanical tools

These usually have some form of power drive these days, with the exception of the hand mower, which relies on you to supply the power. There are hundreds of wonderful and diverse inventions available, most of them expensive and many not particularly useful. The ones I suggest are those which can make life easier if time (or enthusiasm) is limited.

THE MOWER. If you want a lawn, you will need a mower. This is probably the purchase that is going to make the biggest hole in your pocket, so you have really got to try and get it right first time. This is one occasion where you can make considerable savings by shopping around, as you can get sizeable discounts by going to the right place at the right time. A garden machinery specialist might charge slightly more than a DIY 'shed', but he will be able to offer expert advice, and will demonstrate the machine at your own home before you buy, so you run less chance of making a wrong purchase.

This is also the one time that if money is tight, you could pick up a second-hand bargain. Many retailers sell reconditioned models which are quite satisfactory and reliable, and at certain times of the year the local papers are full of small ads for second-hand mowers at realistic prices. But beware – and bear in mind whether the price of the one you are considering, plus the cost of having it expertly serviced before you try it on *your* lawn (you could soon ruin months of work – and enthusiasm – by using a badly aligned or poorly serviced one) compares favourably with the extra security but higher cost of going to a reputable dealer.

Before you make your final purchase, you also ought to decide which type of machine is most appropriate for your particular needs. Always aim to buy one which is tough enough for the work you're going to give it. Mowers come mainly in two forms, the cylinder model and the rotary one. The cylinder mower has a multi-bladed cutting cylinder which cuts the grass against a fixed bottom plate as it revolves. The cylinder usually has 5 or 6 blades, sometimes less, sometimes more. The more expensive models frequently have the most blades. The higher the number of blades, the better the cut, as it prevents the ridging effect often seen on grass cut with fewer blades. At the front of the mower is a set of small rollers, usually plastic or wood, which are responsible for the length of cut of the grass by means of some form of adjusting mechanism. At the rear of the blades is a larger and heavier metal roller which is the part of the machine giving the characteristic striped appearance of a well maintained lawn. Some hand models do not have this rear roller, but two large side wheels instead. Cut grass is fed into a collecting box, usually at the front, but occasionally at the back, of the mower.

Cylinder mowers are made in many sizes, measured by the width of the cutting cylinder, from 12 in. (300 mm) up to several feet, the larger ones often having a removable or fixed seat for ride-on facility. They are generally powered in three ways – manually, by electricity, and by petrol. Occasionally, battery powered models are available.

The rotary mower has a sharpened blade underneath it which rotates horizontally very rapidly to sever the grass. The basic models have four wheels which can be raised or lowered to vary the cutting height, but they cannot collect the clippings or make stripes on the lawn. More sophisticated versions take up the cuttings, and some are fitted with a roller to give the effect of a cylinder mower. These mowers also come in many sizes, the larger ones also having ride-on facilities (some are even fitted under the body of a mini-tractor which is capable of other functions in the garden).

A variation of the rotary mower is the hover-mower, which has the same flat rotating blade, but instead of being moved about on four wheels, when in operation it floats on a cushion of air produced by the motor.

Rotary mowers are powered by petrol or two-stroke engines or electricity.

Cylinder mowers

WHICH TYPE OF MOWER SHOULD I CHOOSE? Choose the hand cylinder mower if you only have a small area, limited cash, or a burning desire to keep fit. Not all hand cylinder mowers are inexpensive − well-constructed, many-bladed ones are available at a higher price. These will give a fine finish to a lawn but can be hard work. Side-wheel versions are cheap, but the wheels can make nasty grooves on a damp lawn and you cannot mow right up to the edge of a bed.

Electric cylinder mowers are probably the most popular for the small modern garden where a source of power is readily available. They are comparatively lightweight and easy to manoeuvre. In many cases the electricity only powers the blades and you have to push the mower along, but some are self-propelled. Cheaper models have fewer blades and so the finish is not quite as good. They are readily available at DIY stores and garden centres and are very competitively priced. The disadvantage is that if the lawn is some distance from the power supply, a lot of extension cable is required. Also there is a chance that the cable could be accidentally cut during mowing. Modern electric mowers are double insulated so this should not prove serious, but for extra safety an appliance known as a residual current device (RCD) (which shuts off the electricity to the machine automatically if anything like this occurs) should always be used in connection with electrically powered garden tools, and you should *never* attempt any form of repair or maintenance to any part of the equipment or its cable while it is plugged into the power supply.

Petrol cylinder mowers are convenient in that providing you have sufficient petrol they can be used on a lawn anywhere. They are also more suitable for mowing large areas of lawn. They are usually heavier than the electric versions and more expensive but, depending on the model, are capable of producing a very good finish indeed. Some have a dual drive which means you can use them with just the blades being driven without the mower being automatically propelled. This gives greater manoeuvrability in awkward places. Modern petrol mowers run on unleaded petrol, but you may find that an older, second-hand one can only use four-star. Petrol and electric mowers are noisy in comparison with hand models and they should be used with the consideration of neighbours in mind!

Cylinder mowers in one form or another are mainly suitable for good-quality lawns of reasonable length and composed of fairly fine grasses and, apart from side-wheel models, can be used right up to the edges of beds and borders. They are not designed for tackling long, tough grass or overgrown lawns, which should be got back into some sort of order using a rotary mower first.

Rotary mowers

When rotary mowers first came on to the market they were suitable only for tackling rough grass such as that found in orchards and the like, and some of the more basic models today should really only be used to tackle hard-wearing areas containing coarser grasses, where finish is not important. However, the better quality versions with fine height adjustments, collecting boxes and large rear rollers can be used on good-quality lawns, and have the advantage of being usable, unlike the cylinder mower, on overgrown lawns. Generally speaking, the same rule of thumb for deciding whether to buy electric, petrol or two-stroke models applies – electrically powered models are usually more appropriate for small and medium-sized lawns and where an electric power-point is accessible. Petrol models are sometimes easier to start than two-stroke, though modern two-stroke engines are nothing like the back-breaking, temperamental demons they used to be – providing the right grade of clean, high-quality two-stroke mixture (petrol and oil) is used. Two-stroke engines are often recommended for sloping areas where four-stroke petrol engines will occasionally stall.

Hover-mowers, once the engine or motor is started, are very easily moved and steered on their cushion of air and are sometimes suggested for cutting steep banks where other mowers would be unusable. However, accidents have occurred by using these machines attached to a rope and it is my opinion that if a bank is so long and steep that it cannot be mown by conventional methods it perhaps should not be grassed at all, but ought to be ground-cover planted instead. Larger hover-mowers can be difficult to transport when not in use unless fitted with transport wheels. Smaller electric models are reasonably lightweight and can be hung up flat on the wall when not in use, which is a big consideration where storage space is limited.

Rotary mowers cannot be used up to the edges of beds and borders. In the case of the wheeled models, the two wheels near the bed must be kept on the lawn to maintain the height of the cut, and although in theory hover-mowers *look* as though they can be run over the edge, in practice the difference in levels affects the cushions of air and causes shaving.

MOWER MAINTENANCE. After every time of use, clean the mower thoroughly and gently remove compacted grass from the blades and, in the case of rotaries, the canopy. Spray the machine with WD40 or wipe it over with an oily rag. Attend to parts recommended in the handbook for oiling and greasing. Re-read the handbook periodically and carry out any other maintenance instructions.

All mowers should be regularly serviced, usually at the end of the cutting season, by an expert. The finish a mower produces is only as good as the maintenance its blades have received, and a sweetly running engine is half the battle on a big or tedious job. Electric models should be periodically checked for faults by a competent electrician, and cables regularly examined for signs of damage.

SAFETY. Always wear stout, well gripping footwear when using power-driven mowers. It is the easiest thing in the world to slip on slightly damp grass if you are wearing inadequate shoes, and toes can be lost very quickly like this. Occasionally – especially with rotary mowers, particularly hover ones – stones are thrown out by the revolving blade. Four-wheel versions usually have a stone guard but hover ones have only the protection of the canopy, and in both cases there is the chance of a stone flying out and hitting your leg. If your shins are protected by trousers, jeans, thick stockings or whatever, it will probably hurt, but no more. If you've nothing on that part of your anatomy, it will probably make a hole in your leg. It never happens to you – until it does!

Never try to free a jammed blade on a cylinder mower or clean out the build-up of clippings on the underside of the canopy of a rotary one while the power is on, and the engine is running (unless of course, you feel some of your ten fingers are surplus to requirements).

HOW TO MOW. It may seem unnecessary to mention this, but the only way to use a mower is to walk up and down behind it. It is dangerous to walk backwards, pulling the machine towards you (you cannot do it anyway if it is self-propelled), you could fall and mow yourself instead, and you will never get neat, straight lines if you cannot see where you're going. It is also not a good idea to walk ahead, dragging it behind you – you cannot see what it is up to. It should not be necessary to cut grass in a series of short pushes and jabs, such as you often see with people using a hand mower. If the mower will not cut properly unless you do this, there is something wrong. In the case of a hand mower, it is usually because the grass is overgrown, the blades need adjusting or the cylinder is just plain blunt, and a good service will put it right. With a powered cylinder mower, it is often because it is attempting to cut grass which is too long. Try raising the blades. If this does not work, the grass is too much for this type of mower, and should be shortened first using a rotary kind. If you have the same trouble with this, raising the blade to its highest point will usually help. With a hover-mower, it is generally because the grass is either too long, or the blade is blunt. It is not a good idea to mow wet grass. This compacts the soil surface, the grass cuts badly, and if there is no grassbox, solid chunks of soggy clippings are left all over the lawn.

THE ROTARY CULTIVATOR. This is a petrol, diesel, two-stroke or, occasionally, electrically powered machine with rotating tillers which will turn over clean soil and produce a fine tilth. It is useful for large, well maintained vegetable plots and the final preparation of soil in new gardens but it is not a substitute for digging, especially in weed-infested ground, where perennial roots can have spread to create a major problem. The most efficient machines are very expensive and the capital outlay is only justified if you think you may need to use it regularly. Cultivators are available from hire shops, which might be a useful consideration for occasional work.

THE SPIN TRIMMER. This is essentially a head containing a reel of nylon cord on a handle supporting an engine or motor which drives the loose end of the cord round at very high speed. The head is held near ground level and the effect of the spinning nylon cord is to sever soft plant growth. Because the nylon is flexible, it does not damage hard material, so it is a useful device for trimming long grass against trees and fences but it can damage the bark at the base of trees. In effect it is the powered equivalent of a pair of long-handled shears – if there is a lot of this sort of work to do, a spin trimmer will do it quicker and more easily. Like the power-driven mower, spin trimmers come in a range of strengths, from lightweight electrical ones for the smaller garden, to heavy-duty petrol-driven machines with a variety of attachments for clearing very rough areas and brushwood.

THE LAWN RAKER. Periodically, a lawn should be raked over with a spring-tined rake to remove dead clippings, the 'thatch' of horizontal grass stems which occurs in older grass, and any moss it may contain. This is a very boring and tedious job, producing masses of rubbish which has to be cleaned up as the work progresses. The electric lawn raker is intended to do the same job only more quickly, more easily and more efficiently. In design it resembles a lightweight electric mower, but instead of a cutting cylinder it has a cylindrical set of wire tines which revolve when the machine is in motion and scratch up the surface of the lawn, bringing off great quantities of debris. This passes automatically into the collecting box fitted to the machine, making clearing up a much less arduous task. It is a reasonably priced piece of equipment which, although not absolutely essential, can be an asset if you are keen on achieving a good-quality lawn. The rakings make excellent compost.

THE HEDGE TRIMMER. This piece of equipment would only be required immediately by a gardener with an inherited hedge, or many bushy plants, such as heathers, requiring regular trimming. But anyone intending to plant a hedge may like to consider acquiring a trimmer when the time comes for regular cutting. Hedges can be clipped with shears, but if the new growth is a bit tough and woody, shears can soon become blunt. Also, if there is a large area to cut, the constant chopping and jarring can be very tiring after a while. Although power hedge trimmers are comparatively heavy, they do the job so much quicker that the user is not as likely to feel as weary at the end of the job. Hedge trimmers are usually powered by electricity and consist of a pair of toothed blades which move backwards and forwards against each other. The tool is passed over the surface of the hedge from the bottom upwards. The new growth is cut as it comes between the teeth of the two moving blades and drops on to the ground. As with other machinery, several sizes are available, but the bigger they get, the heavier they are in proportion, and it is usually less arduous to use a smaller, lighter model unless you have to trim hundreds of yards of hedging. Petrol and two-stroke models are also manufactured but these are considerably heavier owing to the weight of the engine and only come into their own if there is no means of powering an electrically operated model. The main drawback of electric hedge trimmers is the likelihood of cutting the cable. Again, with modern double-insulated models, there should be no real problem but the use of an RCD in connection with the machine, as described for electric mowers, will eliminate the risk of electric shock. A battery-operated machine is useful for trimming shrubs and short lengths of hedge.

While an electric hedge trimmer is a boon to the busy gardener, in careless hands it can become a dangerous piece of equipment. Always wear good footwear and fitted clothing, especially if you have to climb a ladder or steps when using it. Never use an electric trimmer on a wet hedge or in the rain. Undue reaching or stretching is not a good idea either, as you haven't got proper control over the machine. If you do inadvertently cut the cable, it should always be rejoined with a proper connector, not a bit of insulation tape. Modern hedge trimmers have a range of built-in safety devices to reduce accidents, theoretically to a minimum. Always keep both hands on the trimmer – do not pull pieces of trimmings off the hedge with one hand while continuing to cut with the other –

those blades are extremely strong – and sharp; they are no respecters of fingers!

THE CHAIN SAW. The chain saw is a useful but potentially highly dangerous piece of equipment. Professional foresters have to undergo rigorous training before using this machine, but the amateur gardener can go to the nearest DIY outlet, buy one over the counter and immediately put it into operation.

A chain saw is only justifiable if you are reclaiming a neglected garden, or if you intend to set up in the firewood business. It is admittedly useful for removing large branches and unwanted trees quickly, but you must bear in mind the following safety considerations:

1. Use ear defenders and goggles, padded trousers sold for the purpose, stout footwear and gloves, and a safety helmet.
2. Only cut material within easy reach. Ladders must be roped to a firm structure.
3. Large trees should be felled in small pieces.
4. Keep children away completely.
5. Always read the comprehensive literature supplied with the machine.

Chain saws are powered by electricity or petrol. Electric chain saws are lighter and more efficient for light work if care is taken with the cable. For long-term work of a heavier nature, a petrol-driven model is advisable.

THE GARDEN SHREDDER. This piece of equipment has become increasingly popular over the last ten years as an alternative to burning and 'tipping' garden waste. The number of shredders, powered both by petrol and by electricity is legion, but they all have one thing in common – they are noisy, and while they solve the environment problem, they create another (i.e., they use valuable energy resources). Again, you get what you pay for. Cheaper models are underpowered and because of their design, clog easily. More expensive shredders work quicker, tackle larger material and clog less easily, but I would strongly recommend a home demonstration before buying.

Above all, think of your neighbour. Your wish to be environmentally friendly might be the end of your neighbour's quiet weekend.

EXTENSION CABLES. Some electrically operated garden machinery is provided with a certain amount of cable, some only has a short piece long enough to connect it to a separate lead. In most cases it is quite likely you will need an additional length of cable to be able to reach as far as you want to. Do see that it is suitable for what is being connected to it – take professional advice if in doubt.

And a word of warning about connectors. These come in two parts – a 'male' part with two or three pins sticking out of it – usually partly covered by a protective sheath, and a 'female' part with the holes, also protected, into which the pins are fitted. Do make sure that the male part is attached to the machine; if it is attached to the extension cable, the pins will be live when the cable is plugged into the mains. This is not as elementary as it sounds – I have actually seen a mower with an extension cable connected up the wrong way round – if a child had pulled the two pieces apart and touched the live pins the result could have been fatal. If in doubt, buy an extension reel with safety connections at each end.

Other equipment

There are a few other items you might find necessary before you have been at the gardening game for long:

A WATERING CAN is a must for watering small seedlings and new plants. Watering cans usually come in a range of capacities up to about 2 gallons (10 litres) – how large a one you buy will depend on how much you feel like carrying at a time – a gallon of water weighs 10 lbs (a litre weighs 1 kg) – but you can always half-fill a big one. Nowadays, watering cans are usually made of plastic, but metal ones are still available. You can buy fine 'roses' (the attachment at the end of the spout through which the water sprinkles) and coarse ones, your choice will depend on whether you want fine drops for small plants and seeds or big ones for more mature things, and other attachments, like weed applicators.

A HOSE can make watering a lot easier, especially if it has some form of sprinkler attached. Buy a kink-proof, reinforced one; it is more expensive, but worth it. A retractable hose reel is now available. Although pricey, it takes all the hard work out of unwinding and rewinding the hose.

See Chapter 27 (page 358) on water conservation for more details on watering.

A SPRAYER is needed for spraying plants with pesticides, fungicides and foliar feeds. Sprayers can be of several designs. The smallest is a hand trigger-operated model, usually holding about a pint (around half a litre). The largest are the knapsack ones used by professionals and can contain several gallons. They are quite expensive and when filled are very heavy, so they are not really suitable for any but the biggest gardens. In between these two are a range of models usually worked with compressed air pumped in by a pressurizing mechanism screwed into the top, liquid being forced out along a lance and through an adjustable spray nozzle. Some sprayers work on the syringe principle, liquid being drawn up and pumped out by means of a pump barrel on the lance. Because certain chemicals have an adverse effect on the plastic of the sprayers, and because some chemicals do not combine well with others, sprayers should always be washed out well after use.

It is not a very good idea to use watering cans and sprayers for weedkillers unless they are kept and used for this purpose alone. However, if you cannot readily afford two watering cans and two sprayers it is possible to combine their use; but after containing weedkillers, cans and sprayers should be more than thoroughly washed out with hot water and strong detergent, followed by copious rinsing with hot and then cold water.

A WHEELBARROW is useful in a large garden for wheeling heavy or bulky materials around. It should be of strong construction. A ballbarrow has the front wheel replaced with a revolving ball, the theory being that the ball does not make grooves in grass when a load is being carried, whereas a wheel does. This is true, but usually these ruts are not serious and soon disappear. A barrow with a pneumatic tyre is easier to wheel than one with a hard wheel. If a barrow is being moved backwards and forwards a lot over one area, a plank can be put down to save wear and tear on the ground and avoid the wheel getting bogged down.

In small gardens a wheelbarrow can sometimes be un-wieldy, and a carrying sheet for large things or an old bucket for small ones is much more practical.

There are also many pieces of household equipment such as step ladders, stiff brooms and the like which are equally at home in the garden. Experience and individual circumstances will tell you which you may have to acquire for your particular needs.

This is just a very basic list of equipment you are going to need to get started. There are hundreds of other appliances I haven't included, mainly because you can do a good job perfectly well without them. Having said that, if you like the look of something which you feel just might be the thing for *you*, you buy it, and it works, well, fair enough. We all have our favourite tools, purpose-made or improvised. If we feel it does the job best for us, then that's the tool we need. But – when in doubt – ask an expert.

4
GETTING DOWN TO IT

What happens next will largely depend upon whether you're starting from scratch or you have the basis of something pleasant.

The brand-new garden

Assuming that this has been cleared of most rubbish, vegetation, etc., by the builders, the main aim at this stage is to get the ground worked into a state ready to take new plants in due course. Take your time. What you do now will affect the performance of everything you grow in the future, so it must be done right.

First, go over the ground and remove any remaining rubble and rubbish. Rubble which might be useful as hardcore could be stacked in a heap and used later as a foundation for paths or similar, the rest disposed of (see How to get rid of your rubbish, p. 65).

Now, consider the time of year, and the weather. If it is very frosty, snowy, or wet, walking on or messing about with the ground can only do more harm than good. If you are in the middle of a sweltering drought, you probably will not be able to get a spade into the rock-hard, sun-baked surface, and even if you can, it is likely to do *you* more harm than good.

Ideally, any initial preparation should be done in early autumn, then the wind, rain and frost can work on the soil over winter. Ground so treated is much easier to work afterwards and even heavy soil will begin to take on a more manageable structure better suited to the cultivation of plants. In reality, it is not always possible to do the right thing at the right time, so you have to pick the most opportune moment. Gardening is always a balance between ideal theory and practical compromise.

Bearing these remarks in mind, the next stage is to turn over the soil roughly. Unless you have the type and size of plot which is most easily dealt with by tractor and plough, there are two courses open to you: hand digging and mechanical cultivation.

Hand digging is done using a spade, or, in the case of very heavy or compacted soil, a flat-tined spading or potato fork. The perfectionist will recommend some very laborious methods of digging which are guaranteed to put off a new or even a moderately enthusiastic gardener for life, especially if there is a large area involved. For most purposes single or double digging will be quite adequate. The former consists of inserting the spade as nearly vertically as possible to its full depth into the ground, bringing up a spadeful of earth, and then turning the spade over so the spadeful falls back into the hole upside down. This method has two functions – to introduce air into the top spit of soil, and to bury 9–12 in. (225–300 mm) deep any weeds on the surface. At this depth the majority will die and rot down.

Double digging consists of taking out a trench at the beginning of the area to be dug, about 2 ft (600 mm) wide and the depth of a spade. The soil from this trench is barrowed to the end of the piece being dug up. The earth at the base of the trench is then dug over, preferably using a fork, and broken up to the full depth of the fork. Then a further strip of ground, adjoining the original trench, is dug out in the same way, the soil from this being used to fill in the first trench, and the second spit at the base of the trench broken up as described. The whole of the area is worked in this way, the last trench being filled in with the soil originally taken out of the first trench.

The purpose of double digging is aeration and weed disposal as before, but in addition the ground is thoroughly broken up and aerated for at least 18 in. (450 mm) and drainage is considerably improved, especially in heavy soils and where large machinery has compacted the ground. But be warned, it is very hard work – although an excellent substitute for jogging. In the majority of gardens, unless the ground is particularly hard or compacted, single digging will be quite adequate for most parts, individual areas such as vegetable plots being dealt with more thoroughly at a later stage. A large piece of ground may need turning over with a rotary cultivator (see page 54).

Whether or not you disregard the next stage will depend on your impatience to see a show place outside your patio doors, but the more you can bear to prepare your garden methodically and without rushing the job, generally the better the end results will be.

Ideally, you should leave your ground roughly dug for a good time to let the elements have a go at it. If you have done the job in autumn, at least the whole winter should elapse before you do anything else. If you dug the ground in spring or early summer, it is best left until autumn before further work. It is not a bad idea to leave it alone until you have got another covering of weeds. Many of these will be annual ones which have germinated from seeds you have turned up while digging, but some will have grown from the roots of perennial weeds which you buried while digging and which grew again. If you wait until they have grown up nicely but have not yet begun to seed you can deal with them in one of two ways: forking, and using weedkillers.

Forking can be quite a satisfactory job if you have the time. You insert a sharp fork into the top spit and loosen all the weeds by the roots. These can then be removed with the fork or a rake and disposed of (see How to get rid of your rubbish, page 65). Unless you have a lot of almost unremovable weeds such as bindweed (convolvulus) or couch grass, this method produces comparatively clean ground in which to replant and gives you an opportunity to dig and aerate the top layer of soil again. Organic gardeners may prefer the 'smother' approach, which consists of covering the weed–ridden area in black polythene for at least 12 months. This is fine if you are not in a hurry. Very persistent weeds, such as horsetail, may not respond to this treatment.

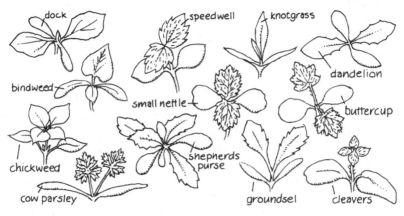

Seedling Weeds

Chemicals for weed control are not entirely essential — but they can make the job of clearing the ground of weeds much simpler. In the case of those perennial weeds whose roots it is virtually impossible to remove entirely, and which will regrow if even a small piece is overlooked, it is possibly more efficient to tackle them with chemicals.

When you have a good covering of active top growth, spray all the weeds, using a herbicide. Do make sure, however, that it is suitable for your purpose. As it is likely you will wish to replant fairly soon, it is no good using a weedkiller with long-term residual effects on the soil, such as sodium chlorate, dichlobenil (Casoron G) or simazine. These herbicides remain in the soil for a considerable length of time after application and are therefore only suitable for areas required to be kept free from weeds for long periods, e.g., gravel paths or the bare ground between shrubs (*not* sodium chlorate for this last purpose as this is highly toxic to *all* plants). Also as you want to kill the *roots* of perennial plants, not just the top growth, there is no point in using a weedkiller such as paraquat which only kills top growth by affecting the chlorophyll and is therefore most suitable for annual weeds. The best chemical to use in such circumstances is one based on glyphosate which absorbs the poison through the green top growth and transfers it to the roots, which are subsequently killed. The chemical is neutralized when it touches the soil and after about 4 weeks (more or less, depending on the time of year and weather), the weeds will have died sufficiently for the ground to be turned over again.

At this point or, if you decide not to use a weedkiller, when the weeds have been forked out, it is a good idea to turn the ground over quickly again (single digging will be enough), incorporating at the same time some humus-forming material such as compost, well-rotted manure, etc. (see Chapter 5, pages 88–93) and possibly some form of fertilizer.

How to get rid of your rubbish

THE REFUSE SKIP. This is a large metal container which is available on hire per day, week, or weekend from waste disposal contractors. It is generally brought to you on a lorry and removed, plus rubbish, at the end of the specified time, for a fee. Some councils put down skips at appointed places and dates, in which local residents can dispose of domestic and garden waste for free. Contact your local environment health department to see if such a system operates in your area. Otherwise the firms providing this service can usually be found from the Yellow Pages and it is as well to shop around as prices vary considerably.

If possible, try to get the skip placed on your own land. It is permissible to site a skip on the highway in certain cases if it is impossible to put it elsewhere, but to get it there is quite a palaver. First you have to request permission from the Highways Department of the council for the area in which you live and fill in the appropriate forms. They will then tell you where to put the skip so it is not a traffic or pedestrian hazard or obstruction. You have to specify accurately the dates on which the skip will be placed on the highway, after which it must be removed, and undertake to have it adequately lit and marked with road lamps, hazard warnings, bollards, etc. What happens in practice is that you go out at night, light your lamps, check that everything is snug, and when you get up next morning, someone has stolen your lamps, put your bollards on next door's gateposts, and the supreme opportunists have been at work in the small hours quietly filling your skip with their old prams and defunct refrigerators.

A skip is a near-essential if you have a lot of non-combustible or non-rottable refuse to deal with, but there are also contractors who will come with lorries or dustcarts and remove piles of rubbish for you, if you have somewhere to stack the stuff till it is worthwhile calling them in.

THE LOCAL RECYCLING CENTRE. This varies from skips in which to dump your rubbish, regardless of origin, to local authorities with the planet's future at heart, who isolate garden rubbish from other forms of refuse, compost it, then sell it back to you, properly treated. If you are concerned about environmental issues, ask around. If your local authority does not offer this facility, you might find your neighbouring one does. For the cost of a short journey, it may be worth it, both to you and the environment.

THE COMPOST HEAP. In broad terms, a compost heap is a collection of green garden refuse – weeds, old pea and bean haulms, soft hedge trimmings, grass mowings, together with vegetable kitchen waste, leaves, straw and any other similar rubbish, such as shredded prunings and newspaper, which is piled so that it rots down by bacterial action. During the process, the part which is rotting becomes extremely warm; the warmer it gets, the better and quicker it rots down and in theory the amount of heat generated is enough to kill weed seeds present, though in practice this is not always the case. Rotting takes place quicker in summer than winter. Don't use big pieces of woody waste as they will take too long, shred or cut them up finely first. Shred weeds with very tough roots finely so they rot.

You can compost a small amount of waste using one of the specially designed bins which can be purchased from garden shops and the like, but large amounts are best dealt with by making an enclosure of timber, or even small-mesh wire netting supported by posts, a minimum of 3 ft (900 mm) square, but 5 ft (1.5 m) is better, into which is piled layers of this soft, green garden rubbish until it forms a cube. Mix coarse rubbish with soft, wet material such as grass clippings so the waste rots quickly and sweetly. Grass clippings and suchlike settle into a soggy blanket which decomposes into a nasty smelly slime because the aerobic bacteria necessary for healthy compost-making cannot exist in such airless conditions, so unpleasant anaerobic ones get to work instead.

It is sometimes recommended that accelerators such as

nitrogen-rich fertilizers, with or without lime or powdered chalk and beneficial bacteria to prevent the heap from becoming too acid during the rotting process, are added as each layer of refuse is placed on the heap, but I find that if the heap is properly constructed it will break down quite adequately without, and the soil acidity can be adjusted after the compost has been dug in if necessary.

It is also suggested that a very thin layer of soil can be spread over each 9 in. (225 mm) of garden refuse on the heap to introduce the bacteria to break down the waste, but if plants with roots have been added to the heap, there could be quite a lot of soil, and therefore bacteria, adhering to these, so I find this is not essential and can actually cool off the heap.

Cover the heap with perforated polythene, sacking, straw or similar when not being added to, to keep out excessive rainwater which would cool down the heap and make the compost soggy, and also to conserve warmth. Usable compost should be available in 6–9 months.

With a proprietary compost bin, you can speed up the rotting process by mixing up the last layer of material with the new waste being added. The already rotting rubbish gets the new refuse to start to rot so much quicker.

Well-made compost should be brown, sweet-smelling, moist but not soggy and look rather like a medium coarse peat. If it is a nasty, greenish-black, evil-smelling goo, it is generally because too much fine soft waste, like grass clippings, has been added at once, especially when steps haven't been taken to exclude as much rainwater as possible.

It is a good idea, when you start composting, to have two heaps, bins, or whatever – one to keep adding to and one which is completed and left to finish rotting prior to digging in.

THE BONFIRE. There is no more contentious subject than the garden fire. In its favour there is the fact that you can reduce enormous piles of combustible refuse into a manageable heap of pleasant-to-handle ashes, which are themselves a beneficial soil additive, providing potash and improving texture. It is also a hygienic way of disposing of pest- and disease-infested material.

Against setting light to garden refuse is the argument that bonfire smoke pollutes the atmosphere, adds to the 'greenhouse effect' and produces a certain amount of substances known to cause cancer. Smoke from fires will nearly always be a nuisance to someone, dirtying washing, forcing people to close windows, staining paintwork. Bonfires can be a traffic hazard if the wind turns and blows the smoke across a nearby road. The site of the fire, if it has been very hot, and burned for some time, can become sterile for a while afterwards, though this is not a major issue, as the existing soil can be replaced or combined with some from surrounding areas.

Before lighting a bonfire, you should consider whether there is a less anti-social method of refuse disposal. If you are new to an area, and especially if you have not noticed anyone else burning rubbish, check with your local council to see if there are any regulations or by-laws about garden fires or smoke emission in general. If not, and you decide to go ahead, light the fire on a still day and well away from houses and roads. Check the weather forecast for 'freakish' changes in wind. If smoke blows over a road, you will be breaking the law, and could be in serious trouble with the police.

When it is cold, bag the ash up in waterproof sacks until it is required, as the potash is easily washed out if the ash is left open to the elements.

It must be stressed that this method should *only* be used where it can cause no offence to others and all other ways of rubbish disposal are impossible.

Dos and Don'ts of Bonfires

DO NOT use paraffin. It makes the fire burn wet and a lot of water vapour is given off which is just what you do not need. It is very rarely you can get a really hot fire by starting it with paraffin.

DO NOT use petrol or any other form of volatile fuel. It flares up with horrific intensity, including the vapour surrounding the spilt fuel which can burn fiercely right back to the container it was stored in and cause a serious explosion. If you are still holding the can at the time, it is unlikely you will be able to make another bonfire for a long time, if ever.

DO NOT start the fire off with any substance other than paper, cardboard or wood. To burn any material which emits black smoke (e.g. polythene or old tyres) is illegal.

DO NOT burn rubbish under adverse weather conditions – high winds, periods of drought, and fog.

DO make sure that you supervise the fire at all times

and ensure any sparks falling in the vicinity are dealt with immediately.

DO keep children and animals well away from the burning area.

DO make sure hot ashes are dowsed with water before you finally leave them, especially in summer.

ALWAYS dig a substantial firebreak into bare earth around the perimeter of the fire.

INCINERATORS. Garden incinerators are not much use if you have vast quantities of rubbish to get rid of. They can also be as much of a nuisance as bonfires, but can sometimes be of benefit in disposing of badly diseased or pest-ridden material. The ones most easily come by are usually of three types.

The *metal mesh incinerator* is in effect a cubic metal mesh basket on four legs. It requires some skill to keep alight; as the bottom also consists of open metal mesh, the base of the burning material soon burns out and the fire requires constant relighting until you get the hang of it. Only small pieces of rubbish should be piled on, as long stalks get caught up in the mesh and won't allow the rubbish to settle on to the burning part, consequently it goes out again. It makes a big burning job rather tedious, but it has its uses in a small area for containing the fire in one place.

The *dustbin incinerator* looks like a dustbin on legs with a hole in the lid attached to an external round chimney and holes around the base to provide the fire with draught. It is made of galvanized iron, so the base eventually burns through after it has been used for a lot of hot fires. It is efficient since by design it ensures small material is burned quickly and without much smoke or many sparks.

The *mobile incinerator* is a large metal box on wheels, with a grid for the base and a sort of pram handle to push it around by. It can be useful for burning up prunings as they are produced by wheeling the bonfire around with you as you work, but again it has the annoying habit of burning out too quickly if it is not regularly fed, and you have to be very careful not to use it on the lawn without putting some form of protection underneath it first, as the heat will scorch the grass and hot ashes will burn holes in it.

The derelict site, the orchard or field site

The trouble with this sort of site is that there will be so much rubbish and unwanted vegetation that you cannot see the wood for the trees. The best way of dealing with it is to consider what is already there and decide the best method of treating it.

TREES. Some of these might be quite useful in forming the framework of the new design, but it is important to find out what they are. Even if they are quite small at the time you take over the plot, they could be saplings of very large forest trees which will eventually become a nuisance. Their leaves will give you, and your neighbours, an endless autumn job, clearing them from lawns, paths and gutters. Leaves left to rot on a lawn will ruin it. Leaves on paths make them dangerously slippery. Leaves in gutters will eventually block downpipes and soakaways, making the walls of the property damp.

Leaves are not the only problem. Roots of big trees spread a considerable distance and can damage foundations, cause settlement and block drains. As a very rough rule of thumb, the roots of a tree spread at least as far in all directions as it is tall. For example, a tree 40 ft tall (just over 12 m) can have a root system of more than 40 ft radius (affecting over 5,000 sq ft or 450 sq m of ground), so it should be at least 40 ft away from any permanent structure. There are many exceptions to this rule, but it is a good guide until you become more familiar with the various species.

A third problem with unsuitable trees is the shade they cast, and the dry area under the spread of their branches. This can become annoying if house light is affected. Also it cuts down quite considerably the types of plant you can grow as those which appreciate dry, shady, impoverished conditions are limited. Remember that this can affect your neighbours just as much as it can affect you if the tree is near their boundary.

Observe also how healthy the trees are, and whether they are well shaped. There is no point planning a garden round an ailing, straggly specimen. However, if it has only small dead and dying pieces, these can be removed – otherwise it is better to lose it altogether.

One word of caution – many mature trees are subject to tree preservation orders, especially in conservation areas or

70

where many properties are 'listed buildings'. If you intend to do anything drastic, check with your local council first. If a listed tree creates certain problems, they will always meet you to discuss them, but if you remove a listed tree without permission, you cannot put it back again!

Assuming there aren't any restrictions, and you decide that a tree has to go, it is far better to deal with it while the garden is being gutted than leave it for a while until it gets out of hand. Tree removal makes a lot of mess and temporary damage to the surrounding area, and lopping back the branches to a more suitable length is no real solution. Lopped trees look ugly and the natural shape, which is often the most attractive thing about them, is permanently spoilt. Also, depending on the rate of regrowth, you will probably have to remove the new branches annually to keep the tree in check – lopped trees always grow faster than ones left alone, until the top growth becomes proportionate to the root system again.

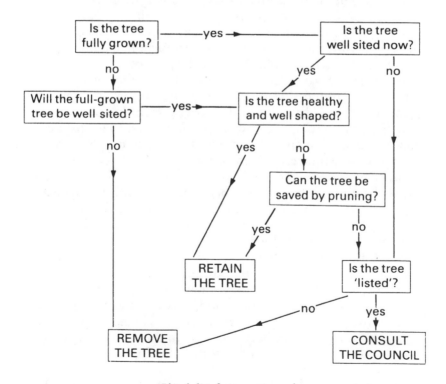

Check list for tree removal

71

Very large trees are best dealt with by reputable tree-felling contractors. A badly felled tree can do irreparable damage. Felling contractors have the machinery for the job, the expertise and protective clothing and harnessing. Personal recommendation is the best way to find a firm specializing in this sort of work. There are probably more unskilled, untrained cowboys in this trade than any other. By the time you realize you have employed one of them, it may be too late. Ask to see their certificate of public liability insurance before entering into any contract.

Some felling contractors will also remove the stump for you if required. If the garden is large enough, they may drag it out with a tractor and chain, or lift it out with a JCB. Otherwise, there are stump-boring machines which will drill most of the stump out. Try and ensure that as much of the old root as possible is removed as certain diseases (e.g., bootlace fungus) can occasionally start this way in a garden.

If the stump is not removed it will sprout again and so should be killed off. One method of doing this is by drilling deep holes in it and filling them up with a brushwood killer, then covering the stump with waterproof material to prevent rain diluting the chemical. The stump will eventually die and rot.

Another alternative is to leave several feet of stump sticking out of the ground, kill it off as before, and grow climbing plants up it. This has a lot of drawbacks, from looking rather odd if in the wrong place, to harbouring pests and diseases, and eventually blowing over when it is rotten and top heavy, so should only be used as a last resort.

Smaller trees can be felled in stages using a hand-saw or small chain saw, which should be quite easy for a handyman. The stump can usually be dug out by hand or covered up as described above. Small trees and stumps can sometimes be winched out using a caravanner's winch.

Small branches and twigs can be burned if convenient or shredded, larger branches and trunks sawn up and used as firewood or burned. If burning would cause problems and the timber is not required for firewood, a skip is the best way to get the rubbish off the site. Large roots do not burn well except when they have been exposed to the air and dried off for a considerable time, so are best put in a skip.

HEDGES. Many neglected gardens have equally neglected hedges. As a good hedge takes many years to establish and is a habitat for wild creatures, it is better not to remove it unless absolutely necessary.

Except for conifer hedges (excluding yew), a neglected hedge will grow up again very well if cut as hard back, using a sharp saw, as you feel necessary. Remember that a hedge will continue to get bigger through all-round growth – not just new shoots – so it is best to cut it back further than you eventually require the height to allow for this. It may take several years of regular clipping to get it into the shape and size you would like to see it, but providing you do not neglect it again, it will eventually come back into form.

Old, bare, coniferous hedges are best removed. Hedge removal is hard work as the roots have to be dug out unless, again, it is possible to drag or push the hedge out with machinery.

Hedges made of quickthorn (hawthorn) and blackthorn (sloe or *Prunus spinosa*) can be 'laid', by splitting the trunks part-way through and then laying them down at an angle. This has the effect of making a very dense, impenetrable hedge. It is, however, a skilled craft, and not a job for the inexperienced amateur. In country districts it may be possible to find a professional hedge-layer, possibly working in farming, to do this job for you. Try ringing your local Agricultural Training Board.

Dispose of rubbish by skip or burning.

BUSHES, OVERGROWN SHRUBS. By the time you start clearing the site, you've possibly got a vague idea of how you are eventually going to lay your garden out. You may be able to recognize some of the bushes growing up in the jungle that faces you. These might be quite ornamental and could be of use in a new scheme, or they might be untidy, wild seedlings. Remember, though, that even ornamental species may not be worth keeping if they have become too old and woody through neglect to be attractive, and if they have been in for many years may have been superseded by better varieties.

To remove unwanted shrubs easily, prune off with secateurs or saw off all but, say, 3 ft (1 m) of top growth, which becomes a useful lever with which to loosen the shrub as you dig it out. Again, a large garden could be cleared using heavy machinery – if this method is at all possible, it is probably worth spending a bit to hire a tractor and driver or a JCB and operator. They can do in a few hours, possibly more efficiently, what it might take you a few years to accomplish.

Dispose of rubbish by skip or burning. Keen vegetable-growing neighbours might be interested in seeing what you have to get rid of which they could use for pea-sticks.

BRIARS, BRAMBLES. Briars are the long thorny stems of wild rose species, and brambles are the matted top growths of black-berries. They are very difficult to dig out, partly because of their thorns and partly because they can become embedded in the soil. Possibly the easiest way of dealing with these is to cut down the top growth and wait until it has made a lot of new strong green shoots, then finish these off with a brushwood killer or broad-leaved herbicide, according to manufacturer's instructions.

Dispose of rubbish by skip or burning.

WEEDY GROWTH. This includes all vegetation such as weed grasses, unwanted perennial garden plants, and those wild plants usually thought of as weeds. If the plot is waist high in a mixture of this sort of rubbish, it is best to decide to start again.

In a small garden, you can cut off the top growth with shears or spin trimmer, and then dig the site thoroughly as described for the new garden (pages 61–5), using suitable weedkillers if and when required.

Dispose of rubbish by skip or composting.

A larger garden is harder work to deal with. Possibly the least arduous method is to cut down the top growth and dispose of it as described above, using a sharp hand-scythe, scythette or grass hook. (Warning: these last three tools can be difficult to wield in inexperienced hands and can be positively dangerous if not used carefully.) A substantial spin trimmer or brush cutter will also usually be able to cope with this sort of vegetation.

When you have cut down the tall growth, leave the un-wanted vegetation to grow up again until there is a good covering, and then treat it with glyphosate. Dig the ground over when the top weed growth has died off thoroughly.

If you do not wish to use chemicals, the only answer is to double dig (see page 62) the area as soon as the weeds are cut down, making sure they are buried at least 12 in. (300 mm) deep. This will not eliminate all weeds from the area, but those regrowing can be dealt with individually on reappearance.

Sometimes old orchards and grass fields used as building plots will still have a good covering of reasonable grass when the house is finished and, unless you intend to become a lawn fanatic, this can often be made the basis of a reasonable piece of lawn. If there are not many weeds, the grass will grow quite well with regular mowing and many very coarse grasses will actually mow out. The best plan is to start with a heavy-duty rotary mower until the surface looks good enough to take a cylinder mower, treating weeds with an appropriate lawn weedkiller (see chart on pages 78–9). With regular mowing, raking, weeding and feeding you should get a lawn that will be at least as good as some of those created from treated meadow turf, and possibly better.

Dispose of rubbish on the compost heap, making sure you mix fine grass mowings with coarser refuse for proper rotting to take place.

OLD FRUIT TREES. Some old apples, pears, cherries and plums, providing they are not in the wrong place, will give good fruit for many years. The ones to get rid of are those with many dead and dying branches, split bark and cankerous growth (this looks like a warty, knotted growth on the branches, and these will eventually die from the canker upwards), also those not making healthy new growth and those of a poor shape.

Those worth keeping should be preliminarily pruned and thinned out by taking out dead branches, unhealthy wood, branches which cross over each other, those which are in the way of mowing and other tasks or features in the garden, and those which grow into the centre of the tree, or are growing too tall and upright. The aim is for an easily managed tree, with an open head of well-spaced branches. Prune plums and cherries in summer to minimize infection by silver leaf disease.

Soft fruit bushes – blackcurrants, gooseberries, raspberries, etc. – have a somewhat limited productive life and whereas they can be pruned and shaped up, they are prone to virus diseases with age, which affect the fruiting and can infect other healthy stock, so it is probably better to scrap them and start afresh.

Dispose of rubbish by skip or burning. Fruit wood,

especially apple, smells lovely burnt on a domestic fire.

RUBBLE. In derelict gardens this usually comes from old paths and hard standings, demolished walls and other features, greenhouse bases, and old rockeries.

Old paths can be very restricting to a new layout so unless they are well constructed it is probably better to scrap them. They might well in any case have deteriorated to such an extent that they can easily be broken up with a pick or crowbar (these can be hired from a tool hire shop). Very well constructed concrete bases, hard standings, etc. are sometimes difficult to remove without professional help, and in such a case it might be better to ask yourself if you could use the concrete *in situ* for something else – the base of a shed or greenhouse perhaps or, properly screened, as a clean working area.

Other refuse which might come into this category is the dumping of years on your derelict site – old beds, cookers, timber, etc. which come to light only when you cut down the jungle, together with demolished fences, collapsed sheds, etc.

If you intend to re-lay paths, drives or a patio, stack rubble such as broken bricks, stone or concrete neatly somewhere until you need it. Unwanted and rotten timber and other combustible rubbish can be burned if convenient, or placed in the skip, as should any other refuse. Sometimes scrap metal merchants will give you a pound or two for good quality metal waste.

It is bad garden hygiene to leave uncontrolled rubbish about on site. Some makes a very good breeding ground for vermin and other pests, while old timber becomes infested with many diseases, the worst possibly being coral spot fungus, which, although mainly affecting dead wood, can infect dead branches on live trees and shrubs, from which it will spread to the live wood, killing branches and sometimes the whole plant.

The established garden

Approach this with extreme caution. Do not tear everything up as soon as possible, regardless of whether it is worth retaining or not. It is a wise policy to give it, and yourself, time. Unfamiliar, seemingly dead bushes may transform themselves, in the right season, into a profusion of spring blossom or stunningly variegated leaves. A bed full of brown, twiggy stumps may turn out to be a thoughtfully planned herbaceous border. Bare earth may be concealing a riot of spring bulbs or lilies. The general rule is to give the garden enough time to show you the best it can do. If after a full season, you still feel that certain things aren't worth retaining or aren't quite *you*, then by all means get rid of them.

This advice does not necessarily apply to the *shape* of an established garden, however. Everyone has preference as to the lines of borders, lawns and other features, and if you want to alter the shape of a certain area, or add something to what is already there, it may be possible to start the work while still evaluating the existing garden.

The main thing, however, is to maintain what you have inherited until you have a clear idea of what you want to do. Keep the plants in good fettle, look after the lawn and stay on top of the weeding. It is not a bad plan, if you are completely new to gardening, to familiarize yourself with what generally constitutes a garden weed. As you get the feel of the garden you will begin to know which plants to leave and which to take out.

If you have a lot to clear out, it may be sensible to hire a skip. However, if you have only a comparatively small amount to dispose of, it might be an idea to find out if you have a local council amenity refuse site or a recycling centre. These are provided by the local authority for residents wishing to dispose of domestic rubbish, and range from very primitive, smelly, messy landfill areas (where you stand a good chance of getting a puncture or stuck in the mud) to skips, compacting bins surrounded by clean concrete roadways and standings and composting receptacles where all you do is dump your gardening waste and the local authority does the rest. They are a godsend to the gardener with rubbish he or she cannot burn or compost but are not so suitable for very large amounts of rubbish because of the problem of carting it to the site – most of these will not take so-called 'trade refuse', so hiring a van or lorry might not be a solution, as often the supervisors look on rubbish from commercial type vehicles as 'trade'. A telephone call to the local environmental health department will tell you what is available and what regulations are in force.

Weeds and green rubbish are suitable for composting. In

HERBICIDES

Chemical	Use
2,4D	Systemic control of broad-leaved weeds in turf and overgrown areas, also for stump treatment and brushwood control, usually in mixtures with other chemicals.
Amitrole	Contact control of weeds in a wide range of situations, in mixtures with other herbicides.
Ammonium thiocyanate	Systemic control of most weeds in overgrown areas, in mixtures with other herbicides.
Chloroxuron	Residual control of moss in lawns, usually in combination with other chemicals.
Dalapon	Systemic control of weed grasses amongst ornamentals, fruit and vegetables.
Dicamba	Systemic control of broad-leaved weeds in turf and overgrown areas, and also stump and brushwood control, in mixtures with other chemicals.
Dichlobenyl (Casoron G)	Residual root-absorbed herbicide for total, long-lasting control of weeds in paths, hard surfaces, uncultivated areas, and between woody plants, including fruit.
Dichlorophen	Control of moss, especially in turf.
Dichloroprop	Systemic control of broad-leaved weeds in turf, and also stump and brushwood treatment, usually in mixtures with other chemicals.
Diuron	Systemic control of weeds in paths and overgrown areas, in mixtures with other herbicides.
Diquat	Combined with paraquat for contact control of all weeds, often in mixtures with other chemicals.
Fatty acids	Organic contact control of all weeds.
Ferric sulphate	Control of moss in turf and some lawn weeds.
Ferrous sulphate	As above.
Glufosinate ammonium	Contact control of weeds in overgrown areas, borders, fruit and vegetables.

Glyphosate	Systemic control of weeds, especially persistent ones, in borders, amongst fruit and vegetables, overgrown areas and areas where recultivation is required within a short period. Also for stump and brushwood treatment.
MCPA	Systemic control of broad-leaved weeds in turf and overgrown areas, and also for stump and brushwood treatment, usually in mixtures with other chemicals.
Mecoprop	Systemic control of broad-leaved weeds in turf, usually in mixtures with other chemicals.
Paraquat	Combined with diquat for contact control of all weeds.
Simazine	Residual, root-absorbed herbicide for total, long-lasting control of weeds in paths, hard surfaces, uncultivated areas and between woody plants, including fruit.
Sodium chlorate with fire depressant	Contact herbicide for all weeds. Unsuitable for use close to plants because of leaching. Some residual effect.

NB Take great care not to apply any herbicide to plants or areas other than those to be treated.

addition, you are quite likely to have large amounts of leaves at certain times of the year. You can stack these separately to break down slowly into leaf mould. This is similar to compost in colour but drier and more crumbly in texture. As it is often quite acid, it is useful for mulching lime-hating plants, but can be dug into the soil in the usual way for humus. (*Note.* Do not compost plant remains containing many pests or known to have been diseased. These are best burned if possible, or taken to the tip.)

If you are not averse to chemicals, an overrun established garden can be cleared up with slightly less effort by the careful use of selective weedkillers. Casoron G and simazine will clear up weeds in paths and vacant ground for up to 12 months. Propachlor will discourage annual weed seeds from germinating once you have cleaned up your borders. You can clear grasses which have grown up through ornamentals with alloxydim sodium and spot-treat broad-leaved weeds amongst cultivated plants with glyphosate gel and spot lawn weedkillers which you paint on the plant to be killed off. There is a variety of herbicides for eliminating weeds in lawns and substances such as dichlorophen and chloroxuron available to clear moss from paths and lawns.

The no-garden garden

Preparing this type of garden is by far the most relaxing, as it consists mainly of studying what area you have for growing plants, looking round to see what is available in the way of containers and researching the type of plants suitable for growing in such conditions.

Safety hints for using weedkillers

ALWAYS read the manufacturers' instructions.

Make sure you buy the right chemical for the job you want to do.

Wear gloves when handling the concentrated weedkiller *and* the diluted solution.

DO NOT get it on your skin or in your mouth and eyes.

DO NOT apply liquid herbicides as a fine mist. Even in still air they will drift where you don't want them to.

DO NOT apply during windy conditions.

DO NOT accept bottles of unknown substances from friends who tell you they're suitable for what you want to do.

These are likely to be agricultural chemicals which are very difficult to dilute and apply accurately in small doses and areas. Potentially toxic substances should not be removed from the original containers in which the manufacturer packed them, and *certainly not* into 'pop' or similar bottles. Many highly poisonous chemicals look very much like soft drinks in their concentrated form.

It is in fact illegal to decant an agricultural or horticultural product into another container, even if it appears suitable for the purpose.

DO NOT apply weedkillers when there are children and animals around.

ALWAYS wash the applicator out thoroughly at the end of applying the herbicide. If possible, keep one watering can or sprayer to be used for weedkillers alone to avoid accidental contamination of other plants.

WASH hands and face well at the end of the job and before meals, even if protective clothing has been worn.

STORE on a high shelf or in a locked cupboard.

5

THE BROWN
STUFF

It cannot have escaped your notice as you fight your way through the jungle outside the patio door that under all this herbage is a substance in varying shades of brown, known as Soil. As soil plays a very important part in the growth, healthy or otherwise, of most of the plants you'll want to grow, it is not a bad plan to learn a little of what it's all about.

The largest part of soil is made up from particles of mineral rock broken down by the action of air, rain, frost, ice, snow, wind, etc. into varying degrees of fineness. Into this, a plant anchors itself with its roots. Where these mineral particles haven't been ground down so finely, they are present in the soil in the form of stones. In addition, a fertile soil capable of supporting healthy plant life contains a high proportion of humus. Humus is the remains of dead plants and animals, which are being broken down by bacteria.

Plants require certain major and trace elements in order to survive. The main elements needed are nitrogen, phosphorus and potassium and carbon, hydrogen and oxygen which are obtained from the air. Magnesium is necessary in smaller amounts, and very small quantities of other elements, known as trace elements, such as boron, copper, iron, manganese, molybdenum and zinc, are also required to prevent the plants developing deficiency diseases. These elements are obtained naturally, mainly from the breakdown of plant and animal remains, but also from the gradual dissolving of the mineral rock particles.

Soil also contains a large number of animal organisms, which play their own part in the way that plants obtain their food. Dead plant remains are pulled into the earth by earthworms and similar creatures for their own nourishment, and are thus broken down into other substances. Also, in taking this dead matter into the ground, these so-called macro-organisms bring about its exposure to soil bacteria, which also break it down for their own food, and in doing so they release plant foods. When such creatures die, the nitrogen given off from their bodies is taken up as well by the plants. Soilborne pests are those which live in the soil, but prefer to eat living plant tissue, causing damage and even death to the plants they feed off.

There are also other primitive forms of life to be found in soil, such as fungi, each playing their own part in the never-ending cycle taking place.

The essential elements are made available to plants in the form of soluble salts and other compounds which are dissolved in the moisture contained in the soil, and taken up through the root hairs at the tips of the plant's roots.

Topsoil is the top layer of soil, which contains most humus and animal organisms, and is therefore the most fertile. It varies in depth from place to place, but is usually about a foot deep. This soil should never be permanently removed as it is that which sustains healthy plant life.

Subsoil is the soil under the layer of topsoil. It can differ considerably from the top layer for geological reasons. It is mainly infertile as the soil organisms do not penetrate so far down – consequently there is little humus in it and therefore few soluble plant foods. However, subsoil can play an important part in the type of topsoil in a particular garden. A free-draining, gravelly subsoil will ensure that surface water drains quickly from the top layer, while a clay subsoil prevents water from draining freely from the topsoil. This can have the benefit of retaining moisture in the upper layers, but can also be disadvantageous if it is so solid or compacted that the surface water only drains very slowly, as it can cause flooding or sour, boggy conditions in the topsoil.

Subsoil should generally not be brought to the surface when digging, as it is of no benefit at all to plants. Neither should topsoil be buried, for example, by covering it with subsoil during building operations. However, if time and energy allow, it is a good practice to break up the subsoil when digging to improve drainage. Subsoil is easily distinguished from topsoil as it is usually lighter or different in colour and has no visible signs of humus (usually identifiable as a brown substance reminiscent of well-rotted vegetation) or organisms such as earthworms in it.

Soil types

Apart from regional variations in subsoil type, topsoils vary considerably. They can even be totally different in different parts of the garden.

Before attempting to do any planting, a prospective gardener should know what type of soil his plot contains. Many plants have a preference for a particular soil, so this can affect the choice of subjects. However, a less desirable soil can be improved by certain treatments so that a wider range of plants can be grown – and more healthily.

LOAM. This is the ideal soil to have and is every gardener's dream. It consists of a well-balanced mixture of large particles (sand), small particles (clay), medium small particles (silt), chalk and humus. A medium loam, which is the best for gardening purposes, has a proportion of about 50 or 60 per cent sand to 30 per cent clay and has twice as much humus as lime (chalk). Light loams have more sand in them than this, and heavy loams more clay. If a loam has a higher proportion of lime to humus than the above, it may well be alkaline (with a pH reading above 7). If there is a proportional imbalance the other way with the humus (i.e. more than twice as much humus as lime), the soil tends to be acid. The type of plants you grow depends on whether the soil is neutral, acid or alkaline. You can determine the pH with a soil-testing kit, available from garden shops and centres. In addition to having a pH indicator, the more sophisticated of them also contain chemicals to show whether a soil is deficient in any of the major elements – nitrogen, phosphorus and potash, generally referred to as NPK. As well as soil-testing kits which work by adding an appropriate liquid chemical indicator to a small amount of soil, shaking, and then comparing the resultant colour with a chart, meters are also available but are not so accurate. Soil pH and nutrients can be adjusted by adding certain substances which will be described later.

A light loam dries out rather more quickly than a heavy or medium one but you can improve the water-retentive properties by adding more humus-forming materials. You can also help a soggy, heavy loam by adding sand or other soil-improving substances (discussed below).

CLAY. This type of soil is the gardener's horror; it sticks to the boots when it is wet, and dries out to a rock-hard crust with deep cracks in it during dry spells in summer. It is composed of very small, even particles which fit closely together, leaving few and small air spaces in between. These spaces soon become filled with water which cannot drain off, and roots find it very difficult to grow healthily because of the airlessness of the soil. Clay soils are cold in winter because of this waterlogging and take a long time to warm up in spring, so plants growing in them are slow to get started – many roots will die and rot off if steps are not taken to improve the texture. Because of the cracks which appear during hot, dry weather, these soils dry out like concrete, which is also extremely bad for anything growing in them. The only advantage of clay is that it can be very fertile as it holds the soluble nutrients well and does not allow them to leach away.

You can improve a clay soil in several ways. You can add lime or gypsum to cause the particles to stick together into bigger ones which can hold more air between. As many clay soils become 'sour' and acid because of waterlogging and lack of air, lime has the additional benefit of 'sweetening' them by increasing the alkalinity. Digging-in humus-forming vegetable matter will also aerate the soil by getting between the fine particles. Sand will do the same job, by introducing bigger grains which do not fit so close together with the existing ones. Heavy clods of clay will also break up and form a better texture if allowed to 'weather', especially during frost.

SILT. Silt soils are a cross between clay and sand. They also have many even particles, but these are larger than clay, although smaller than sand. They are often found near rivers and where ground has been drained. They too are very fertile because of their water-retaining properties but tend to 'pan' when they dry out after a period of wet weather if the surface has been broken down too finely. They can be improved by adding humus-forming materials while digging.

SANDY SOILS. These have a high proportion of large particles (sand) in them, so they are open and free draining. They are easy to dig at almost any time, being light and draining quickly after rain. Roots penetrate readily, and because these soils do not remain soggy in winter, they warm up quickly in spring. The disadvantage is that because water drains away so freely, a sandy soil soon dries out, and a further problem is that as the water runs away, it takes a lot of soluble nutrients with it. This problem can be overcome by adding large quantities of humus-forming materials which will help to hold moisture and retain plant foods.

PEATY SOILS. Peat soils are found in areas which have been water-logged over a long time so that dead vegetation has been unable to rot down properly with the aid of aerobic bacteria. Very peaty soils are extremely acid and light in texture, drying out and even blowing away in dry, windy weather. Most ericaceous plants and many other calcifuges (lime-haters) will only grow well in such conditions, but others need a more alkaline soil to give the best results. You can add lime to increase the pH, and a method of stabilizing the texture to make it less fly-away is to deep dig to bring up and incor-porate some of the subsoil. Many peaty soils overlie clay (this is why they tended to be waterlogged a long time ago), and in such a case this method of soil improvement can be quite successful, but you really have to know what you are doing, as any other subsoil is quite often absolute rubbish as far as the grower is concerned. In any case, often the subsoil is so far below the surface as to make this a totally impossible job for the amateur, so it is possibly better to grin and bear it as most plants will grow perfectly well in a peaty soil, properly managed.

CHALK. This is a thin, dry hungry soil formed from the impurities in an area covered by calcium carbonate (which has been washed away by carbon dioxide from the air dissolved in rainwater). It is not an easy soil to grow plants in, but can be considerably improved by the regular addition of humus-forming material.

MARL. This is a mixture of clay and chalk which on its own is quite difficult to cultivate, but can be improved by increasing the amount of humus in it. It is sometimes possible to obtain marl by the load which can be used as a top dressing for peaty or sandy soils – the chalk increases the alkalinity and the clay gives the soil body.

STONY SOILS. These are soils containing a disproportionate amount of various sizes of stones. They are usually quite manageable, but the stones tend to work their way to the top and look unsightly, and they can be frustrating to dig because the blades or tines hit the stones. Also they have to be raked off a seedbed or the seeds will not come up evenly. You must pick them off a newly seeded lawn or they will damage the mower. Some very stony soils tend to be rather thin and impoverished, but can be improved as described for chalky soils.

SOIL COLOUR. The colour of a soil plays a large part in how well it performs. The colour partly depends on the original colour of the rocks it is formed from, especially those containing iron, and partly on the amount of humus it contains, which tends to make it darker.

Dark soils are preferable to light-coloured ones, as they absorb more of the sun's heat and warm up quicker in spring. Although the colour of a soil is largely a thing you are stuck with, a light-coloured soil can be darkened to a large extent by increasing the amount of humus it contains, which can only be good for it in every respect, or by adding weathered soot.

Assessing the situation

Apart from asking around, a rough way to get some guidance is to one-quarter fill a screw-topped jar with your ordinary garden soil, and then fill the jar almost full of water. Shake the jar briskly for about two minutes until the soil and the water are all mixed up into a brown liquid. Allow the jar to stand for an hour or so, and the soil will have divided up in the water into its basic constituents. On the top will be floating the decaying vegetable matter (humus) while the heavier particles will have dropped down to show the heaviest, and therefore largest, at the bottom, with the finer at the top. Any very fine particles will still be in suspension in the water, between the floating humus and the stuff on the bottom. The more humus that floats on the top, the more the soil contains, and if not much at all is floating, then it needs a lot added to it as it is obviously short of this substance. You will see from the soil particles which have sunk to the bottom how many are coarse, and how many are finer. The coarse particles are an indication of how sandy the soil is; if there is a fairly even balance between these and the finer ones it denotes a loam. If there are a great deal of very fine particles still in suspension, then the soil almost certainly contains a large proportion of clay.

In practice, however, it will soon become pretty obvious how heavy or light your soil is by the mess your boots get into and the ease (or otherwise) with which it falls off your spade.

Soil additives and conditioners

There are very few gardens that can boast an ideal soil for every requirement, and even if you start off with a good-quality loam not lacking in plant foods, as your plants use up what is already there, it will need to be replaced.

Also there are many compounds that can be added to a soil to correct some physical defect. Many of these, such as substances which provide humus, will also improve soil texture as well as breaking down to supply elements essential for healthy growth.

These additives can usually be divided into 3 categories: manures, fertilizers, and other soil conditioners.

MANURES. A manure has come to be regarded as a bulky organic substance which is incorporated into the soil to supply plant foods during its breakdown. Before the introduction of concentrated fertilizers this was the only way in which plant foods could be replenished as they were used up. The drawback of this is that a comparatively large quantity is required to provide enough of every element needed, especially for areas which are heavily cropped. Manures are the humus-forming substances needed for good soil structure; in addition to forming plant foods, they hold water to prevent a soil drying out and the actual digging-in process ensures that air is introduced.

However, during decomposition they give off acids which lower the pH of the soil. As a soil gets more acid, bacterial activity slows down, and foods stop being released, therefore at some point the alkalinity has to be increased to encourage bacteria to continue to break the material down. This is done by adding lime, or calcined seaweed, but lime should not be added at the same time as manure, as it will cause it to break down so quickly that the plants are unable to absorb much of what is produced.

Manures come from many sources and the foods they supply and their relative proportions depend on the type of manure (see the chart on pages 94–9).

FERTILIZERS. Technically, all substances capable of supplying plant foods are fertilizers (that is, they make a soil fertile). However, fertilizers are now thought of as concentrated compounds added to soil for the purpose of supplying one or more elements necessary for plant growth (see the chart on pages 94–9).

NITROGEN. Plants require nitrogen for quick, healthy, green growth, especially leaves and stems. A shortage of this element causes pale green colouring and stunted growth. Too much makes a plant very lush, prone to diseases, and reluctant to flower and set fruit, so it is essential not to create an imbalance with other elements.

PHOSPHORUS (usually in the form of phosphates) is necessary for strong root development. In acid soils, this element becomes 'locked up' in insoluble salts and therefore is unavailable to plants, which is why the soil alkalinity should be increased by careful liming.

POTASSIUM (potash) encourages the development of flowers and fruits and should be added in balanced amounts with nitrogen.

MAGNESIUM assists in the process of photosynthesis and a deficiency is shown by pale areas between the veins in leaves, owing to a lack of chlorophyll. This can be caused by too much potash or lime which 'locks up' the magnesium and can be remedied by the use of Epsom salts.

IRON is also required for healthy photosynthesis. Deficiency is usually brought about by the 'locking up' effect of too much calcium in the soil and is recognized by pale leaves and unhealthy stunted growth. If this chlorosis becomes too severe, the plant will die.

MANGANESE. A deficiency of this element has an effect on plants similar to that of magnesium and iron deficiency and can be recognized by a speckled yellowing of the leaves.

These last three elements can be supplied as a sequestrene, or chelate, obtainable at all good garden shops. This is magnesium, iron and/or manganese in a form which cannot be locked up by an excess of some other substance in the soil, and so will remain in a soluble form available to plants.

Other *trace elements* are necessary only in very small amounts and too much of any one or more of them can be harmful. Trace element deficiencies are unlikely in well manured soils, but certain compound fertilizers, in addition to the major plant foods, have minute quantities of these substances added as well.

Plants obtain nearly all their nourishment from the soil through hairs on their roots, but they are also capable of absorbing small amounts of chemicals, including plant foods, in weak solution through their leaves. The effects of these can be seen much more quickly, and therefore foliar feeding is a useful boost to growth, as well as a supplement to regular feeding through the roots.

Fertilizers can be quick- or slow-acting depending on their composition. Some can be applied in liquid form. These are more fast-acting, but require more regular application. Many manufacturers also produce a range of specific fertilizers formulated with the requirements of a particular type of plant or crop in mind, e.g. tomatoes, chrysanthemums, roses. There are also fertilizers which have been formed into tablets or sticks for ease of application.

Other soil additives

LIME. This is applied to soil mainly to neutralize excess acidity. It also has a conditioning effect on clay soil, causing the very small particles to stick together to form larger ones. This improves drainage and aeration. A third function is to supply *calcium* which is another element essential in moderation for healthy plant growth. The term 'lime' is used to refer to several similar substances containing calcium.

GYPSUM. This is sulphate of lime, and has a similar conditioning

90

effect on clay soils as lime, but has an advantage in certain cases in that it does not make the soil more alkaline.

CALCINED (CALCIFIED) SEAWEED. This is the dried and crushed remains of certain forms of seaweed with calcium carbonate in their cell walls. It is a useful soil conditioner in the same way that lime is, and also contains traces of minerals and other plant foods.

SAND. This is added to heavy soils to improve aeration and drainage, and for this purpose, sharp sand (that with angular particles in a range of sizes up to ⅛ in. (3 mm)) should be used.

PERLITE. This is a type of expanded volcanic rock heated to form holey granules, which are full of air and can absorb up to four times their own weight in water. Perlite can be added to a soil to improve its texture and air- and water-holding properties, and will assist in the formation of a strong, healthy plant root system. Polystyrene granules can also be used for this purpose.

VERMICULITE. This is a substance produced by heating mica-like minerals until they take on a flaky, cellular texture. It can hold air and water as perlite does, so can be used as a soil conditioner in the same way, although the texture does break down after a while so the effect is more temporary than that of sand or perlite. However, it does encourage a fine plant root system to form quickly. Vermiculite can also be obtained very cheaply as an insulation and packaging material, but this grade can be extremely alkaline, and therefore not beneficial as a soil additive. Vermiculite for growing purposes should always be of a horticultural grade.

Seed and potting composts

With an abundance of soil all around you it is tempting to use this if you want to plant things in containers, or re-pot existing ones. After all, it is free, so what's the point of buying something for doing the job?

Unfortunately, it is not as easy as that. For a start, most soils are far from ideal and plants grown under stress – container growing is a sort of stress, because roots are restricted, watering is often neglected (or done to excess), and the growing medium tends to get over-warm in summer and over-cold in winter, especially if the pots are outside, or under glass

– need the best conditions you can provide. Furthermore, even a really good loam tends to lose texture and quality if packed indefinitely into a confined receptacle, and you cannot improve it as you can garden soil by digging it over and adding lots of compost, or other soil conditioners. Another disadvantage of using soil straight from the garden for potting is that it contains many pests and diseases which are fairly insignificant when given an unrestricted area in which to operate, but can become extremely harmful to plants when imprisoned in a comparatively small space.

It is therefore essential, if you want to keep your containerized and potted plants as healthy as you can, to give them something to grow in of good texture and as free as possible from bugs and blights.

SOIL-BASED COMPOSTS. Originally, all seed and potting composts were based on sterilized loam. In the 1930s the John Innes Institute devised standard formulae for seed, cuttings and potting compost comprised of loam, peat, limestone or chalk and coarse sand, with a fairly quick-acting fertilizer mixture added according to what the compost was to be used for. Even today, soil-based composts are still the most desirable for long-term container growing as they encourage the formation of the best type of root system for this sort of cultivation, keep their texture, and do not dry out so readily.

Formulae for John Innes Composts (all measures are by bulk):

Seed mixture: 2 parts sterilized medium loam; 1 part peat, 1 part coarse sand. To each bushel (a bushel is equivalent to 4 2-gallon buckets) add 1½ oz (40 g) superphosphate of lime and ¾ oz (20 g) finely ground chalk or powdered limestone.

Cutting mixture: 1 part medium loam; 2 parts peat; 1 part coarse sand.

Potting mixture: 7 parts loam, 3 parts peat, 2 parts coarse sand. To each bushel add ¾ oz (20 g) ground chalk or powdered limestone and (for JI1) 4 oz (110 g) of a mixture of 2 parts (by weight) hoof and horn meal, 2 parts (by weight) superphosphate of lime, 1 part (by weight) sulphate of potash. For JI2 and JI3, double and treble the fertilizer amount respectively.

John Innes seed compost is used for sowing seeds, using seed trays or small pots.

The cuttings mixture contains no fertilizer and is for use when propagating plants from cuttings.

The potting mixtures are for potting on from the seedling and rooted cutting stages.

John Innes No. 1 (JI1) is for pots up to 4 in. (100 mm) diameter containing young or comparatively small plants.

John Innes No. 2 (JI2) is for potting into pots over 4 in. (100 mm) diameter and contains twice as much John Innes Base Fertilizer as JI1.

John Innes No. 3 (JI3) is for vigorous growing and large plants in containers over 8 in. (200 mm) diameter and contains three times as much fertilizer as JI1.

John Innes-type composts have become modified over the years and often now contain peat substitutes and perlite or vermiculite as well as, or instead of, peat and sand.

JI composts are suitable for filling raised beds and other similar features. Because of the limestone or chalk in them, however, they are unsuitable for lime-hating plants, such as heathers, azaleas, rhododendrons, etc. If you wish to grow these in contained or raised beds, and many of them do lend themselves to this form of cultivation, you should obtain an ericaceous mix from which the limestone has been omitted, or replaced with a non–alkaline substance.

SOIL-LESS COMPOSTS. These were originally developed because of the increasing difficulty of obtaining good quality loam, but are now used as a widespread replacement for soil-based composts. They are much lighter and therefore easier to handle than those containing soil, but watering is more critical – too much makes them waterlogged, too little and they dry out and become very difficult to re-wet satisfactorily, especially when they have been in pots for some time and contain a lot of roots. However, they are very useful for germinating seeds, potting on small plants, especially house-plants, and as a growing medium for temporary container planting – bedding plants, bulbs, etc.

Soil-less composts are based on peat, or a peat substitute, such as coir, bark or composted wood waste, to which may be added sharp or silver sand, perlite, or vermiculite, to improve drainage and aeration, and fertilizers capable of providing all the necessary plant foods for about 6–8 weeks. Many contain ground limestone or chalk to bring the pH up to neutral as

MANURES, FERTILIZERS AND SOIL ADDITIVES

Type of Substance	Source	Function – Plant Food (PF) or Soil Conditioner (SC)	Organic or Inorganic	Foods Contained				Rate of Application		When, Where and How to Apply	Slow or Fast Acting
				Nitrogen (%N)	Phosphate (%P)	Potash (%K)	Trace Elements	Base Dressing per sq yd	Top Dressing per sq yd		
MANURES											
Composted Community Waste	Domestic refuse from waste bin collection with glass, plastic and other non-rotting materials removed	Both	O	Varies but similar to garden compost				Varies according to process but usually about 5–12 lbs/sq yd		As a top dressing in spring or dug into the soil during planting or in autumn. Can contain calcium carbonate so useful for raising pH	Moderately slow
Cocoa Shell	Husk of the cocoa bean – by-product of the chocolate industry	Both	O	Variable					2 in. spread over soil surface	Use as mulch, or soil conditioner, will make alkaline soils more acid	Fairly slow
Dried Slurry	Separated slurry from animals in intensive farming systems, composted and dried	Both	O	Variable but contains a good proportion of NPK and trace elements				4 lb/sq. yd	4 lbs/sq. yd	Top dressing in sping or dug in during planting or in autumn	Moderately fast
Dried Sewage Sludge	Sewage solids separated, composted and dried	Both	O	Variable but similar to above. Contents tend to vary according to process used for preparation				1½ –2½ lbs	1½–2½ lbs	As above	Moderately fast
Farmyard Manure	Farm animal waste and bedding material used (usually straw) stacked in a heap to rot down	Both	O	0.6	0.3	0.5	Yes	10–15 lbs	10–15 lbs	As above	Moderately slow –breaks down over a period
Garden Compost	Composted garden and kitchen refuse	Both	O	2–2.5	0.5–1	0.5–2	Some	10–12 lbs	10–12 lbs	As above	As above
Green Manure	Quick maturing crops dug into soil to break down into humus, e.g. mustard legumes (pea family), rye grass	Both	O	Variable but tends to be high in nitrogen				Crop is dug in 'green'		Useful for soils low in humus and for recycling and fixing residues of previous fertilizer applications	As above
Guano, Pigeon Manure	Bird or bat droppings	Both	O	10–14	9–11	2–4	Some	–	2–4 oz or 6 oz/sq. yd mixed with twice its own bulk of soil or sand	As a quick-acting top dressing around plants. Should not be put on too thick or scorch can occur	Fast

Material	Description			Varies according to source of manufacture but usually:						Application	Speed
Hop Manure	Composted spent hops with plant food additives	Mainly O	Both	3–4	1–2	2	Trace	1 lb	–	Dig into soil in spring	Fast
Spent Hops	Used hops from breweries stacked for a few months	O	Both	0.5–0.6	1–2	a little	–	10–12 lbs	5–10 lbs	Dig into soil during autumn/winter at planting time or use as a mulch in spring	Slow
Spent Mushroom Compost	Medium in which mushrooms have been grown consisting of rotted straw composted with horse manure or nitrogenous fertilizer and some time	Mainly O	Both	2–3	1–2	1–2	Variable	5–10 lbs	5–10 lbs	As above	Fairly fast
Leaf Mould	Autumn leaves cleared up and stacked to rot	O	Mainly soil conditioner Small amounts of nutrients	Trace	Trace	Trace	Trace	5 lbs	–	Dig into ground in autumn or use at planting time mixed with soil	Very slow
Peat	Incomplete decomposition of vegetable remains in waterlogged conditions	O	SC	Trace	Trace	Trace	Trace	10–12 lbs	10–12 lbs	Use in planting mixtures and composts	Slow to very slow
Poultry manure (fresh)	Droppings and cleanings from poultry houses	O	Both	2.5	1.0	0.5	Trace	2–4 oz	2–4 oz	Dig into soil at any time or use as top dressing in spring	Moderately fast
Poultry manure (dried)	As above, dried	O	Both	4–6	3–3.5	1.7–2.3	Variable	2–4 oz	2–4 oz	Incorporate into soil before sowing or planting or use as spring and summer top dressing	Fast
Pulverized bark	Tree bark stripped from timber, broken up and composted	O	Both mainly SC	Variable, depending on type of timber and process, but typically it has a trace of NPK and other elements, although some manufacturers add a fertilizer to improve the nutrient quality and replace nitrogen which tends to be lost as the bark breaks down				10–12 lbs	10–12 lbs	Used in a similar way to peat. Different grades are obtainable for different functions	Fairly slow
Seaweed (fresh)	From the seashore	O	Both	0.5	0.1+	1.0	Very wide range	10–20 lbs	–	Incorporate well into the soil at time of digging	Moderately slow
Seaweed (dried)	From the seashore	O	Both	0.5	0.1+	1.0	Very wide range	2–3 lbs	–	As above	Moderately slow
Seaweed (liquefied)	As above, made into liquid	O	PF	Variable but high potash and wide range of trace elements				According to manufacturer's instructions		Applied as liquid feed during growing season	Fast

MANURES, FERTILIZERS AND SOIL ADDITIVES (continued)

Type of Substance	Source	Organic or Inorganic	Function – Plant Food (PF) or Soil Conditioner (SC)	Nitrogen (%N)	Phosphate (%P)	Potash (%K)	Trace Elements	Base Dressing per sq. yd	Top Dressing per sq. yd	When, Where and How to Apply	Slow or Fast Acting
Seaweed (calcified)	As above made from seaweed from Britanny containing calcium carbonate, dried and crushed	O	Both	Variable but high in potash and trace elements. Contains calcium carbonate which will increase soil alkalinity and improve clay soil structure				2–10 oz/sq. yd according to type of plant/area being treated		Top dressing for flowers, fruit, lawns, vegetables at any time. Dug in in autumn/winter especially in heavy ground or at any time	Moderately fast
Shoddy	Waste wool and other natural fibres	O	Both	5–15	–	–	–	1 lb	–	Dig into soil at any time of year	Very slow
FERTILIZERS Basic slag	Waste product from the lining of blast furnaces	I	Both mainly PF	1.0	8–22	–	–	8 oz	–	Dig into soil in autumn/winter but do not mix with organic manures. Contains about 3% lime so useful on clay and sour soils	Slow
Blood (dried)	By-product of slaughterhouses	O	PF	7–14	1–2	1.0	Some	–	1–2 oz per 1 oz per gallon as a liquid feed	Apply to growing plants as a top dressing in spring/summer	Fast
Bone flour (steamed)	By-product of slaughterhouses	O	PF	1	27–28	–	Trace	3–4 oz	3–4 oz	Apply to soil in autumn around flowers, shrubs, trees and fruit, and at planting time	Fairly fast
Bone-meal	By-product of slaughterhouses	O	PF	3–5	20–25	–	Trace	Up to 8 oz per sq. yd		Similar uses to bone flour but takes longer to break down	Slow
Bonfire ash	Burned wood and vegetation. May contain some burnt soil	O	Both	Variable but contains a very high proportion of potash				Apply liberally at digging time or as a top dressing		As a source of potash at digging time. Also useful conditioner for heavy soils. Can be used as a top dressing to encourage reluctant flowering plants to come into flower and also useful top dressing for fruit	Fairly fast. Quick source of potash
Borax	Occurs naturally	I	PF	–	–	–	Boron	Apply at 2 oz/30 sq. yds to correct boron deficiency		Dig in as a source of boron where it is shown to be deficient. NB: an excess of boron is highly toxic to plants	Fast
Fish meal	By-product of fishing industry	O	PF	8–10	5–10	1–2	Trace	3–4 oz	3–4 oz	Work into soil during spring cultivation as top or base dressing	Fast

								Trace elements				
Growmore (typical balanced fertilizer)	Chemical manufacture	I	PF	7	7	7	7	Not unless these have been added by manufacturer	3–4 oz	3–4 oz	Apply to soil during spring as a top or base dressing	Fast
Hoof & horn (fine)	By-product of slaughterhouses	O	PF	–	12–14	1–3	–	–	3–4 oz	3–4 oz	As above	Fast
Hoof & horn (coarse)	By-product of slaughterhouses	O	PF	–	12–14	1–3	–	–	3–4 oz	3–4 oz	As above	Slower
John Innes base fertilizer	Chemical manufacture	I	PF	–	5.1	7.2	9.7	–	3–4 oz	3–4 oz	As above or used in potting composts	Fast
Magnesium sulphate (Epsom Salts)	Chemical manufacture. Also occur naturally	I	PF	–	–	–	–	10% magnesium	–	4 oz/sq. yd or 2 oz–5 pints water as foliar feed	Apply as a top dressing or liquid or foliar feed to correct magnesium deficiency	Fast
Nitrate of potash (saltpetre)	Occurs naturally	I	PF	–	12–14	–	44–46	–	–	½–1 oz/sq. yd or ½ oz/gall.	Apply to soil round plants in spring and summer to promote fast strong growth or apply as liquid feed	Fast
Nitrate of soda	Occurs naturally	I	PF	–	16	–	–	Some	–	1 oz/sq. yd or ¼–½ oz/gall.	Apply to young crops during growing season	Very fast
Nitro-chalk	Chemical manufacture	I	Both	–	16	–	–	–	–	1 oz/sq. yd.	As above. As it contains some chalk it is useful on acid and heavy soil	Fast but longer lasting action
Soot (weathered)	By-product of domestic fires	O	Both	–	3–6	–	–	–	4–6 oz	2 oz	Dig in or apply as a top dressing before planting. Use as a conditioner to counteract stickiness in clay soils and to darken soil to cause it to warm up faster	Fast
Sequestrenes	Chemical manufacture	I	PF	–	–	–	–	Iron and/or magnesium and/or manganese	–	According to manufacturer's instructions	Water in or apply as a top dressing to counteract iron, magnesium and/or manganese deficiency-induced chlorosis in alkaline soils	Fast
Sulphate of ammonia	Chemical manufacture	I	PF	–	20–21	–	–	–	2 oz	1 oz/sq. yd 1 oz in 2 galls	Add to soil before sowing and as a quick boost to growth as a top dressing or liquid feed during the growing season. Quick green-up for lawns.	Fast

MANURES, FERTILIZERS AND SOIL ADDITIVES (continued)

Type of Substance	Source	Organic or Inorganic	Function – Plant Food (PF) or Soil Conditioner (SC)	Foods Contained				Rate of Application		When, Where and How to Apply	Slow or Fast Acting
				Nitrogen (%N)	Phosphate (%P)	Potash (%K)	Trace Elements	Base Dressing per sq. yd	Top Dressing per sq. yd		
Sulphate of iron	Chemical manufacture	I	PF	–	–	–	Iron	–	½–1 oz in 1 gall.	As a foliar feed to correct iron deficiency chlorosis	Fast
Sulphate of potash	Chemical manufacture	I	PF	–	–	48	–	–	½–1 oz/sq. yd ½–1 oz/gall.	Apply before sowing or planting as a top or base dressing or as a liquid feed for flowering and fruiting plants	Fast
Super-phosphate of lime	Chemical manufacture	I	PF	–	18.5	–	–	½–1 oz	1–2 oz/sq. yd or ½–1 oz/gall.	Apply before sowing or planting or as a liquid feed	Fairly slow
Triple super-phosphate	Chemical manufacture	I	PF	–	47.0	–	–	–	1–2 oz/sq. yd or ½ oz/gall.	As above, but it is 3 times as strong, so use in smaller amounts	Fairly slow
Urea	Chemical manufacture	O	PF	46	–	–	–	–	1 oz/sq. yd 1 oz/2 galls.	As a fast acting nitrogenous top dressing (mixed with sand) or liquid feed during summer. Quick green-up for lawns	Very fast
OTHER SOIL ADDITIVES											
Lime Ground limestone and chalk	Calcium carbonate obtained from natural sources – limestone rock, chalk etc.	O	Mainly soil conditioning but supplies calcium in addition	–	–	–	–	Amount varies according to type of soil and original pH but is around 8oz/sq. yd every 2 years to keep land in good heart	–	Applied as a top dressing in autumn or any other convenient time and can be lightly forked in. It should not be added with manures as it causes them to break down too quickly, so if added at the same time it must be kept separate. Good soil conditioner for clays	Fairly fast
Burnt lime or quicklime	Calcium oxide obtained by burning limestone in a kiln	I	Mainly soil conditioning but supplies calcium in addition	–	–	–	–	Amount varies according to soil and existing pH but is usually about half that of ground limestone (i.e. 4 oz/sq, yd)	–	As above	Fast

Material	Type	Source					Function	Application rate	Use / notes	Speed
Hydrated or slaked lime	I	Calcium hydroxide obtained by treating quicklime with water	–	–	–	–	Mainly soil conditioning but supplies calcium in addition	As above	As above	Fast
Magnesian limestone	O	Obtained from dolomitic limestone and contains calcium carbonate and magnesium carbonate	–	–	–	Magnesium	Mainly soil conditioning but supplies calcium and magnesium as well	As above	Applied as above but useful on soils deficient in magnesium	Fast
Gypsum	I	Sulphate of lime obtained by quarrying	–	–	–	–	Mainly soil conditioning but supplies calcium as well	Amount varies according to soil type but is around 8 oz/sq. yd for a heavy clay soil	Used in the same way as lime for improving soil texture but does not increase alkalinity and is therefore good for alkaline clays. Useful for reclaiming soil affected by flooding	Fairly fast
Perlite, perlag	I	Expanded volcanic rock	–	–	–	–	SC	Added in varying amounts according to original texture and then incorporated well into the soil	Use for lightening clay soils and improving air- and water-holding properties. Used in potting composts	Fast
Polystyrene granules	I	Manufactured	–	–	–	–	SC	As above	As above	Fast
Sand	I	Quarrying	Fairly inert but may contain some minerals depending on origins	–	–	–	SC	As above	Used for improving the texture/aeration of heavy soils	Fast
Vermiculite	I	Heating certain minerals	–	–	Trace	Trace	SC	As above	Used in a similar way to Perlite but on a more temporary basis. Also used as a seed-sowing medium	Fast

Vermiculite note: Can also hold calcium, magnesium, potassium and nitrogen absorbed from other fertilizers without it the materials forming the compost tend to be acid, although many vegetables and ornamentals like slightly acid conditions, provided that a correct balance of plant foods is supplied to counteract any deficiencies because of the low pH. At one time different mixes were available depending on whether you intended to sow seeds, take cuttings, or pot on, but more manufacturers are now making a universal compost suitable for most purposes.

Specialized composts are also available, e.g. bulb fibre has charcoal added to keep it sweet in containers which frequently have no drainage holes, and orchid compost contains a large amount of coarsely pulverized bark to simulate growing conditions in their natural habitat. Ericaceous composts are ones which have no added limestone so are suitable for acid–loving plants. Some manufacturers provide kits from which you can make up your own composts, according to your needs, from peat, or peat substitute, sand, ground limestone and fertilizers, or sometimes supply kits of additives to mix with your own peat, or peat substitute. At the present time, it is my opinion that, while many peat-substitute composts are available, none of them produces the same results as a peat-based compost, and independent trials tend to prove this. They are also more expensive, so you may pay much more for much less – both in quantity and in results. Research continues and no doubt a product comparable with peat will eventually be found.

If possible, plants raised in soil-based composts should not be potted on into peat-based ones and vice-versa, as root systems differ according to which medium they have grown in, and will suffer a check if put into something different.

Growing bags are flattish, heavy-duty polythene bags filled with soil-less compost, the actual ingredients and their proportions varying according to manufacturer. These are useful for growing temporary crops of flowers, herbs, strawberries and vegetables outside or under glass and are especially handy for patios and other paved or concreted areas. They are supplied with instructions for planting up, quantities of plants, subsequent feeding, drainage, etc. depending on maker. Sometimes they can be used for two crops in succession but an imbalance or build-up of fertilizers can occur so, if in doubt, buy new, as spent growing bags will always come in handy for mulching or digging into garden soil to improve texture.

Like soil-based composts, most soil-less ones have a limited shelf-life because of the inclusion of quick-acting fertilizers. This can be considerably reduced if the bags are stored under less-than-ideal conditions, for example, in a wet yard. It is as well to purchase growing bags and compost from reputable suppliers who are aware of this, to avoid the chance of buying compost containing useless or even harmful fertilizer additives.

Potting composts are usually manufactured by well-known and highly respected firms and by buying names you recognize or those recommended to you, assuming they have been properly handled by the retailer, you should have no problems.

Growing bags, on the other hand, are a different matter. For a start, there tends to be a cut-price war among retailers, even with the 'famous names'. These are always the ones to look for, and you ought to be all right, but some less responsible shops are able to cut their prices only because they are selling off old stock, which may or may not have deteriorated. A further complication arises in that many supermarkets sell cut-price bags under their own name. Some of these are actually made for the supermarket by the major manufacturers and there should be no trouble with these. Unfortunately, others produced by less scrupulous firms contain dubious ingredients producing poor results.

It is difficult to give any hard and fast advice, therefore, on how to choose growing bags. Perhaps the best way to go about it is to stick to the names you know. If anything should go wrong, these firms will always do tests for you to see if it is anything to do with them which is at fault. If so, they will be glad to know for their own reputation and will willingly replace. If the trouble lies with the retailer, they will be able to make the particular stockist aware of what is going wrong and give suggestions for improved storage. If the likelihood is that it is your technique which is lacking, they have advisory departments happy to put you back on the right road. So treat the nameless, cut-price offer with caution – it may not turn out to be the bargain you thought it was!

6

HOW TO BECOME A CAPABILITY BROWN

Hints on Planning Your Garden

If you have eased yourself gently into a relationship with your plot as suggested, you will have begun to feel the mood of the thing. As you have cleared it and worked the soil, you will have started to get ideas for how you would like to put something back into it. A garden should contain things *you* like, within reason, where *you* want to see them, as it is *you* who is going to have to live with them. There are only two fundamental planning considerations to bear in mind: first, the plants should be suitable for the area you want to put them in; and second, big plants should not be placed in front of small ones. All other aspects of planning are purely personal ones: what suits one person's tastes or needs may be an offence to another. You might like borders with crisp, straight lines and plants placed like rows of soldiers. Your next-door neighbour may tell you this is wrong – borders should have wavy informal edges with what they contain allowed to natural- ize into an informal jungle. But this is *his* taste; if intricate geometric designs full of bedding plants please you, then providing you have the time and money to maintain them, have them.

What is important is to get your ideas and observations into some sort of order. The best way is to start with a scale plan. Obtain a large sheet of graph paper and decide on a scale which will enable you to draw the whole of the part you are designing (back, front or whatever) comfortably on it.

The next step is to go outside and measure up boundaries, with a check on diagonal measurements, positions of existing features, trees, shrubs, beds, walls, paths, patios, sheds, clothes lines, etc. that you intend to keep, and transfer these accurately to the plan. You should also indicate which way the garden is orientated. (North can be determined using a compass, but another way – if it is the right time of year – is to see where the sun rises and sets on 21 March or 21 September. On these dates it will rise due east and set due west.) This will affect the areas of shade in it. For example, if your property is at the southern end of the garden, it will exclude a lot of midday sun and so the house and therefore the garden is said to be north facing. It is well to know these things at an early stage in designing as a north-facing part will be cool and shady, a south-facing one hot and sunny, a west-facing area will have hot afternoon sun in summer, and be sheltered from cold, easterly wind in winter and an east-facing aspect will receive cold winds and early morning sun which can be harmful to buds and new shoots during frosty weather. You can then choose suitable plants for each type of situation.

Indicate on your plan any areas which receive an appreciable amount of shade from high walls, big trees, buildings, etc. and show the extent of this shade if such features obscure the sun for a fairly long period of the day. It will be useful later when you come to deciding what you can have in a particular area.

The next thing is to consolidate your wants, needs, likes and dislikes by preparing some sort of questionnaire. This all sounds rather unnecessary, but it does save you making a lot of mistakes in the long run. Ask yourself some simple questions, give honest answers, and you are well on the way to planning your patch the way *you* want it.

WHAT CAN I AFFORD? Try to have some sort of target figure in mind when embarking on a planning scheme. Even if you are going

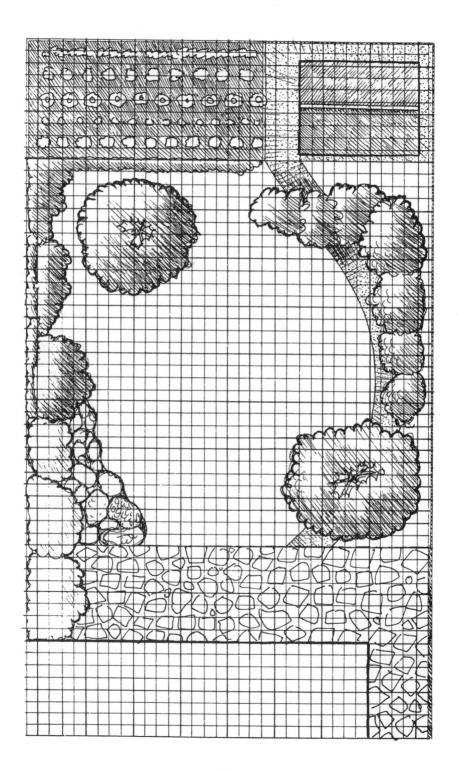

to do every bit of the work yourself, trees, shrubs, slabs, fencing materials, grass seed, all run away with the spare cash. If you are young, of course, chances are that you will be able to spread the cost over several earning years, so there is nothing to stop you from aiming at something you cannot afford all at once. However, if this is the way you intend to go about it, do try to plan the work so that every stage is an entity. Nothing is worse than a job that looks as though you have run out of money. For example, if cash is really short, plan the beds, borders, lawns, paths, etc. in advance, then tackle each job *and finish it* as funds allow.

If, on the other hand, your first real garden is going to be your retirement hobby, aim for something simple (you'll be glad you did as the years go by, anyway!) and put any spare money into maintaining it properly.

HOW MUCH TIME DO I HAVE? Do not overestimate the amount of time you will have for maintenance, as it will soon get the upper hand if you do not stay on top of it. It is no good thinking how much time you *may* be able to give, the chances are you can divide this figure by half as other more interesting activities jostle for your free time. If it is a toss-up between weeding the rockery or taking the children for a picnic, the rockery is unlikely to win! If you are retired but like to spend six months of the year abroad, you will have to plan your garden to be self-maintaining, or else be prepared for a jungle, or a gardener's wages. Paved areas instead of lawns, shrubberies which can be kept weeded by the careful use of selective herbicides instead of fussy flower beds, well designed fences or walls as a substitute for hedges which require clipping, all cut down on maintenance without affecting adversely the attractiveness if properly thought out.

WHAT IS MY LIFESTYLE? A garden should be a pleasure and an extension of your life, not a burden and a chore. You should therefore think very carefully about major factors affecting you and your family, and how the garden can be planned to accommodate and suit them.

CHILDREN? It seems a pity if children have to go and play elsewhere because they could spoil your masterpiece. If you have a young family, try to make the garden fun to be in. No fancy or expensive treasures, but tough shrubs which can take the

105

knocks. No Cumberland turf, but a hardwearing grass mix; even better, if you have the space, give children a play area of their own and cover it in bark chippings, available from most garden centres – they are kinder to small knees than slabs and gravel. They can have all their toys, swings, climbing frames etc. neatly concealed behind a substantial fence – children appreciate somewhere of their very own and, if you can do this, you save your part of the garden from looking a cross between a well used rugger pitch and Steptoe's yard.

Do try, however, to involve the children in the cultivation of the garden. Nearly all youngsters enjoy growing things, so try to incorporate a small patch of land where they can sow a few flower and vegetable seeds. Children who have been encouraged to garden from an early age are more likely to make keen gardeners in young adulthood.

PETS? It is no good planning something exotic if you are going to be constantly nagging once the garden is planted up. Dogs have the most devastating effect of all pets, especially in quantity, converting lawns into muddy skating rinks and well turned soil into padded earth. Male dogs 'cock their legs' on your favourite conifers, leaving them eventually bare and stinking. Bitches 'wee' all over the grass, covering it with a rash of dead and dark green spots where the concentrated nitrogen in their urine has burnt it off. They cannot help it, so it is better to prevent the problem by avoiding evergreens and expensive turf. The answer might even be to replace the lawn with a well designed gravel area, or, if it is feasible, cut the bottom of the garden off and give them a place where they can romp and widdle to their hearts' content, not forgetting that what *your* eye cannot see may be only too apparent to your neighbour's eyes – and ears, and nose.

Other pets do not cause quite so much havoc, though cats tend to view your fine seed beds as their equally fine loos, so if there is any danger of your vegetable patch becoming the neighbourhood feline public convenience, it might be worth planning your seed bed areas so they can be covered with crop protection fleece or mesh. From personal experience, there is nothing that will deter persistent moggies other than a physical barrier of some sort.

Rabbit cages, aviaries and pigeon lofts do not contribute much to the domestic landscape, so these should be sited if possible where they can be screened. Dovecotes are a more attractive proposition, but doves, pigeons, call them what you like, have a thing going for brassicas (cabbages, sprouts, etc), so if you like the friendly sound of cooing birds, be prepared for emergency action with plastic netting down on the cabbage patch, or buy your vegetables instead!

WHAT WILL BE THE PRIMARY USE OF MY GARDEN? Every garden, backyard or window box has a predominant function: it may be to give the owner pleasure by presenting a riot of colour or a subtle blending of flowers and foliage. Other gardens may be the basis of a collector's paradise, provide plants for flower arranging or provender for the hungry flock which returns to the roost at the end of every school or working day, as well as giving the dog a place to run after his ball, or the children somewhere to bring their friends to play. A garden's main use plays a large part in its design.

If you just want to relax and admire the wonders of nature without too much effort, you should aim for a lot of permanent, low-maintenance tree and shrub plantings with plenty of low-growing evergreen ground cover, and comparatively large areas of attractive paving. If, on the other hand, you cannot resist buying something every time you go to a garden centre and intend to cram every plant in creation into your piece of God's earth, you will want more space given over to beds and borders than lawned and paved areas. If you are heavily into self-sufficiency, you will need to give far more of your garden over to fruit and vegetable production than ornamental plants, terraces, and lawns. If you are a pillar of your local flower arranging club you will be looking for sites for cut flowers and shrubs which do not take exception to being hacked about for greenery. If barbecues and alfresco meals and parties are your thing of the moment, then you should be thinking about sunny, sheltered sitting and patio areas, and perhaps a tree of two to provide some light shade in the hottest part of the day.

Once you have a general idea of what you are looking for in the way of a garden, you must then give some thought to the permanent features which will affect your design.

THE PROPERTY. Gardens attached to bungalows require slightly different treatment from those belonging to houses, as it is very easy to dominate a low building by planting too much tall stuff, especially if it is not a very big plot. Taller properties are not affected quite as much by this sense of proportion, though bear in mind the detrimental structural effect of planting unsuitably large trees too close to buildings. Cottage gardens can benefit from an informal approach, especially if suitable subjects (hollyhocks, herbs, etc) are favoured. Of course, if it is a balcony attached to a tenth-storey flat, then the style is a bit limited!

The period of construction can sometimes play a part in design – for example, ultra-modern architecture blends well with mass plantings, paving features and ornamental walling constructed of contemporary building materials, whereas a pre-war semi or a Nineties neo-Tudor, half-timbered and leaded-paned des. res. can benefit from a slightly more traditional approach, though again personal preference is possibly a more influential factor.

WALLS. The materials of which a property is constructed can also have an effect on garden planning, especially in relation to patios, walls and plant colours. Stone walls and concrete paving have to be matched carefully for style and colour – there are some very good imitation stone slabs, and some very basic concrete ones which are sometimes better used in connection with modern architecture, especially when the concrete is coloured with a pigment. Some colours work quite well with twentieth-century buildings, some colours are frankly crude and should not be used in any location. Brick paths and patios will fit in well with most old buildings, gravel and cobbles can be effective with certain types of stone and brick.

On the subject of plant colours, bear in mind that red flowers do not usually look good against or near red walls, white ones are lost near white walls, and so on. Choose the colours for contrast or harmony.

A final consideration while on the subject of walls is their subsequent maintenance if you want to grow climbers up them. If a wall is painted or rendered, self-clinging climbers should be avoided as you will have to cut them down to the ground and remove the clinging bits every time you want to get at the wall for maintenance, which is a pity, and also causes a lot of extra work. It is best to consider a moderate-growing plant which will attach to some form of easy-to-remove trellis, or forget wall-plants in this situation.

WINDOWS. In Britain much of the time spent looking at the garden will be done through one window or another, so these should be marked on the scale plan to remind you when you are trying out some ideas on paper of just how the design is going to be seen, from which angles, and when.

COLOUR SCHEMES. Some people like to look on their gardens as a continuation of their living-rooms – their co-ordinated fabrics being equally co-ordinated with the colour that is beyond the window. Before you install a bed of 'Blue Moon' roses which do not quite tone with your brick-red carpet, give some thought to whether this aspect bothers *you*.

BOUNDARIES. Most gardens have some form of delineation between them and other properties – quite often house deeds specify that there should be one, though many place restrictions on type, and especially height.

Boundaries are generally formed by fences, walls or hedges, though occasionally the hedge concept goes a step further by being a mixed screen of shrubs, conifers and small trees. When you take over a garden there is usually some form of boundary demarcation already. Because the materials of which these are made are pretty pricey, unless the wall, fence or hedge is in poor condition, totally wrong, or an offence to you, it is as well to make the best of what you've got, rather than tear it down and start again. Perhaps the most fortunate person is the one who has only a post and wire, or a post and chain link fence, often provided by builders to fulfil the legalities of the situation, because then you can do your own thing in front of it if you wish, without the existing structure being too much in the way.

However, the type of boundary you have will affect the planning of the garden in front of it. Boarded fences do not look particularly pretty, so think about ways of concealing them. Some walls also are best covered up; however, some stone and well designed brick walls have a beauty of their own which should perhaps be shown off.

Another point to bear in mind is that open-mesh fences, hedges and screens tend to filter wind rather than exclude it, which as far as plants are concerned is a good thing, since where wind is blocked by a solid structure, such as a wall or a heavy close-boarded fence, it tends to hop over the top and create peculiar down-draughts which can be damaging to a lot of plants – a point to remember when planning things to go immediately in the lee of a wall.

Apart from indicating the extent of your property, boundary screens do shelter a garden from winds, subject to the limitations just mentioned, so this is another argument in favour of not tearing everything up or knocking it down immediately you arrive, because an existing windbreak will give new plants a head start. Therefore, if your fence is just of the open post and wire variety, consider the amount of wind your garden receives and think about providing some shelter.

Fences, hedges and walls not only screen your garden from the elements, but can also give privacy if you want it, as well as providing a certain amount of protection from straying animals and children. This can be quite important in rural areas where farm animals are no respecters of gardens, and while a lot of the legal responsibility is on the farmer to ensure his stock is kept under proper control, this is no consolation if years of work are razed to the ground by a flock of wandering sheep.

The snag here is that on new estates the trend is towards open-plan front gardens. These might look very spacious and aesthetic to the planners, but can turn into a trampled morass, well seasoned with doggies' calling cards. This understandably causes many enthusiastic gardeners not a little irritation. Before you rush out and buy a load of timber, conifers or bricks, however, check your deeds, as many specifically forbid the erection in an open-plan situation of any form of barrier, so you're well and truly stuck with the problem. A point to bear well in mind when house-hunting, unless that sort of nuisance doesn't bother you.

Boundary screens are also a very effective way of camouflaging eyesores beyond your property and therefore your control. On the other hand, they can also obscure pleasant views, so if the prevailing winds aren't in this quarter, this could be an argument for removal, or at least perhaps a reduction in height.

VIEWS. While you are getting the hang of your plot, make a note on the scale plan of all desirable views and also those you would rather shut out. When you come to replanting, you can do a lot towards developing an attractive vista, as well as obscuring a tatty one. Try to see these from as many angles as possible, including upstairs and downstairs windows. In this way you will make fewer mistakes in siting the plants chosen for the purpose. Remember, also, that a few shrubs and suitable trees can prevent you from being an eyesore to others!

SOIL AND LOCATION. As we have already seen, soil types play a large part in the choice of plants for a garden. The most sensible ones to choose at first are always those that will do naturally well in a particular locality or type of ground – for example, tamarix does nicely in a seaside position where some conifers would turn brown with the salt. Bay trees, being not entirely hardy, are likely to do better outside in the southern counties of Britain than the north. Rhododendrons thrive in acid peat, but sicken on chalk, while clematis and pinks would much prefer such alkaline conditions. It is certainly better, and cheaper, to have things growing healthily, even if perhaps they are not what you have chosen for preference.

Human nature being what it is, however, you have probably got a burning desire for something which would normally be quite unsuitable for your plot. It *is* possible to alter conditions to please your pet fancy – boggy areas created with a hose and buried polythene, dry areas made by draining a naturally soggy piece of ground, screens provided round wind-hating plants, winter protection given to tender treasures, alkaline soil removed to make way for peat beds for acid lovers, etc, etc. But these are the first things to suffer when something occurs to upset the status quo. An artificial bog may dry out in a drought, when restrictions are placed on watering from the mains supply; you may forget to provide winter protection for your temperamental prima donnas (or be in hospital, or working away) and in the event of a particularly severe frost, you will probably lose the lot.

Artificial habitats can be extremely expensive, not to say time consuming, to build and maintain, and are often very much less successful than the so-called experts would lead you to believe. Far better, for a start at least, to ask yourself 'What am I stuck with?' 'Is my soil naturally clayey, light, peaty, etc?' 'Is my site sheltered, or is there nothing between it and the Urals?' 'Have I boggy areas, or is the whole plot hot and dry

111

all summer?' 'Have I a damp and dark backyard, two acres of loam, or a balcony sixty feet up, overlooking Waterloo Station?' Then choose suitable plants accordingly.

WHAT DO I WANT? Unfortunately, because of the limitations and restrictions already described in this chapter, what you actually *want* comes a long way behind what you have already *got* or, more accurately, in the case of time, money and ideal conditions, what you have *not* got. Perhaps it would be more accurate to head this section, 'What do I want that I can have?'

Although gardens are not divided up nearly so much these days into clearly defined areas and features, mainly because of the diminishing size of the average domestic plot, much of what you're likely to want can still be separated into different categories.

Here is a list of the sort of things you are likely to find, or want, in a modern garden. In the next chapters they are described in some detail to give you an idea of what you could be letting yourself in for.

BOUNDARIES: Walls, fences, hedges, screens.

SURFACING: Patios, paths, paving, drives.

LAWNS

FLOWERING AND OTHER PLANTS: Annuals, biennials, bedding plants. Herbaceous perennials and herbaceous borders. Roses. Trees. Shrubs and shrubberies. Bulbs. Climbing plants. Herbs. Vegetables. Fruit.

SPECIAL FEATURES: Ponds. Water gardens. Bog area. Acid gardens. Pergola and arch. Greenhouse and frame. Shed and summer-house.

7

BOUNDARIES

This topic has already been touched on in the preceding chapter. Assuming you have now decided you want or need something to divide you from the rest of mankind, you are faced with several alternatives.

Walls

ADVANTAGES. They are permanent structures and require little maintenance when properly constructed. They can add considerably to the attractiveness of the garden when the materials are properly selected to complement the surroundings. They can provide support for climbing plants. They give a high degree of privacy and act to some extent as a sound barrier.

DISADVANTAGES. Unless you are lucky enough already to have a supply of new or good quality second-hand bricks, they can be very expensive items in a garden. They require a certain amount of skill in their construction – a badly erected wall is both an eyesore and a danger. Some preliminary excavation work is needed in order to provide satisfactory foundations to carry the rest of the wall. If the area to be screened is comparatively small, solid walls, especially brick, can give a rather shut-in feeling. They can encourage down-draughts at their bases which may have a detrimental effect on plants growing there. The area of ground at the base of a wall is often drier than the rest of the garden, especially that side in the lea of the prevailing wind, because the wall tends to shelter it from any rain not falling straight down. High walls can create shade, which may or may not be a disadvantage. Because walls are so permanent, you have to be absolutely sure you have got it right – it is no good deciding in a couple of years you would have been better with something else.

Because walling is a skilled job it would be frivolous to describe in a few words what it might take a building apprentice years to accomplish. And because a wall is such a costly item, it is well worth considering employing an expert builder to get it right. Failing that, you must equip yourself at the outset with the tools to get it upright and level – a plumb line and long spirit level are essential. Certain DIY shops sell aids for ensuring that you use the correct amount of mortar at each 'dollop'. It is not beyond a handy person to produce a nice piece of walling, but – remember – a badly executed bit of work looks, and is, a disaster. A good book on do-it-yourself projects is a wise investment.

What materials?

BRICK. Brick garden walls are quite attractive if the property is made of a similar brick. Some old stone properties will take a garden wall of mellow coloured or second-hand brick without its looking odd. A few of the cheaper facing bricks are rather soft, and need a capping and foundation of harder or engineering bricks to give extra strength and keep the weather out. The use of contrasting bricks in this way can give quite an interesting effect.

STONE. Stone walls are the Rolls-Royces of garden walling but look best used where the property is built of stone, especially if the stone for the walling is rough-cut. Modern buildings and rustic garden walls do not go together nearly as well as might be imagined. The stone should be in good condition or it will suffer frost damage, and high-quality stone is very expensive.

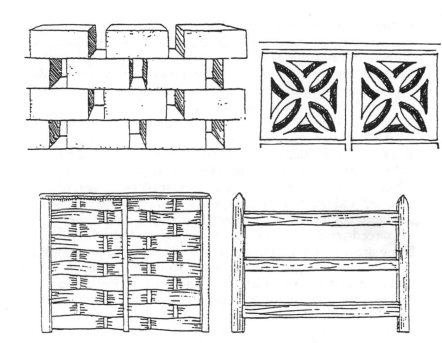

Dry (unmortared) stone walls of more than a foot or two in height are really a craftsman's job to erect safely.

RECONSTITUTED AND IMITATION STONE. This is another expensive building material but much easier to work with than real stone as it is manufactured in standard shaped pieces which are laid much like bricks. Several finishes are available, from blocks which simulate rubble walling to those which look like dressed stone. There are many arguments for and against the use of reconstituted stone where the natural building material of the district is real stone, but if the work is well executed and the materials chosen with care it can blend in quite well. Reconstituted stonework also seems to co-ordinate better with modern materials and designs than some forms of natural stone.

PIERCED-SCREEN WALLING. Pierced-screen blocks are made of concrete and are open-work in the centre with a design of one sort or another. They are mortared together like bricks but because they are intended to create an overall open pattern, they are laid on top of one another with corresponding horizontal and

115

vertical joints and not broken bonded like brick and stone. This means they do not have the strength of bonded bricks and stone, but for garden walling they are usually quite adequate. Because they are bigger than bricks and do not require bonding they are much easier for the amateur to lay, but they must be provided with a good foundation.

They can be erected to quite a height and are usually finished off with a precast concrete capping to tidy the job up and keep the weather out. Generally, unsupported runs need a pillar at each end and long stretches require intermediate pillars as well. Pre-formed concrete pillar blocks (pilasters) are available and are easy to erect, or the pillars can be made of toning or contrasting brick which can look very effective.

Pierced-screen blocks come in several shades and qualities. Some are very crude, but the better quality blocks are quite attractive. Moulds are also available, complete with instructions, for making the blocks at home – how satisfactory the results are largely depends on how good you are at this sort of thing and the raw materials you use for the job.

A section of pierced-screen walling incorporated into a solid brick wall can look quite pleasant and eliminates to some extent the shut-in feeling of high solid brick walls.

Because of the open nature of this kind of walling, the down-draughts experienced at the base of solid fences and walls are considerably reduced.

Pierced-screen walling is particularly useful for making certain recreational areas like patios more private without shutting them in entirely. Privacy is achieved as it is difficult to see through properly without actually peering through one of the holes, but behind such a screen you can get an impression of something beyond, and sun and air can penetrate to a certain extent. You also avoid the very claustrophobic feeling a solid wall or fence might induce.

HONEYCOMB WALLING. The function and effect of honeycomb walling is similar to that of pierced-screen walling but it is created with bricks, laid so that there is an open gap between the vertical joints, which leaves a hole between each brick in the course. The bricks are bonded in each course so that where there was a brick last time, there is a hole the next course up. These holes should not be too wide or it makes the wall weak. More skill is required to construct such a wall safely and effectively, though properly done it can be a very attractive feature.

CONCRETE BLOCKS. This is a pretty austere material requiring almost the same skill and effort to erect as any other walling material, and the effect is so bleak that apart from cost it has little to commend it. Concrete blocks can be either solid or hollow – the hollow ones are slightly more useful in a garden as alpines can be planted into the holes in the top. Concrete blocks can of course be rendered and/or painted but this increases considerably the amount of maintenance work sub-sequently required and reduces the choice of plant you can grow up them, as you need to have regular access to the surface of the wall.

HOLLOW WALLS. These are constructed in exactly the same way as solid walls except they comprise two skins with a cavity in between, the purpose of this being that dwarf plants can be grown on the top of the wall. Hollow walls should be kept low so that you can see the plants better, but if you want a higher one, trailing varieties can be used. Hollow walls are also best used as internal divisions within a garden because of the temptation to children to walk along the top – if it is accessible to them – and trample all the plants down.

RETAINING WALLS. These are not really boundary walls but have been included here because of the similarities between them and other walls.

Retaining walls are open at one side and are backfilled at the other to support ground at a higher level. They can either be constructed formally and mortared to give a formal terraced effect, or made of stone laid dry which can provide a useful rockery area. The dry stone wall is probably most satisfactory sloping back at an angle into the ground and backfilled as the work proceeds. The stone is then built into the ground and the joints between are filled with the soil from the back of the wall which can then be planted up with alpines as each course is laid.

If the wall is vertical and has been mortared, it can be finished off with a line of paving slabs on top, flush with the upper level, or a border created at the back of it on the higher ground containing plants which can trail down the face of the wall.

117

Foundations are needed as for any other type of wall and, especially with a dry wall, the earth should be replaced very firmly at the back of the structure as the work proceeds.

Fences

ADVANTAGES. They are probably the quickest and easiest way of reminding people where their responsibilities end – and yours start.

They come in all shapes and sizes to suit every taste and purse.

The materials are easily obtainable from a variety of retail outlets.

They take considerably less time and skill to erect than a wall.

They can have things grown against them to soften and disguise them.

DISADVANTAGES. They tend to look rather utilitarian and a lot of them used in a built-up suburban area give a 'boxy' feel, especially where the fences are solid.

They require a certain amount of after-care – treating with a wood preservative, painting, replacing rotted or rusted parts, etc., where appropriate.

It is highly likely that most gardens will contain some form of fence or other. There are so many different types that a whole book could be devoted to fences alone, so this is just a quick round-up of what is available, with a few hints on uses and erection.

Open fences

POST AND WIRE. These are used mainly to indicate legal boundaries of plot. They can have plants trained against the wire if convenient to the person owning the adjoining plot. They are useless for excluding children and small animals from gardens. They consist of 6 ft (2 m) long 3 in. (75 mm) diameter or square wooden or concrete posts, driven firmly into the ground for 2 ft (600 mm) at 10 ft (3 m) intervals. Heavy-gauge wire is then run between the posts, the first one at 9 in. (225 mm) from the ground, and then at 1 ft (300 mm) inter-vals to the top. Every tenth post should be a straining post. The wire should be attached firmly at one end and tightened by means of a wire strainer. Barbed wire is sometimes used instead of ordinary wire but is a nasty dangerous material not to be recommended.

WIRE NETTING, CHAIN LINK. These are used to protect the garden from intruders, children and domestic animals. Climbing plants can be grown up them to disguise them. They consist of posts inserted into the ground as before and wire netting or chain link stapled or wired to them. Galvanized wire netting has a limited life and tends to get bent or trodden down. Chain link is more costly but lasts longer and can be obtained with a green plastic coating which makes it unobtrusive. Straining wires should be used top, bottom and at intervals in between to keep the wire netting or chain link rigid. Chain link fencing can be of any height and is often used around play areas and as stop netting for tennis courts.

Some manufacturers now make all-plastic link or netting fencing which is used in the same way.

Galvanized wire netting can be buried 9 in. (225 mm) deep to give protection from rabbits which will burrow under a normal fence.

POST AND RAIL. These have a similar function to post and wire but are more aesthetic and substantial, though considerably more costly. They consist of 3 ft (1 m) wooden posts driven into the ground as before with flat rails attached to them at intervals. It requires a certain amount of elementary carpentry skill to get a really professional finish. The upright posts need to be about 6 ft (2 m) apart. Some woodyards and DIY timber merchants sell post and rail kits cut to the correct sizes and lengths for immediate erection.

POST AND TRELLIS. These are rather fragile types of fence similar to post and netting but using 6 ft (2 m) wide square trellis panels, strengthened with thicker timber top and bottom, instead of chain link or netting. They look very attractive but they are not strong, although useful for growing climbing plants up.

RANCH FENCING. This is similar to post and rail except the cross pieces for it are usually deeper (about 6–8 in./150–200 mm). Again, if made in wood some basic dexterity is required, but plastic ranch fencing kits are now available consisting of hollow plastic uprights with grooves into which the plastic cross rails are inserted as the work proceeds. This can be quite effective if properly erected, but in areas likely to be vandalized the posts are best set in concrete and the hollow centres filled up with fine concrete as well.

POSTS AND CHAINS. These are used generally to keep vehicles off certain areas or as decorative front garden fences. They consist of 3 ft (1 m) wood, concrete or plastic posts set firmly into the ground, in concrete if necessary, with plastic or metal chain hung between them, attached firmly to 'eyes' in the top of the posts.

There are also many other plastic and plastic-covered wire ornamental fences available from DIY shops and garden centres which have very little function other than to decorate the edges of paths and beds.

SPLIT CHESTNUT. This is used as temporary fencing or a windbreak or snow-break when something more permanent will eventually be used. It consists of chestnut palings wired together to leave gaps between of 1 and 3 inches (25–75 mm) and attached at intervals to posts driven into the ground. It looks somewhat functional but has the advantage of being able to be rolled up and removed when not required any more, and can be used again elsewhere.

Solid fences

These are used to provide total privacy, hide an eyesore or shelter a very exposed plot. They can cast shade in the same way as a wall, so height should be chosen carefully.

Solid fences are usually of three types – overlap, when thin pieces of timber are attached to battens for strength; interwoven, which has similar thin strips woven in and out of vertical battens; and close-boarded, which is vertical wooden boards nailed to rigid substantial cross-pieces. Interwoven fencing is the cheapest and least substantial, while close-boarded is very expensive, but, properly maintained, will last a lifetime.

These forms of fencing vary considerably in price and quality according to manufacturer and it pays to shop around. They are usually made in 6 ft or 2 metre widths and up to 6 ft (2 m) in height in 12 in. (300 mm) stages from 2 or 3 ft (600 or 900 mm) minimum height. They are usually supported by substantial wooden or concrete posts sunk well into the ground, or brick pillars. Concrete posts can be set in concrete but research has shown that wooden ones rot less quickly if they are just rammed firmly into the earth. Metal post-supports are now available – these are driven into the ground first and the posts set into them afterwards. Later models have adjusting devices to compensate for not getting the socket absolutely vertical, which would prevent the post, and therefore the panel attached to it, being upright. These gadgets can be quite handy, but add greatly to the cost of the fence. A similar metal socket is available for replacing a rotted wooden post in a concrete base.

The solid appearance of this type of fence can be considerably reduced if the top foot or two is replaced by open square trellis panels. These are usually sold by fencing manufacturers as well as the solid panels, or can be made to order.

Remember that you can get down-draughts from close-boarded fences like those from walls, so any floppy plants near the base should be given adequate support.

An interesting variation on this theme is a brick wall with close-boarded panels built in along the length of it. This reduces the cost of materials, i.e. the bricks, and also introduces a different texture, breaking up the length of brickwork.

IRON FENCES AND RAILINGS. These are becoming popular again with traditionalists. They are, however, expensive and require regular maintenance to prevent rusting.

Maintenance of fences

TIMBER FENCES. All wooden parts should have been treated with wood preservative before the fence was erected. Panels and fencing posts are usually treated under pressure by the manufacturer. If you are buying timber to make your own fencing, probably the best preservative is still creosote, but this is highly toxic to plants when fresh. Other spirit-based preservatives are very effective, and treated wood can be used near plants only a short while after application, but are a lot more expensive.

If possible hardwood (oak, elm, etc.) should be used for all solid parts but this is very pricey and not always easy to come by. Creosote should not be used on hardwood as it can cause it to split and crack, but spirit-based wood preservatives are quite suitable.

Periodically, exposed timber should be re-treated. Water-based stain-preservatives are useful for this as they give the wood a long-lasting colour in addition to deterring rot. They are not suitable, though, for the parts of a fence in permanent

121

contact with the soil. The thin timber of which interwoven and close-boarded fencing is made is not quite so vulnerable as regards rotting because, provided it has a free circulation of air round it, it dries out quickly.

If you grow plants against timber fences, especially solid ones, they should be provided with a secondary means of support (plastic mesh, wires, etc.) so air can circulate behind and also to enable them to be pulled away from the fence so you can reach it easily for maintenance.

Timber, of course, can also be painted. White paint looks good on ranch fencing, but once you start painting wood it has to be done regularly. Certainly most forms of timber fencing look better with a natural or wood-coloured finish.

Check all wooden fences regularly for signs of rotting or damage and replace the defective parts as soon as possible. This could save a major repair job later on.

PLASTIC FENCES, NETTING, ETC. Most plastics deteriorate gradually owing to the action of sunlight on them, but better quality plastic building materials have been specially developed to withstand outdoor conditions over many years. Ornamental plastic fences look better if they are washed regularly to restore their original finish, and should be checked occasionally for broken parts. The durability of plastic posts, imitation boarding, etc. depends largely upon the care given to its erection. Do not forget that plastic is inflammable and bonfires should be kept well away, especially from plastic-covered chain link, a fact which can be easily overlooked.

WIRE FENCES. Fences consisting largely of tensioned wire between posts should have the wire re-tensioned from time to time as it is inclined to slacken off slightly.

Well galvanized chain link fencing should require very little attention for many years. Galvanized wire netting eventually rusts and, if a similar fence is still required, it will be necessary to replace the netting every few years. Wire netting fences are perhaps best used as a temporary measure, for example, while a hedge is growing up, then the need for periodic replacement is avoided.

Hedges and screens

ADVANTAGES. A well-maintained hedge is a delight in a garden. Even formal evergreen ones look different depending on the time of year. Birds nest in them readily, so wildlife is attracted.

There is a very wide choice of suitable subjects for every purpose.

Hedges tend to filter wind, rather than block it, doing away with down-draughts created by solid screens.

They are comparatively inexpensive to establish.

By choosing the right plants, they can be made impenetrable to both animals and humans.

Hedges of a reasonable height are very effective for absorbing and deadening traffic and other noise.

DISADVANTAGES. They take some time to establish themselves and so often a temporary fence is needed in addition. They require some form of regular maintenance, usually clipping, to keep them within bounds. This also means you have to have a good relationship with the neighbour whose garden is the other side. They can harbour insect pests.

It is said they absorb a great deal of moisture and food from the soil in the vicinity, though good garden practice should prevent this by regular feeding and providing mulches if the ground seems always dry at the base of the hedge (water the soil first, though!).

Deciduous ones, especially beech, make a lot of leaves at certain times of the year.

Tall, thick hedges cast a lot of shade.

Choosing a hedge

The labour involved in maintaining a good hedge might have deterred you from going any further into whether you should plant one or not, but if you look at what is suitable and available you might be able still to have one and not land yourself with a lot of hard work.

Hedges can be broadly divided into those which require a lot, some, or minimal maintenance.

'Cheap and cheerful' hedges

Into this category come all the well known, and somewhat out-dated, hedges which are inexpensive to buy, quick to establish themselves, and give their owners a lot of work.

PRIVET. This is semi-evergreen or evergreen depending on locality and hardness of winter. It can be obtained in green and several variegated forms (the latter are more expensive but more decorative). It may be clipped into shapes if required. It is quite dense if planted closely (about 9–12 in. (225–300 mm) apart) but not impervious to small animals. It can often be infested with greenfly and other insect pests. It is quite a greedy feeder so plants nearby should be fed. It is best restricted to about 6 ft (2 m) in height or the top can blow out of shape. It is very susceptible to armillaria disease (bootlace fungus, honey fungus) which lives on dead wood in the soil and can spread to healthy nearby roots by means of black, bootlace-like threads running through the soil. The infected plants begin to die off and eventually the wood rots. There is a white, fan-like growth under the bark, and in the autumn honey-coloured toadstools appear at times. There is no cure. Remove and burn the infected plants and those nearby and treat the soil with a proprietary chemical such as Armillatox. Once a privet hedge is infected, the disease usually spreads throughout the whole of it. Armillaria is not confined to privet but privet is especially prone to infection.

The biggest drawback of privet is that it needs trimming frequently to keep it in good shape. This can be as much as two- to three-weekly intervals in certain seasons.

LONICERA NITIDA. This is another evergreen or semi-evergreen with tiny, round leaves and a rapid growth habit which can give you an unending job for the whole of the summer. You can take cuttings easily from friends' hedges – indeed, clippings dropped on to the soil and not cleared up will root where they lie. Against it is its untidy habit – it gets woody in the middle with a lot of dead stalks all through the bush, but it can be cut back quite hard if it gets into too bad a state and it will shoot again. It is useless for tall hedges as it flops if it gets too high.

HAWTHORN (quickthorn). This is another easily obtained hedge but is considerably more useful, as close-planted it can be an animal deterrent. It grows fairly rapidly and should be cut back early in life in order to encourage it to bush out. It can be allowed to grow to almost any height and reduced virtually to ground level if required. It is spiny but if clipped regularly, usually in early summer and again in the autumn, this will not become a problem. Neglected quickthorn hedges can be 'laid' by half splitting the trunks and bending them over at an angle, supported by sticks. The result of this is to thicken the base. It is a craftsman's job, but worth it. If you cannot find a hedge layer in your district, your local branch of the Agricultural Training Board (see Yellow Pages) may be able to put you in touch with someone, as they organize hedging courses in certain areas.

Hawthorn hedges attract a number of insect pests, including caterpillars. Occasionally young shoots are affected by mildew, but these are usually cut off when trimming.

BLACKTHORN (sloe) makes a similar hedge to quickthorn, with the same advantages and disadvantages. It can be mixed with quickthorn to form the basis of an English-style mixed hedge, together with field maple.

Coniferous hedges

The main attraction of these is that you can get away with clipping them only once a year. The three most commonly planted coniferous hedges – *Chamaecyparis lawsoniana* (Lawson's cypress), *Thuja plicata*, and the ubiquitous x *Cupressocyparis leylandii* (Leyland cypress) – can look pleasing if well trimmed in late May (with a possible tidying up in early autumn). *Thuja plicata* is the least rapid growing of the three, is a nice fresh green colour with some bronzing in winter, and has a pleasant piney smell when brushed against. The best Lawson's cypress are raised from seed and so vary slightly in form and colour. This breaks up the potential monotony of a large area of dark green foliage which does not drop off in winter. Leyland cypress is a very rapid grower and so forms an obvious hedge very quickly. Unfortunately it has been so overplanted in recent years as to have become boring, though for the nearest thing to an instant evergreen hedge, it still cannot be beaten. If you want to interplant with a golden variety, choose the form 'Robinson' which has a similar habit. Most other golden forms are much slower growing than the green form.

Thuja plicata takes some while to establish but gives a neater hedge eventually. It is also reasonably inexpensive and will withstand some shade.

Lawson's cypress does not move well bare-rooted, so always obtain container grown plants. Inexpensive bare-root plants are often advertised at low prices but these frequently die, so it is a false economy. Lawson's cypress also browns in cold winds so is no good for very exposed areas. It tends to die in prolonged drought.

Leyland cypress is the most expensive of the three and is virtually always container grown. The best height for replanting is about 18–24 in. (450–600 mm) – larger ones are often straggly at the bottom and smaller ones can easily get overlooked!

Place hedging conifers about 2 ft (600 mm) apart. Although they can be planted at any time of the year if in containers, early autumn gives them the best chance to re-establish. Water well and spray with water for the whole growing season after planting, and stake firmly to prevent them blowing about and working loose in the soil. Clip tightly before the required height is reached, especially if a tall hedge is wanted. This encourages the hedge to thicken up well.

It is no good planting conifers of any sort, especially small ones, where every passing dog can 'wee' on them – they will always remain brown at the base and unhealthy. Neither is there any point in planting coniferous hedges in waterlogged places – they will eventually sicken and die.

Yew (*taxus*), both the golden and deep green forms, can be used in much the same way as the three conifers mentioned above. It makes a hedge for posterity, but is very slow, and is deadly poisonous to all animals, so should not be used for hedges bordering fields where livestock is kept.

Any conifers planted in straight lines will make some sort of hedge given time. This is a point worth remembering if you want something slightly different from the usual. Most of them are much slower than those suggested above, although many could make tall screens in time. If you are intending to mix conifers, do make sure they all have a similar habit and growth rate. For example, it is possible to mix runs of *Chamaecyparis lawsoniana* 'Stewartii' (golden foliage), *Chamaecyparis lawsoniana* 'Pembury Blue' and *Chamaecyparis lawsoniana* 'Green Hedger', planted about 4 ft (1.25 m) apart. They all grow at about the same speed, have a similar shape and will take clipping when they get to the required size. However, it could be argued that to use specimen conifers for such a purpose is a waste when cheaper and less shapely varieties are available, though there is no doubt that, especially in the early years, it is a very effective planting.

Other formal evergreen hedges

You really need quite a lot of space for some of these. *Common laurel* and *Portugal laurel* make a good shelter but look better in bigger gardens where they can be allowed to put on some height and width. Young plants are reasonably inexpensive and an established hedge given plenty of room needs trimming only once a year in spring.

Holly, green or variegated, is a good animal deterrent but expensive to buy and slow to get started. It is also rather unpleasant to clip and the dead leaves that drop off make kneeling and hand-work (weeding etc.) nearby a hazardous job. It is prone to a pest known as holly leaf miner which makes tunnels in the leaves which eventually drop off. It is a difficult pest to control because it gets in between the waxy layers of the leaves where it cannot be reached but a systemic insecticide will have some effect against it. Unless the infestation is severe, it is unlikely to do any lasting harm, even if untreated. It is suggested that this type of hedge should be pruned with secateurs and not clipped with shears as the half-severed leaves look unsightly, but I find that if you are short of time it does not really matter.

Green box will make a good formal hedge up to 6 ft (2 m) high – the slow-growing, variegated form makes an attractive dwarf or low-growing one.

Beech is not evergreen, but it retains its dead leaves all winter so in that respect it remains 'clothed'. *Hornbeam* is similar, but will stand soggy clay soils better. Beech and hornbeam are slow to reach their eventual height, but spaced at 12 in. (300 mm), eventually make a good, dense screen. They have two drawbacks. One is that they become horribly infested with aphids and their sticky honeydew on the young shoots, but this can be controlled with a good insecticide, which is a good idea if you are due to trim it, as clipping a hedge full of aphids and their by-products is not to be recommended! The other snag is that the dead leaves are shed over a long period of autumn, winter and spring which makes clearing them up an endless task.

Clipping formal hedges

All regularly clipped hedges should be thicker at the bottom, tapering towards the top. This enables more water to reach the base of the hedge and also makes for greater stability, especially where the hedge is a tall one.

Informal hedges and screens

These are by far the easiest to maintain, providing you choose the right plants and have a good bit of space to play with. Just as conifers planted in straight lines can constitute a hedge, so can many shrubs. The most successful shrubs for this purpose are the easily grown ones which will stand some hacking about if necessary, without taking offence. Prickly shrubs are ideal dog deterrents if planted close enough together. The *berberis* family is very useful for this purpose. Taller-growing, deciduous shrubs – e.g., *philadelphus*, *weigela*, *forsythia*, *lilac*, etc., – providing they are matched for habit and size, can be used as single species or mixed together.

Low hedges can be made with shorter-growing shrubs such as *potentilla*, *Spiraea 'Anthony Waterer'*, *fuchsias* (in warmer parts of Britain), *Hypericum 'Hidcote'* and many shrubby *herbs*.

Informal evergreen hedges can be formed from almost any evergreen shrub – *Viburnum tinus*, *escallonia*, *elaeagnus*, *pyracantha* and the evergreen and semi-evergreen forms of *cotoneaster* are particularly suitable.

Controlling informal hedges can be done in two ways: You can prune each shrub in the hedge individually after flowering by removing the oldest flowered wood and generally thinning out the crowded stems and reshaping the plant – which is most suitable for shrubs flowering on old wood before the end of July – or you can shorten back the whole hedge all round once a year, or even less than annually if space will allow. This is a useful method for dealing with mainly foliage subjects such as berberis, elaeagnus, etc. Because these hedges are designed to be informal, you should confine trimming to keeping them within bounds without losing the natural habit, although most of them can, if necessary, be clipped or sheared back like any other hedge; sometimes, however, you will lose flowering wood in this case.

SHRUB SCREENS. These can be treated in the same way as hedges, but for the sake of density you can plant at least two shrubs deep, those at the front should be a little lower so the back row can also be seen. In this case, initial spacings would depend on the eventual natural spread of shrubs chosen.

Rose hedges

In their simplest form, rose hedges are just bush roses of one or two complementary varieties planted reasonably closely (18–24 in. (450–600 mm)) to form a hedge. Usually they are lightly pruned in spring (see chapter on roses, page 185) so there is always some obvious form of barrier. A mature rose hedge will usually range in height from between 3 ft and 4 ft 6 in. (1 m–1.50 m) depending on soil, area and variety, but if 'Queen Elizabeth' is used it could reach as much as 7 feet (over 2 m).

Many of the shrub ('old-fashioned') roses also make good hedges, and as these need hardly any pruning other than the removal of very old twiggy growths and dead wood, they aren't a lot of bother. A lot of these 'species' roses have the added bonus of colourful hips in the autumn, and birds are attracted by them. Of all the shrub roses, seedlings of *Rosa rugosa* provide perhaps the cheapest and among the most effective hedging subjects as, having been grown from seed, their flowers vary from deep magenta to white. They have large hips and their leaves turn a clear golden yellow in autumn before falling.

How to plant a hedge

An old forestry worker once told me the best way to plant young hedging was to insert the spade into the ground, work it backwards and forwards to make a slit in the soil, drop in the root, then close up the slit by shoving the spade in at either side. While this might be all right for millions of young plants, where half of them are expendable, there is no substitute for well-prepared ground – after all, the hedge may be there for a hundred years.

Dig the whole of the area where the hedge is to go thoroughly, add plenty of humus-forming material and also bone-meal (if the hedge is to be planted in autumn or winter) or a good balanced fertilizer, such as growmore, if it is to go in in the spring. Late October to early April is the time for planting bare-root hedges, including roses; late September and October, or April, for conifers. Most hedging plants can now be bought containerized, which means that provided it is not frosty or the middle of a drought, if necessary you can plant a hedge at any time, but the after-care is greatly increased.

A hedge is just as much a part of the ornamental garden as any other plants in it, and deserves the same treatment. It will always respond to annual feeding and the addition of manure and/or compost to the surrounding soil. A mulch is especially beneficial in early years as it helps to conserve the soil moisture which is so necessary for a fast-growing young hedge.

8

SURFACING

There can be few gardens which do not need some form of hard-standing, either to step out on to from the front or back door, or to leave the car on. Apart from absolute necessities, how much of your patch you bury beneath something solid is really a personal matter.

For example, you do not *need* a terrace or patio as an essential requirement of your plot. If you like grass, you may prefer to lounge about on a hard-wearing lawn rather than a lot of concrete or stone. On the other hand, you may feel that for you a firm, clean, dry, sitting area is an absolute must. Similarly, if you do not have to keep walking regularly from one part of the garden to another, apart from the possible aesthetic interest of such a feature, you do not have to lay a solid path. Getting your feet dirty round the outside of the house when you wash the windows may not bother you. Then, again, it well might.

The choice of materials for hard surfacing plays a large part in the overall effect of the garden, as already mentioned in

Chapter 6. If in doubt, the plainer the better. If you are not sure whether tinted or coloured materials look right in your particular environment, stick to a neutral shade or try to pick out one of the 'quieter' colours of the building materials used to construct the property. Above all, if you are doing the job yourself, or getting someone not skilled in paving work to help you, do ensure that you get the job right. Uneven slabs not only look unsightly, they are a positive menace to even the sure-footed, let alone the elderly and infirm. Too much gravel can make it impossible for a car to get on and off, or a wheelbarrow to be moved. Skimped concreting will need to be re-done after the first hard frost. Remember, too, that path-laying is very hard work. Slabs are heavy and difficult to handle. Concrete takes some effort to mix and barrow about, especially if you are mixing by hand. The base for any path, patio, drive, or whatever has to be firm, level and solid. If you cannot manage this efficiently because of sheer physical limitation, cut your losses and get the job done professionally.

Surfacing materials and their possible uses

GRAVEL. This is obtainable in several graded sizes, most of which are suitable for garden use. Pea gravel (the smallest grade) is inclined to tread off on wet or muddy shoes and boots and become embedded in car tyre treads. Gravel can be used for paths, patios, drives and hard-standings. It has a natural look and blends well with most surroundings, but it is unsuitable for sloping paths and other non-level areas as it tends to work down to the lowest point. Many people say they find gravel drives a useful deterrent to intruders who cannot move around quietly outside the house. It is available from builders' merchants, larger garden centres, or direct from the gravel pit and is now sold by the tonne, which is approximately 1 cubic metre, depending on how wet it is.

METHOD OF LAYING. Remove about 8 in. (200 mm) of soil and level the area to be gravelled. For small areas the easiest way to do this is using a straight, flat piece of wood and a long spirit level. Then put down and roll a 5-in. (125 mm) layer of 'hoggin', a mixture of coarse gravel and clay. Fill the top 3 in. (75 mm) with the chosen grade of gravel, and roll or firm this as well, and then rake it smooth. A neater job is made if you use pre-cast concrete or wooden kerbs at the edges of the gravelled area. This prevents the gravel working off on to the surrounding garden.

MAINTENANCE. Very little maintenance is needed, other than regular raking to keep the surface tidy. Before putting in the hoggin, it is a good idea to treat the soil surface with a long-lasting total weedkiller (see the chart on pages 78–9) and thereafter give the surface an annual application of a similar suitable herbicide. (Try ICI Pathclear or Casoron G if in doubt.) Eventually the surface will settle and become low in parts and generally rather tatty, but it can be revamped by covering with a 1 in. (25 mm) layer of new gravel.

Tarmacadam and asphalt

These are available cold from local dealers and DIY stores. Hot asphalt is usually provided and laid by specialist surfacing contractors. *Warning*: this is another area where 'cowboys' run rife. Never succumb to someone who comes to your door wanting to do you a quick, cheap job – you will almost certainly be sorry. If in doubt ask someone who has recently had a job done. In this field, personal recommendation is certainly the best way of finding a reliable contractor.

Tarmacadam is used for drives and hard-standings likely to be subjected to heavy wear and vehicular traffic. It can be used for paths but does not look very attractive.

METHOD OF LAYING. Prepare the area in a similar way to that described for gravel, including treatment with a persistent weedkiller if a lot of deep-rooted weeds can still be seen. First lay and consolidate hoggin, then spread and roll about 2 in. (50 mm) of coarse tarmacadam, followed by 1-in. (25 mm) top coat of ¼-in. (5 mm) graded tarmacadam, rolled in with a heavy roller. It is essential to get a slightly higher 'crown' in the middle or the area will flood, also there should be no 'high points' and definitely no depressions or puddles will collect. If you are using concrete kerbs – and these certainly finish the job off better – you should leave holes for drainage between each section on to the surrounding garden.

Hot asphalt makes a harder surface and can have pea-gravel or coloured chippings rolled into it for a better decorative effect.

MAINTENANCE. If the area is properly prepared and laid, little will be

133

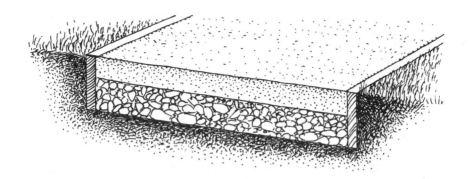

needed for several years. After a while, weeds tend to grow in the dirt which collects in the rough surface, and their roots will damage the tarmacadam unless they are removed quickly, apart from looking untidy. An annual application of a total long-lasting weedkiller as suggested for gravel will prevent this happening.

Eventually even the best laid surfaces will start to break up a little, especially after a bad winter. A new 1-in. (25 mm) top coat may then be put down on the cleaned up and re-levelled surface.

If the budget will allow, a way of preserving the finish of a tarmacadam or asphalt drive is to get a contractor to spray the surface with hot tar, into which chippings or pea-gravel are rolled while the tar is still liquid. This considerably lengthens the life of a drive and improves the rather sombre appearance.

Concrete

This is usually used for drives and hard-standings. Paths and large concreted sitting areas look a bit spartan, although they are long-lasting and serviceable and do not have the problem of weeds growing between the joints. A simulated slab or crazy paving pattern can be marked on the surface of drying concrete if liked. A rough, slightly grooved finish can be given with the edge of a plank while the concrete is still wet, which makes the wet surface easier to walk on, especially for the infirm. Concrete is obtainable as ready-mix from some suppliers, as separate materials (cement, sand, aggregate) from builders' merchants and DIY stores, or in bags as the dry mixed ingredients. It really depends on how much you need as to whether you buy a load of ready-mixed concrete or mix your

134

own. Tool hire shops usually have concrete-mixers for loan if you have enough work to justify hiring one. Bags of cement and sand are comparatively expensive and are best used for small areas and patching jobs or where transport of large quantities of cement and loose sand is a problem.

LAYING CONCRETE. Excavate and level the area to be concreted to about 5-in. (125 mm) depth, and place kerbs or wooden formwork at the sides to contain the concrete. Lay a layer of ashes or fine rubble in the bottom of the excavation, then pour the wet concrete on top to the required level. Paths need not have quite so much depth of concrete as suggested above if they are not intended to carry heavy loads. Level the concrete with a rake and consolidate by rolling or tamping while it is still wet enough to be worked but not so liquid as to be unable to support the roller or rammer.

The most suitable mix is one part cement, two parts clean sand and four parts shingle or other similar aggregate. Mix these together thoroughly by placing the cement on top of the sand and turning it over until the cement is evenly dispersed. Add the aggregate afterwards and incorporate it properly, then add the water slowly, mixing all the time, until the concrete is of a porridgy consistency. Alternatively, you can use a concrete-mixer. The less water, the better the concrete is, provided it is workable. Concrete should dry slowly, and in hot weather the surface should be covered with damp sacks or similar to prevent it 'going off' too quickly. Never lay concrete in frosty weather, or it will not set – just dry off into a lot of shingle, sand and useless spoilt cement.

MAINTENANCE. Properly mixed and laid concrete should require little maintenance for many years. If odd holes do appear, they should be patched, first cleaning out and wetting the hole to ensure the adhesion of new concrete.

Paving slabs, sets and bricks

It is not so long ago that when you thought of using slabs you more or less had two choices – crude grey concrete, perhaps garishly coloured with unnatural looking dyes, and real stone. Unless you could get the latter second-hand, cost alone put them out of reach for most people.

Now, however, the choice is unending. New manufacturing methods have introduced man-made paving which is a

135

fair imitation of the real thing, with a choice of different finishes, textures and patterns to suit every style and taste. Interesting effects can be obtained with plain slabs by using several different sizes – the design can be drawn out on graph paper first to make sure it works. Paving slabs with a definite pattern or part pattern can be laid different ways to produce larger patterns. It is not out of the question to use more than one colour providing they are chosen with care. Hexagonal and circular slabs can provide interesting effects in the right places. Some firms manufacture '*sets*' which are smaller than slabs and can be used at times to give a less stark feel to a paving scheme.

It is often felt that too big an expanse of plain paving is uninteresting, though this is very much a personal opinion and it is unquestionably far better to have a neat stretch of well-laid slabs than a wilderness if for some reason you can't cultivate the site properly. Many ideas have been put forward to break up a large paved area. In addition to using different colours, different materials are also suggested. Leaving out some slabs and replacing with *cobbles* or large stones, either loose or set in mortar, is one alternative which should certainly be considered, but these pieces should not be placed near a sitting area as it can be difficult to get a table or chairs level on this sort of finish. Cobbles can also be difficult to walk on, especially for the wearers of high heels and for the elderly, and they can cause the visually impaired to trip. *Bricks* are another method of adding interest. These are also set in cement and, properly laid, make a more even surface than do cobbles. Bricks for this purpose should be hard enough to withstand frost and wear – many second-hand rustic bricks and cheaper facing bricks are not suitable and soon break up. Paving bricks are a popular alternative. They are hard and will in dry sand withstand even vehicular traffic. These can be laid in a variety of patterns and are quite successful. Whole paths and patios can be surfaced using bricks – or paving bricks.

Still on the subject of the informal, crazy paving fits in quite well with old buildings, particularly of the cottagey type. Many garden centres sell broken slabs by weight which are suitable for the purpose – you get about 9 square yards to the ton (about 7.5 square metres to the tonne).

A much easier and cheaper way to break up a large area of paving which is only intended for walking on is to leave out

The author's garden – a small plot where available space is maximized.

Unusual shapes and mixed textures add interest to hard surfaces.

Crazy paving makes an ideal patio surface in a cottage garden setting.

The author's vegetable garden in June produced an abundance of mouthwatering crops by August. *(Colin Leftley/Garden Answers)*

A greenhouse can blend in unobtrusively with the garden if thought is given to the overall design.

Newly planted hanging baskets bene-fit from greenhouse protection for a few weeks until established.

A frost free greenhouse is a boon for overwintering slightly tender shrubs.

Bubble polythene insulation will reduce fuel bills when making early sowings.

Good light is necessary for flowering plants under glass in early summer.

An attractive container of well grown bedding plants is an asset to any garden.

Regular feeding and watering is essential for a healthy hanging basket.

A colourful hanging basket will brighten a plain wall.

A magnificent specimen of *Wistaria sinensis*.

Clematis 'Miss Bateman' – a first rate climbing plant for a trellis.

Lonicera periclymenum 'Red Gables' has a very long flowering period.

A water feature can be large and spectacular . . .

. . . or a miniature aquatic delight.

areas of slabs at random and use the spaces as beds for dwarf shrubs and conifers, low-growing perennials, bedding plants and bulbs. These areas can even have dwarf walls erected round them to make raised beds. In certain areas creeping plants – e.g., dwarf thymes – can be planted in the cracks between the slabs. These look especially nice with crazy paving but if there is likely to be a lot of foot traffic, such plants can get trodden on.

Gravel and slabs can also be mixed to good effect in certain places. While this idea is not particularly advisable for patios and terraces, as the gravel tends to get kicked off and it is difficult to get chairs, tables, etc., to stay even on it, the drive leading to a garage can well consist of two tracks of slabs or concrete for the wheels with the area to each side and in between filled with gravel.

Paving, sets and bricks can be used for patios, terraces, working areas and paths, also for drives and hard-standings provided that an adequate foundation has been laid and the slabs are perfectly firm and even. Single slabs of all shapes, including broken ones, can be sunk into the lawn or a border to form stepping stones. They are available from DIY shops, builders' merchants and garden centres. Sometimes they are sold off second-hand by councils and other public bodies. If you're doing your garden very much on a budget, check with the social services department of your local council – some have sheltered workshops for the mentally and physically handicapped which produce and sell slabs to the public at very reasonable prices.

HOW TO LAY PAVING, SETS, COBBLES AND BRICKS. Prepare the area for paving slabs, sets and heavy-duty bricks designed to support the weight of a vehicle, as for laying gravel, with about 4 to 5 in. (100–125 mm) of well-rolled hoggin put down first. Bed the slabs on a 1-in. (25 mm) layer of sand, or fine concrete. Fill the joints between with sand – in which case an annual application of a total weedkiller may be necessary – or mortar. In the case of sets, it is preferable to bed them in concrete and mortar the joints between. If you only intend the paved area to be walked on, it is enough to excavate, level and consolidate the area under the slabs and lay them on a 1-in. (25 mm) bed of sand. This would mean that 3 or 4 in. (75–100 mm) of excavation would be enough. The ground should be treated with a total weedkiller after the sand has been laid down. The joints between can be treated as described above.

Lay bricks and paviors for footpaths on 4 in. (100 mm) of consolidated hoggin and embed them in a 1-in. (25 mm) layer of levelled sand. Do not cement them in. Kill the weeds when necessary.

Cobbles can be laid loose on a bed of sand but are perhaps safest embedded in a cement and sand mix.

Lay crazy paving in exactly the same manner as paving slabs but ideally bedded in sand and cement. Do not use pieces that are too small. The joints between the slabs should be between ¼-in. (5 mm) and ½-in. (10 mm) wide but may have to be wider in parts because of the random nature of the broken pieces. Point these joints with mortar except where plants are to be grown in between. When slabs are used for stepping stones in grass, you should take care to sink them slightly below the surface of the lawn, or their edges and corners will play havoc with the mower blades.

MAINTENANCE OF SLAB PATHS. Weathered slabs, bricks, etc., will eventually begin to grow algae, mosses and lichens on the surface. Some of this can be extremely slippery, and it is important to clean it off regularly with a suitable chemical (see Herbicides chart, pages 78–9). Alternatively, clean off the algae with a pressure washer, which can be hired by the day, or weekend, from a tool-hire shop.

If the joints between have been mortared, they will eventually start breaking up, and should be removed and replaced.

Otherwise an application of a total weedkiller to the cracks when needed is all that is required (do not use this near or on any plants growing between the slabs though!).

Organic gardeners will prefer to hand-weed their patios, or use one of the new weedkillers based on fatty acids.

Other surfacing materials

Timber paths have become quite popular in recent years. Rustic paths can be made from thin logs laid across their width, and stepping stones from slices of tree trunks set into the ground. Although they eventually rot, they can give quite a sylvan feel to a wild garden. They are not for the feeble-footed however. Covering the surface with fine-mesh chicken wire helps to provide a non-slip finish. Log-paths are difficult to walk on steadily because of their ridged surface and the wooden slices can become very slippery.

Maintenance consists of treating the exposed surfaces periodically with a spirit-based preservative.

Grass paths are aesthetically pleasing but have a limited use because if they get a lot of walking on or constant barrowing over them the grass will wear and in winter they soon become muddy. In addition there is a great deal of maintenance required in keeping the edges neat and regularly clipped. Only use hard-wearing grasses. A grass path grown from seed could take several years before it can accept any hard usage. Turfing is the most satisfactory way to create a new grass path, but you have really got to be something of a fanatic to keep one looking good. As there are so many pleasing alternatives, there are not many arguments in their favour.

Some tips on the design of drives, paths and patios

DRIVES should be made big enough to accommodate both your own vehicles and those of visitors if space will allow. Neighbours do not appreciate their gateways being obstructed by guests at your party while you have got a big empty space at the front of your house. If you do not have a double entrance (and many local authorities will not allow this), incorporate a turning bay into your drive so you do not have to back out into oncoming traffic on the road outside your property.

If you are making a gateway, do not forget to make it wide enough to take a big vehicle – it is surprising how many removal lorries cannot gain access to the drive because the gates are too narrow to squeeze through. However, there can be local-authority constraints on the making of new gateways and vehicular accessess – if in doubt, check with the Planning or Highways Departments.

If your drive slopes down towards the garage or house, it may be necessary to put in a soakaway and grating to prevent water running under the door. This makes it more difficult to get the levels correct, as there should be a fall in every direction towards this drain, and especially *away* from the garage. If the slope is not quite so steep, an alternative is to embed a piece of guttering or form a channel in the surface near the garage door to drain off on to the garden at one side or the other. This should be deep and wide enough to take what runs into it even during heavy rain. A drain is also useful in a level drive for catching water used for car washing.

PATHS. Dead-straight paths do not look particularly attractive unless you are set on a very formal, geometrically laid out garden. Unfortunately, though, if a path does not go from A to B by the shortest route, you can be sure everyone wanting to reach B from A will do it as directly as possible. A compromise is to curve the path very *gently*, perhaps first in one direction and then another, but not making any bend so sharp that it is easier to cut straight across the lawn and miss it out. The theme of these curves can maybe be taken up and amplified by the edge of any bed or border nearby to give the path curves some purpose.

If you have enough ground, the wider the path the better as it makes it easier to move barrows, machinery, etc. Many gardening books recommend that a path should be no narrower than 3 feet (900 mm), though most modern gardens would not be able to afford the room, apart from which it could look very unbalanced in a small area. If space is restricted, a guide to width would be what you could manage to walk up and down comfortably without feeling you are walking a tightrope. This is generally about 2 feet (600 mm) wide.

Do not forget, if you are wanting to grow plants up the walls of your house, and you are running a path around it, to leave enough spaces for the things you are likely to plant. It is much easier than hacking holes out afterwards!

Place stepping stones close enough together to walk on comfortably without having to take large strides or walk on the spaces in between. The gap therefore should be no more than 7 or 8 in. (175–200 mm), and could be as little as 6 in. (150 mm).

Gravel paths are not a lot of use in parts of the garden where you may walk off the soil and down the path with muddy boots. Concrete and slab paths will get dirty but can be swilled or swept – gravel will stick to your soles and tread all over the lawn and everywhere else you do not want it.

PATIOS. It is customary for a patio area to be placed adjacent to the house, but this is not always the best place for a sitting-out area. Patios facing due south can become unbearably hot on a sunny day at the height of summer. Patios facing due north never get any sun and so are only useful in a heatwave. If the conventional patio area has to be in one of these extreme positions and you can spare the land, try making a second paved sitting-place in another part of the garden – one in a sunny spot if your house faces north, or one that gets some shade if your property faces south. If you shape this second area correctly, it can fit in quite well with the design of the surrounding borders and will not look out of place.

Always make a patio as big as you can afford – space or money-wise. A small area looks large on paper – once you have laid it out and filled it with chairs, tables, loungers, barbecues, paddling pools, sunbeds, hammocks, pots of flowers and all the other hopeful summer paraphernalia, the thing is full to overflowing. A depth of 12 or even 16 ft (3.75 or 5 m) by the width of the property is not unreasonable, even in a comparatively small garden. It can always be made to look more interesting by combining different materials, as already described.

9

THE LAWN

A lawn is to a garden what a carpet is to a room: and a smooth green grass 'carpet' does indeed show everything else in the garden to its best advantage. But remember that, just as bare polished boards look better than a scruffy carpet, paving might be better than ill-kempt grass!

It is curious that despite the fact that a decent lawn can be quite a lot of hard work, and will set you back a good bit into the bargain, it is usually the first item included in the plan when starting on a new garden site.

ADVANTAGES. A well maintained lawn is the best foil for other features, both constructed and living, in an ornamental garden.

It is the second easiest – and probably in the long run, the least expensive – way of covering big areas of ground to eliminate the necessity of regular weeding and large-scale tidying up operations.

It can be walked on, sat on, lain on, played on (in moderation) without doing undue damage either to it or you.

Drought-resistant mixes can now be obtained which, even if they turn brown in hot, dry weather, soon recover after the first rain.

DISADVANTAGES. A poor lawn makes the whole garden look un-cared for, even if all the other features are first class. It requires regular maintenance; between mid–March and October it has to be cut on average once a week, and as much as every three days at certain times if it is growing well. Unless it is regularly fed and weeded it can soon deteriorate, and fertilizers and chemicals are definitely not cheap. For a first-class lawn the clippings should always be removed, and these produce a considerable amount of rubbish which is difficult to compost properly unless you have enough coarser material to prevent the heap from turning into a slimy and evil-smelling morass.

The edges need trimming regularly if the effect is not to be spoilt.

Although a hard-wearing lawn will tolerate some running and playing on it, it soon succumbs to really rough treatment, and boisterous children and dogs are definitely out.

Taken on balance, however, there are few substitutes for a lawn, especially one covering a large area, though anyone with a severe physical disability, or who spends a lot of time away from home, would be better considering some alternative, of which perhaps the most practical is large shrub borders which can be kept free of weeds by using a weedkiller annually (e.g. Casoron G), and an open, gravelled area, which can be kept free of weeds in the same way.

Making a new lawn from seed

The two best times for seeding a new lawn are April and September, though I know many good ones which were sown during the summer. The important thing is that the new grass must never be allowed to dry out, so you are very much more dependent on watering if you risk sowing in the warmer months of the year. Before April the ground has not really warmed up enough for germination to take place. In a cold, wet spring seed which is put down too early will often rot, and what does not becomes a welcome addition to the birds' menu. Grass seed is usually treated with a bird repellent, but this largely washes off with the first rain after sowing. If the autumn has been a good one and the ground is still warm, seeding can be done until mid-October. Providing it has germinated properly, the seed will continue to make roots during winter and will grow away quickly when the weather warms up the following spring. Ideally, September is the optimum month for sowing as the grass germinates rapidly in the mild dampness of autumn and will be quite well established before the weather deteriorates.

You must prepare the prospective lawn area properly. Whatever the time of year, dig thoroughly and clean it of as many perennial weeds as possible as described on pages 63–5. Lawns grow best in soil which is not too heavy or soggy – if your ground is regularly waterlogged you may have to consider installing a drainage system, but most bad drainage is due to heavy machinery compacting both the top- and subsoil so that surface water cannot escape. If you have prepared the ground well and broken up any hard areas, the problem should resolve itself. At the time of digging add as much fine humus-forming material as possible – spent mushroom compost, very well rotted manure, dried concentrated manure, are all suitable – what you do not want is clods of it on or near the surface which could give the germinating grass seed problems with growing properly. If the soil is still very heavy after all this, dig in about 14 lb per square yard (7.5 kg per square metre) sharp sand as well. If because of the time of year, or the weather, you cannot sow the lawn, you can leave the ground in this state until conditions are right, though you may have to turn it over again to bury any young weeds which have grown from seed in the meantime.

About two weeks before you hope to seed the lawn, break down the big clods of soil and do some preliminary levelling. There is nothing wrong in having gradual slopes and falls on a lawn – it adds interest to an informal landscaping scheme – but what you do not want are craters and bumps; in addition to looking most unprofessional, the bumps get scalped by the mower and the craters fill with water, causing growth problems and diseases. Do not do this too early or the surface may 'pan' and set hard, which means you will have to break it all up again. At the same time, add 2 oz per square yard (60 g per square metre) of growmore or similar balanced fertilizer to the soil.

A week before you sow the seed you can do your final levelling. If you cannot judge by eye whether you have any holes or bumps, use a long, straight piece of wood across the surface to show up any problem areas. If you have done your preliminary levelling properly, you can do any refinements with a rake, and you should rake the whole surface thoroughly now until it looks like fine crumbs. In between each raking you should tread the whole of the area to settle the soil. Any soft spots will show up and can be filled in and firmed gently. What you are aiming for finally is a smooth surface with no large stones, pieces of root, etc., which is firm enough to be walked on at any part without your feet sinking in, but crumbly enough for the germinating seed to get an easy root-hold.

You can sow seed on this finish at any time after preparation, but if you can let a week elapse it will give it another chance to settle down overall. The best time for sowing is on a still, dry day when the soil is nicely moist. Sow the seed at a rate of 1½ oz per square yard (50 g per square metre); if you sow the grass seed too thickly the seedlings will be overcrowded and will run the risk of 'damping off' or dying through fungal infections.

An easy method of making sure you have an even distribution is to divide the seed for a given area into 4 parts – sow ('broadcast') 1 part from left to right across the plot, 1 part from top to bottom, 1 part from right to left and one from bottom to top. Then rake the area lightly to mix the seed into the crumbly surface.

The time taken for germination depends largely on temperature and rainfall. A lawn sown on warm ground during damp weather may only take a few days to appear, but during cooler or drier conditions it could take a fortnight or more. It is not desirable to sow in weather which would necessitate a long germination period or the seed could start to rot.

WHICH MIX? The majority of gardeners will need one of three mixes.

If you are aiming for a really super lawn, you will want a *luxury grade mixture*. This contains seeds of the finest grasses only. But before you rush out and buy a bagful, beware. Fine grasses can be mown shorter, but they need more regular feeding and general care. If your soil still tends to be on the solid side, or you do not have much time to spend on the lawn, it is not the mix for you. There is really no point considering a high quality grass mix if you intend to use a rotary, or hover-mower. And if you have energetic children and/or lively dogs, forget it.

There has been a great deal of improvement in *hard-wearing lawn mixes* over recent years. In the past most of these incorporated a proportion of perennial ryegrasses, which because of their toughness and ability to root down well into less than perfect soils, were added to improve the durability of turf likely to be subjected to adverse conditions and heavy use. Unfortunately these were inclined to make the lawn rather rough as they were coarse bladed, and also they could not be mown closely or they would die out. Furthermore, they grew very quickly, making cutting a never-ending job.

However, a whole new generation of 'tough' mixes is now available, based on mixes containing a high proportion of dwarf ryegrasses. These are less coarse and have a slower growth habit, and for the majority of domestic lawns where a good-natured sward and a respectable finish are required, these new mixes take a lot of beating.

The third major type of seed is that needed for areas in a lot of shade, especially under trees, and for this a shade-tolerant mix is available.

If you are still in doubt as to which seed is really *you*, the salesperson should be able to advise you, and all the major producers of grass seed have an advisory service to help you to get the best from their products.

AFTER-CARE. When the new grass is about 1–1½ in. (25–35 mm) high, on a dry day, sweep it gently to disperse any worm casts and then roll *lightly* with the back roller of a cylinder mower. An ordinary garden roller is too heavy for most newly sown lawns. Make the first cut when the grass is approximately 2 in. (50 mm) high, preferably using a good cylinder mower with very sharp blades, and the clippings should be removed.

If the lawn is autumn sown, this cutting may not be necessary until the spring. For the first season, you should always treat the lawn with care. Regular mowing takes place when it becomes evident it is necessary, but do not shave right down to the ground. It will need plenty of water in dry weather, and traffic on it should be kept to a minimum.

Because new grass is very easily scorched by chemicals, it is probably best to avoid feeding and weeding in the first season.

There should be enough residual food in the soil to get the lawn through to its first autumn, when a proprietary autumn lawn food can be given, strictly according to instructions. From then onwards, for the purposes of fertilizing it can be regarded as an established lawn.

If the ground was thoroughly prepared before sowing and the grass gave a good quick coverage of the soil surface, you should not have many weeds. Some seeds still in the soil which were turned up during preparation may have germinated. These will be small and will almost certainly mow out after the first two or three cuts. You can dig out the bigger ones by hand, using an old table knife. There are no weed-killers on the market suitable for lawns under two years old. You could try using a 'spot' weedkiller – then if the grass does not like it you will only get a small bare patch to reseed instead of ruining the whole lot. In any case, you may find you have to patch the odd bald place, so keep a bit of seed over from the main sowing for this purpose.

Turf

It takes time and patience to establish a good lawn from seed, and the temptation is always to do too much on it before it is ready for it. This is especially true where there are children in the family.

A more instant solution is the use of turf. Turves are pieces of grass and roots skimmed from the surface of the ground where they originally grew. They are about 1 in. (25 mm) thick or less and usually come in long rolls comprising a square metre.

Turf in quantity is usually obtained from turf suppliers, though many garden centres sell small amounts for patching. Most turf is what is known as 'treated meadow turf' – grass from pasture land which has supposedly been treated with selective weedkillers some time prior to lifting. Some arrives looking as if it has come straight out of a botanical collection.

A better alternative is to find a supplier who cultivates his own. The grasses in this will be much more suitable for a domestic lawn. It will be more expensive but it pays dividends in the long run.

If you are hoping for a good-quality lawn, it is no good ringing up the first supplier you come to in the Yellow Pages and ordering a load. You should first enquire whether theirs is specially grown turf, or is cut from a meadow. Try to see someone else's load if you spot one being delivered in your district. Never consider very rough and especially weedy turf, or there will have been no point in your attempting to get the site weed-free in the first place.

You should prepare the area to be turfed in exactly the same way as for seed up to the point of sowing. Just because you are covering up the surface, it is no excuse for covering up a multitude of sins as well.

Purists will tell you that turf should be laid in October, then it has the whole winter to settle down, knit and re-establish itself. In practice it is quite permissible to turf at any time of the year providing it is not snowy, frosty, or in the middle of a drought. Summer turfing, however, will require constant watering, and if there is a prolonged hot spell and consequent water shortage, you risk losing the lot. If you can bear to wait, it is probably wiser.

The turf will arrive by lorry, rolled root side out, and you should lay it as soon as possible to prevent undue drying out. You must handle turves gently, supporting them underneath. If you pick them up roughly or by a part only, they will drop to bits.

Lay the individual turves a row at a time, broken bonded so that there are no long vertical cracks between them. It is best to work forwards, off a plank placed on the already laid turf so you do not spoil your levelling or compact the ground too much in parts. It is not a good idea to end a row near a border with a small piece as this often keeps getting dislodged – a firmer edge is made if you run the turves right round the outside of the area first, then any small filling in pieces will be inside and will re-establish better. The soil you are laying on should be just nicely damp. There is no need to roll the finished turfed lawn if you have patted each piece into place to make sure all parts of the roots were in contact with the soil. Rolling can be positively harmful and can consolidate the ground underneath so that the turves cannot root easily into it.

Some people recommend brushing a mixture of soil and sand into the joints between the pieces, but providing you have butted the turves up close together and you never let them dry out, it is not really necessary.

AFTER-CARE. The after-care of a turfed lawn is very similar to that of one which is seeded, except you can begin to walk on it sooner. Plenty of water is the thing for at least the first, and preferably the second, summer – it should never become dehydrated. The time which elapses between laying and the first cut varies – often the grass is long when the turf arrives, and you can give a very gentle mowing a week after it goes down, even in winter, if it is very overgrown and the weather is mild and dry. The first cuts, like those of a seeded lawn, should always be light ones, the blades being gradually lowered when you are sure the grass is growing strongly and has rooted into the soil beneath.

Because turfed grass is not newly germinated grass, it is not quite so delicate when it comes to using chemicals, but you should still use these with discretion in the first year. In any case, if you have bought decent turf and prepared your ground properly, you should not have many weeds – few enough to be spot-treated. Usually turf has been well fertilized in the season before lifting, so, with what you have added to the ground before laying, the grass should not need much feeding before the autumn after the first full summer season of growth.

The inherited lawn

Having a lawn tailor-made to suit yourself is all very well if you are starting from scratch but what if you inherit something? A good lawn will be free from weeds, bare patches,

149

bumps, depressions and coarse grass, and start growing well when spring arrives. All you have to do is mow it carefully and frequently, make sure it does not dry out in summer, and feed it. Any weeds which do appear can be dealt with immediately by spot treatment before they become a problem.

Unfortunately, though, most lawns are not like that. They are probably full of moss, a thatch of tangled stems and dead clippings, uneven areas, bare patches, clods of coarse grasses, weeds and annual meadow grass. They most likely look pale and are not growing well. Hopeless as it may seem, they can be renovated to a reasonably high standard providing there is enough good grass amongst it to make it worthwhile. A really bad lawn, which is thin and unhealthy, has more weeds than grass in it, and is smothered by thatch and moss, is not worth starting on and is best dug up and renewed completely.

TO RENOVATE A POOR LAWN. You really need to start in spring, and it will take about twelve months to see the benefits.

First, in late March apply a moss killer – see chart on pages 78–9. (Some contain urea to give a quick green-up if the grass is looking tired.) Any moss will die out in a week or so, and when you are sure the moss killer has worked, give the whole lawn a thorough raking with a spring-tined rake or mechanical lawn-raker to remove as much dead moss and thatch as possible. Then spike it all over with a fork inserted to the depth of its tines to let in air.

By now the grass should be long enough to cut, and during mowing much of the straggly grass which has been teased up by raking will be cut off. A cylinder mower is much the best machine for a good-quality lawn, and the blades should be as sharp as possible (see page 54 for hints on using a mower). There is no point in dealing with bare patches yet as you are quite likely to make a few more before the summer is out.

At the end of April it will be possible to start feeding the lawn. For this you can use either a dry fertilizer applied by hand or by mechanical spreader according to the makers' instructions, or a liquid one applied by watering can. Spring and summer feeds contain a lot of nitrogen to encourage a healthy top growth, and less phosphates and potash. Dry feeds usually have a longer residual effect but can scorch if you do not apply them evenly. The results of liquid feeds can be seen within a few days, but they need applying at regular intervals throughout the summer as they are soon used up or washed out.

By mid-May the grass, and the weeds in it, will be growing very strongly. Now is the time to apply a selective weedkiller (see Herbicides, pages 78–9 for suitable products), as the weeds will take it up quickly. Fertilizer/weedkiller mixes are available but I find that it is better to apply the fertilizer first, following it with the herbicide when the weeds are growing strong and lush. They should die off over about 10–14 days.

In the meantime, you should continue to mow regularly, but preferably not too closely. Gaps will start to appear where the weeds used to be – if the grass is growing well enough it will thicken up sufficiently to fill many of these, otherwise they can be patched later. As you mow you will become aware of any serious bumps and lumps – it does not really matter if you shave the high spots because you will be dealing with these as well in due course.

After about eight weeks some of the persistent weeds which were not properly finished off by the weedkiller will be starting to grow again, so it is a good thing to apply another dose of herbicide, but only when rain is forecast within 24 hours, unless you are using a liquid.

Coarse grass cannot be killed out chemically, but if you slash the crowns of clumps of coarse grass with a sharp knife periodically, much will die out. If this method does not work for you it is best to remove the coarse grass entirely and patch these areas at the same time as you do the rest of the patching.

By this time you will have a good idea of the work you are going to have to do on the lawn in the autumn with regard to levelling and patching. You should stop using a summer food by early August as it will make the top growth too soft to survive winter conditions without damage.

In early September, rake the lawn *gently* again to remove any dead clippings, and spike it again, especially if it is hard. You can now remove any high points and fill in any hollows. You can then apply a top dressing of equal parts peat, or peat substitute, loam and river sand at 2 lbs per square yard (1 kg per square metre) (if you cannot get good loam, equal parts of peat, or peat substitute, and sand will do). To each 2 lbs of top dressing you can add about ½ oz (about 15 g to each kilo) of grass seed and a high-phosphate, dry autumn lawn fertilizer at the rate per square yard or metre recommended by the manufacturer. Spread this dressing evenly over the surface of the soil and work it well in with a stiff broom or the back of a rake. The existing grass will soon grow up strongly through this dressing and the added seed will germinate and thicken the lawn up where it is sparse. At the same time as the dressing is applied, you can loosen the surface of the bare patches and evened-out parts with a hand-fork, and sow seed on them at 1 oz per square yard (around 30 g per square metre) in addition to that in the dressing. After about a fortnight, you can mow the whole area with the blades raised high enough just to top both the old and the new grass. By the following season you should have the makings of a reasonably good lawn which, with regular maintenance, will continue to improve.

In recent years, with the rise in interest in organic gardening, there has been a tendency to worry less about weeds in lawns, except in broad ones like docks, thistles and dandelions, which can be dug out or spot treated individually.

Routine care for an established lawn

MOW regularly from late March to mid-October and occasionally during mild spells in winter if it is in active growth. If possible change the direction of the cut every time you mow to prevent the grass from lying down one way. Raise the blades for early and late mowings, and gradually drop them as summer approaches. You should also raise them in hot dry spells.

Clippings should be removed for the finest-quality finish, except during very hot weather when you can leave them on to protect the grass from the intense heat of the sun at such times.

FEED regularly.

WEED chemically only when there are actually weeds present.

MOSS KILLING may be necessary if moss is present, but it should not be if you look after the lawn properly. Many people do not object to a mossy lawn. Leaving the grass slightly longer will give it a better chance of competing with the moss.

RAKE annually to remove thatch.

SPIKE to let in air in spring or autumn, but it is not necessary on very light or sandy soils.

152

TOP DRESSING in autumn as described for improving tired lawns above is always beneficial. It is not necessary to add grass seed unless you feel the grass is thin.

PATCH bare areas in autumn or spring. Do not allow bare patches to remain too long or weeds and coarse grasses will move in.

Problems

Fortunately, the problems of a healthy lawn are few and can be eliminated by good cultivation.

WEEDS are caused by seeds falling on the lawn and germinating. They can be eliminated as already described by hand weeding, chemical control or spot weeding with a suitable herbicide. A dense sward of healthy grass is not as likely to become infested.

ANNUAL MEADOW GRASS seeds freely and is virtually impossible to eliminate entirely. It can be reduced to a certain extent if the lawn is always mown with the box on, and no clippings ever allowed to fall back on the grass.

MOSSES, LICHENS AND ALGAE. These are caused by bad growing conditions and cultivation. Heavy shade, compacted soil, bad drainage and too close mowing early in the year are usually responsible. The remedy is to kill the moss and then improve conditions by regular raking, spiking, sensible feeding and raising the mower blades somewhat. Resow shaded areas with a shade-tolerant mix. If the area is very densely shaded, you should not really expect to grow there at all.

DEAD PATCHES. The sudden appearance of dead patches in an otherwise healthy lawn can have several causes:

Bitch spots occur when a bitch urinates on the lawn. The very high concentration of nitrogen in the urine burns the blades of the grass, which eventually re-grow, if the dead area has not been invaded by weeds in the meantime. Bitch spots can be identified by the ring of lush dark green grass stimulated by the nitrogen which appears around the edge as the area 'heals up'. There is no solution to this on-going problem other than following Mrs Dog around with a bucket of water. If you like your bitch to have free access to the lawn, you cannot have a perfect finish.

Petrol will kill off grass more effectively than any weedkiller if accidentally spilt on the lawn. It will be a long time before soil so polluted can support growth again and the affected area is best excavated, the soil replaced with new, and the patch re-seeded. This kind of problem does not usually arise if you take your petrol mower right off the grass to refill or adjust it.

Dollar spot is a disease of fine lawn grasses and creates dead spots only about 2 in. (50 mm) across, but badly disfiguring to a good lawn if the patches run together. It should not occur in lawns that are correctly fed and regularly aerated and de-thatched, but it can be treated with a fungicide if it does appear.

Fusarium patch is a common disease which usually appears as patches of yellowing and dying grass in autumn or spring and after the lawn has been covered with snow, hence it is also called 'snow mould'. Sometimes a white fluffy mould grows on the dead patch in damp weather. To prevent this happening, do not use a high nitrogen fertilizer after the end of July, do not walk on the lawn in frosty weather, and do not pile up snow from paths and the like on the lawn. Over-feeding with nitrogen is by far the commonest cause, but if you de-thatch and spike regularly, the chance of the disease coming in is reduced. Fungicide will help to control it if it has already arrived.

Leatherjackets and chafer grubs will eat the roots of grass, causing dead patches to occur. *Birds* will also scratch up the surface in an attempt to find these pests to eat. There are few soil insecticides effective against these pests that do not do more harm to the environment than good.

MOLES can be a nightmare with their tunnels that undermine the surface and their destructive 'hills'. There is no real answer to this problem; theoretically they can be trapped, but this is a skilled job, or gassed, which does not always work. They can be discouraged to some extent by putting strong-smelling substances – mothballs, creosote, etc., down the runs, but they often pop up elsewhere. Ultrasonic devices are expensive and do not always work. Moles are attracted by earthworms, which are their main food. A deterrent which is ineffective one year can be effective the next, so it is worth trying a variety of remedies.

RED THREAD is another disease of fine-leaved grasses which are underfed. It appears as patches of bleached grass which in time take on a pinky tinge owing to infection by a reddish fungal growth. Good regular maintenance is the way to avoid this, or if your lawn has already become infected, treat the patches with a fungicide.

TOADSTOOLS AND FAIRY RINGS. These are the fruiting bodies of fungi growing on decaying organic matter buried in the soil. Clumps of toadstools and rings of dark green grass indicate the presence of one or other fungus which is feeding on something in the centre of the ring. Toadstools can be very little bother, or they can cause havoc, as some fungi kill the grass in the vicinity of the fairy ring.

Eliminating toadstools is difficult. When the lawn was prepared all old timber and woody decaying matter should have been removed, but that is no help if you have got the problem now. You could try digging down to see if you can find the food source (a piece of rotting wood, perhaps) but this could be some feet under. You can disguise the rings by keeping the lawn well fed and therefore a deep green colour all over (but this can encourage fusarium!), and the toadstools should be picked off as they appear.

10
ANNUALS, BIENNIALS AND BEDDING PLANTS

Even though it is perfectly feasible to create a garden using no flowers or plants other than grass, most people like to have a go at growing something.

Annuals, biennials and bedding plants can be looked at together because of their similarities, although annuals are plants which germinate, flower, seed and die in a period of one year, biennials do not reach maturity until the second season, and many bedding plants are actually perennial but are considered expendable at the end of one season. Some years ago bedding became somewhat unfashionable because of the work involved, but with new varieties becoming available and the enormous contribution these plants make to colour in the garden, it has experienced a new lease of life.

ANNUALS

Annuals can be divided into two groups, hardy and half-hardy.

Hardy annuals

These are capable of withstanding reasonably cold conditions without frost damage, and their seed germinates at a comparatively low temperature.

USES. In mass bedding schemes, when they are sown *in situ* in their flowering positions in blocks of one variety or genus. They have a slightly less formal appearance than half-hardy annuals.

In tubs and other containers.

As temporary flowering plants in between herbaceous perennials and shrubs and to fill in space until the permanent plants reach their required size.

The shorter ones can be used for edging if sown in a line at the front of a bed or border.

To provide temporary colour where the area is intended to be stocked with permanent plants at a later time.

ADVANTAGES. Hardy annual seed is reasonably inexpensive and consequently the use of these plants is probably the cheapest method of stocking a garden.

Many of them make very good cut flowers.

No special equipment or skill is required to raise the plants from seed.

They provide a quick method of filling in a space colourfully.

DISADVANTAGES. The ground into which they are sown must be as free from weed seeds as possible or the annuals will become weed infested as they and the weeds germinate together. On newly cultivated ground this is very difficult to ensure.

When they have to be weeded at the seedling stage, it is sometimes very difficult to distinguish the weeds from the hardy annuals. (This can be made easier by sowing the seeds in drills within the allotted patch instead of broadcasting it all over the surface. The straight lines of flower seedlings can soon be identified and anything else removed.)

Hardy annuals do not grow well if planted too thickly. This means that they have to be thinned out according to type when they are big enough to handle properly. This can be a fiddly job.

Many hardy annuals grow quite tall and will fall over and become untidy if not supported. The best method is to push twigs into the ground as soon as possible for the plants to grow through, but this makes it more difficult to weed round them, or to thin them out.

The majority of hardy annuals seed readily into the surrounding soil. This can be an advantage if you want them to keep coming up year after year but they can be as big a problem as the weeds if you do not want them all over the garden.

Generally speaking, they do not have as long a flowering period as most half-hardy annuals or bedding plants. Some continue to flower longer if they are regularly dead-headed, but this is a fiddly and time-consuming job.

Most of them do not like shady conditions.

How to grow hardy annuals successfully

The ground should be thoroughly cleaned, dug, broken down and firmed. The same preparation as that for sowing a lawn is suitable except the soil should not be made quite so firm (see pages 144–5 for how to prepare the ground).

Hardy annuals flower best in ground which is not too rich in plant foods. A general balanced fertilizer can be raked in during preparation if the soil is really hungry, but perhaps the cheapest and easiest method is to water weekly during the growing and flowering period with a high-potash, soluble plant food.

Seed is obtainable in packets from garden centres and garden shops, some supermarkets and general and multiple stores, and by mail order from the seed companies from their annually produced catalogues. A wider selection is usually available by mail order.

Some seed companies even offer 'package deals' of seeds for whole borders, and supply well thought-out plans to work to.

In warm parts of the country seed can be sown in early autumn while the soil is still warm enough to germinate it. The hardy annuals will then over-winter as small seedlings. It is best not to thin these too much until the spring to allow for some natural wastage.

In most parts of Britain, and especially if you are in any doubt, it is better to wait until March and April when the air and soil temperatures are getting higher. Short-lived annuals can be sown at any time of the spring and summer to provide a succession of flowers.

Hardy annuals do not transplant well, but if you require more control over their positioning you can sow two or three or a pinch of seeds into individual pots, either outside or in a cold greenhouse for slightly earlier flowering, then the pots are planted out when the young plants, thinned if necessary, are big enough. You should use a good potting compost for this, which increases the cost of the scheme.

METHOD. Mark out the patch to be sown by drawing a line round it in the tilth with a stick. This is not vital if you are just sowing odd groups, but is more or less essential if you are making a whole border out of hardy annuals, so you can see where each type starts and finishes.

Draw shallow drills across the area about half an inch (10 mm) deep. Sow the seed thinly into these. If you cannot sow thinly enough, you can mix the seed with a little sand to make it easier to handle. Alternatively, if you prefer, you can broadcast the seed over the surface.

Rake the area *very lightly* to cover the seed.

The time taken to germinate varies according to type of plant, time of year and kind of soil, but is usually somewhere between 1 and 3 weeks.

AFTER-CARE. Keep the soil moist. If you are watering, a *fine* rose on the watering can is best. Keep the area as free from weeds as possible.

Once the seedlings are showing, thin them out as soon as they can be handled. You might have to thin them out two or three times over a period until the required final spacing is reached. The instructions on the packet will tell you how much space you should leave between seedlings.

As with everything connected with gardening, always read the instructions first!

As soon as you have thinned out enough, you should provide twigs as supports for the plants. Eventually you will not be able to see the twigs as the annuals grow through them, provided you do not make the supports too tall.

For the rest of the season, maintenance consists of a high potash feed as previously described, and some dead heading if you can manage it.

At the end of summer, pull the plants up and put on the

compost heap. You can replant the vacant area with spring bedding subjects, bulbs, or permanent plants, or dig it over and leave it to lie fallow till the spring.

PROPAGATION. Hardy annuals set seed very easily and when this is ripe it can be removed, dried off in an airy place for a day or two, and then stored in airtight containers until required for re-sowing. Plastic margarine tubs are ideal for this. Most hardy annuals come true to type when grown from saved seed.

A dozen hardy annuals to get you started. For named varieties, consult a seed catalogue. (The illustrations in the margin are to enable you to distinguish the seedlings from weeds.)

Calendula (pot marigold). Big double flowers in various shades of yellow and orange. Height up to 2 ft (600 mm). Good for cutting.

Candytuft. Heads of flowers in pink, mauve, purple and white. Height up to about 12 in. (300 mm). Useful as an edging plant.

Annual chrysanthemum. Large flowers in a range of colours. Height up to about 2 ft (600 mm). Good cut flower.

Clarkia. Spikes of frilled double flowers in peach, pink, cerise, purple and white. Height up to 2 ft (600 mm). Good for flower arranging.

Cornflower. Double pom-pom flowers in blue on stems up to 12 in. (300 mm) high. Also available as mixed colours. Good for cutting.

Eschscholtzia (Californian poppy). Single or semi-double flowers in shades of reds, oranges and yellows. Ferny foliage. Height up to 15 in. (375 mm). Good for cutting and edging.

Godetia. Single or semi-double flowers in many colours from cerise to white. Dwarf and taller varieties available. Useful for cutting.

Larkspur. Resembles an annual delphinium with long flower spikes in pink, blue, purple, cerise and white. Very good for cutting and drying. Up to 3 ft (900 mm) tall.

Lavatera (mallow). Red, pink or white trumpet-shaped flowers up to 4 ft (1.25 m) high but shorter varieties available. Makes a well-shaped, bushy plant.

Linaria (toadflax). Like an annual antirrhinum in a wide range of colours. Up to 12 in. (300 mm) high.

160

Linum rubrum (scarlet flax). Scarlet flowers on dainty stems 12 in. (300 mm) high. A useful colour in an annual bedding scheme.

 Nigella (love-in-a-mist). Feathery leaves and pom-pom flowers in blue and also in mixed pastel shades. 18–20 in. (450–500 mm) tall. Useful for cutting.

Half-hardy annuals and other bedding plants

These are the plants usually seen for sale in trays and boxes in nurseries, garden centres and outside the corner shop at the beginning of summer. As already mentioned, there are many half-hardy perennials which, if treated as half-hardy annuals, make good, compact plants the first season with plenty of flowers, and are inexpensive and easy enough to produce and to discard at the end of the summer and raise new ones each year. What they all have in common is the fact that they are not tough enough to tolerate the frosts and low temperatures of winter.

USES. As mass bedding plants for colour during the summer months.

In tubs, boxes, hanging baskets, etc.

To add colour at the front of shrubberies and fill in spaces in all types of ornamental beds and borders.

As a temporary fill-in prior to permanent planting later.

ADVANTAGES. They provide instant colour – they are usually either in bud or in flower when planted out.

They require very little maintenance once established in their permanent positions – many modern varieties do not even require dead-heading.

They come in a wide range of types suitable for most positions – one or two will even put up with some shade, if it is not too heavy.

DISADVANTAGES. If you raise them yourself from seed you need to give them some warmth until the time approaches for planting out. This means that the seed has to be germinated in a heated propagator in a cold greenhouse, or in a warm greenhouse with a temperature of about 65°–70°F (18–21°C), which is expensive. Alternatively, they can be raised on a windowsill in a light room but they take up a lot of space ultimately and tend to become drawn and 'leggy' because they lack the overhead daylight of a greenhouse.

If you do not raise them from seed they are expensive to buy.

They need quite a bit of attention – watering, weeding, etc. once they are planted out until they become rooted into the soil and start to grow and spread outwards.

OBTAINABLE as seed from usual sources (the choice of varieties is wider if purchased by mail order from seed merchants), or as plantlets to grow on, also from seed companies. Ready sown and ready-to-sow starter packs are available for ease of raising though these are expensive compared with packeted seed. Plants ready for planting out can be bought from nurseries, garden shops, etc.

Raising bedding plants from seed

Do not sow the seed too early in the year or the plants will be ready for planting out too soon, before the danger of frost is past. Late February and March is quite soon enough – the later sown ones eventually catch the others up because of having more daylight and natural warmth.

Nearly fill seed trays or small pots with a good moist seed-sowing compost and sprinkle the seed thinly on top, then cover *lightly* with more compost. If the compost was damp enough in the first place, it should not need watering again now, otherwise damp the surface with a watering can using a very fine rose, or a trigger-spray of tepid water. This is a tricky job because if you are not careful you will wash all the seed out. Cover the trays with a piece of clear plastic, glass, or cling film and a sheet of newspaper, or the plastic dome of the propagator and keep at a constant temperature of no lower than 65°F (18°C), either in the house, greenhouse, or heated propagator. Germination time varies according to the type of plant being grown. Remove the glass and newspaper as soon as the seed germinates (you can leave the propagator lid on with the vents open). When the seedlings are large enough to be handled, prick them out by lifting them gently from the compost with the end of a knife or similar small tool, and replant in trays of potting compost about 1½ in. (40 mm) apart. Only handle seedlings by the leaves, never the stems, which may be crushed so they rot off at the base. You can also pot up the baby plants into individual containers. This makes it easier to plant them out without damaging the mass of fibrous roots they make.

Grow the plants on in the warmth in these trays or pots, and a week or two before they are due to be planted out in the garden, harden them off. This means that they are gradually introduced to the cooler conditions they will meet when they are outside. If you have an opening cold frame, place them uncovered in this during the day, but cover them over at night to avoid damage by frost. Otherwise, place outside during the daytime and bring into a cool room, shed or garage for the night.

Treat starter kits similarly – follow the instructions, which vary according to the producer, until the plants are ready for pricking out, then follow the above procedure.

Seedlings bought from the seed producers are usually despatched to the purchaser at the right time for potting on into bigger pots.

If you have nowhere to raise half-hardy annuals indoors, many of them will germinate in their outdoor flowering positions if sown like hardy annuals in May. They will be later coming into flower, but you may feel it is worth a try.

Buying bedding plants

If you only want a few annuals to give some summer colour, it is cheaper to buy them ready for planting out than go to the trouble and expense of the equipment and heating needed to raise them yourself. Points to watch when buying bedding plants are:

Do not get them too early if you have nowhere inside to keep them until it is safe to plant them out – mid-May to mid-June is the time, depending on which part of the country you live in. Before this it is quite likely a late frost will finish the lot off if you put them in the open garden too soon.

Plants which have been brought on too early become pot-bound. All the compost and nutrients have been used up, and you will find a hard tangle of fine roots when you remove the plants from their trays, which are difficult to separate without damaging them, and often these roots never manage to grow out into the surrounding soil. You can usually tell which plants are in this state as they look woody and overcrowded, seem to have stopped growing and are well in flower. The foliage often looks pale and starved of nutrients. Healthy plants will still appear to be making new growth, be green and bushy, and be in bud or just coming into flower.

163

Sometimes nurseries which have over-estimated demand have trays of 'remainders' for sale at reduced prices at the end of the season, usually about the beginning of July. These will be pot-bound and not in first-class condition, but if they are cheap enough and you have a gap to fill it is worth a chance, though you could be disappointed with their performance, so do not spend a fortune.

Planting out

You should have previously prepared the ground to be used by digging it well, breaking it down to a 'tilth' and adding a balanced fertilizer. Remove the bedding plants from their trays or pots, disturbing the roots as little as possible. Place each plant in its own hole, which has been watered well to make a damp environment to root into. Carefully replace the soil and firm it round the stem − it should not be any higher up the stem than the compost was when it was in the box. You can give the whole area a thorough watering when you have finished, although sometimes this causes the moisture to evaporate more quickly from the soil.

AFTER-CARE. You will have to make sure that the plants do not dry out until they become established, and they will need some weeding until the top growth joins together and covers the soil. Give a weekly liquid feed. If the dead heads do not drop off naturally, or if seed pods start to form, some dead-heading will be necessary to keep the plants in full flower and looking neat for as long as possible.

PROPAGATION. You can save seed from the ones already in the garden, but many of the best bedding plants are F1 Hybrids, so the seedling plants will not be like their parents. Some perennial bedding plants can be increased by cuttings, e.g. bedding geraniums (zonal pelargoniums). Trim off 3−4 in. (about 10 cm) long unflowering pieces below a leaf joint and remove the lower leaves. Insert the pieces into pots almost full of potting compost with a little extra sand or perlite added to improve drainage. Keep under frost-free glass in winter or in a semi-shaded place outside in summer. Do not overwater when temperatures are low, as they will rot off. You can take cuttings at any time, but those done in July, August and September will be ready for flowering in summer bedding schemes the following year. Many other perennial bedders can be treated in the same way, but if you are short of overwintering space you may find it easier to start again each spring.

At the end of summer, pull up and compost all true annuals and those perennial bedding plants you do not want to keep. If you wish to retain the perennials, pot up fairly tightly, or pack together in wooden boxes, and keep in a frost-free greenhouse, conservatory or light room for the winter.

Twelve favourite bedding plants

Ageratum. Blue (or sometimes white) powder-puff flowers on compact plants. Good for edging.

Alyssum. White or mauve low-growing edging plant. Easy to grow and can be sown in situ if necessary.

Fibrous-rooted begonias. Pink, white and red flowers and fleshy leaves ranging from red to pale green in colour. Dwarf habit, useful for edging. Will stand some shade. Can be potted up for winter and will last for many years, or cuttings can be taken in spring. Outdoor plants brought into a warmish room will flower inside for several months.

Bidens. A comparative newcomer to the bedding plant scene, with yellow, daisy-like flowers, fern-like leaves, and a sprawling habit which makes it excellent for basket, window box and tub planting.

Cineraria maritima. Grey-leaved, perennial useful for foliage effects. Will survive outside most winters. Has yellow daisy-like flowers but these tend to make the plants look untidy and should be removed. Old plants must be cut hard back several times a season to keep them in shape.

French and African marigolds and tagetes. Yellow and orangey-red flowers, ferny leaves. French marigolds are shorter and generally have smaller flowers. African marigolds are more suitable for the back of bedding schemes. Tagetes are similar to French marigolds but have masses of small flowers and finer leaves. This group of plants varies in height from a few inches for the dwarf French varieties to more than 3 ft (900 mm) for some African cultivars.

Bedding geranium (pelargonium). Well known bedding and pot plant in a wide variety of colours from deep red to cerise to white. Sometimes leaves are zoned or variegated. Can be grown from seed and cuttings, and kept from year to year. Older plants tend to be leggy and need to be cut hard back in spring. Trailing forms available for container planting.

Impatiens (busy lizzy). Compact perennial bedding plants easily raised from seed in a wide range of colours. Tolerant of a wide range of conditions.

Lobelia. Low-growing annual in blue, red, white, pink and mixed shades. Useful as an edging plant either on its own or in combination with other dwarf bedders. Trailing forms good in window boxes and hanging baskets.

Mimulus (monkey flower). An increasingly popular bedding plant with similar advantages to impatiens.

Nicotiana (tobacco plant). Trumpet-shaped flowers in most colours and large leaves. Heavily scented at night. Dwarf and taller growing varieties available.

Scaevola. Another semi-trailing newcomer with striking blue flowers and a semi-woody habit. First-class on its own in a hanging pot, or mixed with other bedding plants in containers.

HARDY BIENNIALS

These are usually sown in April-June one year to flower in spring or early summer the next. Many plants described as biennials are really perennials but for best effect are treated as biennials.

ADVANTAGES. They flower at a time when not a lot else is happening in the flower garden.

They can be used to replace summer bedding plants so the ground is not bare all winter.

Some are reasonably shade tolerant.

DISADVANTAGES. Because many have a long flowering season they tend to run over into the time when you might want to be putting out your summer bedding plants.

They require three lots of handling before they are finally installed in their permanent position.

Space is needed for nursery beds to bring the plants to the final transplanting stage.

OBTAINABLE as seed from the usual sources of supply, or as transplants from nurseries, garden centres and 'garden-gate sales' (if you are buying from the latter, make sure you buy healthy plants or you could infect your soil with diseases you do not already have).

USES. For mass spring and early summer bedding schemes, sometimes underplanted with bulbs.

As blocks of planting amongst permanent subjects e.g., in shrubberies and herbaceous borders.

In tubs, planters, window boxes and other containers.

Method of cultivation

Sow the seed in nursery beds (in the vegetable garden, for instance) in drills, ½ in. (15 mm) deep, in late April to June.

Either thin out in the drills until the correct spacing recommended for the type is reached, or plant the seedlings out to provide space between.

Some biennials (e.g., wallflowers) benefit from having the tops pinched out to encourage busy growth. The instructions on the seed packet will usually tell you where this is appropriate.

Plant out the well grown plants in their permanent positions in autumn (September to November). This is the stage at which you will buy them when you are not raising your own plants. Some growers are now selling biennials in individual container-grown packs to obviate root disturbance, though I have not found any improvement over the bare-root ones by the end of winter. Do make sure the plants you buy are bushy and well shaped, and have not been spoilt by overcrowding in the nursery bed.

AFTER-CARE. Add a slow-acting fertilizer such as bone-meal while preparing the site before planting, and give a top dressing of quick-acting balanced feed in the spring. Otherwise the plants require little attention. If they are big and bushy, check from time to time throughout the winter to make sure they have not rocked loose in the wind, and re-firm them if necessary.

Six favourites

> *Brompton stocks.* Really perennial, and left in the ground can form large plants of almost shrub-like (and rather untidy) habit. Although used mainly for spring bedding they will flower for quite a long time if the original flower spikes are removed after they start to set seed. Heavily scented.

167

Canterbury bells. Spikes of bell-shaped flowers in a range of pastel shades and deep blues up to 3 ft (900 mm) in height.

Forget-me-nots. Dainty blue spring flower. Look well in bedding schemes with bulbs, early pansies, and wallflowers.

Winter-flowering pansies. Technically perennials, but the flowers on young plants are the best and largest. A very popular winter bedding plant with a long flowering season.

Sweet williams. Again, can be kept from year to year but best grown as a biennial. Double or single carnation-like flowers in large heads in a wide variety of colours, pinks, reds, and whites. Very good for cutting and popular because of the delicate scent. Up to 2 ft (600 mm) high.

Wallflowers. Really another perennial, but always look best in their first flowering year. Now available in a range of colours and heights to suit every scheme, all heavily scented.

PROPAGATION. Enthusiasts can save seed at the end of the flowering season, but as so many new varieties are brought out every year, it is wise to keep an eye on what can be purchased.

The 'perennial biennials' can sometimes be propagated from cuttings taken from the base of the plant but they are so easily raised from seed that there is little point in doing this.

AND NOW FOR THE NASTIES

Annuals and other bedding plants, if given good growing conditions, are not troubled with a lot of problems, but they do get the odd pests and diseases which should be dealt with as soon as spotted. Here is a list of all the major symptoms, with the probable causes and suggested remedies:

Plants wilting, roots eaten, or plant severed just below soil level

> *Cutworms* – grey-brown, soil-living caterpillars.
> *Chafer grubs* – revolting fat curved grubs, dirty white in colour.
> *Millipedes* – leathery and segmented bodies, black or spotted, many legs. Curl up when disturbed.
> *Vine weevil grubs* – curled white grubs which will also affect pot plants.

To give you some idea of what damage caused by various pests and diseases looks like.

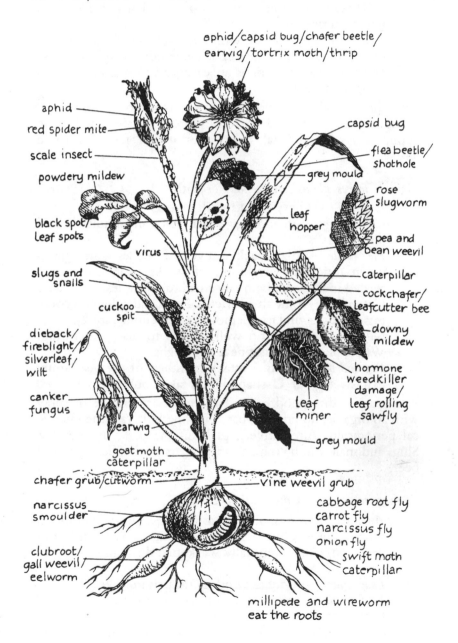

aphid/capsid bug/chafer beetle/
earwig/tortrix moth/thrip

aphid

red spider mite

scale insect

powdery mildew

black spot/
leaf spots

virus

slugs and
snails

cuckoo
spit

dieback/
fireblight/
silverleaf/
wilt

canker
fungus

earwig

goat moth
caterpillar

chafer grub/cutworm

narcissus
smoulder

clubroot/
gall weevil/
eelworm

capsid bug

flea beetle/
shothole

grey mould

rose
slugworm

leaf
hopper

pea and
bean weevil

caterpillar

cockchafer/
leafcutter bee

downy
mildew

hormone
weedkiller
damage/
leaf rolling
sawfly

leaf
miner

grey mould

vine weevil grub

cabbage root fly
carrot fly
narcissus fly
onion fly
swift moth
caterpillar

millipede and wireworm
eat the roots

Wireworms – thin, hard, shiny worm-like pests which move slowly when touched.

These pests often occur in grassland which has been newly cultivated.

Cabbage root fly – small, white maggots which tunnel into the roots of plants of the cabbage family, including stocks and wallflowers. This is an easy pest to introduce with bought-in stock.

REMEDY. Apply a soil insecticide if problem is severe. Vine weevil grubs can be controlled to some extent organically by the application of beneficial nematodes which feed off these larvae.

Holes in leaves, plants eaten wholly or partly

Earwigs – leathery insects with pincers on tail.

Capsid bugs – green bugs which make small holes in and distort leaves.

Flea beetles – small black and yellow beetles which jump when touched. Very fond of stocks, wallflowers and related species. Make many small round holes.

Caterpillars – come in a variety of sizes and colours according to species, and can demolish a plant quite rapidly.

Slugs and snails – too well known to need describing. Whole plants can disappear overnight.

Pea and bean weevils – attack members of the pea family (e.g. sweet pea). U-shaped bites taken out of leaves.

REMEDY. Spray with a good general inorganic insecticide or spray with an organic, liquid soap-based compound. Vary the chemical periodically. Alternatively, pick off the pests and destroy. Slugs and snails can be trapped in jam jars partly filled with old beer.

Damage to young growths, marking on leaves

Aphids – otherwise known as greenfly, but they come in other colours as well. Young growth distorted and buds damaged. Plant eventually weakened through sucking of sap.

Leaf miner – produces winding tunnels in leaves.

Leaf hopper – yellow-green insects causing mottling and flecking of foliage.

REMEDY. Spray with an inorganic or 'environmentally friendly'

170

insecticide, except for leaf miner, which can only be controlled by a systemic insecticide.

Damage to flowers

Earwigs and *capsid bugs* eat the petals.

Aphids distort the blooms.

Thrips – recognized as the tiny black thunderflies which become such a nuisance in hot thundery weather. Cause silvery flecking of flowers and leaves.

REMEDY. Spray, as above.

Rust-coloured dust on leaves, leaves distorted and bronzed

Red spider mite – small red mites which suck the sap. Often found on plants in hot, dry places, e.g. sunny patios.

REMEDY. None, other than regular misting with water.

Swollen roots

Club root disease. Affects stocks, wallflowers, etc.

REMEDY. Keep soil pH high. Dip plants in a fungicide dressing at planting time. Do not replant in infected soil. Make sure you do not buy infected plants. Plants raised in individual pots are less likely to be seriously affected.

Wilting plants

Wilting can be caused by pest or disease damage to roots or stem or insufficient watering in dry spells, especially with newly planted subjects. Also –

Black root rot. Blackened, rotten roots.

REMEDY. Do not replant in infected soil. If condition occurs in containerized plants, do not use unsterilized compost in future. There is no cure for affected plants.

Wilt

Leaves wilt, although soil is moist, and tissue inside stem stained brown. Caused by verticillium or fusarium fungi, and there is no cure. Do not replant susceptible plants in same soil.

Damping off

Fungal disease of seedlings. The stem wastes and rots at ground level and plants fall over and die.

REMEDY. There is no cure for affected plants, which should be removed immediately. Do not keep compost too damp and give plenty of ventilation. Watering newly planted seeds or seedlings with Cheshunt compound, or a fungicide will help to prevent and control the disease.

Foot rot

Also known under other names, e.g. geranium blackleg, pansy sickness etc. The stem base turns black and rots.

REMEDY. Do not overwater. Try not to inflict damage with tools, etc., while cultivating round plants. If the disease occurs to plants in containers, the compost was not sterile or the containers were dirty. Destroy affected plants and water the rest with Cheshunt compound, or other fungicide.

Grey powder or mould on leaves, stems or flowers

Powdery mildew – plants become covered with a white mealy deposit and begin to distort.

REMEDY. Do not overcrowd. Susceptible plants (e.g. cornflowers) should be sprayed regularly with a fungicide *before* the disease occurs. Mildew is much easier to prevent by good growing conditions and regular spraying than it is to cure.

Grey mould (botrytis). Fluffy grey mould appears where affected – stems, leaves, flowers. Worse in wet seasons.

REMEDY. Remove badly affected parts on plants immediately and spray with a fungicide regularly.

Downy mildew. Upper leaf surface becomes yellowed, the undersurface is covered with a greyish mould. Not common but more prevalent in damp weather.

REMEDY. Fatal in severe cases, but try spraying regularly with Dithane 945 before giving up completely.

Coloured swellings on leaves and stems

Rust. Yellow, orange or brown pustules on leaves, which often drop off.

REMEDY. Infected leaves should be removed immediately and regular spraying with propiconazole started. Susceptible species, e.g. antirrhinum and sweet williams, may be sprayed as a preventive measure before the disease is noticed. Do not use propiconazole on fuchsias and young bedding geraniums as damage to young growth will occur. Propiconazole is not permitted for use on food crops or other plants which may be eaten.

A general note on pesticides and fungicides

Many similar chemicals are sold under different manufacturers' brand names, and new sprays are being introduced all the time. If you feel bewildered by the overwhelming selection on the shelves of your local garden shop and you cannot get good personal advice, send for a copy of the *Directory of Garden Chemicals*, produced annually by the British Agrochemicals Association, 1 Lincoln Court, Lincoln Road, Peterborough, which lists every garden chemical at present available, including the trade names each is sold under and the purpose for which it is used.

Do not forget whenever you are handling chemicals to observe the basic safety rules of all garden sprays. These are listed on pages 78–9 in connection with weedkillers but apply equally to all potentially toxic chemicals used for one purpose or another in the garden.

Chemicals for the control of pests and diseases can be purchased in various forms: as liquids, granules, aerosols, dusts, and even smokes. Liquids are the most easy to use, diluted according to instructions, but sometimes to use a dust is more convenient. Ready-to-use sprays are comparatively expensive but useful for spot treatment of small areas. Granules are used for soil treatment, smokes for the disinfection of greenhouses.

Only mix chemicals together if it is recommended by the manufacturer.

Most insecticides and fungicides are still considered to be inorganic, and therefore unsuitable for true organic cultivation. 'Organic' pesticides based on fatty acids, similar to those in soft soap, and fungicides containing sulphur, are generally permitted.

11

HERBACEOUS
PERENNIALS AND
BORDERS

Broadly speaking, hardy herbaceous perennials are those garden plants which go on from year to year, but die down either
completely or to a rosette or crown of leaves for the winter, to
start into new growth the following spring. They conjure up
visions of the long sweeping masses of foliage and colour so
beloved of the owners of large houses and stately homes in
times gone by when labour was cheap. A properly maintained
border was (and is, for those of us who are still able to have
one) a never-ending job – manuring, dividing, splitting,
planting and replanting, staking, tying, dead-heading, cutting
back, forking, fertilizing and spraying, though when all this is
done to perfection, there is perhaps no more beautiful living
feature than a herbaceous border in summer.

However, the majority of garden owners today simply
cannot afford to devote such a disproportionate amount of
time to any one area, especially as for a large part of the year
the herbaceous border is doing nothing – from October to
April very little of most of the plants can even be seen at all.

Nothing looks worse than a neglected bed of perennials. A further argument against giving a whole part of the garden over to this type of plant is that in most modern plots there just is not room – not if you want to have a go at several aspects of plant cultivation, at any rate.

Just as annuals and bedding plants went out of favour twenty or so years ago, so herbaceous plants have been through a very untrendy phase for all except the dedicated plantsman. They had a reputation for being rampant, and disease-prone, and designers were pointing out the greater benefits of shrubberies, which provided something to see at all times of the year, even if it was only the tracery of the bare branches, colour being provided as much by contrasting foliage effects as by the flowers. Herbaceous plants fell into some disrepute with uninitiated garden owners mainly because the only experience they had of them was through 'gifts' from friends of rampant golden rod, mildew-ridden Michaelmas daisies, and other subjects off-loaded because they were threatening to take over the whole neighbourhood. And if the novice did succumb to what was bestowed so graciously, and planted them, what happened? They ran riot all over the place, shot rapidly up to a height of five feet or more with spindly stems and sickly leaves and, come the first high wind or heavy rain, they were all down on the ground again.

Things have changed considerably in the last few years. Shorter growing, less invasive varieties have been produced, many having greater disease resistance. The old-fashioned concept of large borders with tall plants backed by a high wall or thick hedge – which in itself produced stability problems because of the down-draughts created – has to some extent been superseded by island beds of short-growing cultivars, or mixed borders where a shrub framework helps to support the herbaceous perennials.

A true herbaceous border or bed is supposed only to contain herbaceous perennials, but a way round winter bareness is to plant strategically placed patches of spring bulbs throughout the area. These clumps can then be removed for the summer, and the spaces filled with summer bulbs (say gladioli), dahlias, or properly chosen bedding plants.

However, many plots just cannot afford the space for such a scheme, nor their owners the time for maintenance, but herbaceous perennials still have a purpose in a modern garden

175

as the colours and flowers they supply are so totally different from those provided by trees and shrubs. One solution to the problem of trying to get a quart into a pint pot is the mixed border, where annuals, bulbs, shrubs, conifers, roses and herbaceous perennials all have a contribution to make. It is fairly important to spend some time planning such a bed or border properly or it can look unbalanced or bitty, but it can also be a very interesting feature if you get it right. If you are not keen on mixing everything up you can achieve some segregation by keeping the shrubs to the back (or centre in an island bed), and planting the perennials, and annuals if you want them, together towards the front.

If you want only a few perennials for additional summer interest, you can leave odd spaces for them in what would otherwise be an all-shrub border. When they are cut down in winter you hardly notice it, but make sure you position the clumps properly, or the effect can be rather gappy.

Similarly, if you still fancy the idea of a true herbaceous border but you are not keen on its aspect in winter, you can plant at regular intervals just a *few* shrubs which do not get too big and provide winter flower or foliate interest. These have to be chosen carefully for suitability – many of the winter- and spring-flowering viburnums are fine, also the daphnes and the witch hazels for flower (and a bonus of scent), whereas variegated evergreens such as some hollies, elaeagnus and photinia would provide leaf effects. If you are a real pedant and you want nothing but herbaceous plants in the bed or border, you could liven it up with evergreen perennials evenly distributed throughout the planting. Some suggestions for these are given at the end of this section.

To summarize therefore, the *advantages* of herbaceous perennials are that they can provide flowers and colour for both garden decoration and flower arrangement; they come up every year and do not have to be removed and replaced annually, and many of them attract wild life – mainly bees and butterflies – to the garden. The *disadvantages* are that they must be chosen carefully to make sure you have not landed yourself with the most awful rubbish; many of them require staking and tying during the growing and flowering season; they usually need dead-heading to ensure a subsequent flush of flowers; they have to be cut down at the end of the season; many of them only have one flowering period (e.g., irises and

176

oriental poppies) so are not contributing much to the overall design for a large part of the year, and every three or four years, or when the clumps begin to look played out, they need to be dug up, split, and the newest growth replanted.

Obtaining herbaceous perennials

Herbaceous perennials are obtainable by collection from specialist and general nurseries and garden centres, and occasionally a limited selection can be found in garden shops. They can either be purchased with bare roots or, more commonly nowadays, in some form of container.

By mail order from specialist nurseries.

By growing your own from seed (see notes on propagation on pages 180–2). Seed can be bought from the usual sources, or collected from the plants of friends or neighbours.

Beware of accepting gifts from well-meaning friends. Do not introduce anything into your own garden unless you know what it is and what it does – otherwise you may have cause to be sorry. Thankfully, most of the older atrocities are no longer available for sale. Treat yourself to a good reference book if you want to study plants seriously. Otherwise buy by mail order from some of the better-known nurseries which produce comprehensive catalogues. Many of these catalogues are a mine of information in themselves and some are so explicit and profusely illustrated with colour photographs that you cannot go wrong.

Planting herbaceous perennials

Always prepare the ground intended for herbaceous perennials well in advance. You can, in theory, plant container-grown herbaceous subjects at any time of the year when the weather is suitable, but even so there are still two optimum periods – in early and mid-autumn (September to the middle of October), when the soil is still warm enough to help re-establishment, and in March to early April when the hardest weather is (with a bit of luck) over. Spring is the best time for perennials which have a tendency to be slightly tender. Bare-rooted perennials should always be planted during these periods.

A month or two before you want to plant, dig in some well rotted manure, compost or similar, and if the soil is at all on the heavy side, you should try to improve the texture

with sand, gypsum or perlite, and plenty of humus-forming
material. If you are planting in the autumn, add some bone-
meal or other slow-release, high-phosphate fertilizer to encourage good root formation without stimulating the top into
premature sappy growth. For spring planting, a top dressing of
a balanced fertilizer is more suitable.

Dig a hole large enough to take the roots comfortably and
break up the bottom so they can grow out of it properly. Set
the plant at about the same depth as it was in the container or
open ground from which it was lifted, or only about half an
inch below so you can work a little soil into the crown. Some
plants, such as peonies, will not flower if they are replanted
too low, and others will not if the crown is deeply covered, so
take some trouble over the job. Firm the perennials and fork
over the whole area lightly to tidy the bed and remove the
unavoidable consolidation which occurred during planting. A
mulch of organic material, or even polythene or mulching
sheet, at this stage is beneficial.

Planting mixtures of peat, or peat substitute, sand and
fertilizers are now obtainable. If you have a lot of planting to
do and you are fairly happy with the soil the stock is going
into, you might find this an unnecessary additional expense. If,
on the other hand, you have never planted anything before,
you have only a little planting to do, and/or you are not sure
whether your soil is as good as it ought to be, these mixtures
would give the new things a sporting chance of getting away
well if you follow the instructions properly.

After-care

All except the most sturdy subjects will need staking to prevent them falling over when they are in full bearing, and this should be done as soon as possible after growth recommences in spring, *not* when it's too late and they are all laid flat! At one time the most widely used way of providing support over a large area was to push twiggy branches into the ground around the plants, which grew through, and eventually hid them. This method is still seen quite frequently in very big gardens where they have large quantities of woody prunings which can be saved and used for this purpose. In the autumn the whole lot − herbaceous top growth and supporting timber, can be burnt. It is better to use new twigs every year as they become brittle and less supportive as they dry out, and can also become infected with coral spot fungus which may spread and seriously damage healthy shrubs and trees.

The main drawback of this method in the small garden is how to find regular annual supplies of stout twiggy branches, and sometimes there is a problem disposing of the additional amount of rubbish it creates. A simple alternative is to drive stakes or strong canes of a suitable length in around the plants and then to run raffia or garden string round them as the plants grow. This encloses the whole plant in a kind of string tube but by the time it is in full leaf the foliage hides nearly all the support. It is *not enough* to shove one cane in at the side and then tie all the stems together to it in a bunch − it is not healthy for the plant, and it looks really dreadful.

Purpose-made herbaceous plant supports are now available from many sundriesmen, and sometimes nurseries sell them mail order as a sideline. The principle of design varies according to the product, but it is usually a set of metal stakes with round or linking cross pieces which can be attached in some way to the stakes to support the whole clump. You can buy various sizes, and some can be joined together to enable you to encircle larger clumps. They are comparatively expensive but unobtrusive, effective and permanent, and make staking very much easier than using canes and string, or brushwood, and if you are starting a high-quality border from scratch, or only have a few treasures to tend, are probably worth the cost.

Newly planted perennials will need a lot of water in the first season after planting, especially in warm spells, and this is where a mulch can be beneficial in keeping the surrounding soil damp. Most established herbaceous plants are not keen on drought conditions and should be kept moist in hot, dry weather.

Top-dress every spring with a balanced fertilizer and, if you have access to it, you can fork in gently some very well rotted manure or fine compost in the autumn. Herbaceous plants do get a few pests and diseases, so keep an eye open for these and take action if necessary.

When cutting the plants down in the autumn leave about 6–9 in. (150–225 mm) of old stalks attached to the plant. This ensures that you know that something is growing there even when the plant is dormant, and it also helps slightly to keep the worst of the frost out. You can remove the rest of the old stems the following spring when new growth has started.

As well as benefiting from dead-heading, many plants will make new growth and a second crop of blooms if they are cut back during the summer. Some need to be cut right down, others can be taken back to a leaf joint on the stem. Experience as much as anything will tell you which method is best for individual types.

Eventually the clumps of perennials will become old and woody in the centre and need digging up and replanting. Save only the newest, strongest and healthiest growth from round the outside – the rest is best discarded. The length of time which elapses between the original planting and the need for splitting and dividing depends on many factors and varies quite a lot, but is usually between 3 and 8 years. If possible, you should redo a whole area at the same time, as it gives you the chance to dig it over thoroughly and work in a good helping of manure, compost, etc. before replanting. The best time of the year for doing this is in late September and October when you can still remember, and see, what you have got.

Propagation

The easiest and most popular method of increasing your stock is by dividing up existing plants. This works for nearly all the popular herbaceous perennials. You can always tell whether it is a practical idea or not by examining the clump: if it has a lot of stems and has grown bigger over the years, it can almost certainly be split. September–October and March–early April are the best time for doing this.

Many perennials can be grown easily from seed. Often it germinates best when sown fresh and just ripe, but some seed needs to have a period of cold before it will sprout.

You can generally find out which plants need which treatment by referring to a good book on perennials – it would be beyond the scope of this one to give cultural and propagation advice on every individual herbaceous subject. Most perennial seed can be sown into seed beds in the open or under cold glass in trays of compost, and young plants overwintered in a cold frame. It will be a year or two before the seedlings will have formed plants large enough to put out in their permanent positions, also many youngsters may not be quite like their parents. Raising perennials from saved seed is therefore often more in the interests of curiosity for the majority of amateur gardeners; whether the end results justify the amount of time involved and space occupied is debatable, but generally speaking the safest way of obtaining top-class varieties is by vegetative propagation - division or cuttings. However, if the whole concept of raising plants this way interests you, you can obtain seed of some very good varieties from the major seed companies.

You can also take cuttings of many herbaceous perennials. The most popular method is to remove young shoots with a 'heel' from the base of the plant when they have just started into growth in spring.

Tidy these up and insert them into a sandy compost, usually under cold glass. Pot them up individually when the cuttings have formed roots. This is a suitable method to use to increase stock of perennials which do not divide up very well, such as delphiniums and lupins, but these two also propagate very well and easily from seed.

You may come across the expression 'Irishman's cutting' – this term is used to describe a piece of plant removed from the base of the parent as a cutting but having a few roots already attached to it.

Root cuttings are sometimes used to increase the stock of fleshy-rooted perennials like Japanese anemones and oriental poppies. Plant pieces of root 2–4 in. (50–100 mm) long in sandy compost under cold glass or well drained light soil outside with the top of the cutting just above soil level. (You can identify top and bottom by cutting the top flat and the bottom slanting.) New plants will grow quite quickly from these cuttings if taken in the spring.

Bugs and blights

Most of the pests and diseases which affect bedding plants, (pages 168–73) also attack herbaceous perennials, given the chance. Well established plants under good growing conditions will be less susceptible to many diseases, with the possible exception of mildew, which should be sprayed as a preventive measure if plants are known to be prone to the disease.

All the remedies suggested for annuals and bedding plants are suitable for use on herbaceous perennials, but certain chemicals can have disfiguring effects on some plants. Where this is the case, it is stated on the label, so be sure to check *first*.

In addition to the problems already described, there is a further one connected with the rhizomes of bearded irises, which can start to rot and turn slimy. This usually happens if the plant is growing in less than ideal conditions – damp and shady, for example, instead of the dry, sunny position it likes, especially if the rhizome has been physically damaged in some way, or if it has been planted too deep – the *roots* only, not the rhizome itself, should be buried in the soil. The plant can be saved in some cases, if the rot has not spread too far, by cutting off all the soft parts and treating the remainder with sulphur. You should disinfect all the tools used in this operation before using them again. The rhizome can be replanted after this treatment, preferably in a different position, and it will probably survive.

Twenty good perennials to get you started

Five tall ones for the back

> *Aruncus plumosus* 'Glasnevin' (5 ft/1.5 m) Creamy white plumes of flowers June–July.
> *Delphinium* 'Pacific Hybrids' (6 ft/1.8 m) Huge spikes with large florets in a selection of pinks, blues and white. June–August.
> *Helianthus* 'Lodden Gold' (6 ft/1.8 m) Double golden yellow flowers July–September.
> *Ligularia clivorum* 'Desdemona' (5 ft/1.5 m) Orange flower spikes, large purplish leaves. July–September.
> *Sidalcea* 'Nimmerdor' (6 ft/1.8 m) Deep pink mallow-like flowers. June–August.

Five of medium height

Anemone japonica 'Bressingham Glow' (20 in./500 mm) Semi-double, rose-red Japanese Anemone. August–October.

Aster nova-belgii 'Marie Ballard' (36 in/900 mm) Light blue, double Michaelmas daisy. September–October.

Helenium 'Golden Youth' (30 in./750 mm) Large golden yellow flowers with prominent dark centres. June–August.

Hemerocallis 'Stafford' (36 in./900 mm) Day lily. Large tubular flowers, deep red with orange throat. June–August.

Lupin 'Russell Hybrids' (39 in./1 m) Long spikes in a wide selection of colours and bi-colours. June–July, but will produce smaller spikes regularly throughout the rest of summer if dead-headed.

Five low growers for the front

Geranium 'Russell Prichard' (8–10 in./200–250 mm) Creeping habit. Carmine red flowers for many months. June–September.

Oenothera missouriensis (10 in./250 mm) Large, bold, yellow evening primrose blooms June–September.

Potentilla 'Gibson's Scarlet' (12–14 in./300–350 mm) Bright red flowers. June–August.

Sedum spectabile (14 in./350 mm) Ice plant. Fleshy leaves. Large light pink flower heads. August–October. Good butterfly plant.

Veronica teucrinum 'Kapitan' (10–12 in./250–300 mm) Bright blue flowers on short spikes. May–July.

Five evergreens for added interest

Bergenia (10–15 in./250–380 mm) All varieties recommended. Leathery 'elephant's ears' green leaves, often turning purple in winter. Red, pink or white flowers. March–May.

Dianthus (pinks). Grey-green spiky leaves and pink, red or white single, semi-double or double flowers. Very fragrant. Modern varieties are perpetual flowering. Make good edging plants.

Euphorbia robbiae (24–30 in./600–750 mm) Deep green leaves, sulphur-yellow flowers. May–June. Spreads and seeds easily and needs careful placing.

Helleborus corsicus (24–30 in./600–750 mm) Leathery green leaves and apple-green flowers. April–May.

Iris pallida 'Variegata' (30 in./750mm) Cream and grey-green variegated sword-like foliage, blue iris flowers. May.

Grasses

Ornamental grasses have become very popular in recent years. As a contrast to other foliage plants they are unrivalled, and there are few more attractive sights in winter than the frost-covered dead heads. Ornamental grasses can be found in a wide range of colours and heights – for an unusual effect, a bed consisting solely of grasses of differing heights and hues is certainly worth considering.

Six eye-catching ornamental grasses

Acorus gramineus 'Ogon' (8 in./200 mm) Gold-variegated rush.

Carex morrowii 'Evergold' (8 in./200 mm) Brightly gold-variegated sedge.

Deschampsia caespitosa 'Gold Veil' (4 ft/120 cm) Dark green overlapping leaves and plumes of green stems and flowers, turning yellow.

Festuca glauca (1 ft/300 mm) Silver-blue, fine-leaved grass topped with wispy, pale flower heads.

Hakonechloa macra 'Alboaurea' (10 in./250 mm) A brightly variegated grass for a moist situation.

Miscanthus sinensis 'Purpureus' (5 ft/150 cm) Stems and foliage tinted purple and a profusion of striking flower heads.

12

ROSES

Roses are still probably some of our most popular garden plants, although the attitude towards them has changed somewhat in the last decade. Hybrid tea and floribunda types have declined in favour, partly because of the skill required for pruning and partly because of the increasing popularity of the cottage garden which suits today's more traditional architectural styles so well and which is better served by the less formal shrub, or 'species', types of rose.

There are few gardens, however, which cannot accommodate a few of these delightful plants to good effect.

ADVANTAGES. Modern miniature, bush and standard roses have a long blooming period with probably one of the most beautiful flowering habits of any ornamental plant.

They are tolerant of a wide range of reasonable soil conditions.

Many have a strong scent.

Shrub roses introduce something different into the shrub or

mixed border – many have coloured thorns or hips to increase their value as garden plants.

They make good cut flowers.

DISADVANTAGES. They require some knowledge of pruning techniques to keep them at their best. (Though research has it that an annual cutting back all over is just as satisfactory.)

They do not like hot and dry or waterlogged conditions or shallow soils.

Climbing forms require some training. Standards need staking.

They get their fair share of pests and diseases.

Most of them have thorns.

They look rather uninteresting in winter.

Uses

FOR FORMAL BEDDING SCHEMES. The beds are usually of simple geometric design – circles, squares etc., each bed containing just one variety, unless the bed is very large, when the roses can be planted in blocks of one colour. Hybrid teas, floribundas, patio roses and miniatures are most suitable here.

FOR INFORMAL BEDS AND BORDERS. Most types of rose can be used in this situation. There are a lot of arguments for and against mixing colours and varieties; I feel this is a matter of personal taste, but large areas tend to look better if more than one of each variety is planted, either in blocks of, say, three or more, or in sequence using possibly three toning or contrasting varieties.

For example, if you were using 3 roses of varieties A, B and C, you could plant one row in the sequence A, B, C, the next in the order B, C, A, and finally C, A, B, throughout the bed. This gives you an overall colour effect which is quite interesting if you like that sort of thing. Smaller borders in 'cottagey' gardens look all right with varieties completely mixed. Remember to make sure you match the heights – you cannot mix them if some grow four feet high and others only two feet, unless you put the tall ones at the back (or in the middle of an island bed), coming down to the shortest at the front, but you have to do your research first, preferably locally, as different areas affect plant habits differently. If in doubt, stick to one sort.

IN A MIXED BORDER. Real enthusiasts may throw up their hands in horror at this suggestion, but it is perfectly feasible to use roses in a mixed border provided you do it properly. Bush hybrid tea and floribunda roses look better planted in groups of three or more. Old-fashioned shrub ('species') roses are generally less formal in habit and grow bigger, so can be planted individually.

IN CONTAINERS. Bush and climbing roses can be grown fairly successfully in large tubs provided they are planted correctly and regularly fed and watered. Miniature roses are suitable for smaller troughs and window boxes, again making sure they are looked after properly. Although this is possibly the only way the patio, roof or balcony gardener is able to grow roses, it has to be remembered that they do not look very interesting in winter.

AS SPECIMENS. Some shrub roses and standard hybrid teas and floribundas can be used as individual specimen plants in a lawn or paving. Bush roses can also be used for this purpose in paving or gravel, but look 'bitty' if planted like this in a lawn, are difficult to mow round and look untidy if the edges of the planting holes are not properly maintained, making a lot of work. Climbing roses can be grown up poles in shrubberies to give extra height.

AS CLIMBING PLANTS. Climbing, rambler and some shrub roses make good wall plants and can also be used to cover pergolas, arches and rustic screens.

FOR HEDGES. Most bush and shrub roses, planted in rows of one variety, make very attractive flowering hedges.

AS GROUND COVER. Some ramblers, dwarf climbers and prostrate shrub roses can be used for this purpose if allowed to scramble over the surface of the soil.

Types of roses available

BUSH ROSES. These are roses of a bushy habit as opposed to ones which grow on a single stem. The term 'bush' usually applies to the bush form of miniature, hybrid tea and floribunda roses, but technically most shrub roses are 'bushes' too.

STANDARD ROSES. These are hybrid tea and floribunda roses budded on to a tall stock to form a 'standard'. Miniature standards are budded on to a thinner and shorter stock. Weeping standards are roses of lax habit such as ramblers and some climbers and shrub roses which are then trained down to form a small weeping tree.

HYBRID TEA AND FLORIBUNDA ROSES. Some years ago these were reclassified as 'large flowered' and 'cluster flowered' respectively. The new names have never really caught on and the old classifications still tend to be widely used, both by amateur gardeners and professionals. They are roses which have been produced by plant breeders over the last century for vigour, colour, good flowering habit and, to some extent, fragrance. As with all roses, their ancestors were the 'wild' species, discovered by explorers and plant collectors over many centuries, but new varieties are now largely bred by the crossing of shrub roses and/or existing varieties of hybrid teas (HTs), floribundas, climbers, ramblers and miniatures known to be good parent stock. HTs and floribundas are today the most widely planted types of rose. Large flowered (HT) roses are those generally producing a single flower or only a few per head, whilst cluster-flowered (floribunda) roses usually produce many.

PATIO ROSE is a new expression describing a short-growing, usually floribunda, rose.

CLIMBING AND RAMBLER ROSES have a lax, spreading habit which makes them useful as climbing plants, given some support or tying in. Rambler roses usually have only one flush of flowers, though a few are remontant (repeat flowering) and they have quite a rampant growth habit. In modern gardens they have largely been superseded by the repeat flowering climbers which are either 'sports' of bush roses with a stronger growth habit than the type, or are found to have a form which makes them suitable for this purpose during the production of new seedlings.

MINIATURE ROSES are bush roses with an especially dwarf growth habit.

SHRUB ROSES are frequently 'wild' rose species originally occurring naturally, but can be sports and hybrids of these originals.

Where to buy roses

FROM ROSE AND GENERAL NURSERIES AND GARDEN CENTRES. This is probably the safest way. They can these days either be bought as bare-root or root-wrapped plants during the dormant period (late October to early April), or containerized for all-year-round planting. The choice from such nurseries ranges from very wide to fairly limited.

MAIL ORDER through nurseries or home shopping catalogues – usually in the dormant period. This should be a safe enough way to buy if both the nurseries and the mail order firms are reputable. Rose nurseries offering mail-order facilities usually have a wide selection to choose from.

SUPERMARKETS, CHAIN STORES ETC. These are largely either prepackaged in cardboard cartons or polythene bags. If you know what you are doing you can pick up a bargain, otherwise it is a dear way of buying material for the compost heap. Try to buy them when they have just arrived and make sure the roots are moist, the stems plump and there are no pale, long shoots growing from the buds – this often happens if they have been kept too long in a moist, warm, dark position. If they do not look as though they have just been dug up – do not touch them. The choice of varieties is usually limited and often the varieties are misnamed.

MARKET STALLS. You can pick up a bargain – but beware! Take care with choosing individual plants.

SEED. Some seed companies offer rose seed for sale. This is no good if it is reliable named varieties and instant colour you have in mind, but interesting for the experimenter. You can also experiment with seed saved from your own hips.

What to look for

There should be at least two branches on new plants and these ought to be no thinner than a pencil. They should not be dried up and wrinkled. If bare-rooted, the roots must not be dry. Containerized plants should also have a strong, healthy top growth and not look as though they have just been planted up at the end of the season. If you buy containerized plants in summer there should be no pests and diseases, and no weeds growing in the top of the pot. Some rose nurseries sell 'seconds' (bushes which are not quite up to their usual standard) at reduced rates and if you are prepared to give them the best growing conditions they can be quite a bargain. Not so, however, the job lots of lost-label bushes offered by some nurseries. You have no idea what you are getting, either with regard to colour or habit, and by the time you do find out, it is probably not kind to give them another move.

What varieties shall I choose?

If you can, try to visit a display garden, trial ground or nursery in the summer when the roses are in flower. This will give you a better idea of colour, scent and perhaps habit, than a catalogue or reference book. Viewing nursery stock is not probably quite as useful as visiting the other two venues, as the young plants have not really settled in to their permanent ways at that age, but it is better than picking varieties 'blind'.

Once you have decided on the right form for the job, colour and scent are more a personal matter, but a no less important issue is cost. You will find that some roses are more expensive than others at the same nursery, these generally being more modern varieties involving what is known as Plant Breeders' Rights, where a proportion of the cost is paid each time to the breeder who produced the plant. Newer roses are not all affected by Plant Breeders' Rights and you do not automatically get a better product by choosing the latest names, but it has been found that as certain varieties are reproduced over the years, they begin to become more susceptible to certain diseases, although this is not always the case. For example, the HT rose 'Peace' was introduced just after the Second World War and continues to be a best-seller because of its strong constitution and resistance to disease, whereas 'Super Star', the vermilion rose which was a must for every rose buyer in the early Sixties because of toughness as well as its new, almost luminous colour, has become progressively more prone to mildew and blackspot as time has passed until these days it is hardly ever recommended by experienced rosarians. This is another argument for seeing the variety before you make a commitment to buying it, especially if you want a lot.

You will have noticed that the number of petals varies according to variety from a single ring to over 60 in some cases. Whether you choose singles or doubles depends on you, but do not be put off by varieties only sporting a few petals. Their overall flowering effect or shape may warrant your buying them.

If you are completely in the dark, here are a few to start you off.

Ten good large-flowered hybrid tea bush roses

> *Alexander.* Bright vermilion, slight scent.
> *Elina Cream.* Moderate scent.
> *Fragrant Cloud.* Coral red, heavily scented.
> *Freedom.* Deep yellow, moderate scent.
> *Just Joey.* Copper pink, moderate scent.
> *Paul Sherville.* Pink with yellow base, fragrant.
> *Peace Yellow.* Slow growing, slight scent.
> *Royal William.* Deep red, fragrant.
> *Silver Jubilee.* Peach pink, slightly fragrant.
> *Wendy Cussons.* Pink, fragrant.

Ten reliable cluster-flowered floribundas

> *Amber Queen.* Amber, moderate scent.
> *Anna Harkness.* Apricot yellow, slight scent.
> *Arthur Bell.* Yellow, tall, fragrant.
> *Hannah Gordon.* White-edged, deep pink, slight scent.
> *Iceberg.* White, slightly fragrant.
> *Korresia.* Yellow, moderate scent.
> *Margaret Merrill.* Blush white, fragrant.
> *Mountbatten.* Gold, tall.
> *Southampton.* Apricot orange, upright, fragrant.
> *Trumpeter.* Orange-red, slight scent.

I purposely have not included any so-called 'blue' roses on this list as no real blue rose exists, and the ones at present so described really vary from lavender to washed-out pink, depending on where you are growing them. You either like them or not but they have their uses as cut flowers. 'Blue Moon' is the strongest grower, 'Charles de Gaulle' perhaps the best colour but rather a weak variety. 'News' is a floribunda of a shocking beetroot-purple shade. Similarly I have not mentioned the greeny-brown roses popular with flower arrangers. 'Julia's Rose' was about the first to be widely available. It certainly has some charm in an arrangement but is not much good as a bedder for garden colour. The bigger specialist rose nurseries usually have a selection.

Half a dozen miniatures

> *Angela Rippon.* Carmine pink.
> *Baby Masquerade.* Red/yellow bicolour.
> *Darling Flame.* Orange.

Easter Morning. Ivory.
Pour Toi. Cream.
Stacey Sue. Pink.

Some reliable climbers

Bantry Bay. Pink, very vigorous.
Climbing Iceberg. White flushed pink 'sport' of the floribunda bush rose.
Compassion. Salmon orange, very fragrant.
Danse du Feu. Orange-red. Will grow fairly well on a north wall. Can be trained up a pillar.
Golden Showers. Golden-yellow. Good for walls, fences and pillars and will tolerate a north position. Fragrant.
Handel. Cream-white edged red. Bronze-tinted foliage. Will train up a tall pillar.

Recommended ramblers

Alberic Barbier. Yellow buds opening white, scented. Almost evergreen.
Albertine. Copper salmon. Fragrant.
Emily Gray. Golden-yellow. Shiny almost evergreen leaves. Fragrant.
Paul's Scarlet Climber. Bright scarlet.
Wedding Day. Small cream-tinged pink flowers with yellow stamens. Very sweet scent. Small glossy leaves. Very strong growing.

Six shrub roses for ground cover

Nozomi. Prostrate. Single pearl pink flowers, small glossy pointed leaves.
Pink Drift. Pale pink, large clusters of flowers.
Red Blanket. Rose-red, perpetual. Not quite as prostrate as Nozomi. Glossy foliage.
Rosy Cushion. Rosy pink, semi-double flowers with ivory centres.
Swany. Very double, snow-white flowers. Prostrate. Small glossy leaves.
Yellow Dagmar Hastrup. Fragrant yellow flowers, semi-double.

192

Twelve really good shrub roses for informal planting

Boule de Neige (*Rosa x borboniana* – 'Bourbon rose'). Creamy white, tinted pink, camellia-like flowers. Scented. Perpetual flowering. 6 ft (1.8 m).

Buff Beauty (hybrid musk). Apricot-yellow, scented, repeat flowering. 5–6 ft (1.5–1.8 m). Like a strong-growing floribunda.

Cecile Brunner (*Rosa chinensis*). The Sweetheart Rose. Tiny double flesh-pink flowers. June. 3 ft (900 mm).

Celestial (*Rosa x alba*). Shell-pink double flowers, fragrant. June/July. Oval hips. 6 ft (1.8 m).

Fruhlingsgold (Modern hybrid shrub). Semi-double scented yellow flowers. May and June. 7 ft (2.1 m).

Nevada (Modern hybrid shrub). Pale pink opening creamy white, semi-double. May–June and at intervals afterwards. Has a similar pink sport called Marguerite Hilling. 7 ft (2.1 m).

Rosa moyesii. Single dark red flowers, lacy foliage. Flagon-shaped hips. 10 ft (3 m).

Rosa rugosa. An easy, inexpensive shrub for specimen planting or hedging. Single crimson purple flowers, cream stamens. Recurrent flowering. Heavily scented. Yellow autumn colour. 6 ft (1.8 m). White version also available.

Rosa sericea var. pteracantha. Single white flowers, black hips. Large ruby-red thorns. 8 ft (2.4 m).

Rosa xanthina 'Canarybird'. Canary-yellow scented flowers May/June.

Tuscany Superb (*Rosa gallica*). (The Old Velvet Rose). Velvety purple-crimson double flowers, June and July and at intervals throughout summer.

William Lobb (*Rosa x centifolia* – 'moss rose'). Crimson purple double flowers tinted lavender grey. Repeat flowering. Scented. Moss-like growth around the buds. 4 ft (1.25 m).

Planting new roses

CHOOSING THE SITE. The reputation that roses have for liking clay soils is no excuse for bad preparation and planting. Roses like *good* conditions – plenty of water, regular feeding, their pests and diseases kept at bay, not too much lime in the soil, and

193

above all, a well worked site with plenty of organic matter added. They like a fair amount of sun, too, and although a very hot, sunny site can cause moisture problems and blooms which fade and 'go over' very quickly, there is also no point in expecting them to give of their best in dense shade, or planted under trees, because they will not.

PREPARING THE PLANTING AREA. Dig the spot you have chosen for your roses very thoroughly and remove all perennial weeds. Add as much humus-forming material – well rotted manure or compost, peat, spent hops, etc. as you can get hold of. This will supply some nutrients, but mainly it will help to open up a very heavy soil and retain water in medium and light ones. If you are planting in autumn and early winter you can add some bone-meal, but from February onwards you should apply a proprietary rose fertilizer according to the maker's instructions. Some experts recommend mixing up a planting medium of loam, peat and sharp sand, plus a handful of bone-meal or rose fertilizer according to planting time, with which to backfill the planting holes, or alternatively you can buy some bags of proprietary planting compost, but I prefer the whole site to be so thoroughly prepared that the soil you take out of the holes is good enough to be put back in again round the new roses. You should always do this preliminary work, whether you are planting bare-root stock during the dormant period or containerized roses at any time of the year.

CHECKING THE NEW PLANTS. Inspect the roots of bare-root roses and cut off any damaged or broken ones cleanly with secateurs. Shorten the roots of very strong plants by about one-third. This is not an excuse for you to dig a smaller hole, but to encourage the plant to make new fibrous feeding roots from the point where they were pruned off. Similarly, you should remove any branches which were damaged low down during lifting or transporting. If you are planting in the spring (or even if you are planting in autumn and winter in mild parts of the country), you can give the bushes their first prune *before* you plant them – then you do not have to bend!

The pruning of new HT, floribunda and patio bushes consists of taking out any weak, dead or damaged wood, and shortening the rest back to an outward pointing eye (bud) about 3 buds up from the base. Depending on variety, the wood that is left will be about 6–8 in. (150–200 mm) long.

194

This method does not apply to miniatures, shrubs, climbers and ramblers. Miniatures require little pruning except trimming back and the removal of dead wood. Remove just the green tips of young shrub roses – these will probably die off anyway. *Climbers* are inclined to lose their climbing habit if pruned back too hard, so just take off spindly, dead, and badly placed shoots and shorten the soft tops back a little to a bud pointing in the direction you want the climber to grow – usually across the wall or whatever support you are using. *Rambler roses* probably will not need anything doing at all, as they will most likely have been tidied up at the nursery, but if you like you can remove any thin and badly shaped or placed wood.

Standard hybrid teas, patios and floribundas are treated in the same way as their bush counterparts, the 'base' being the point at which the branches come out of the stem at the top.

(If you are planting containerized roses in full leaf, they will not require any pruning other than dead-heading until that autumn or the spring following.)

At this point, it is a good idea to soak the roots of dormant bare-root roses in a bucket of water for 24 hours. They can be taken to the site in this bucket and removed as required so they will not dry out.

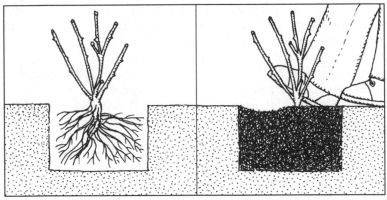

PLANTING. Take out a hole big enough to accommodate the roots comfortably (or the root ball in the case of a containerized plant). Some people recommend shaping the bottom of the hole to fit the roots, which usually slope downwards to one side at an angle, though I do not find this is necessary, providing you spread the roots out properly and don't bunch or bend them.

195

With climbers and ramblers grown against a solid support (a wall etc.) the hole should be a little way (about 15 in./375 mm) from the wall or whatever, and the climber or rambler sloped back to the support.

Place the plant in the hole (do not forget to remove any container). Most commercially grown roses are produced by 'budding' the desired variety on to the base of a type of wild rose stock. The buds then grow out and the top of the stock is removed. It is quite obvious where this has been done as it is the point at which the branches start to grow. Place this 'union' an inch (25 mm) below soil level. Where it is not obvious that this was the method of propagation (for example, with miniature roses grown on their own roots and some shrub roses propagated from seed), you should plant them so that the soil is up to the original soil line on the bush – this also applies to standard roses, where the 'union' is at the *top* of the stem. Standard roses must also have a stout stake driven into the ground at the side of them before backfilling – then you can see the roots so you do not damage them. When the soil has been returned, you can secure the standard to the stake with one or two plastic rose tree ties, one of which should be just under the head to stop it blowing right off.

If you are planting roses from containers, you should still make sure that the union is an inch (25 mm) below ground level. Some badly containerized roses have their unions sticking out of the compost several inches and the instinct is to plant to the depth of the compost, but this is one occasion when you should plant *deeper* than originally.

You can then fill up the holes with soil, treading gently and making sure the new bush is still in position. When you have finished, the plant should be firmly enough in the soil for you not to be able to pull it out again with a *gentle* tug.

Prick over the soil lightly to remove footmarks and any consolidation, and then mulch with organic material. Containerized plants put in during summer will need plenty of water – water the hole and the root ball before it is removed from the container and water the whole site thoroughly before you apply the mulch.

Give roses to be planted in tubs and the like a container big enough for them to grow away healthily. Plant in a similar manner to that described above, using John Innes No. 3 compost. Make sure the tubs have adequate drainage holes.

What if I cannot plant my new roses straight away?

If they are in containers they will manage quite happily until you can deal with them, providing you don't let them dry out.

Roses sent mail order by reputable firms are so well packed that they should survive at least a fortnight in a cold shed or garage if the packing remains unopened. This means that if you cannot deal with them immediately, because the weather is snowy or frosty, for example, they will be all right for 2 or 3 weeks as they are. At the end of this time open the parcel and cover the roots in the same cold but frost-free conditions, with damp sacking or similar.

If it is likely that you will not be able to plant them for several weeks, and the weather is open enough to put them outside, they should be temporarily 'heeled in' until you can plant them in their permanent positions.

After-care of new and established bushes

Roses like a routine – mulching, pruning, feeding, dead-heading, spraying. In addition they should be kept free of weeds. This is best done by hand, or light hoeing.

The subject of when to prune perhaps causes more argument between gardeners than any other garden practice. The autumn pruners (of whom I am one) say that unless you live in a very harsh environment, autumn pruning removes all unripe tissue liable to damage by frost and forces the bushes into a necessary period of rest and dormancy. If new shoots do start to appear during the winter months, they have grown during a time of lower temperatures and will therefore be more hardened to frosts and bad weather. The spring pruners contend that if you get a spell of really severe frost, the pruned roses will become damaged so close to the base that they will not be able to recover. It is really a matter of trial and error as to which method suits your particular case best, but I find that spring-pruned roses, which produce new growth during April, are very liable to have this new, soft growth produced at warmer temperatures cut back by late spring frosts.

Be that as it may, all bush roses and many others will require some form of pruning in autumn (mainly November) or spring (usually March).

You can also mulch in early autumn or spring; the main

thing is to make sure you are applying it to comparatively warm, moist soil, and not sealing in cold and drought.

There are two types of feeders, the two or three times a year brigade, and the little and often lot. The first group feeds in spring when the buds are beginning to grow out, and after the first flush of flowers is over, to promote a further one. In addition they give a slow, high-phosphate food such as bone-meal in the autumn to promote root production. This is a quite adequate feeding programme for medium and heavyish soils, but on lighter ones when rainfall or watering has been excessive a lot of the food will have washed through before it has been absorbed by the plants.

The other lot feeds monthly, with a small amount of proprietary rose food, backing it up with an autumn feed as before. This is fine for roses grown on light soils, but you can get something of a build-up on heavier ones. Whichever method is most suitable, the food should be the same – fast-acting, high-potash food in summer and a slow-release, high-phosphate one in autumn. Proprietary feeds have the necessary trace elements such as magnesium, manganese and iron added. Without these, leaves can show deficiency signs such as browning or yellowing and 'veining', and the plant loses its vigour. A happy rose has a good appetite and objects to feeling hungry. There are pest and disease sprays which incorporate a suitable foliar feed to give the plants a summer boost.

Modern hybrid roses are more or less perpetual flowering, but can be encouraged to flower better if the dead heads are removed. In theory the correct way is to take off the spent head, plus a length of the stem, to a well placed bud, which gives the bush some summer pruning and shaping. In practice, if you cut the head off down to the next leaf it will still probably shoot again just as well, but the bush might need more shaping up during its annual prune.

You must be careful when pruning shrub roses as many produce coloured hips which are part of the attraction of the species – if you dead-head you will cut them off. Do not let hips form on hybrid roses, they tend to weaken the bush slightly as they are taking nourishment from it.

Roses look less than their best if they are not treated regularly for pests and diseases. It is a good thing to spray monthly as a matter of routine as soon as the new leaves begin to come in spring, *before* the problems start.

Do not forget to check stakes, ties and supports regularly.

Sometimes from the base of budded bushes, or the stem of standards, you will find a strong vigorous growth which looks nothing like the rest of the plant. This is usually a sucker produced by the stock and should be removed right back to the root it came from. Once the suckers are allowed to take over, the budded part will soon die as the suckers take all the strength from it. They are often produced from damaged roots so rose beds should never be dug over deeply, just the surface hoed or pricked over from time to time.

In very hot dry periods you will find your roses give much better service if they are well watered. Do this thoroughly, so it gets right down to all the roots, and not a little dribble applied to the surface of the soil. Thorough, regular watering is especially important for roses grown in containers, and roses grown at the base of walls and fences.

You should always check regularly that the bushes are firm in the ground, otherwise root damage may occur. Particularly risky times are during windy weather and after frost, when you should go round your bushes and tread them in firmly.

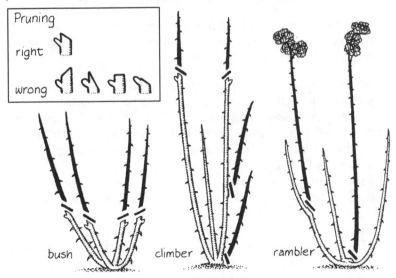

Pruning

Modern HT and floribunda roses produce the best flowers on young bushes. In pruning, you aim to encourage the production of young wood from the base of the plant, which left to itself, would eventually become an unhealthy and untidy tangle of old, diseased and dead wood, shortening its useful life considerably.

In addition, all roses benefit from the removal of very old, woody branches, those badly positioned, and dead tissue which can become a breeding ground for all sorts of nasties.

Make all pruning cuts with clean, *sharp* secateurs to a position just above a bud (eye) pointing in the direction from which you want the new branch to grow. The cut should be slanting *away* from the eye at an angle of about 45 degrees, starting about $\frac{1}{4}$ in. (5 mm) above the eye. By this method, water drains off the cut away from the eye. Whole branches are best removed using heavy-duty sharp loppers or a pruning saw with a narrow blade. If possible, burn all prunings.

SHRUB ROSES. These vary slightly according to species but can be left alone for several years apart from the removal of very weak, diseased, dead and dying growths and badly placed and crossing branches. You can remove the oldest, twiggy, flowered wood in autumn or spring, and the very strong shoots produced by some can be shortened by a third.

MINIATURES. Just remove the old flower trusses and any dead wood. You may find that very sharp scissors are easier to use for these tiny plants than secateurs.

BUSH, PATIO ROSES, LARGE-FLOWERED HYBRID TEAS, CLUSTER FLOWERED FLORIBUNDAS AND STANDARDS OF THESE. There are many methods suggested, some of which are very complicated. To simplify matters, what you are aiming for is a cup- shaped bush with well spaced branches, an open centre and plenty of young wood.

First, remove all weak, dead, dying and diseased shoots entirely. Then take out completely all branches growing into the centre or, if two are crossing each other, one should be removed.

Next, shorten all remaining branches back to about 3–5 eyes from the base of the previous season's wood, cutting to an outward pointing eye as described above.

As the bush gets older, some of the really old and increasingly unproductive branches should be taken right out annually to encourage young ones to be made from near the base.

WEEPING STANDARDS are pruned like the climbing or rambling varieties from which they have been produced. Some lax growers will weep naturally from the budding union at the top of the stem, ones of stiffer habit may need some training by tying down on to an umbrella framework of plastic-coated metal which is attached to the top of the supporting stake.

CLIMBERS. Prune back flowered shoots to about 4 eyes. Remove old or weak shoots. Tie in new growths when long enough. If you find your climbing roses are growing strongly upright with only a few shoots and the flowers are at the very top and it is convenient to do so, try training the main branches out horizontally. Sub-laterals will be produced from the leaf buds, and these will flower at a lower level.

RAMBLERS. This is the only group of roses which should be pruned immediately after flowering, removing dead, diseased and old flowered wood and tying in the strong new shoots which will flower the following summer.

GROUND-COVER ROSES. Little regular pruning is needed. If they begin to get overcrowded and out of hand, prune as ramblers (i.e. by removing a proportion of the oldest branches).

Pests and diseases

Fortunately, if the roses have been planted correctly in good soil in the right position, root troubles are mercifully few.

PESTS.   *Holes in the leaves*, in addition to being caused by the pests on page 169, are also produced by cockchafers and leaf-cutter bees, which take bites out of the edges.
Damaged flowers can be caused by chafer beetles, tortrix moths, capsids, aphids or thrips.
Marked leaves and damaged young growths are a sign of the pests on page 169, and also rose slugworm, which skeletonizes the leaves.
Rolled leaves are usually produced by tortrix moth caterpillars, leaf-rolling sawfly, or damage by hormone weed-killers.
White froth on stem (cuckoo spit) is caused by frog-hoppers.

DISEASES. *White patches and powder on leaves, which become distorted –* powdery mildew.
Black spots with yellow edges, leaves turn yellow and drop off – black spot.
Orange swellings on undersides of leaves – rose rust.

REMEDY. If you are spraying regularly with both a fungicide and insecticide at monthly intervals, your problems will be controlled to a large extent. Sometimes bugs and blights develop a certain amount of resistance to chemicals used regularly and so some variation should be introduced.

Other problems

LEAF DISCOLORATION. Healthy roses have nice green leaves. They can be dark green or lighter, depending on variety, but should be of one colour. Sickly leaves with pale green parts or reddish or purple tinges or spots are almost certainly an indication of a shortage of major and/or trace elements. You can avoid to a large extent the problem by regular feeding as described. Occasionally the condition can be caused by virus and although there is no remedy, regular feeding will improve the symptoms.

SUNKEN, BROWN PATCHES ON THE STEM. This is caused by the canker fungus, which enters through a small wound, insect damage, frost, etc. After a while the canker encircles the whole of the stem and the part above it dies. There is no cure for this and the affected stem should be cut back to a healthy bud.

REDDISH, FURRY GROWTH ON LEAVES (robin's pincushion). A gall caused by the gall wasp. It does not hurt the plant but if you do not like it you can cut it off.

SHOOTS OR STEMS DYING BACK. This condition is known appropriately enough as die-back. It has several causes: frost, canker, other diseases, water logging, plant food deficiencies, etc. A common cause is faulty pruning when the cut has been made too high above the bud. The stem between the cut and the bud often dies back right into the new growth coming from it. The treatment is to remedy the trouble that has caused the die-back where possible, and to cut the affected part back to a healthy bud below the dead piece.

BLINDNESS. A term used to describe a new stem where the terminal bud does not develop into a flower. Some roses are more prone to this than others, but frost damage and poor feeding are a contributory factor. Sometimes if you leave it alone, the shoot recovers itself and puts on more growth which eventually ends in a flower bud, or sometimes buds in the leaf axils grow out into flowering lateral branches. If this does not happen, cut the shoot back to half its length to a well positioned bud which will then develop into a flowering stem.

A word about hygiene

Plant diseases are infectious, just like any others. When you cut out diseased parts, you will almost certainly contaminate your secateurs. If you then use contaminated tools on healthy tissue you will probably pass the infection on to that as well. It is advisable that whenever you use secateurs on infected parts you wipe them over, especially the blades, with neat Jeyes Fluid or methylated spirit. Do not handle infected tissue and then immediately touch healthy growth without washing your hands first. Bear in mind that dirty gardening gloves can also spread infection.

Propagation

As already stated, at present the majority of roses are produced commercially by inserting a bud of the variety to be propagated into the bark of the stock. The commercial rose grower finds this method advantageous as he is able to produce many new plants from one stem off a stock plant. Also the vigour of the 'wild' stock is passed on to the variety under propagation. However, this method is not very practical as you have to obtain suitable stocks, and budding takes some skill and experience.

For the amateur, taking cuttings is perhaps the simplest method. It is very successful for ramblers, strong-growing climbers, miniatures, shrub roses and some floribundas, but less successful for hybrid teas, though in every case it is worth a try.

In September, take ripened shoots of the current year's growth about 9 in. (225 mm) long and as thick as a pencil and trim them above and below a bud at each end. Remove all the leaves except the top two, and all thorns below the second leaf from the top. Dip the base of the cutting into hormone rooting powder, then dig a 6 in. (150 mm) trench in a spare piece of good ground. Place cuttings in this, 6 in. (150 mm) deep and about 6 in. (150 mm) apart. About half fill the trench with sharp sand, then backfill the remainder with the soil and firm it. Leave the cuttings where they are for 12 months, then plant them in their permanent positions in the November following. Deal with miniatures similarly, but because the cuttings should only be about 3 in. (75 mm) long, they are best inserted into a seed-sowing compost in pots and kept in a cool, light place inside over winter. They will be ready for planting out the following spring.

Seed saved from hips which have formed on HTs, floribundas, climbers and hybrid shrub roses will not come true to type, so raising plants from seed is more to satisfy one's curiosity than anything else as it will be some time before the results can be evaluated. Species roses do breed true, but take some time to reach a useful size. Miniatures grow quite well from seed sown in April in a heated greenhouse or heated propagator. Germination can be erratic but you should be able to prick some promising seedlings out in the summer. These are repotted when necessary and kept under cold glass that winter for planting out the following spring.

Some ramblers and shrub roses can be layered. Peg down long, flexible stems after making a cut (held open with a matchstick) on the underside of the part where the layering is to take place. Bury this section an inch or two (2–5 cm) in the ground and tie the loose end of the shoot to a strong cane pushed securely into the ground. Done in July and August, roots will have formed by March and the young plant can be severed from its parent and replanted.

13

TREES, SHRUBS AND CONIFERS

This group is the backbone of any garden design. Properly chosen for the particular spot, they are indispensable. In the wrong place, they are a disaster.

ADVANTAGES. There is always something to see. Even bare branches can be attractive. Most conifers, many shrubs and some trees are evergreen. A lot have very colourful or variegated foliage, often in addition to flowers or ornamental fruit. Some trees and shrubs have coloured bark.

There is usually a shrub for every position, hot, dry, cool, shady, or moist.

Correctly sited, trees and taller shrubs and conifers give height and, therefore, a different dimension, to a garden.

They require very little maintenance other than some careful shaping and pruning (not necessarily every year), and an eye kept open for the odd bug or disease.

Weeds can be kept under control with suitable herbicides.

DISADVANTAGES. You must research your plants carefully. Shrubs and conifers vary in size from a few inches to many feet, both in height and spread, but young ones straight from the nursery are all pretty much the same. It is only when they are planted out that they reveal their true selves. Nor is it any good buying one conifer or shrub at 3 feet and one at 9 inches and expecting them to stay that size, for good, or even relative in size to one another, because what you may actually have bought is a big specimen of a hebe at 3 feet which will only ever get perhaps a foot (300 mm) bigger, and a very young plant of a variety of philadelphus which will rapidly reach 10 feet (3 m).

Do not buy on impulse. Make sure you have an adequate space for whatever takes your eye as you walk round the nursery, and if you do not know what it is – find out before you buy. Nothing is easier than to spot something really eye-catching and put it on your trolley before you have thought about it properly. Once you get it home, you have no idea what to do with it, so you shove it into the first spare spot you can find. You are well on the way to an untidy, uncontrollable jungle.

It is probably wise to take a good reference book round with you. Many good garden centres have experts to ask, but they are not always there when you want them. Nurseries which put descriptions of the plants either on a board near them or preferably on the labels themselves are to be commended.

If you feel you could run into problems in this way, it might be better to get your shrubs either mail order or for collection later from one of the major nurseries producing large, comprehensive, fully descriptive catalogues which include a guide to sizes – though bear in mind that sizes quoted are usually those expected to be reached a specified number of years after planting, and trees, shrubs and conifers will almost certainly continue to get bigger thereafter.

The temptation to overcrowd young shrubs and conifers is a clear argument in favour of a scale drawing indicating the spread of the particular types you've chosen before you start.

But it is not just the fact that unsuitable and over-crowded specimens do not look right – they can be a positive danger. Large ornamental and forest trees have no place in any but the largest gardens. They obscure light, their leaves and fallen branches are a nuisance and a hazard to the infirm, but above all, their roots can damage drains and foundations, and on clay soils the great amount of water they take out of the ground during dry spells can cause subsidence.

Some large shrubs can also cause their fair share of problems, so always go for varieties suitable for small modern gardens and site taller shrubs and any ornamental trees you do feel you have space for well away from *all* buildings, not just your own. (Away from boundaries, too, if the plants you have chosen are inclined to be bushy. Better still, go for upright varieties.)

Do not expect to keep a large shrub small by cutting it back – if such is its habit, it will just grow all the stronger for being cut back, and you could lose any flowers as well.

Remember that evergreens, especially conifers, do not appreciate the lavatorial attentions of male dogs, so do not plant them where they are likely to be used as canine urinals.

Do not let all this put you off. Most gardens look better with at least a few of the right shrubs, conifers or trees, properly sited, so let us look at how you can make them work.

Using trees, shrubs and conifers in the garden

AS SPECIMENS IN PAVING, LAWNS, ETC. Well shaped, suitable shrubs and trees and most conifers are very useful for this. Trees and conifers look quite nice either singly or in correctly spaced groups. Be careful with shrubs planted this way – they can sometimes look fussy and make a lot of work mowing and trimming round.

AS HEDGES AND SCREENS. See pages 122–30.

IN TUBS AND OTHER CONTAINERS. See Chapter 25, 'The Invisible Garden', page 325.

AS WALL PLANTS (not trees and conifers). See Chapter 16, 'Climbing Plants', page 235.

IN 'SPECIALIST' BEDS AND BORDERS. Whether you fancy this is largely a personal matter. You might like large areas given over to, say, all conifers of contrasting forms, all heathers similarly contrasted, all grey or yellow foliaged shrubs, all evergreens, all rhododendrons, etc. Conifers and heathers treated this way are quite attractive, but some one-colour borders can be frankly dull. In any case, only those garden owners who have enough space to try this will be able to consider it.

IN MIXED BORDERS. See Chapter 11, page 174.

IN SHRUBBERIES. Strictly speaking, shrubberies are beds and borders containing only plants of permanent woody top-growth, and this can include trees and conifers. The inclusion of any other subjects – bulbs, hardy or half-hardy herbaceous plants, annuals, perennials, etc., technically makes such a planting a mixed border or bed.

When designing a shrubbery, remember the following points: Leave sufficient space between individual permanent plants. If, like Nature, you abhor a vacuum, you can always fill the bare ground up with something temporary.

Try to include subjects which do not all do the same thing at the same time – use flowering shrubs which come out during different months, evergreens, plants which have berries as well as flowers, leaves with good spring or autumn colour, shrubs with variegated foliage, or coloured bark, etc.

Arrange your shrubs so that they contrast and complement each other – different coloured leaves, different foliage or habits, a good balance of evergreens to deciduous shrubs, and so on. As a general rule, shrubberies should be designed with the taller plants towards the back (or middle, in an island shrubbery), the shortest at the front, but providing you do not obscure the ones behind, you can bring a few taller subjects nearer the front to break up the rather regimented effect. There should be a reasonable difference in height between the taller shrubs and the ones in front in every case so you can see the maximum of each individual. Do not plant the more tender sorts where they can be damaged by cold winds – at the front, or, more commonly, the back. Sometimes conifers can 'brown off' considerably during periods of frosty wind, so ones for exposed places should be chosen with care. Position conifers so that as much as possible of each one can be seen.

Ornamental trees are used in a shrubbery, apart from other effects of foliage, form, flower or bark, to give additional height. Do not choose ones that will eventually make a very big canopy, and remember that the head of the tree will get bigger in time, so plant shrubs nearby which are suitable for growing under trees.

If you have only a limited space, choose shrubs that do as

much as possible – for example, if they only have a short flowering period, don't include them if the out-of-flower habit is dull or untidy unless they have, say, berries, good autumn foliage, or coloured bark.

Do some research first on the conditions preferred by the shrubs you have in mind. Whereas most favourites will tolerate a range of soil conditions, there are many which will not thrive in a limey soil – rhododendrons, azaleas, pieris, for example. Others, like cornus (dogwood), prefer the ground to be moist but most conifers will not put up with a constantly soggy position. Of course, you can try to alter conditions in the locality of the shrub if you simply *must* have that particular thing, but in the main it is best to choose varieties suitable for what is already there, and create whole areas elsewhere in the garden to provide special conditions of some kind if you must go against nature.

Where to obtain trees, shrubs and conifers

NURSERIES AND GARDEN CENTRES, EITHER BY COLLECTION OR MAIL ORDER. Some nurseries and garden centres will deliver bulky items and large orders, either free or for a small fee.

A small selection is sometimes offered by *other garden shops* and even greengrocers. You could pick up a few basic shrubs here but you are rarely likely to find anything very special.

MAIL-ORDER CATALOGUES. Those offered in the gardening section of home shopping catalogues are usually good, if rather expensive, but the choice is very limited. One or two mail-order-only firms produce very glossy catalogues which belie the poor size and quality of the stock you eventually receive. If in doubt try to buy from personal recommendation.

MULTIPLE STORES AND SUPERMARKETS, PREPACKED. The warning given in Chapter 12 (Roses), page 189, applies equally well here.

MARKET STALLS. Often held by reputable nurseries who want to increase their exposure to the general public. These are reliable, and give a fair selection to choose from. Unfortunately, during periods of recession, some uninformed people obtain market stalls to sell plants. Their stock, and especially their information, may be of dubious quality.

WELL-MEANING FRIENDS. Many keen amateur gardeners love to propagate their plants and it gives them great pleasure to offer rooted cuttings to friends. Never look a gift horse in the mouth, but do make sure it is what you really want before you plant it.

SEED. Some large seed companies list seed of some trees, conifers and shrubs that germinate easily and come reasonably true. It is quite an interesting exercise, but the results are not usually very ornamental and it will be some time before they are big enough to plant out permanently. Also, many trees will probably end up far too big for most gardens.

What to look for when buying trees, shrubs and conifers

The stems – and leaves, if you can see them – should be healthy, and the whole head should be even and well shaped. In the case of evergreens, especially conifers, there should be no brown patches on the outside; though the oldest inner foliage eventually dies and drops off, there is nothing wrong with the plant.

Do not automatically buy the biggest – get the bushiest and one that looks happy.

Bare-root shrubs and trees should have healthy, reasonably undamaged roots and shoots and should not be dried out. Most shrubs are now sold containerized as a matter of course. Many young trees as well are available grown this way for out-of-season planting. In general, conifers do not move well and should be purchased container grown if possible.

Container-grown shrubs should not look as though they have been in the same pot too long. Signs of this are hard, dry compost on the surface, moss and weeds growing in the pot (this is also a sign of neglect, and if a lot of plants look like this in the nursery or wherever, go elsewhere), arrested growth, and roots which have grown out of the bottom of the container into the soil or sand underneath. Plants like this will not re-establish well in their permanent positions. Other indications of neglect are obvious signs of pests and diseases, and sick, dying and dead stock not removed from the display beds.

Root-balled plants are ones which have been grown in the open ground, but lifted with a good ball of soil or packed round with peat held in place with hessian or netting, so the roots do not dry out. They are more likely to experience problems re-establishing themselves than plants grown all their life in a series of containers, but much less likely to suffer a severe check than bare-root stock.

Planting trees, shrubs and conifers

As with all plants, you can plant bare-root stock during the dormant winter period, weather permitting, and containerized plants all the year round, again providing the weather is suitable – do not plant during conditions of water-logging, frost or drought.

The same method is used as for any other garden plant (see pages 177–8 and 194–6) – well dug and prepared soil, plenty of rotted organic matter, and planting holes large enough to take the root or root ball without trouble. If you are planting in the spring and summer, you can use growmore or other quick-acting fertilizer as a top-dressing, bone-meal being more suitable for autumn and early winter. Always make sure that the new soil line is at the same height as the old one on the stems or trunks in the case of bare-root and root-balled stock. If it has been grown in pots or other containers, the tree, shrub or conifer should be planted no deeper than for the soil just to cover the compost round the roots.

Always plant trees, shrubs and conifers firmly, and if there is any chance of the wind rocking the plant before it is established, support it with a strong cane or canes, or a stake, otherwise it will probably die. All young trees, unless they are very small, need a strong stake (about 2 × 2 in., 50 mm sq.) preferably of hardwood, but treated softwood (not with creosote) will do. This should be long enough to support the head of the tree. Knock it well down into the prepared hole first, then put the tree against it and spread the roots out around it, before you backfill the hole. Secure the tree to the stake with one or more proprietary tree ties, making sure that no part of the trunk or any branches are rubbing against the stake before anchoring it finally. Mulch the tidied up, newly planted shrubbery to conserve moisture.

If you cannot plant newly arrived stock straight away, it should be dealt with in the same way as for roses, see page 197.

WHAT ABOUT THE CONTAINER? One of the aspects of planting new stock which seems to worry inexperienced gardeners more than anything else is – what do you do about the container or other root wrapping that bought plants frequently come in these days?

Polythene containers, plastic solid or open pots and plastic netting will *not* rot and must *always* be removed. Some nurseries use an automatic root-baller which encloses the bare roots in peat or compost held in place with a kind of elastic net. You will often find that the roots inside are bunched and constricted, so this also should be cut off and the roots properly spread out.

Pots made of treated cardboard, peat or other consolidated organic materials will eventually rot, if they are well soaked before planting. However, it is sometimes difficult for the novice to identify these, so, if in doubt, unless there are actual signs of the roots growing through the sides of the pot, the container should be removed.

Hessian sacking was once used a lot for root-balling but has now largely been superseded by non-rotting, man-made materials. If you are sure it is real hessian, the whole rootball can be wetted and planted intact, but if you are not certain, the best thing is to place the plant in the hole in its final position, then loosen the sacking from the stem with a sharp knife. It will fall away, but the ball should remain intact long enough for you to fill up the hole without disturbing the roots.

After-care of new plants

Give all new trees, shrubs and conifers plenty of water for the first season after planting, especially if containerized stock has been used during the summer months. In addition, evergreens, including conifers, lose a lot of moisture through transpiration and must be syringed all over in hot weather, sometimes several times a day. New shrubs in general require little pruning except for the removal of damaged branches and some preliminary shaping. Control weeds by hoeing or hand weeding.

Looking after established trees, shrubs and conifers

Ornamental trees will take some years to reach the size at which they can support themselves. Until then they should always be adequately staked. You must check the stake regularly for rotting and replace it immediately if necessary. At the same time, make sure no parts of the tree have started to rub on it. If you do see this happening, wrap the branch where it touches with hessian or old nylon tights. Also check the ties, and loosen them if they are becoming rather tight. They should not be allowed to cut into the bark at any time.

Once trees, shrubs and conifers have become established for more than a year, you can eliminate weeding to a large extent by using a suitable weedkiller such as Casoron G (dichlobenil). Applied in spring, it should remain active, if the surface of the soil is undisturbed, for up to twelve months. Do make sure you follow the instructions, especially for any shrubs you should not use it near. If you suspect any plants are growing less well, you can refrain from using weedkiller for a year or two. You will get fewer weeds anyway if you mulch regularly. You cannot use total weedkillers if you intend to interplant with bulbs, annuals or herbaceous perennials.

Once they have been established for a few years, most trees, shrubs, etc. will not require watering in the same way as annuals, herbaceous perennials and the like, as they have wide-spreading roots capable of seeking out moisture in the soil.

An annual top-dressing of a slow-release, balanced fertilizer in spring is beneficial.

Pruning

If you have to prune, do not 'snip and clip' indiscriminately.

Most ornamental trees require no pruning other than the removal of unwanted branches growing on a bare trunk, especially where the tree has been top-grafted, and the taking out of badly placed and rubbing branches and dead and diseased wood. These should be removed completely, leaving no snags or stumps.

Conifers not used for hedging purposes need not be pruned except to remove pieces which have grown out of shape, but sometimes an all-over trim will improve the colour and form. You should choose subjects which will only grow to the size you want them to, not try to cut them to fit the hole!

The majority of shrubs, unlike roses, do not deteriorate greatly without regular pruning, although if they are never touched they will eventually get into a bit of a tangle, and end up woody and leggy. (Do not forget to use clean, sharp secateurs and make a sloping cut just above a bud or eye.)

For pruning purposes shrubs can be divided into 4 categories:

1. *Evergreens.* No pruning is necessary except light shaping if required, and the removal of dead and diseased wood, preferably in late spring or August. Some can be cut hard back in spring if necessary (but not conifers).

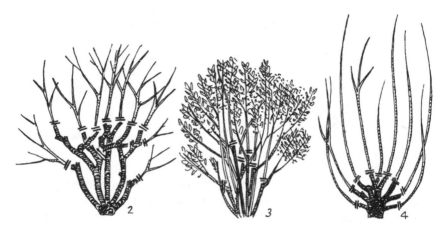

2. *Shrubs flowering on old wood produced the previous season.* These are mainly spring-flowering shrubs. Remove all old flowered wood after flowering, and badly placed branches, also dead and diseased growths.

3. *Shrubs flowering on old and new wood.* These are the early summer-flowering ones. After flowering, remove completely some old flowered branches and shorten back some of the younger stems to fresh growths on the main branches. Thin out crowded growth and remove weak, dead and diseased stems.

4. *Shrubs flowering on the current season's wood.* These are mainly the late summer- and autumn-flowering ones. Cut back to within two or three buds of the base or of the main branch framework in early spring.

This method of pruning is also used for shrubs grown mainly for their coloured stems in winter, and also for some quick-growing deciduous ones planted for the colour of their young foliage.

Note. Research has proved that treating the cut surfaces with a pruning paint is unnecessary.

Problems

Trees, shrubs and conifers get pests and a few diseases, just like any other plants, but if they are growing healthily they are not bothered by them very much.

Holes in leaves or edges notched – leaf cutter bees, vine or leaf weevils, leaf or chafer beetles, caterpillars. Spray with insecticide as recommended for annuals on page 170.

Shot hole disease – appears as brown spots which turn into holes. Prunus family is particularly susceptible. It is a deficiency disease and regular feeding with a balanced fertilizer containing trace elements should help.

Bronzing of leaves, with silky webbing – mites. Spray regularly with cold water.

Distorted shoots – usually aphids. Controlled by an insecticide, as recommended on pages 170–1.

Yellowing leaves – chlorosis. Usually found on plants which do not like an alkaline soil, but can be caused by waterlogging or induced by weedkillers. Immediate action is to treat the affected plant with sequestrenes (chelated iron, magnesium and manganese), but the long-term remedy may have to be to give the plant more favourable surroundings.

Tunnels or blisters in leaves – leaf miner – see pages 170–1.

Galls – swellings on leaves or stems which can be caused by insects or fungus. They are not harmful but are best removed.

Patches of scale on branches – caused by infestation by one or other of a large group of scale insects. Manual removal is best, but if impracticable, spray with malathion in May.

Grey powder or mould on leaves, stems or flowers – powdery mildew, see page 172.

Orange, yellow or brown swellings on leaves – rust, see page 172.

Orange pustules on dead and live branches. Coral spot, which breeds on dead wood and infects live tissue through a wound. Remove all affected parts and burn. Do not leave dead timber lying about.

White 'wool' on leaves and branches – woolly aphids or adelgids. Spray in spring at fortnightly intervals with malathion, other suitable insecticide, or wash deciduous shrubs with tar oil in winter.

Cracked bark – split bark or canker. See remedy in Chapter 22 (Fruit), page 301.

Damaged or tunnelled wood under the bark – bark beetles or goat moth caterpillars. Healthy trees and shrubs are rarely affected. Remove and burn affected branches, or entire subject if badly infested.

All-green branches on variegated shrubs and trees. If the whole plant is turning green it is a sign that it needs better light and therefore is unsuitable for the position it is in. If just one or two branches are involved, it is attempting to revert to the unvariegated parent form. These strongly growing branches should be cut right out as soon as possible to avoid spoiling the shape of the plant. Root stock suckers are another cause and should be removed if they occur.

Propagation

LAYERING. See method for roses on page 204.

HARDWOOD CUTTINGS. Use pieces of ripened stem of the current year's growth generally varying from 6 to 12 in. (150–300 mm), trimmed above and below a node. Insert into a well drained or sandy soil in autumn, and bury except for about 1 to 2 in. (25–50 mm) sticking out at the top. Protect evergreen cuttings and conifers in a cold frame over winter. These root best if taken with a 'heel' (where it is attached to the main branch).

SOFTWOOD CUTTINGS. These are the tips of the new growths, taken from April to July before they begin to ripen. Cut off just below a node and take off the bottom leaves, then dip the stems in rooting powder and insert into a good cutting compost. Shade the cuttings and cut down transpiration as described for taking cuttings of herbs (see page 246).

SEMI-HARDWOOD CUTTINGS. Many common deciduous shrubs strike well if the semi-ripened shoots are inserted into compost in a similar manner in July and August.

SEED, but see the remarks on page 204.

BUDDING AND GRAFTING. This is the way many trees and shrubs, and some conifers, are propagated commercially. This method serves three purposes – to produce a great many new plants from one stock plant, to slow down the growth of certain strong-growing species, or to improve the root-system of shy-rooting subjects. You have really got to know what you are doing, both in relation to the choice of stock and the actual method, and it is perhaps best left to the professional or experienced enthusiast.

A selection of trees, shrubs and conifers to suit every garden

Five trees for a garden of reasonable size, to be placed at least 30 feet (9 m) from a building

> *Acer pseudoplatanus 'Nizetti'*. Variegated sycamore. Leaves variegated golden, white, pink and purple.
>
> *Betula alba 'Youngii'*. Young's weeping birch. Silver bark, weeping habit, good autumn colour.
>
> *Crataegus prunifolia*. A type of hawthorn. Shiny dark green leaves which turn orange and scarlet in autumn. White flowers, big red berries.
>
> *Malus 'Royalty'*. Purple-leaved form of crab apple, large pink flowers in spring and wine-red fruits.
>
> *Prunus 'Pink Perfection'* flowering cherry. Double, rosy pink flowers.

Five trees for smaller gardens, to be planted at least 15 feet (4.5 m) from a building

> *Acer pseudoplatanus 'Brilliantissimum'*. Shrimp-pink young leaves.
>
> *Cotoneaster hybridus 'Pendulus'*. Weeping cotoneaster. White flowers, red berries, evergeen.
>
> *Gleditsia triacanthos 'Elegantissima'*. Fern-like, dainty leaves.
>
> *Sorbus scopulina*. Small, compact form of mountain ash. Big red berries in autumn.
>
> *Malus sargentii*. Small, white-scented flowers and currant-like fruit.

Note. Trees are usually sold as standards, short- or half-standards or feathered, and sometimes as quarter-standards. Full standards have 5 to 6 ft (1.5–1.75 m) of clear trunk before the branches start, half- or short-standards around 4 ft (1.25 m) of trunk and quarter-standards about 2 or 2½ ft (600-900 mm). Feathered trees are young ones with branches still growing right down to the base. It is advisable to leave your standard or short standard tree in the form in which it was purchased, partly because to allow young branches to grow out down the trunk would make it look unsightly and spoil the shape, and partly because many have been top-grafted, so the new branches would be those of the stock, and not the named variety. On the other hand, you can turn a feathered tree into a standard if you wish by removing the lower branches, but some, e.g. silver birch and many bottom-grafted weeping or fastigiate (upright) trees, look better with their 'feathers' left on, at least until they reach semi-maturity.

Five taller shrubs

Amelanchier lamarckii. Snowy mespilus. Up to 18 ft (5.5 m). Pink young leaves, starry white flowers in spring. Red berries turning black. Brilliant autumn colour.

Arbutus unedo. Strawberry tree. Up to 10 ft (3 m), more in warm districts. Evergreen. Ivory flowers come out October/November at the same time as ripening orange-red, strawberry-like fruits of previous season.

Cornus mas. Cornelian cherry. 12 ft (3.5 m), or more. Masses of tiny yellow flowers in February. Good autumn colour.

Magnolia soulangiana. 12 ft (3.5 m), or more. Tulip-shaped flowers, purple tinged outside, white inside, appear before the leaves in spring.

Stranvaesia davidiana. 15 ft (4.5 m), or more. Evergreen leaves brightly tinted red in spring and autumn. White flowers followed by red berries.

Five for the middle

Berberis thunbergii 'Rose Glow'. 4 ft (1.25 m). Purple leaves variegated pink, yellow flowers.

Elaeagnus 'Limelight'. 6 ft (1.8 m). Grey-green leaves variegated yellow and lime green. Evergreen.

Hydrangea villosa. 6 ft (1.8 m). Grey-green leaves, large blue and lavender flowers in late summer.

Philadelphus coronarius 'Aureus'. 5 ft (1.5 m). Golden mock orange. Yellow leaves, scented semi-double white flowers in May/June.

Viburnum 'Park Farm Hybrid'. 5–6 ft (1.5–1.8 m). Evergreen. Pink buds opening to pure white clusters of fragrant flowers in April. Good autumn colour.

Euonymus fortunei 'Variegata'. 15 in. (375 mm). Evergreen green/cream variegated leaves.

Hebe armstrongii. 30 in. (750 mm). Golden, cord-like evergreen foliage and white starry flowers in spring.

Phlomis fruticosa. Jerusalem sage. 36 in. (900 mm). Grey evergreen leaves. Yellow flowers.

Potentilla 'Goldstar'. 3 ft 6 in. (1 m). Large golden yellow 'buttercup' flowers, grey-green leaves.

Weigela florida 'Foliis Purpuriis'. 4 ft (1.25 m). Purple leaves, rose-pink flowers, early summer.

Five conifers for height

Chamaecyparis lawsoniana 'Pembury Blue'. 12 ft (3.5 m). Silver-blue foliage.

Cryptomenia japonica 'Elegans'. 10 ft (3 m). Japanese cedar, best on good, lime-free soil, sheltered from cold winds. Bronzy-green feathery foliage in summer, turning copper in winter.

Picea abies 'Aurea'. 10 ft (3 m). Golden form of spruce. Bright gold new growth turning green. Very spectacular.

Pinus strobus 'Pyramidalis'. 8–10 ft (2.5–3 m). White pine. Light blue needles and large pendulous cones.

Taxus baccata 'Fastigiata Aurea'. 6–8 ft (1.8–2.5 m). Golden upright form of yew.

Five conifers that will not get out of hand

Chamaecyparis lawsoniana 'Golden Pot'. Soft, bright golden yellow foliage. Probable height after 10 years, 36 in. (900 mm).

Juniperus communis 'Compressa'. Column shaped, blue-green foliage, compact. Height after 10 years, about 15 in. (375 mm).

Picea pungens 'Globosa'. Slow-growing, globular, silver-blue form of spruce. Height after 10 years, about 24 in. (600 mm).

Pinus sylvestris 'Beuvronensis'. Dwarf form of Scots pine. Dark, grey-green foliage. Height after 10 years, up to 30 in. (750 mm), 36 in. (900 mm) spread.

Thuya plicata 'Stoneham Gold'. Deep golden yellow. Height after 10 years, up to 36 in. (900 mm).

14

ALPINES AND ROCK GARDENS

Nearly every inexperienced gardener seems to hanker after a rockery. One wonders why, because the only really decent ones you ever see belong either to botanic gardens or to the real alpine enthusiast.

More often you see a hideous mound of poor soil, the surface punctuated at intervals with small, badly chosen pieces of stone, rather in the manner of almonds on a Dundee cake, where a battle ranges between every pernicious weed in creation and those invasive horrors euphemistically known as 'easily grown rock-plants' – *Sedum acre* (stonecrop), *Cerastium tormentosum* (snow-in-summer) and *Sedum spurium*.

Probably you were first tempted by the sight of attractive spring displays of pink or mauve aubrieta, yellow alyssum, blue *Campanula carpatica*, pink, white and red mossy saxifrages and white iberis which can look so effective planted together and hanging over a wall, but apart from a later half-hearted flush, the party's over by mid-summer and the whole thing looks a bit dull.

Rockeries are about the only feature in the garden today that have not been made easier to maintain by modern science. They require regular weeding, because once weeds get amongst the rock-plants and under the stones they are almost impossible to get out, except by spot treatment with glyphosate or alloxydim sodium for weed grasses – a chore which is as fiddly as the weeding in the first place, and which can lead to accidents if you are careless. If you can't spare the time to look after it properly, don't have a rock garden.

Of course, rockeries are not the only places you can grow alpines, and in this category of plants I am including many dwarf subjects appropriate for this kind of situation, not only true alpines (i.e. those originating in mountainous areas). Suitable varieties can also be used to effect (and generally speaking, are easier to maintain) in sinks, troughs, pots and windowboxes; in raised beds; as edging plants at the front of borders; to hang down over walls; in dry stone and peat walls; in scree gardens; in between paving stones and other surfaces; as specimens in specially manufactured 'rock pots', which resemble large rocks with planting holes in them; in cold greenouses ('alpine houses').

However, if you are still determined to grow your rock-plants in a rockery, here are a few rules.

DO NOT site the rockery under a tree – alpines dislike dripping branches – or in the wind tunnel between two buildings.

DO NOT make the rockery too tall. For every foot of height, the base should be 4–5 feet wide.

DO make it as big as possible.

ALWAYS use light, free-draining soil. If yours is not naturally suitable, you will have to improve it, with organic material and sharp sand.

BE SURE to remove all perennial roots before you start. If you do not, you will probably have to dismantle the rockery before long and start again.

DO NOT leave holes and gaps where slugs and snails can make a home.

DO obtain professional advice when choosing your rock-plants. As a general rule, most alpines like an open, well drained, slightly alkaline, reasonably sunny site, but there are others which prefer cool, shady and/or moist conditions, and acid soils, or to be planted in a gravelly scree or in a 'fissure'.

They can all be used to effect in different parts of the rockery. For example, it is damper at the base of the rockery than at the top. If you have a south-facing, free-standing rock-garden, you will also have a cooler, shadier north face. If you want to grow lime-hating plants, you can construct one terrace (not where alkaline water can seep into it from above, though) with an ericaceous mix of soil-based compost. However, there are quite a few alpines which, although they can stand any amount of dry cold, simply cannot tolerate the cold, wet conditions of the British winter and should only be grown indoors in an unheated alpine house.

DO NOT choose plants which are too rampant. If you have a big area to fill, plant, say, three of a slow-growing sort rather than something which covers the area quickly and gets out of hand.

DO NOT plant in winter, if it can be avoided. Although in theory you can construct and plant up a rock garden at any time of the year, spring and autumn are best.

DO plant your alpines and other dwarf subjects in the rockery with the same care that you would use elsewhere in the garden (see appropriate sections).

STONES should blend in with local building materials if possible. They should be well shaped, with reasonably flat surfaces, though not flat in themselves. They should be big enough to look obvious, though not so big you cannot handle them. They should be built into the rockery as you go on, and at least a half and preferably two-thirds should be buried to give stability. The soil at the back must be well rammed and the stone should be able to bear your weight without rocking. The strata of the stones, where obvious, should run horizontally.

You may find it easier to construct your rockery as a series of terraces, with a layer of stones supporting one flat terrace from

which is built up the next, and so on. Crevice plants can be inserted between the stones as you progress and other alpines, miniature roses, dwarf shrubs, conifers and small bulbs can be planted on the terraces or allowed to hang down the face of the wall of supporting stones. The soil between the plants on the terraces can be covered with chippings or pea gravel – this helps prevent the plants from rotting off in wet weather – and the odd 'outcrop' of stones can break up the flatness if you like, providing it looks natural.

Alpines are obtainable

From specialist growers, either for collection or by mail order. They are almost invariably grown in small pots.

From alpine societies.

As seed from certain companies, usually those specializing in alpines, or alpine societies.

A reasonable selection is usually available from garden centres and general nurseries, but beware – some that are offered as 'alpines' should not be within a hundred miles of a decent rockery.

Be cautious of gifts from well intentioned friends, unless the giver is an experienced rock-gardener or unless you have some idea of what or what not to plant.

After-care of alpines and rockeries

Correctly chosen rock-plants are very little trouble, and maintenance is usually confined to weeding and making sure the more vigorous ones do not smother the slower plants. Conditions would have to be very dry before you needed to water, unless you have particularly chosen moisture and shade lovers, but these should have been planted in a suitable position in the first place. Stronger growing trailing and carpeting plants (aubrieta, etc.) require cutting back regularly after flowering if they are not to get straggly.

Because most true alpines occur naturally in soil that does not contain large quantities of nutrients, they do not require much feeding – certainly no nitrogen, but you can give them an occasional top dressing of a high-potash fertilizer.

Pests and diseases

Because most alpines are technically herbaceous perennials, they are prone to the same problems. The most common troubles are listed on pages 168–72 (as for annuals and bedding plants) and page 182 (for herbaceous perennials).

In addition, you may have some dwarf shrubs and conifers, so see pages 215–16, miniature roses (pages 201–2) and small bulbs (pages 233–4).

Pay particular attention to soil-borne pests and if you find root damage you should water regularly with an insecticide. Slugs and snails are also a serious problem and should be trapped regularly.

If you find certain plants rotting off in damp weather, this could be a sign of poor drainage so when you replant, you should incorporate more sand into the soil round the new alpines and surround the plant with chippings. However, if the dead plant is one with very soft or woolly leaves, it is probably unsuitable for the amount of rainfall in your area.

Propagation

BY DIVISION. Most clump-forming alpines will divide into several pieces, in late summer or early autumn for preference, but you can try spring as well.

BY CUTTINGS. Insert inch-long (25 mm) shoots with their lower leaves removed into a sandy compost in August and early September. Use the same method for woody alpines, but take the cuttings with a 'heel' (i.e. by pulling it gently off the main stem, then trimming off all long or ragged strips of bark). These can be overwintered in a cold frame, or taken in wooden boxes and covered with glass during the worst of the weather.

ROOT CUTTINGS. A few alpines have fleshy roots and can be propagated by root cuttings as described for herbaceous perennials on pages 181–2.

SEED. Many alpines can easily be raised from seed, but hybrids will not come true to type. Clay pots and pans are best but are expensive; plastic ones can be used, though achieving and retaining the right amount of moisture in the compost is more difficult. Place some drainage material (sharp crocks or stones) at the bottom and top up with a suitable compost, such as three parts John Innes seed compost and one of coarse sand. Sow seed in March and April and prick out the plants when large enough to handle.

Some ideas for a new rockery

FOR HANGING OVER A WALL. *Alyssum, arabis, aubrieta,* most *campanulas,* many *geranium* species, *gypsophila, helianthemum, iberis, Lithospermum 'Heavenly Blue', penstemon, alpine phlox, saponaria, alpine veronicas.*

FOR PAVING. *Acaena, antennaria, arenaria, prostrate thymes.*

WALL CREVICES. Many of the above, and also *saxifraga* ('silver' or encrusted types), and *sempervivum* (house leeks).

FOR GROUND COVER. Many of the plants suitable for hanging over a wall make good ground cover, and also *ajuga* varieties, *armeria* (thrift), *Sedum 'Weihenstephaner Gold',* and *Sedum spurium* varieties. *Note.* If you wish to plant any of these as single specimens in the rock garden itself, they will need careful siting or they will swamp choice varieties.

SHADE TOLERANT PLANTS (not heavy shade). *Acaena, ajuga, campanula, dodecatheon,* some *gentians, gypsophila, iberis, Lithospermum 'Heavenly Blue', Nierembergia rivularis, alpine phlox,* some *primulas, violas.*

FOR HOT, DRY, SUNNY SITES. *Acaena, alyssum, arabis, aubrieta, crepis, dianthus, erinus, gypsophila, helianthemum, hypericum, iberis, penstemon, sedum, sempervivum, veronica.*

FOR SINKS AND TROUGHS. *Androsace, dwarf campanulas, dwarf dianthus, draba, erinus, saxifraga* (dwarf slow-growing ones), *sedum spathulifolium, sempervivum.*

MINIATURE ROSES (see pages 191–2).

SOME DWARF SHRUBS. *Berberis 'Bagatelle'* (purple leaves), *Cytisus decumbens* (prostrate broom), *Hebe 'James Stirling'* (golden cord-like leaves), *Hebe pagei* (grey, white flowers), *Potentilla mandschurica* (12 in. (300 mm), white flowers grey foliage).

FIVE MINIATURE CONIFERS. *Chamaecyparis obtusa 'Nana Lutea'* (golden), *Cryptomeria japonica 'Vilmoriniana'* (green, globular), *Picea abies 'Gregoriana'* (miniature spruce), *Pinus mugo 'Humpy'* (dwarf pine), *Thuja plicata 'Rogersii'* (golden bronze and green).

SUGGESTED BULBS. *Crocuses, miniature daffodils* and *narcissi, 'species' tulips,* hardy *cyclamen, scillas, dwarf iris, Anemone blanda, puschkinia, allium, brodiaea, dwarf fritillaries.*

225

15

BULBS

There is probably not a home in Britain that cannot contain a few bulbs (I am using the term loosely to include corms and tubers as well). Even if you have no garden at all you can force them in pots for indoor decoration. Given a reasonable amount of care, these little powerpacks of colour will reward you handsomely.

USES. To fill whole beds, borders and other areas for spring display.
In groups and clumps in between other plants.
Spring bulbs (excluding tulips) can be planted under trees to provide early colour.
In tubs, pots, window boxes and other containers for outdoor (or, in some cases, indoor) decoration.
In rows in the vegetable garden for cutting.
Smaller growing bulbs may be planted in the rockery.
To naturalize in informal borders and rough grass areas (spring bulbs only).

ADVANTAGES. They are easy to grow and most of them require little attention once correctly planted.

They quickly increase in numbers to provide additional stock if required.

They can be planted between other permanent subjects without fear of overcrowding as their foliage dies down for a large part of the year.

They are widely obtainable from a variety of sources.

DISADVANTAGES. The foliage should be left on the plant to die down after the flower has faded (or for at least 6 weeks in the case of strong growing ones such as daffodils), to build up food reserves in the bulb for the following year. As it yellows it looks increasingly untidy.

Naturalized in grass, bulbs prevent the grass from being mown until their leaves can be trimmed off.

Many summer-flowering bulbs are not entirely hardy in this country and have to be lifted in the autumn.

Large-flowered hybrid tulips deteriorate unless regularly lifted.

They will not tolerate very damp or waterlogged conditions.

Bulbs are obtainable from

> *Mail order bulb specialists.* Many bulbs available in Britain are bought in from abroad, mainly from Holland.
>
> *Garden centres and retail nurseries.* Sometimes a more limited choice.
>
> *Seed companies.* Some offer bulbs, often summer-flowering ones, as a sideline.
>
> *Market stalls.* Usually fairly good quality. Choice generally restricted to the more popular varieties.
>
> *Home shopping catalogues.* Reliable, if rather poor choice.
>
> *Supermarkets, chain stores, DIY superstores and general stores.* Often prepackaged, so check packs for deterioration. Choice limited.
>
> *Friends.* This is a fairly safe way of getting free garden stock and an especially good way of obtaining snowdrops, which are about the only common bulbs which re-establish better if planted 'in the green' (i.e. straight after flowering while the leaves are still green). Daffodils are very susceptible to virus disease, so if someone promises you daffodil bulbs in the autumn, check the leaves if you can the previous spring. If there are signs of yellow or red streaking, distortion or weak growth, give them a miss.

A LIST OF COMMON BULBS, CORMS AND TUBERS

Name	Planting Time	Depth in. (mm)	Distance Apart in. (mm)	Flowering	Colour	Remarks
Allium	Sept/Oct	2–6 (50–150)	3–6 (75–150)	May/July	Several	Many species available, depth and planting distances vary accordingly.
Anemone St Brigid	Oct/March	2 (50)	4–5 (100–125)	Variable	Several	Good for cutting, needs sun.
Anemone blanda	Oct	2 (50)	4–5 (100–125)	March/April	Mauve/blue/pink/white	Good for rockeries.
Begonia	April	1 (25)	6 (150)	All summer	Several	Start off indoors in tray or pots and plant out when frost is past.
Brodiaea (Missouri hyacinth)	Sept	3 (75)	6 (150)	June/July	Blue/pink/yellow	Sunny well-drained position, useful on rockeries.
Camassia	Oct	4 (100)	3–4 (75–100)	Long flowering period	Blue/white	Useful for naturalizing – not heavy shade.
Chianodoxa	Aug/Sept	3 (75)	3 (75)	March/April	Blue	Naturalizes well but can become invasive.
Colchicum (autumn crocus)	Aug	4 (100)	4–6 (100–150)	Sept/Oct	Usually mauve	Flowers appear before leaves.
Spring crocus	Sept/Nov	2 (50)	3–4 (75–100)	Feb/April	White/blue/yellow/cream/striped	Good for naturalizing, many varieties seed well.
Autumn crocus	July	2 (50)	3–4 (75–100)	Sept/Oct	Blue/white/yellow	Good for rock-garden planting.
Cyclamen hederaefolium (neapolitanum)	March	Just under surface	4 (100)	July/Nov	White/rose	Seeds freely, good for rockeries.
Cyclamen coum	June	Just under surface	4 (100)	Feb/April	White/rose	Naturalizes well.
Endymion (bluebell)	Aug/Sept	6 (150)	4 (100)	May/June	Blue/white/pink	Useful bulb for wild gardens and dappled shade.
Dahlia	May	8 (200)	18–24 (450–600)	July to frosts	Several	Full sun necessary, not fully hardy.
Eranthis (aconite)	Aug/Sept	2 (50)	3 (75)	Jan/March	Yellow	Also useful in wild garden. Difficult to establish then becomes invasive.
Erythronium (dog's tooth violet)	Aug/Sept	4 (100)	3–4 (100–175)	Mar/April	White/yellow/pink	Acid, leafy moist soil and some shade needed.

Name	Plant time	Depth cm (mm)	Distance apart cm (mm)	Flowering time	Colour	Notes
Fritillaria Imperialis (Crown Imperial)	July/Sept	6 (150)	8–10 (200–250)	April/May	Orange/yellow	Full sun best
Fritillaria Meleagris (snake's head)	Aug/Sept	6 (150)	8–10 (200–250)	April/May	White/purple/spotted	Some shade and damp soil.
Galanthus (snowdrop)	March	3 (75)	3 (75)	Jan/March	White	Useful early spring flower.
Galtonia (cape hyacinth)	Nov	5–6 (125–150)	8–9 (200–225)	July/Aug	White	Good for mixed borders.
Gladiolus	April/May	4–5 (100–125)	8–12 (200–300)	July/Sept	Many	Not really hardy. Good cut flower.
Hyacinth	Sept/Oct	4–5 (100–125)	4–6 (100–150)	April/May	Several	Strongly scented useful for tubs and indoor planting.
Iris – Dutch and English	Sept/Oct	5 (125)	4–6 (100–150)	May/June	White/blue/yellow	Good for cutting.
Iris reticulata	Sept/Oct	4 (100)	3 (75)	Feb/March	Blue	Useful rock garden shrub.
Ixia (African corn lily)	Sept/Oct	2 (50)	3 (75)	June/July	Many	Warm, well-drained position essential, not entirely hardy.
Leucojum (snowflake)	Aug/Sept	3–4 (75–100)	4–6 (100–150)	Feb/March	White	Sunny position.
Lilies	Sept or March	6 (150)	6–10 (150–250)	June/Sept	Several	Good acid soil with some leaf mould.
Muscari (grape hyacinth)	Oct	3 (75)	3 (75)	March/April	Blue/white	Can become invasive.
Narcissus	Aug/Nov	5–6 (125–150)	6 (150)	Feb/May	Yellow/cream/white	Good all-round spring bulb.
Nerine	March	2–3 (50–75)	3–4 (75–100)	Sept/Oct	Pink	Needs warm sunny spot.
Ornithogalum	March or Sept	3–4 (75–100)	3–6 (75–150)	April/Sept	White	Some varieties not winter hard.
Scilla	Aug/Sept	3 (75)	3–4 (75–100)	April/May	Blue	Useful for shade, spreads quickly.
Sparaxis	Sept	2–3 (50–75)	3 (75)	April/May	Many	Not really hardy. Warm sunny position needed.
Tulip	Nov	4–5 (100–125)	6–8 (150–200)	March/May	Many	Species tulips can be naturalized. Hybrids should be lifted annually.

Note: Planting depths are from *top* of bulb

Choosing bulbs

Healthy bulbs should be firm, not at all soft when squeezed *gently*, have no damaged or diseased patches or mouldy parts, and wherever possible, be as large as you can get them, according to variety. Do not plant bulbs that are not in first-class condition – at best they will not do much and at worst they can introduce all kinds of problems.

Planting

Grow bulbs for formal bedding in straight rows and blocks, otherwise plant in clumps, spaced out according to type and variety.

Bulbs for naturalizing schemes can be positioned in large areas by throwing handfuls and planting them where they fall.

All bulbs like good, well prepared soil, and as much attention should be given to the site as for any other type of plant.

Make sure they are planted deep enough and at the correct time of year (see Table, pages 228–29). Autumn-planted bulbs should be given a slow, high-phosphate fertilizer (bone-meal or similar), and spring and summer planted ones the correct amount of a balanced feed.

Bulbs for indoor cultivation in winter are planted in bowls of bulb fibre from August onwards and placed in a cool dark place until the flower buds are showing in the neck of the bulb. The compost is kept damp but not soggy. The pots are then gradually accustomed to conditions of warmth and light.

At flowering time

Support tall varieties (gladioli, dahlias, lilies, etc.) as they grow, either by tying the individual flower spikes to canes, or in the case of a bushy habit, with herbaceous plant supports (see page 179).

Even bulbs can suffer from drought, though this is usually more applicable to summer-flowering ones. If the ground becomes very dry, give a good soaking of water, but on no account must you make the ground waterlogged.

After flowering

You will find that the leaves of many bulbs continue to grow – this is so they can make food to store until the next season in their self-contained underground larder (the bulb itself). A regular soluble feed helps the leaves in their food-making task; whenever possible, you should leave them undisturbed to die off naturally.

Dead-head regularly unless you want to save the seed.

If you have to lift spring-flowering bulbs because you need the room for something else, they should be heeled in to die down in an empty part of the garden. They die down more quickly because their roots have been disturbed, so this is not an ideal method, and the bulbs may give poorer performance the following year, but they will get over it. One solution is to plant small numbers of bulbs in well drained containers and then sink the whole container in the ground. This can be removed after flowering and the leaves left to die off naturally.

Before the first frost (or, in the case of dahlias, after the first frost), summer bulbs unsuitable for naturalizing should be lifted, dried off, cleaned, tidied up and stored in a cold, dry, frost-free place until the next planting season. (Some purists might question the inclusion of dahlias in this section, as they are really half-hardy herbaceous perennials with tuberous roots, but the similarities to other bulbs are so marked that it is perfectly reasonable to include them here.)

Treat spring bulbs which have been lifted in a similar manner and store in an airy shed until the autumn.

Bulbous plants which are really corms (crocuses, gladioli, etc.) form an entirely new corm on top of the old one; you should discard the latter as it will not grow again.

Only store firm, healthy bulbs from plants which have performed well and check them over regularly in store to make sure none is deteriorating. If any are found to be rotting, you should dispose of them hygienically at once or the problem will spread. Treating with a fungicide according to instructions at storage time sometimes helps to prevent storage rots.

Bulbs which make a great many offsets, such as daffodils, can be left intact until they get too big and overcrowded, when they should be separated. Otherwise you can remove the young bulbs and grow them on somewhere until they become big enough to produce a flower.

Some corms, particularly crocuses and gladioli, make a lot of small corms around the main one. These can be detached and grown on in nursery beds until they are big enough to plant in their flowering positions.

Bulbs used for indoor decoration can be hardened off and put outside in the garden to die down. They will not be any good for indoor growing a second year and it might take a couple of years for them to get their strength back outside after the forcing, but they will eventually flower properly again.

Propagation

Most bulbs increase readily by offsets in the ground or, occasionally, on the stem (e.g., lilies). The young bulbs, corms, etc. will take a year or two to reach flowering size but this is the best and easiest way of propagation.

Some tubers can be *divided* carefully before planting, for example dahlias and begonias. Do this with a sharp knife, making sure that there is a healthy stem bud at the top of each piece of tuber, otherwise it will not grow. It is a good idea to dust the cut surfaces with a fungicide before planting. Sometimes, small pieces of a bulb can be grown on into a great many whole new ones, but this is tricky for the completely inexperienced.

CUTTINGS. Again, this method is suitable mainly for tuberous-rooted plants such as dahlias and begonias. Start the dormant tubers into growth in gentle warmth in early spring and remove the young shoots when about 2 in (50 mm) long. Root in suitable compost in a heated greenhouse or heated propagator.

SEED. Many bulbs seed quite readily and seed is best sown when ripe. The length of time taken to germinate and the time needed to reach the flowering stage varies according to the type of plant. Some spring bulbs – bluebells, aconites,

232

chianodoxas, scillas, snowdrops, etc., seed themselves but larger bulbs are best dead-headed – unless you want to sow seed out of curiosity.

Troubles

Most problems with bulbous plants concern the part underneath the ground.

Bulbs eaten

> If the bulbs have disappeared entirely, *mice* are the cause.
> *Swift moth caterpillars* remove pieces from the bulbs. These are whitish caterpillars with brown heads. Even if the bulbs are not eaten entirely, the damaged ones will probably rot. Regular hoeing disturbs the swift moths' life cycle. Attracting birds into the garden can help.
> *Bulb aphids* are small insects which collect on stored bulbs and feed under the outer scales, damaging the young growth which appears after planting and causing localized rotting. Dust with derris at storage time.

Bulbs eaten, uneaten parts rotten

> *Narcissus fly.* Bulbs are eaten in the ground by maggots about half an inch (15 mm) long, and go rotten. Watering the leaves and ground with an insecticide regularly after flowering will control this pest, as will hoeing around the foliage.
> *Eelworm* affects daffodils, tulips, hyacinths, etc. Bulbs are soft and rotten with dark rings inside. Leaves (if any) are pale with small yellow swellings. There is no cure. Do not plant bulbs, corms, tubers, etc. on infested land for at least 3 years.
> Do not plant soft bulbs. Be careful when accepting gifts.

Bulbs rotten in store or in the ground

> *Narcissus smoulder.* A storage rot, characterized by small dark fungal growths on the outer scales.
> *Basal rot* starts at the basal plate and spreads upwards through the bulb. Affects daffodil and narcissus bulbs in store.
> *Tulip fire.* Black fungal growths appear on outer scales of stored tulips; leaves and flowers of affected bulbs are streaked, with brown ends.

Dry rot occurs on crocus and gladiolus corms in store and appears as black spots which eventually merge and all the tissue goes rotten.

Hard rot also occurs on stored corms. The spots are brown and the corm shrivels.

Scab is a corm rot which starts with brown, round, shiny scabby spots.

Core rot is a wet rot occurring in the central core of corms.

The control for rots is to dip stored bulbs in a fungicide before storage and dry off, and dip again before planting. With bulbs left in after flowering, watering with a fungicide may help a little. Dispose of all rotten bulbs and corms immediately.

Rotting is made much worse in cold, waterlogged soils so this type of environment must be improved if you intend growing bulbs there.

Tuber rot occurs in stored dahlia and begonia tubers. The usual cause is insufficient cleaning and drying off. A fungicidal dip at storage time will help, but make sure the tubers are dried off thoroughly afterwards. Small rotten parts can be trimmed off to healthy tissue. Regular inspection in store is essential.

Vine weevil grubs can eat tubers which then rot. Dust with HCH, or use one of the new organic nematodal controls now available.

Other problems

Virus causes distortion, mottling and streaking of leaves and sometimes flowers. All affected bulbs should be dug up and burnt as soon as the disease is spotted, as there is no cure. Be careful of cheap bulbs and gifts.

Thrips cause mottled streaking of gladioli leaves and flowers. Spray regularly with any insecticide (malathion, derris, etc.).

Birds will peck at crocus flowers and tear them to pieces for no apparent reason and there is little you can do about it. There are proprietary bird repellents you can water on, but they are not very effective and, in any case, they wash off when it rains. Plastic humming line can be a deterrent.

16

CLIMBING PLANTS

Plants that grow better if given the support of a wall or trellis play a useful part in the landscaping of any plot, large or small, but especially in the very tiny garden where you gain extra space by growing vertically. They also help to soften harsh buildings and solid boundaries but before you completely conceal your property under a jungle of tendrils, there are certain points that ought to be considered.

The term 'climbing plants' is generally used to describe any that are suitable for growing against a supportive barrier – wall, fence, trellis, etc., but in fact they really fall into four distinct categories, obtainable in the main from outlets selling other shrubs.

1. *Free-standing and self-supporting plants.* These are mainly shrubby and would grow perfectly adequately in the open garden, but their habit makes them suitable for standing or training against a wall or fence. They will generally grow taller and spread wider if given such support, and a warm wall can provide a more clement microclimate for less hardy subjects.

Many do not require artificial support, unless you intend some form of formal training, when a system of wires or some trellis should be provided. Examples of shrubs in this category are:

Pyracantha – evergreen, white flowers, followed by red, orange or yellow berries, suitable for any position. Trains well.

Cotoneaster horizontalis – Fishbone cotoneaster. Deciduous but has red berries and good autumn colour. A tough shrub for all sites and completely self-supporting.

Escallonia. This genus is one which varies in hardiness depending on where it is grown. It is perfectly hardy in mild districts and on the coast but does not like cold inland positions, so if given a south or west wall it will grow considerably better. Escallonias are evergreen or semi-evergreen with shiny leaves and pink, red or white tubular flowers.

The dividing line between this type of plant and any other, especially shrubby ones, is very fine, and in theory any shrub which does not object to some formative pruning can be used to disguise a wall.

2. *Self-clinging climbers.* These stick themselves to the wall with modified aerial roots which act like suckers and require no additional support, for example, *ivies (hedera),* of which a considerable number are available, with both plain green and variegated leaves. Also in this group are *Hydrangea petiolaris,* a climbing hydrangea with white flower heads in summer, and *Parthenocissus veitchii,* the well known Virginia creeper, which turns a brilliant red in autumn.

3. *Climbers which support themselves by means of twining stems, leaves or tendrils.* Typical examples of these are the well known large-flowered hybrid and smaller-flowered species *clematis,* the rampant *Polygonum baldschuanicum* (Russian or mile-a-minute vine) and the various climbing forms of *lonicera,* the honeysuckle family.

These do not require any tying in usually, but need a trellis or netting to climb on to, or stakes, canes, poles, etc. to twine round.

4. *Lax growers requiring training and support* – e.g., the yellow winter and white summer jasmines and most climbing and rambler roses.

DISADVANTAGES. First, you must be sure to pick the right plant for the job. It is no good choosing something which grows only 6 feet high if you want to hide an eyesore, and many climbers, given the right conditions, are far too rampant for most house-wall decoration. You will need access to the windows for cleaning and maintenance, so do not plant bushy or prickly things underneath.

If you grow plants up a free-standing trellis, pergola, arch, poles, or similar you often find that you have to renew the support periodically. Even if plastic mesh is used, you generally have to use wooden support stakes driven into the ground to attach it to, and eventually these could rot. You may not find out they are rotten until the whole thing blows over, and then you more or less have to start from scratch in order to sort out all the muddle. The same thing applies if you plant climbers up a dead tree stump – the lot can fall down eventually, demolishing quite a bit of other stuff with it.

Timber trellis is comparatively fragile and the weight of a strong growing plant can distort or even break it down.

It is often recommended that rampant climbers, such as *Clematis montana*, Russian vine, honeysuckle, and some roses – notably *Rosa filipes* 'Kiftsgate' – should be encouraged to grow through a living tree. This can be done, but the climber may spoil the shape of it, and when entangled in the branches, it can make the canopy much thicker and shadier, thus reducing the selection of plants you are able to grow underneath. Eventually, the tree may become choked, and die.

But perhaps the main snags are encountered with plants growing up house walls and garden fences that require periodic maintenance such as painting or the application of preservative or stain. This means that no self-supporting plants are suitable, because you would have to detach them to paint or treat behind. This would almost certainly damage the plant and it would be difficult to make it stick back on again when you had finished. As the plant grew bigger, so the difficulty would increase.

Incidentally, it is somewhat of a myth that this type of climber damages the fabric of the wall – good brickwork and sound mortar would not be affected – only crumbling walling could be damaged when you pulled the creeper off, which is an argument for letting well alone if you have something mature and healthy climbing all over your property and you

237

do not want to get behind it for maintenance.

Free-standing shrubs are perhaps the best solution, providing they are not too prickly and you do not want them formally trained. You can then put a rope round the whole bush and pull it right off the wall or fence. In this case, there is no point in attaching wires to the wall to train the plant to, as it would be virtually impossible to remove the plant temporarily from the wire.

Another solution is to allow the plant to grow on or through trellis which has been fixed to the wall so it can be removed, either by using non-rusting screws and plastic plugs, or by obtaining some of the plastic-coated, rigid wire trellis where the support is screwed to the wall, then the trellis clips into the support. Trellis plus plant can then be detached and laid down to give access to the wall or fence. This is a particularly successful method in connection with twining or tendril-producing plants, as they are usually pliable enough not to break off at the bottom when bent over gently.

A final point must be made that where certain types of damp-proof course have been installed during modernization, some contractors claim that climbing plants bridging the DPC can cause the work to become ineffective, and thus would invalidate the guarantee.

Possible means of support

GALVANIZED WIRE AND STRONG PLASTIC-COATED WIRE. This should be pliable but not flimsy, so it can be pulled taut without kinks or sagging. It is usually wound round screws plugged into the wall or run through eyes and attached firmly at each end. Horizontal stretches at 1 ft (300 mm) intervals are usually adequate, but a mesh can be made by doing the same thing vertically as well. If the mortar is good, this can be drilled to take the plugs and screws, otherwise the bricks themselves should be used. You will probably need a hammer power drill, and certainly a strong masonry bit, to drill the hole as some bricks and mortar can be very hard. This method has its limitations, as already discussed. You also might prefer not to drill the wall.

WOODEN TRELLIS can be made from cedarwood or whitewood and should be thoroughly treated before erection. It is obtainable in concertina-like panels which pull open to give a diamond pattern, or in rigid squared panels. Different thicknesses and qualities are sometimes available – the thicker the timber the longer it lasts. Whitewood can be painted but once the plant is climbing up it you cannot paint it again – unless you cut all the climber off before you start. It is manufactured in several widths and lengths and can be screwed directly to the wall or attached to 1½ × ½ in. (40 × 15 mm) battens fixed to the wall first.

All trellis should be fastened to the *posts*, not the panels, if used against boarded fencing. It is a good idea to fasten it so that it stands off the boards a few inches to allow air to circulate. You can use cotton reels for this purpose, or for any other fixing job where the trellis is required to stand slightly off the wall.

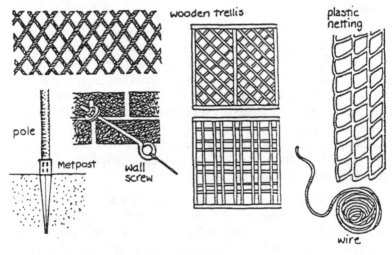

If you feel handy and can afford it, you can make your own trellis by nailing together sawn lathes or roofing battens, which gives you a much stronger job.

PLASTIC TRELLIS. This is a plastic version of the wooden sort. It requires no maintenance and is much stronger, but is used in the same way. The squared panels are also made to fold up, which facilitates transporting them home.

Trellis panels can also be used to form a fence for climbing plants using 3 × 3 in. (75 mm sq.) treated softwood or hardwood stakes driven firmly into the ground for 2 ft 6 in. (750 mm), or fastened into Metposts, to which the trellis is nailed. You can strengthen it by giving it thicker top and bottom rails. Trellis panels are available with convex or concave curved top rails for additional effect. Climbing plants can then be grown up this to form a living screen.

PLASTIC-COVERED METAL TRELLIS. This is rigid or semi-rigid, thin metal rods or wire covered by a substantial coating of plastic. Various designs and colours are available. The semi-rigid sort is bought off the roll by length and it can be obtained in several widths. It can also be used as an open fencing material. The rigid type is usually found as standard-sized panels, though fan-shaped designs are sometimes seen. They are attached to the wall by purpose-made clips supplied with the trellis, the clips being screwed to the wall first. These panels are strong and virtually indestructible as long as the plastic coating is not damaged.

PLASTIC NETTING. A heavy duty, small gauge plastic mesh which is available in several colours and makes an unobtrusive support against a fence or wall. For installing against a wall it is best attached with metal staples to horizontal battens at 2 ft 6 in. (750 mm) intervals. There are several widths obtainable and the beauty of this method is that you can cover as much or as little of the length and breadth of the wall or fence as you want without the joins showing, as it can be cut to whatever length you want (within reason) off the roll, and joined up widthwise on the horizontal battens.

POLES. These are useful for pillar roses (e.g., 'Golden Showers') and some twining climbers like clematis and honeysuckle. The poles should be of treated rustic timber or 3 × 3 in. (75 mm sq.) sawn treated softwood or hardwood embedded at least 2 ft 6 in. (750 mm) into the ground, or fastened to metal post supports, and must be of sufficient length to accommodate the plant (usually up to 8 ft (2.5 m)). Site with care as they can look rather obtrusive until the climber is well established. This method can be quite effective at the back of a shrubbery.

FASTENERS. All wall shrubs which are unable to support themselves either directly or by clinging to a trellis will need tying in to whatever means is used to hold them to the wall. You should always make sure that the ties are soft enough not to cut into the bark or shoot. Old tights cut into strips are useful for this. If you use plastic coated wire, it should be put fairly loosely around stem and support. Check all ties at least annually, sometimes more with a quick growing variety to make sure they are not getting too tight. Once they have cut into the wood it is too late.

Propagation

Most climbers can be increased in number by using the same methods as for shrubs (see page 216).

Pests and diseases

As climbing plants are nearly all shrubs or sub-shrubs, they are prone to the same troubles as free-standing ones (pages 215–16), and the same action should be taken for control. The problem is, because climbing and wall plants are generally grown against some form of solid support, or bunched together up a pole, anything they get is generally on a much worse scale, because of the additional warmth, crowding of the foliage, and lack of free circulation of air. For example, a rose can experience mildew to a much greater degree in such a position.

Clematis wilt sometimes occurs with large-flowered hybrid clematis species, when parts or the whole plant wilt and die suddenly, apparently without reason. Often the plant can be saved by cutting out the parts affected, and drenching the rest with a fungicide.

It might appear that the complications involved in the cultivation of climbing and wall plants are so many and so great as to make it not worth while. But do not discount it. Growing plants up walls opens up a whole new field of gardening; it could be a particularly attractive aspect of your overall garden design, and certainly it is indispensable for toning down the harshness of man-made structures. Suitable climbers can be used for disguising clothes posts, rambling over old unsightly buildings, and various other cosmetic jobs. Do not use thorny plants for clothes posts or ones which get out of hand, but large flowered hybrid clematis can be quite effective. You will need a fairly rampant climber to conceal an eyesore – Russian vine, *Clematis montana* and varieties of Vitis (ornamental vine) are handy for this, but do make sure you don't need to get underneath again!

241

17

HERBS

Gone are the days when home cooking confined itself to a roast and two veg. The trend towards eating out more, especially in foreign-food restaurants, has made everyone more aware of different tastes and flavourings – and there is no doubt that the subtle use of herbs, preferably fresh, can enhance even the most mundane meal. Most aromatic plants are no more difficult to grow than any other ornamentals, so it is surprising they are not more widely cultivated. There is no comparison between dried herbs and fresh ones out of your own patch.

How to use herbs in the garden

Most are very decorative in their own right, and the only thing to distinguish them from other plants is the fact that some part of them has a strong smell or flavour. There is no reason at all why the ones with a herbaceous habit (e.g., angelica, mint, fennel, tarragon, parsley, chives, basil, marjoram, balm, borage, lovage, coriander, dill and sweet cicely)

242

should not be incorporated in a herbaceous or mixed border, while the shrubby ones (thymes, sages, bay, rosemary, lavender) make a useful addition to any shrubbery.

Many people like to keep their herbs to one part of the garden, and this need not look boring. In many big and old-fashioned gardens the herbs are each given a formal square demarcated by rustic bricks, or something similar. This serves the dual purpose of keeping them in tidy clumps, while the solid partitions prevent the rampant ones from running amok. In the majority of smaller plots, however, it is better to lay your herb garden out as an informal mixed border or bed, arranging it so the different habits, foliage and colours complement each other like any other ornamental combination.

Grow herbs as near the house as possible, preferably just outside the kitchen door, for while it is lovely to be able to pick sprigs fresh as you need them, you are not likely to do this if you have to don mac and boots and trail down to the bottom of the garden in a torrential downpour to get your bouquet garni. But it is essential to keep them looking as neat and decorative as possible, as they are always in view. Many of the shrubby types need regular clipping or cutting to keep them in good shape – the bushes will last longer, too; left to their own devices they are inclined to go woody and untidy and so will need replanting frequently. Quite a few of the herbaceous herbs, mint and tarragon being the best examples, have to be restrained or they will run everywhere. The best method is to plant them in a bottomless bucket with the rim slightly proud of the ground so the runners do not hop over the top into the open soil.

The shorter-growing herbs can be planted as an edging to a bed or border – parsley, basil and chives are especially useful for this. In any case, it is always a good idea to put scented foliage plants near a path where you can get the benefit in warm sunshine or after rain or when you brush against them. Some herbs not suitable for culinary purposes can be grown for this function alone, like cotton lavender (*Santolina*), lad's love (*Artemisia abrotanum*) and, best of all, lavender itself.

Several shrubby herbs can be used as hedging; Old English and the dwarf lavenders are the most widely planted – they are easily kept tidy by pruning back after flowering, but not into the old wood, or they will probably not shoot again. Other suitable plants are cotton lavender, bay (in milder areas), rosemary and many forms of sage, which can be trimmed back quite hard.

Most herbs can be grown quite successfully and decoratively in some form of container – smaller tubs, hanging baskets, herb pots and window boxes for the shorter-growing ones and large tubs for the tall types. In very cold parts of Britain this is the only way to grow many of them as a lot tend not to be quite hardy at very low temperatures. As they will get too big and straggly for pot cultivation after a while, you should consider them a temporary planting and be prepared to replace them regularly with fresh young stock. Herbs are often recommended for indoor cultivation but – unless you have a suitable sunny window-ledge in a cool, light room or a cool greenhouse or conservatory – you must like their taste a lot; in a warm room with poor light, they soon become pale and drawn, and not very decorative. A few pots of those herbs which normally die down at the end of summer like chives, can be useful kept on the kitchen window sill over winter.

The *advantages* of growing herbs are that they taste so much better than the dried, bought variety, they are easy to grow, and they make a useful contribution to the overall planting effect of a garden.

The *disadvantages* are that the shrubby types are comparatively short-lived and require regular replacement and frequent attention to keep them in good order, while the herbaceous forms are often invasive. Many herbs are not entirely hardy, especially as young plants, in colder districts. A further snag is that most herbs do not like shady, draughty, heavy or waterlogged positions.

Obtaining and cultivating herbs

Herbs can be *obtained* as young plants by collection and/or mail order from most nurseries and garden centres, but a better selection is usually found at specialist herb nurseries which will also be able to give you other tips in connection with their uses – in cookery, or pot-pourri, or for medicinal and cosmetic purposes, for example. Some health food stores and supermarkets are now offering limited varieties in small pots.

If you know anyone who has particularly good plants you can take cuttings quite easily from shrubby and many perennial sorts, and in addition you can split up clumps of most herbaceous types.

Seed companies sell packets and kits of seed of the most popular varieties.

Herbs in general prefer a lightish soil in a sunny, sheltered position and if your land is inclined to be heavy you should try to dig in as much sand and humus-forming materials as are necessary to make it pleasant to handle.

Most of them are best planted in the spring after the worst of the weather is over and they can then make plenty of good strong growth before the following winter. The method of planting is the same as for other herbaceous and shrubby subjects.

AFTER-CARE. Young plants should not be allowed to die of drought the first year after planting but in general most shrubby herbs prefer a position which is on the warm, dry side. The herbaceous sorts need more moisture, but should not be drowned.

Evergreen shrubby ones need clipping over or cutting back once during the summer so they can make new and hardened growth before winter. Cut back herbaceous sorts regularly to ensure a supply of young, tender shoots. Cut down in the autumn to tidy up the plant.

Herbaceous perennial types will need splitting periodically to keep them young and in bounds, usually about every three years.

A few herbs, like dill, coriander, basil, borage, and parsley are actually annuals or biennials, and should be resown every year.

Slightly tender perennial varieties in cold areas will need to be given some protection in winter. Some form of shelter can be erected if they are subjected to cold winds, or a 2 in. (50 mm) mulch can be used to keep the frost out of the roots, and the crown of the plant, where appropriate. Containerized herbs should be put in a cold greenhouse, or light room or garage when the weather is really severe.

PROPAGATION. Because young plants are best, keep a supply of replacements handy.

You can save seed from your own herbs, especially the annual ones, and sow it under cold glass or in a sheltered spot outdoors in spring and early summer, though this hardly seems worth it for the cost of a packet of seeds, especially as if you once let them seed, they will come up all over the garden, often where you do not want them to.

You can also save seed from the perennial herbaceous and shrubby types, though there are easier and more effective methods. Most herbaceous perennials are best propagated by division, or by removing small rooted portions and growing on in a pot.

Shrubby herbs grow well from cuttings. Insert 3 in. (75 mm) long tips of shoots or branches 1 in. (25 mm) deep in a good potting compost in small pots in late April and May. Remove the leaves first from that part of the stem which is in the compost. You can dip the ends in a hormone rooting powder, but they will root quite readily without. To cut down transpiration and water loss from the compost you can keep the cuttings in a big, inflated, clear polythene bag for a week or two, but be very careful they do not touch the bag sides or they will start to rot – in fact, all cuttings are inclined to rot more easily with this method, though you will not get problems with wilting in the early stages. Keep in a sheltered, shaded position outdoors until they have rooted, which only takes a few weeks for most types.

Some perennial herbaceous ones, like mint, can also be propagated this way, but are more satisfactorily propagated by division.

Preserving your herbs

The best time of year to harvest is July, before they get too tough, but when they have a nice length of growth on them, though if you keep cutting them back regularly and using them fresh, you can preserve the new young shoots at any time of summer and autumn. Herbs just before flowering contain the highest concentration of volatile oils and therefore have the strongest flavour.

The conventional method of laying in a store for winter is to harvest bunches of leaves and stems, hang them up in a warmish, dry place until they are brittle, then the leaves can be crumbled from the stalks, rubbed fine and stored in the dark in screw-topped jars. Bay leaves are stored whole.

An altogether fresher taste can be obtained by freezing the herbs green when they are still young and tender. When you need some for cooking they will crumble easily if you do it while they are still frozen solid. Of course, evergreen ones can be picked off the bush at any time when required.

246

Plagues and pestilences

The troubles that affect shrubs, annuals and perennials (see pages 168–73, 182 and 215–16) can also afflict herbs. Earwigs and caterpillars can defoliate a sage bush if not dealt with quickly. Mint is particularly susceptible to rust. Occasionally parsley can have its roots eaten away by larval grubs of the carrot fly.

The problem with controlling pests and diseases on herbs, like vegetables, is that they are likely to be required for eating a short time afterwards, so a suitable chemical must be chosen which will leave the plants safe for consumption one or two days after spraying. Many of the products containing permethrin are suitable or you could safely use a soap-based organic spray.

There is no satisfactory remedy for mint rust, except to dig up and burn or otherwise safely dispose of affected plants, and start again elsewhere in the garden, with new, clean stock, preferably from a herb specialist.

A beginner's collection of herbs

Twelve good perennial culinary species

> *Angelica (Angelica archangelica)* (6 ft/2 m). Tall and short-lived. Stems can be crystallized for cake decoration.
> *Sweet bay (Laurus nobilis)* (20 ft/6 m). Evergreen shrub. Can be damaged by frost in bad winters. Will clip well to control size. Used in casseroles and puddings.
> *Chives (Allium schoenoprasum)* Herbaceous. Onion-like leaves and mauve flowers. Delicate onion flavour.
> *Fennel (Foeniculum vulgare)* (5–6 ft/1.5–1.75 m). Herbaceous. Feathery leaves, yellow flowers. Bronze-leaved form available. Good with fish.
> *Lemon balm (Melissa officinalis)* (2 ft 6 in./750 mm). Herbaceous. Strong lemon flavour. Golden and variegated forms available. Useful in stuffings and seasonings.
> *Lovage (Levisticum officinalis)* (6 ft/1.75 m, and taller). Herbaceous. Leaves look and smell like celery. Yellow flowers. Stems, shoots, leaves and roots used.
> *Wild Marjoram (Origanum vulgarem)* (18 in./450 mm). Herbaceous. Lilac, pink or white flowers, green, golden or gold variegated leaves.
> *Mint (Mentha)* (12–18 in./300–450 mm). Herbaceous.

Many forms and variations of flavour available, some with variegated leaves.

Rosemary (Rosmarinus officinalis). Evergreen shrub, grows tall but can be clipped. Blue, lavender or white flowers. Upright and prostrate varieties also available. Young plants slightly tender. Good with fish and lamb.

Sage (Salvia officinalis) (2 ft 6 in./750 mm). Evergreen shrub. Lilac flowers. Grey, purple, gold variegated and tricoloured varieties obtainable. Used in stuffings for pork and game.

Tarragon (Artemisia dracunculus) (2 ft/600 mm). Slightly tender, spreads if happy. Excellent with poultry.

Thyme (Thymus) (prostrate, 10 in./250 mm). Evergreen shrub. Many forms available both for culinary and decorative purposes, some with variegated or golden leaves, some with lemon flavour and scent. Prostrate varieties good for edging, ground cover and planting between paving. Used in stuffings for poultry.

Five for aromatic and ornamental use

Cotton lavender (Santolina incana) (2 ft/600 mm). Evergreen shrub. Silvery aromatic leaves, yellow button flowers. Cut hard back after flowering.

Golden feverfew (Chrysanthemum parthenium 'Aureum') (12 in./300 mm). Evergreen, herbaceous perennial. Daisy flowers, strongly scented. Golden chrysanthemum-like leaves.

Lavender (Lavendula) (18–36 in./450–900 mm). Evergreen shrub. Grey or grey-green leaves, pink, white, blue or violet flowers.

Rue (Ruta graveolens) (2 ft/600 mm). Evergreen shrub. Strongly scented leaves, yellow flowers. Slightly tender. 'Jackman's Blue' has bluer, less filigree leaves.

Southernwood (Artemisia abrotanum) (3 ft/900 mm). Deciduous shrub. Feathery green leaves smell like pine disinfectant!

Five to sow every year

Sweet Basil (Ocymum basilicum) (18 in./450 mm). Half-hardy annual. Likes a hot spot. More compact and purple-leaved forms also obtainable. Used with eggs, tomatoes and salad.

Borage (Borago officinalis) (2 ft 6 in./750 mm). Hardy annual. Coarse hairy leaves, blue flowers. Tastes and smells of cucumber. Used in summer drinks and salads.

Caraway (Carum carvi) (12 in./300 mm) Hardy biennial. Leaves, seeds, roots all used for flavouring.

Dill (Anethum graveolens) 12 in./300 mm). Hardy annual. Leaves used in cooking, seeds in pickles and with vegetables.

Parsley (Petroselinum crispum) (12 in./300 mm). Hardy biennial. Stems, roots and leaves all used for flavouring sauces and stuffings.

18

PERGOLAS AND ARCHES

Definition of a pergola

A pergola is really only a construction to give support to climbing plants. In its simplest form it consists merely of upright posts and longitudinal pieces, usually along the top, but sometimes there are intermediate ones as well. More elaborate pergolas have diagonal infilling, or trellis nailed to the uprights and longitudinal members.

Double pergolas usually comprise lengthwise and cross-pieces as above, but there will be two of these, often straddling a path, with cross-pieces forming an open roof between the two to join them up.

Ideally, the width between the two sides of a double pergola should be equal to the height, but as the height really has to be at least 7 ft (2.15 m) the width may have to be slightly less in a smaller garden, in which case the design should be kept as open and simple as possible, otherwise you tend to get a claustrophobic tunnel effect.

Again, the distance between the uprights should be about

6 ft (900 mm), but can be reduced if space is limited. You can reduce all spacings in a small garden without it looking odd, but where the pergola is viewed from a distance in a large garden, having the members too close together will make it look fussy.

Another type of pergola is one attached to the house, where there is a single row of uprights and the cross-pieces are supported by the house wall at one side. This should be constructed of substantial timber, or it will look spidery against the solidness of the property. Also, you should be sure that the rooms looking out on to this construction can afford the marked reduction in light once the pergola is covered with plants.

Definition of an arch

An arch is essentially any framework under which you can walk. You can buy ready-made rustic or iron-work ones – some are very attractive but a few of the self-assembly metal ones tend to be in the plastic gnome category, although once they are well covered with plants it is difficult to see the difference.

A very simple arch can be made from two uprights and a cross member, possibly with diagonal corner pieces at the top for strength and stability. This really needs covering with plants quite quickly as the initial effect is more like a gallows than a garden decoration.

Again, the arch should be sufficiently tall for a 6 foot–plus (2 m) person to walk under comfortably without losing an eye when the climbing roses have covered it.

Suitable climbing plants are planted at the base of the uprights and trained as required along the longitudinals and over the cross-pieces.

The gazebo, or bower

This is a modified pergola, with the effect of a skeletonized summerhouse. It makes a cool, shady, sitting and eating place, especially when covered with suitable, preferably fragrant, climbers.

Uses of pergolas and arches

To accentuate a change of scene in a garden. An arch or short pergola can be erected, for example, where you pass from the ornamental garden into the vegetable area, or from one part of the garden to another out of view.

To shade a hot sunny area. This is an especially useful function of a pergola attached to the main structure of the property, where it can shade a very hot patio and/or hot, south-facing windows.

To give height. For example, a rose arch joining together two informal rose beds will take away the uniform flatness of the bush roses.

To accentuate a path. If you must have a long, straight path in the garden and space will allow, you might as well make a feature of it and put a pergola over the top.

Disadvantages

These are few, if the construction was properly done in the first place. Tying in and training is the main chore. Eventually, of course, timber will deteriorate and have to be renewed – even the best-cared-for constructions have been known to collapse unexpectedly, so be prepared! If you decide to embark on regular painting or treatment, it can be a fiddly and time-consuming job, necessitating a lot of cutting back and removal of tangled growths.

Some suitable plants for arches and pergolas

> *Akebia quinata*
> *Large-flowered clematis*
> *Eccremocarpus scaber*
> *Some ivies*
> *Lonicera (honeysuckles)*
> *Passiflora caerulea (passion flower)*
> *Most climbing and rambler roses*
> *Solanum crispum*
> *Vitis (ornamental vines)*
> *Wistaria varieties*

What should they be made of?

TIMBER. There are three types of timber suitable for the construction of a pergola or arch.

1. *Sawn timber.* This gives a fairly formal but very neat and substantial effect. If you can afford it, hardwood is best – some timber yards will cut it to size while you wait. It should be well treated with a spirit-based preservative before assembly.

If you decide to use softwood, the preservative treatment should be very much more thorough. Pressure-treated timber is best, otherwise you will need to give the timber several coats of a suitable spirit-based preservative before it is ready for use.

The uprights should be 3 × 3 in. (75 mm square), or 4 × 4 in. (100 mm square), longitudinals 2 × 2 in. (50 mm square) or 3 × 3 in. (75 mm square), and cross-pieces and diagonals 1½ × 1½ in. (35 mm) square) or 2 × 2 in. (50 mm square). The thinner timber is more suited to arches and smaller pergolas.

At least 2 ft (600 mm) of the timber must be firmly buried in the ground so you should buy uprights 2 ft (600 mm) or more longer than the eventual height of the pergola or arch. Alternatively, use metal post-anchors and buy posts the same length as the height of the pergola. The longitudinals and cross-pieces should project for 9–18 in. (225–450 mm), according to the size of the structure, at the ends and sides, so these will be 18 in. to 3 ft (450 to 900 mm) longer than the length and width of the construction.

2. *Stripped poles.* These are softwood poles which are stripped of their bark. They are usually graded at the sawmill or timber yard into nominal sizes based on the diameter near the base. They will, of course, taper slightly but there should not be too much difference between the diameter at the top and the bottom otherwise once they are in position they look very odd. You will require 3–4-in. (75–100 mm) diameter timber for the uprights, 2- or 3-in. (50 or 75 mm) for the longitudinals, and 1½- or 2-in. (35 or 50 mm) for the cross-pieces and diagonals. Stripped poles must also be buried at least 2 ft (600 mm) in the ground if metal posts are not used, and the cross-pieces and longitudinals should project as described for sawn timber, so estimate the lengths in the same way. You should pay special attention to treating this kind of timber with preservative. Some garden centres sell these poles already treated.

3. *Rustic Poles.* These are similar to the above, but the bark has been left on. They are usually made of larch, but other timbers are sold for the purpose as well. The sizes required are the same as for stripped poles. They give a very natural, rustic effect, but, in general, need renewing much more often than the other two types as they cannot be effectively treated with

253

preservative. Any timber below ground level should be soaked in creosote for 2–3 days and allowed to drain before use. The problem with that part of the wood which is above the ground is not so much rotting, but infestation with timber-boring beetles under the bark which eventually reduces the strength of the construction so much that the pole can snap in a high wind, especially if there is a lot of foliage on it. A further drawback of this kind of wood is that occasionally it can become a breeding ground for coral spot disease which may then spread to live plants elsewhere in the garden.

METAL. Many attractive, good-quality iron and aluminium arches, pergolas and gazebos are advertised in specialist garden magazines. They are comparatively expensive but, in general, will last much longer than timber. Their thinner framework can be an advantage in some circumstances. Metal structures are usually purchased fully or partially constructed and should be erected according to the manufacturer's instructions.

Constructing the timber pergola or arch

Position the uprights first. Ram rubble around the base before backfilling with soil. The use of metal-post anchors will

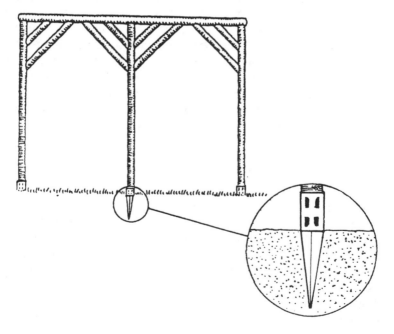

lengthen the structure's life. Concreting is not necessary and can do more harm than good as it causes premature rotting. In the case of a double pergola, erect pairs of uprights together. Make sure the uprights are truly vertical and all at the same height. This is easy enough to check with a spirit level if you are using sawn timber, but with rustic poles you have to rely heavily on your eye for vertical accuracy, though you can check the heights by putting a straight piece of wood across any two uprights and using a spirit level on this.

Nail the longitudinals to the tops of the uprights. You do not have to be an expert carpenter to make this sort of construction as it does not matter if the end result is slightly less than perfect, but you must make sure that the members are joined firmly and that the whole thing does not look drunk when you have finished. It is as well to drill the nail holes first, especially in sawn hardwood, or you can often split the timber. Then nail the cross-pieces to the longitudinals and, finally, add any diagonals, trellis-work or other in-fill timber.

Planting up and after-care

The method of planting suitable subjects and their care in subsequent seasons is exactly the same as for planting other shrubs (see pages 211–13).

Tie them securely to the supports on planting. Training and tying in must be done regularly otherwise the whole thing will quite quickly turn into an impenetrable jungle. Problems of water reaching the roots will not be great as with plants grown up a solid structure such as a fence or wall, neither will that of pests and diseases (see pages 201–3, 215–16, and 241), as air can circulate more freely.

Maintaining the structure

If you have bought a ready-assembled structure or self-assembly kit, follow the manufacturer's instructions. Wrought-iron arches need regular painting, first removing as much rust as possible. This can be a very awkward job if it is thickly covered with plants, so bear maintenance in mind when you choose the plants, and use those which can be easily removed or cut down if necessary – for example, the late flowering group of large-flowered clematis which can be cut right down in spring.

Timber pergolas, arches and the like should last many years

if properly constructed. There are two schools of thought about regular preservative treatment – either you should continue to treat the timber regularly or it considerably reduces its life, or there is no need, as the circulation of air around the wood will prevent rotting to a large extent. In practice, if you have plants nicely trained over the structure exactly where and how you want them, you will not be too keen to take them off to treat it with anything. Probably, once you have got the pergola or whatever up, you will not give another thought to preservative treatment. More important is to check the construction over regularly and if you see any signs of rotting, holes bored in the wood, or other deterioration, to remedy them immediately. This is especially relevant in the case of bark-covered rustic poles – you will have to pull a bit of bark off here and there to see what is happening underneath.

19

THE WATER GARDEN

Next to rockeries, inexperienced gardeners seem to want a water garden more than any other feature, usually without understanding what they are letting themselves in for. Admittedly there are very good arguments in favour of considering water when planning your garden:

ADVANTAGES. The effect of light on the surface and reflections in the water give a feeling of tranquillity.

The sound of running water from a fountain or cascade is very pleasing.

It gives you the chance to explore new aspects of plant cultivation.

You can introduce wildlife into the garden in the form of fish (and the tomcat from next door, and the heron which clears out your collection in one sitting!).

DISADVANTAGES. A pool must be maintained properly at all seasons or it can quickly become an eyesore.

If you are intending to make a boggy area and have no suitable natural part of the garden, you will have to rely very heavily on regular irrigation during dry weather or the plants will die. To provide moving water in a garden, you have to install comparatively expensive equipment and know what you are doing regarding the electrical supply to this, or alternatively pay for a qualified electrician to do the job for you.

Where small children are concerned, you will have to fence off any water deeper than a few inches if you are not to keep them under constant supervision – it is surprising how shallow a depth of water a child can drown in.

How to use water in the garden

FOR SOUND. If you just want the soothing sound of splashing water without all the hassle of maintaining a pool, there are many pieces of equipment these days which can enable you to do this. A typical example is a fountain kit attached to a sunken reservoir, on top of which is some stone feature, probably containing cobbles or similar. The water is pumped up through the fountain and runs back through the cobbles into the reservoir. This is essentially a formal feature, probably best situated in a patio. On the other hand, if you want sight as well as sound, you can achieve this by installing a fountain in a conventional pool, and/or pumping the water up to run back down the face of a rockery through a channel and rock pools back into the pond. This has the additional advantage of aerating the water, which is of considerable benefit to any fish.

AS A FORMAL FEATURE. In this case, the shape of the pond is confined to a geometric shape. The edges are best kept plain by paving. This type of pool can be quite satisfactory as an inset in a terrace or patio and can be raised above ground level.

AS AN INFORMAL POOL. Possibly the most successful for the majority of gardens. The shape is asymmetrical and can be sited in grass and/or surrounded with informal paving or stones. The 'spoil' from the excavation can be used, if it is suitable, to create a rockery area flanking the pool, in which case it can contain a waterfall if required.

AS A MOIST BED OR BORDER AREA. Here the pool excavation is not filled with water, but with soil which is kept moist all the time.

258

An area such as this may be attached to an informal pond, or can be a feature on its own, without the inclusion of a piece of open water.

Siting the pool

Water gardens, except bog areas, which can stand a certain amount of shade, are best situated in an open, sunny position, otherwise the water tends to green up with algae. If you are using a fountain or similar, place the pool where you are most likely to get the benefit from the sound of splashing water, otherwise an informal pool is sometimes better in a peaceful spot away from the house.

Never install a pond where it can fill up easily with leaves – for example, near deciduous trees or shrubs. This might look picturesque, but debris dropping off the branches soon rots and fouls the water, and can be fatal to fish.

Always make the pool as big as you can manage it in proportion to the rest of the area.

Constructing your pool

There are many materials which can be used for holding water, some better than others.

NATURALLY MOIST AREAS. A few people are lucky enough to have a part of the garden which is always wet, either because of springs, seepage, or a stream. In this case, if the bottom is dug out, water will usually stand in it, although the natural level might be lower than that in an artificial pond, but the banks can be planted up with suitable pondside plants to very good effect. If the site is soggy, but does not contain standing water, it can be used for growing bog-loving subjects in a similar manner to a herbaceous border.

CONCRETE. Once this was about the only reliable method of making a pool. As it requires a lot of heavy work to get it right and there are other problems concerning possible leaking and contamination of the water with salts out of the new concrete, it is not a method to be recommended nowadays for the amateur gardener with so many other materials at his or her fingertips.

PUDDLED CLAY. Another outdated method sometimes used in localities where a lot of heavy clay was freely available.

Basically, it consisted of ramming wet clay and sometimes straw into the hole until it was so solid the water could not drain out. Apart from the sheer physical effort involved, this method had its drawbacks in that if the water level was allowed to drop and the sides dried out, they would probably crack and the pond would start to leak. There are other methods more suitable.

POLYTHENE. Heavy duty polythene sheet is available from water gardening suppliers. This is used, often as a double thickness, to line the hole before filling it with water. Its main advantage is the reasonable cost, but it punctures easily if the hole is not completely free of sharp stones, and deteriorates rapidly in sunlight, so the lining needs renewing after a year or two.

SEMI-RIGID PLASTIC SHAPES. These are made, usually in a neutral shade, of stiff but flexible plastic and simulate a rough, informal pool bottom. The hole is dug out to fit the plastic shape and then soil is rammed in around the sides at the same time as the pond is filled. They are reasonably priced but, not being entirely rigid, if not installed properly, once the pool starts filling with water, the pressure will push it out of shape and it can collapse and distort in all directions.

FIBREGLASS AND PLASTIC PREFORMED POOLS. These are quite expensive but available in a whole range of sizes and shapes to suit every requirement. They are usually stone-coloured but some are made in a garish blue or very light colours which look totally unnatural and do nothing for any landscape. They can be obtained with imitation stone edging or plain edged for covering with your own material – crazy paving or grass, for example. They are much easier to install once the hole is there than the semi-rigid sort, but the base must be smooth, level and firm before the preformed pool is finally placed. The levels in each direction should be meticulously checked before backfilling and running water into the pool. They should incorporate a shelf for marginal plants.

POOL LINERS. These are probably the easiest to use, although good ones are expensive. However, unlike polythene, they do not deteriorate in sunlight so should last for many years provided that they are installed correctly in the first place, that you do not tread in them, and that you do not stick a fork through the bottom. These days they are usually made from PVC, nylon-reinforced PVC or butyl, the latter a very expensive material, but being of toughened rubber material, very strong. PVC sheets are usually coloured grey or blue, sometimes one colour on one side and one on the other, while butyl is an unobtrusive charcoal grey.

To make a simple pool using a liner

To obtain a suitable environment for growing the widest range of plants possible, the depth of the pool should vary. To do this, a marginal shelf is necessary around or against part of the outside. This could be at the back and/or one or both sides in a square or rectangular pool, and around the back and part of the sides of a round or informally shaped pool. Large, deep pools can be constructed to have shelves of various depths.

The pool at the deepest part need be no deeper than 24 in. (600 mm) deep. A single marginal shelf should be about 9 in. (225 mm) below the surface of the water and 12 in. (300 mm) wide.

TO CALCULATE THE SIZE OF THE LINER. The *length* is the overall length of the pool, plus twice the maximum depth; the *width* is the overall width of the pool, plus twice the maximum depth.

As you cannot satisfactorily join a liner yourself, check first to see what widths are available. The maximum width obtainable will dictate the width of your pool. Butyl liners can be supplied in most sizes by aquatic specialists.

First, mark out on the ground the outline of the pool and the extent of the marginal shelves. Excavate the deepest section, then the area covered by the shelves. The walls of the pool should have a slight slope inwards. Reinforced PVC and butyl liners are usually laid over the hole and the edges weighted with stones, bricks, etc.; polythene and unreinforced PVC are mainly laid into the shape of the excavation, but do check the manufacturer's instructions before you begin. When you start to fill the pool with water, the weight will stretch those liners which are laid across until they fit the hole. The hole itself should be absolutely smooth before being lined, and you can add a layer of sand if desired. Leave a flap of liner all round the outside to anchor it, which can be covered over later with rockery stones, slabs or similar. If you want to make a bog garden at the side of the pool, you should use an extra liner, buried about 18 in (450 mm) deep with the three sides not adjoining the pool brought up to form a basin. This is kept constantly moist – the sides will prevent the water in it from seeping into the surrounding soil – but mind how you dig, once it is installed!

Remember to make allowance for burying any cables for pumps, fountains, underwater lighting, etc. at the time of construction. These should be of approved standard only, and purchased from reputable aquarists. As there is a safety hazard when installing permanent electricity supplies out of doors, if you are at all in doubt, use a qualified electrician.

Cascades and waterfalls

Unless your garden has a substantial natural or man-made slope, you will have to provide height for this type of thing by some kind of raised feature, the most popular being a rockery. Follow the same principles of construction, planting, etc. as for any other rock garden and remember to bury cables, hoses, and so on where you can get at them but not where you are likely to shove a fork or trowel through them – make a mark on the rocks or draw a plan to remind you where they are.

Preformed waterfalls are now available – these can lead into a series of manufactured rock pools if you like. They look rather stark on the face of a new rockery, but the edges can be easily disguised by low, spreading plants.

Obtaining the materials

Water gardening is becoming increasingly popular so many garden centres now have a special section selling a whole range of aquatic equipment. There are also major national firms specializing entirely in aquarists' materials and many of these have a mail order department. If you are in any doubt, this is probably the best way to buy, as the catalogues most of these firms produce are as helpful as any book on the subject.

If you have friends with an established pond, they may be wanting to split the plants, and even give away a few fish. This can be a good way of getting started, but first inspect the pool in question, checking that the size and habit of the water plants are suitable for your enterprise. Make sure, if possible, you are not importing pests, diseases or aquatic weeds, like duckweed.

Timing

Between April and early August is the best period for stocking the pond, because the water is warm enough to get the plants growing away strongly. In winter the disturbed roots would probably rot, although there is nothing to stop you constructing the pool then, and stocking when the time is right.

Stocking the pool

The plants you are likely to encounter when beginning to plant up the pond can be divided into 6 categories.

1. *Waterside plants* require moist soil but should never be waterlogged and must always be planted above water level. They require a fertile loam and are best planted in spring, although with containerization the summer months are suitable as well. They are also suitable for a drier bog garden.

> *Astilbes* – feathery flower spikes in pink, white and red.
> *Hostas* – large-leaved herbaceous plants, some with variegations. Lily-like white or lilac flower spikes in summer.
> *Rheum* – ornamental rhubarb. Huge leaves, suitable for large damp areas.
> *Rodgersia* – cream or pink feathery spikes, spectacular bronze leaves.

2. *Shallow marginal plants* are equally at home in permanently wet soil or shallow water up to 6 in. (150 mm) deep. Suitable for wet bog gardens or marginal shelf planting.

> *Caltha palustris* (marsh marigold). Yellow or white 'kingcup' flowers in spring.
> *Iris.* Water loving varieties such as *laevigata* and *pseudoacorus.*
> *Pontederia cordata* (pickerel weed). Light blue flower spikes.
> *Veronica beccabunga* (brooklime). Dainty marginal plant with blue flowers.

3. *Deeper marginal plants* will grow in water up to 12 in (300 mm) deep.

> *Alisma plantago* (water-plaintain). Spikes of pink and white flowers.
> *Scirpus lacustris.* Strong-growing bulrush for larger pools.

263

4. *Oxygenating plants* grow below the surface and are used for keeping up oxygen supplies in the water, which is essential for fish.

> *Elodea canadensis* (Canadian pondweed). Strong growing.
> *Potamogeton crispum* (pondweed). Seaweed-like foliage.

5. *Surface flowering aquatics* root into the bottom and require water at least 12 in. (300 mm) deep. They often have big leaves which provide useful shade for fish.

> *Aponogeton distachyum* (water hawthorn). White flower spikes all summer and floating oval leaves.
> *Ranunculus aquatilis* (water crowfoot). Dark green foliage and white flowers in high summer.
> *Water lilies.* Many varieties and colours available. Some are more suitable for small areas than others so check with supplier before buying.

6. *Free floating aquatics.* The roots of these plants float in the water so do not require any soil. Some, like *azolla* (fairy floating moss) and *lemna* (duckweed) are too invasive for most ponds but *Stratiotes aloides* (water soldier), which looks like the top of a pineapple with white flowers and sinks to the bottom for the winter, is interesting.

Planting up

Although with modern pond-making materials it is perfectly feasible to dig the pool, line it, fill it and stock it all in a weekend, it is wise to let it settle down for a while after putting the water in. You may find the water turns green a few days after filling – with or without plants present; this is due to algae but the problem should go away of its own accord once the water stabilizes.

Unless you have a natural pool with sides and bottom of soil, rather than cover the shelves and bottom with soil it is much easier to plant aquatics in special open-work plastic planting crates first, then these, plus plants, are gradually submerged in the required places; this method makes eventual cleaning out so much simpler.

Do not overplant your pool – water plants are usually fairly strong-growing and can quickly overrun the area allocated to them. For example, a small pool with an area of a square yard (or square metre) could accommodate a dwarf water lily, up to

4 suitably slow-growing marginals, and 6 oxygenators. A larger pool of about 130 sq. ft (12 sq. m), say 10 × 13 ft (3 × 4 m) could take 4 suitable lilies or other surface-flowering aquatics, up to 16 marginals (depending on type), and 20 to 30 oxygenators, but it is always better to underplant. A lot depends, of course, on how much bog area you have provided around the outside, if any.

Heavy soil is the best for using in planting crates and you can line the crates with hessian or old nylon tights to keep the soil from getting into the water. Gravel placed on the surface will prevent particles from floating off and dirtying the water.

You can adjust the height of the water over the crown of the plants if necessary by placing the crates on bricks or similar.

Fish

Fish are not an essential part of a water garden; but most people decide to have them. As with plants, it is best to under-stock rather than over-stock. As a guide, to allow for growth no more than 3-in. (75 mm) length of fish should be added for every square foot of surface area.

Ideally, you should let a few weeks elapse so the plants have a chance to settle down before you put the fish in. You do not need to stick to the common goldfish these days as most aquatic centres have a wide range of other types but, before buying any, you should research the subject.

When you buy your fish, you will usually be given them in a polythene bag partly inflated with air. When you get them back to the pond, you should submerge them, still in the bag, for about an hour (not too long or they will run out of air) to let them become used to the different water temperature gradually, then they can be released gently under water – that will probably be the last you see of them for several days while they recover from their traumatic experience!

You may get casualties, either at the beginning, or from time to time in the established pool, as fish suffer from pests and diseases just as all other living things do. If you see a sick or dead fish, remove it immediately from the pool – a poorly fish must be isolated and can be treated with one of the potions that fish specialists will sell you for whatever condition it is they think yours has got, but it will probably die anyway – they have this unhappy knack – so you may find it less heart-breaking to practise euthanasia by killing it by dashing it hard on to a firm surface – it will be an instant happy release in most cases. Do not flush it down the loo, as I have often heard is done – choking them to death in sewage is not the answer.

FEEDING. Once the pond is established, there is really no need to offer 'artificial' food as in a short while larvae of certain insects will appear in the water and these provide natural nourishment, but if you must, you can give a little supplementary food once a day during summer. In winter feeding should be discontinued altogether.

Watersnails

These are the scavengers of the pool. They can often be introduced as eggs on new plants, though they are generally offered for sale where fish are sold. They are not considered as useful as once thought, as they can damage the plants.

Frogs and newts

These may be temporary summer visitors for breeding purposes. They usually do no harm – in fact, they eat many small garden pests like slugs and the tadpoles eat green algae in the water. Occasionally, they can damage a fish by mistaking it for another frog during the mating season.

After-care

Treat marginals growing in the soil surrounding the pool as any other herbaceous plants (see pages 170–80). With regard to those aquatic plants growing in the water area, if you have stocked and planted up your pond as suggested, maintenance need only consist of an annual spring clean sometime during April, May or June. Remove the crates, pull off dead material and clean out all debris which has accumulated at the bottom.

After a few years, the plants in the crates will become overcrowded and need to be divided and replanted as before in fresh soil. This is the best method of propagation.

Most ponds will develop blanket weed at some time or another. There is not much you can do about it other than remove it manually. If you just twirl a stick around in the water you can attach a lot of it to the end of the stick – rather like candyfloss – and if you do this regularly (several times a week sometimes in summer as it spreads rapidly in warm weather) you will generally manage to keep on top of it. However, as the pool surface becomes covered with lily and other flat leaves, light will gradually be excluded and it will eventually be greatly reduced.

You will have to keep your eye on the pool in autumn to make sure large quantities of leaves do not fall in. These gradually sink to the bottom and rot, giving off poisonous gases and polluting the water. It pays to cover the pond with fine mesh netting if you do find a lot of leaves blowing into it – you can remove the cover when the leaves have stopped coming down.

The pond in winter

All activity, of both plants and living creatures, is reduced to a minimum. Aquatic plants become dormant and fish just 'tick over' in the cold water. Providing the pool is clean and well maintained, there is nothing to worry about – things can be left to look after themselves until the spring.

The only problem you are likely to encounter is that of ice. In very cold weather the whole surface freezes over and although there is nothing to worry about for a day or two, eventually the water becomes depleted of oxygen and any fish will die, so an air hole has to be kept in the ice. It is not easy to do this in very cold conditions, because the free water soon freezes over again. Pond keepers all have their own pet methods for letting air in, some more successful than others:

FLOATING A CHILD'S BALL ON THE WATER. Works all right in thin ice, but in very bad weather can freeze in and get stuck. Can be dangerous if small children are around.

FLOATING THICK PIECES OF POLYSTYRENE ON THE SURFACE. These are often used as packing round fragile objects such as television sets, so are usually readily available. The idea is that they are slightly warmer than the surrounding water, and so keep an unfrozen area around their edges. If the temperature drops really low, and this area freezes as well, you can easily make holes gently through the polystyrene itself. The two drawbacks here are that the sheet can float away out of reach if your pool is fairly large, or, if you can reach it and you start making holes, if the cold spell goes on a long time you can run out of material to make holes in, so you have to remove it and replace it with a new piece.

HOT WATER. A large, thin tin can full of boiling water will thaw a hole in ice which is not too thick. This may have to be repeated several times a day in the same place but is reasonably successful if done before the ice gets really thick.

POND HEATER. This is probably the most efficient way of keeping an open area in an icy pool and works rather like an immersion heater, but you do have to have a safe electricity supply, and if the cold spell goes on a long time it can cost you a bob or two.

NEVER make holes in the ice by banging or cracking it. The shock waves it creates can give the fish a fatal headache!

Pests and diseases

Herbaceous plants growing on the margins of pools can get any of the troubles listed on pages 168–73 and 182. The problem is not so much the affliction, but the fact that it is very difficult to deal with if you have livestock in the pond. Most garden chemicals are highly toxic to fish and should never be used anywhere near them if there is a danger of run-off or spray drift.

Fortunately, aquatic plants are not too badly affected by nasties. The most serious problem is that of the *water lily beetle*, which eats big holes in the leaves. The best remedy is to remove the leaves in question complete with the beetle, its larvae and the eggs.

Infestations of any other pests are best hosed off into the water, where they will be received with delight by the fish.

Herons and cats are the most serious pests as far as the fish are concerned. The only remedy is to net the pool securely and permanently, which does nothing for its appearance, but in areas where either or both of these are a nuisance there is no other practical answer. The *large black water beetle* is also an undesirable addition to the wildlife of the pool, as it can eat small fish. It should be netted out as soon as spotted.

20

THE ACID
GARDEN

You will have gathered by now that I am not a great advocate
of going against natural conditions in order to plant something
you fancy, though one way you can beat nature to a certain
extent is by creating an acid garden.

The majority of calcifuges (lime-hating plants) have a particular attraction all their own, which is why they are so much
in demand. Perhaps a quarter of the plants featured in a typical
catalogue are of this nature; but most of them just will not do
well in a soil containing lime. If you live an an area which has
a naturally acid soil (with a pH of around 5–6), you will be
able to plant these acid lovers wherever you want in the
garden (having regard, of course, to other special conditions
they might need – sun, shade, damp, dry soil, etc., as with any
other plant).

If your soil is neutral or slightly acid, then the addition of
some peat – preferably sphagnum moss peat, which has a
lower pH, leaf mould or cocoa shell – is all you need to create
the right environment for this type of plant. But if you have

got a really alkaline soil – above pH 7, you are going to have to make a special area to suit these lime-haters.

Construction of an acid garden

The easiest method is to excavate the whole area you wish to give over to calcifuges to a depth of about 2 ft 6 in (750 mm) and replace the natural soil with an acid medium. You can use all sphagnum moss peat for this if you wish, but this would be very acid, and you would find you had to feed carefully as plants can have as many deficiencies in too acid a soil as in too alkaline a one. The best mixture is about 1 part of good garden soil to every 2 or 3 sphagnum peat, depending on the alkalinity of the soil you are using – you will have to check with a soil-testing kit to see what pH you are getting as you mix. You are aiming for something in the region of 4.5–5.5. You will run the risk of getting beaten over the head by the green movement but see Chapter 28, pages 372–3.

An alternative to peat is the correct grade (fairly fine) of pulverized bark, but this is still more expensive and as it has not the same composition as peat, it breaks down rather differently. Otherwise, use leaf mould if available.

Lime in the soil always washes down. It does not work upwards (or outwards, to any appreciable amount) in a well drained, well worked soil, so once you have created your acid medium, it should remain fairly stable, but it is possibly as well to check the pH from time to time.

If you do not fancy digging out, you can also make a similar acid garden in a raised bed. Peat blocks are quite a good building medium for this as you can plant acid-loving trailing plants amongst them as you build, which helps to consolidate the whole thing.

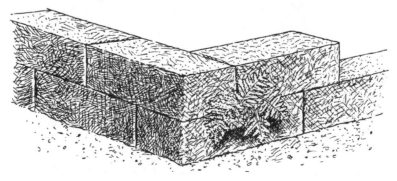

DISADVANTAGES. If you get your conditions right in the first place, and choose suitable plants to fit the spot, the drawbacks are surprisingly few. The main problem is with watering as chances are that the water that comes out of the tap is as limey or even worse than the soil you have removed. Generally speaking, watering should not be too much of a problem if you've thought the exercise out properly; for example, heathers like a sunny, fairly dry position, rhododendrons a cool spot with some shade, which in the normal run of things ought to be fairly damp anyway. The odd watering with tap water should not matter, but it would be better to get a rainwater butt before you start your acid garden and situate it under one of the downspouts of your house.

The real snag occurs when you get a prolonged period of dry weather and you are forced into regular watering. Even if you have a rainwater butt it will eventually run dry. Your only alternative in this case is to use tap water, but apply the necessary iron, magnesium and manganese (which will eventually become locked up in the soil by the lime in the water and therefore unavailable to the plants) in the form of sequestrene or chelates, which are available at most garden shops and garden centres.

Obtaining acid-lovers

Acid-loving plants are available from the same sources of supply as other herbaceous perennials and hardy shrubs (see pages 177 and 209–10). Some nurseries specialize in the raising of such plants, particularly rhododendrons and heathers. Most young plants will be containerized in a special acid compost.

The same rules for choosing acid-loving plants, particularly shrubs, including rhododendrons and heathers, apply as to the selection of other subjects (see pages 163–4 and 189). Choose healthy-looking specimens, as ericaceous plants soon begin to reflect poor maintenance in loss of condition, particularly with yellowing leaves which are a sign of lime-induced chlorosis, possibly owing to watering with hard water, or potting on into the wrong compost.

WHAT TO BUY. This is mainly a matter of personal preference. The term 'acid gardens' is a very loose one, only describing the type of soil found in such an environment, although it conjures up pictures of heather beds, rhododendron collections,

271

azalea borders and the like, but there is nothing to stop one making a mixed shrubbery in such an area, or even a mixed border, using acid-loving herbaceous plants as well. In fact, many lime-tolerant plants will grow just as happily in acid soils, although if you have gone to considerable labour and expense in creating these conditions, it seems rather a waste to occupy space with plants which would be perfectly contented elsewhere in the garden, unless there is something which is essential to the overall effect – e.g., ornamental conifers in a heather bed.

Many rhododendrons are now raised by micropropagation, resulting in sturdier, healthier plants which flower earlier and better.

Planting

As the only important thing which distinguishes acid-loving plants from others is their inability to tolerate lime, all the general rules for planting – times, methods, etc., still apply, although many ericaceous subjects originated in impoverished soils and therefore require less feeding than the majority of plants. A good rule of thumb for feeding is to give about half the amount you would to a similar lime-tolerant plant. Rhododendrons, azaleas and many other acid plants are surface rooting and should never be planted any deeper than they were in the nursery, but heathers can be planted slightly deeper.

After-care

Regular mulching with bark, cocoa shell or leaf mould helps to conserve natural moisture and keep the pH low.

Pruning is more a matter of the type of plant in question rather than the fact of whether it is or is not lime-tolerant, so the general principles of pruning apply.

Heathers can be just clipped over with shears after flowering to keep them compact and bushy. Rhododendrons and azaleas should never receive regular pruning other than the removal of dead or diseased wood and badly-placed branches, but should have the dead flower-heads *only* (not the wood underneath them, which contains next year's flower buds) removed. Very overgrown bushes, however, will regenerate if cut hard back.

Feeding is not really necessary on a routine basis. When it is needed, the rough rule of half the recommended dose will usually be enough. If you find growth is poor and the plant looks generally yellow and unhealthy, it is a sign that too much lime is getting to the plants, either through tap water or leaching from the surrounding soil (the latter is unusual, though). This can be corrected with sequestrene as already described. If you live in a very alkaline area, give an application of sequestrene annually in spring as a matter of course.

Pests and other problems

The pests and diseases described on pages 168–73 and 215–16 can occur, and should be treated similarly. *Chlorosis* as described above is the main worry.

Many ericaceous plants can contract a *wilt disease* known as *Phytophora cinnamonii* which attacks the roots. There is no cure for affected plants, but the surrounding ground should be treated with mancozeb to prevent the infection from spreading.

Bud blast is the only other major problem, which is confined to members of the rhododendron family. The flower buds turn brown with black fungal bristles and do not open but go hard and remain on the bush. This disease can sometimes be confused with frost damage, but in the latter case there are no black bristles present and frost-affected buds can drop off by themselves eventually. There is no remedy, but as the disease is spread by leaf-hoppers, the bushes should be sprayed in August with a suitable insecticide.

Propagation

Propagation is no more difficult than with lime-tolerant plants of similar type – e.g., herbaceous plants can be increased as described on pages 180–2 and shrubs as on page 216.

Remember to use a lime-free compost and water with soft water.

Heathers strike particularly well as inch-long (25 mm) cuttings taken in July and August and inserted in a compost of sandy peat.

Some suggestions for acid gardens

Trees

Acer palmatum (Japanese maple). Decoratively-shaped purple or green leaves, good autumn colour.

Liquidambar styraciflua (sweet gum). Silvery grey bark and maple-like leaves which turn crimson, purple, bright red and gold in autumn.

Magnolia. Tulip-shaped flowers of pink, white or purple, depending on variety. Some species will tolerate some lime, but in general these trees prefer a lime-free soil.

Shrubs

Camellias. Evergreen. Many colours and forms available.

Corylopsis pauciflora. Primrose-yellow flowers before leaves in March. Some shade required. Slow growing. 4 ft (1.25 m).

Enkianthus campanulatus. Pale cream flowers tinted bronze or red in May. Woodland conditions preferred. Brilliant autumn colour. 6 ft (1.8–2 m).

Hamamelis. The witch hazels eventually form small trees. Yellow or red flowers in December to March and bright autumn colouring.

Kalmia latifolia. Laurel-like evergreen leaves and pink flowers not unlike that of a rhododendron. 6 ft (1.8 m).

Leucothoe fontanesiana 'Rainbow'. Evergreen leaves variegated cream, yellow, pink and green. Pitcher-shaped white flowers, May. 3 ft (900 mm).

Pernettya mucronata. Small leathery evergreen leaves, white flowers and white, pink or red berries on female plants. Will tolerate some shade. One male plant will pollinate 3 females.

Pieris. A genus of evergreen plants requiring similar conditions to rhododendrons. Flowers appear in spring and resemble lilies-of-the-valley. Some varieties have bright red young shoots and a variegated form is available. Most are slow growing.

Skimmia. Small evergreen shrubs with pink flowers and red berries on female plants. Can be grown on an alkaline soil, but tend to become chlorotic so are at their best in lime-free conditions.

Rhododendrons and azaleas

Cool woodland conditions and dappled shade best. There are many types available but the following are good for starters.

Hardy hybrid rhododendrons. All evergreens.

> *'Britannia'*. Scarlet-crimson. May—June. 4 ft (1.25 m).
> *'Pink Pearl'*. Huge pink flowers. 7—8 ft (2.1—2.5 m).
> *'Purple Splendour'*. Hardy hybrid. Purple flowers with black markings, June. 5 ft (1.5 m).
> *'Sappho'*. Hardy hybrid. White flowers with dark blotch. 6 ft (1.8 m).

Dwarf rhododendrons. Evergreens, suitable for rockeries and can be grown in full sun.

> *'Blue Diamond'*. Lavender-blue flowers. Scented leaves.
> *'Curlew'*. Large yellow flowers.
> *'Linda'*. Pink flowers, new leaves chocolate-brown.
> *Rhododendron praecox*. Semi-evergreen. Mauve, scented flowers, March. 4 ft (1.25 m).

Deciduous azaleas. May-flowering, flowers often scented, good autumn colour.

> *'Gibraltar'*. Glowing orange flowers. 4 ft (1.25 m).
> *'Homebush'*. Deep rose, double flowers. 4 ft (1.25 m).
> *'Hotspur'*. Flame-red flowers. 4 ft (1.25 m).
> *'Persil'*. Pure white flowers with orange flare. 4 ft (1.25 m).

Japanese azaleas. Evergreen. May-flowering. Useful for tubs.

> *'Blue Danube'*. Violet-blue flowers. 2 ft 6 in. (750 mm).
> *'Hinomayo'*. Pink flowers. 2 ft 6 in. (750 mm).
> *'Vuyk's Scarlet'*. 2 ft (600 mm).
> *'Palestrina'*. Ivory-white flowers. 2 ft 6 in. (750 mm).

Heathers

There are many attractive varieties, both winter and summer flowering. *Erica carnea* and × *darleyensis* will tolerate some lime, but in general, all heathers do best on a lime-free soil.

Heathers look best planted in groups of the same variety spaced about 12—15 in. (300—375 mm) apart. A good collection to begin with would be:

Calluna vulgaris 'J. H. Hamilton'. Bright pink, double flowers. August–September. 10 in. (250 mm).
Calluna vulgaris 'Silver Queen'. Silvery-grey foliage, purple flowers. August–September. 10 in. (250 mm).
Calluna vulgaris 'Wickwar Flame'. Lavender flowers, orange-yellow foliage in summer, turning flame-red in winter. 12 in. (300 mm).
Erica carnea 'Ada S. Collins'. Dark green foliage, white flowers, November–April. 8 in. (200 mm).
Erica carnea 'Myretoun Ruby'. Dark green foliage, ruby-red flowers, February–April. 10 in. (250 mm).
Erica carnea 'Westwood Yellow'. Golden foliage, lavender flowers. February–April. 6 in. (150 mm).
Erica cineria 'Cindy'. Bronze-green foliage, bright purple flowers, July–September. 6–8 in. (150–200 mm).
Erica cineria 'C. G. Best'. Salmon-pink flowers, July–September. 12 in. (300 mm).
Erica darleyensis 'Arthur Johnson'. Rose-pink flowers, November–May. 30 in. (750 mm).
Erica darleyensis 'Silberschmelze'. White flowers, November–April. 18 in. (450 mm).
Erica tetralix 'Pink Star'. Bright pink flowers, June–October. Grey foliage. 10 in. (250 mm).
Erica vagans 'Valerie Proudley'. Golden foliage, white flowers, August–October. 8–10 in. (200–250 mm).

Herbaceous plants for acid gardens

Lime-hating herbaceous plants are not as common as calcifuge shrubs, but the following are useful in a mixed border.

Gentians. Most prefer acid soils. Tall and low-growing forms available.
Lupins. Although these will tolerate lime, the best flowers are produced on lime-free soil and the plants last much longer.
Iris kaempferi. Blue and purple flowers. Moist soil necessary.
Lithospermum 'Heavenly Blue'. Prostrate, suitable for rockeries and the front of borders.
Meconopsis baileyi (Himalayan blue poppy). Cool, leafy soil essential.

Conifers

There are a few conifers which grow or colour better on lime-free soils. Among these are –

> *Chamaecyparis pisifera 'Boulevard'*. Steel-blue.
> *Ch. thyoides 'Andleyensis'*. Dark green, pillar-shaped.
> *Ch. thyoides 'Ericoides'*. Sea-green, turning bronze in winter.
> *Cryptomeria japonica 'Hegans'*. Feathery foliage turning red-bronze in winter.

21

VEGETABLES

If you had asked me a few years ago whether growing your own vegetables was worth it, I would probably have said 'no'. But then vegetables were inexpensive to buy, and I was not living in an intensive farming area constantly drenched with the drift from crop-spraying, so that I began to wonder just what I was eating along with my sprouts. Now two of us are more than self-sufficient from a patch 40 ft by 20 ft (12 m by 6 m), and even taking into account the price of buying fresh seed every year, providing fertilizers and sundries, it only costs me a fraction of what my annual vegetable bill would be from a greengrocer or supermarket – and it cannot be much fresher than straight out of the garden and into the pot. I do not use insecticides and fungicides as I am not growing prize-winning vegetables for show and do not mind sharing them with the odd bug providing they leave a proportionate amount for me.

Of course, you will not get reasonable vegetables if you do not look after them and observe certain principles, but anyone can produce a respectable crop, bearing the following in mind.

The Ten Commandments of happy vegetable growing

1. Always make sure your soil is in good heart. In spite of the 'no digging' cult that has sprung up in recent times, I am a firm believer in attempting to dig the area thoroughly once a year (see pages 62–3 for suggestions on how this should be done).

2. Attempt to add as much humus-forming material as possible (well-rotted manure, garden or mushroom compost, etc.) about once every three years. Some vegetables will not grow well on freshly manured ground, so the suggested crop rotation on pages 284–5, should be used if possible.

3. You will need to 'top up' the plant foods in the soil periodically when you start to crop the ground regularly. Once you begin to go into vegetable growing seriously you will encounter many specific fertilizers which can be used for individual crops, but these are bewildering to the new gardener, so for a start you can add a balanced fertilizer such as growmore or blood, fish and bone to the ground a week or so before sowing or planting out with quite satisfactory results. If you use fertilizers as suggested in the cropping plan you should not get a build-up of nutrients.

4. Make sure you break the soil down to a fine tilth before sowing seeds. If you are planting out young plants the surface need not be as fine.

5. Always read the seed producers' instructions on the back of the packets. These are put there to enable you to get the best results from the kinds of vegetables and the varieties you have chosen, but you may be able to space them slightly closer than the recommendations on the packet. The yield per plant may be reduced but the overall crop may be as high, or higher. However, if in doubt, stick to the instructions.

6. Keep the ground moist in dry spells. If not, leaf crops will be small and tough, roots will be woody, and crops such as runner beans will cease to produce their beans. Mulch if necessary.

7. If possible, try to rotate your crops so that no two similar types are grown consecutively on the same piece of ground. As well as utilizing the plant foods in the soil to the best possible advantage, it also prevents the build-up of pests and diseases specific to a certain type of crop. (There is a cropping plan on pages 284–5.)

8. Do not sow too much of a certain thing. Although home freezing has eliminated to a large extent the 'glut' experienced in the past when too much of too many crops all matured at the same time, there is nothing like fresh food – and, in any case, many vegetables (for example, salads) cannot be frozen. Small amounts of a crop should be sown at intervals to mature so that some are always ready.

9. The use of crop-protection fleece, or netting, will considerably increase your yield and substantially reduce pest infestations.

10. Do experiment with new vegetables and varieties. Once you have achieved satisfactory results with a certain thing, the temptation is to stick to it. Of course, you may find you still prefer the variety you always grew, but you do not know until you try.

Obtaining vegetable seed

The most reliable seed is that produced by the major seed companies who work to strict regulations, so you are almost certain that what you buy has a high standard of purity and germination. Most seed now is packed in moisture-proof and air-tight inner packets – these are filled with seed which has been kept under optimum temperature and moisture levels and should germinate well if you follow the instructions. Most seed gradually loses its viability as it ages, though new packaging techniques provide something like a time capsule environment – normal ageing does not start until the packet is opened, so seed from unopened, moisture-proof packets should still be usable several years after the packaging.

Saving unused seed once you have opened the packet is rather a different matter as the germination rate will normally start to drop but if you store the remainder in an air-tight tin in a cool, dark, dry place you should certainly get enough seedlings the following year for your needs, especially as one always tends to sow too thickly anyway and the original germination rate was very high. The exception is parsnip seed, which ages rapidly, even in ideal conditions and which has a low germination rate anyway.

The widest range of vegetable seed is obtained by ordering around Christmas and the New Year from the major seed-producing companies. These companies also packet their most popular varieties for retail sale in shops, supermarkets and garden centres. Shops, supermarkets and DIY outlets do not offer as big a choice, but unless you're going into vegetables in a big way, you will still be able to pick up your year's supply of vegetable seeds when you do your weekly shopping.

You may be offered home-produced seed from other amateur growers but you will not necessarily find home-saved seed as satisfactory as bought seed, either from the germination point of view, or with the varieties. Certainly there is no point in saving seed from F1 Hybrid vegetables as you will get a very assorted crop next year once the plants have interbred with themselves and others in the area, and while open-pollinated varieties generally come true to type to a greater or lesser extent, variations, good or bad, can creep in, and if you want the same variety the following year, you must be sure that the seed you are using came from a typical plant of its kind. The same applies if you are intending to save seed from your own vegetables. Seed companies operate strict quality-control standards which ensure that only the best and most true-to-type seed from suitable plants is saved for future 'sowings'. For the price of a few packets, it is hardly worth bothering to mess about with saving your own.

Having said this, amateur growers who exhibit a lot of vegetables often have their own (frequently very secret, too!) strains of seed from which they know they get results, but they are pretty experienced in this sort of thing – it takes time to recognize when you could be on to a winner.

Early crops

Early crops can be produced by covering the prepared soil with horticultural fleece, black polythene or cloches to warm up the soil for two to three weeks before sowing and again after sewing.

Catch crops

Catch crops are quick-maturing vegetables which can be sown between slower, long-standing crops to utilize the space between rows until required by the main crop itself. Suitable catch crops are radishes, small lettuces, spring onions, turnips and seed rows of brassicas. In small gardens where spacings tend to be closer than generally recommended, you may find you are no longer able to squeeze catch crops in satisfactorily. In the case of salad crops (radishes, onions), a bed can be made

281

near the main sowings of lettuces for convenience in picking if you cannot fit them in between other crops.

A word about sowing and thinning

When you sow rows of seeds, you will need to sow as thinly as possible to avoid having to thin out unduly. With small seeds, this can be quite difficult, and you may find it less of a problem if you mix the seed with a small amount of dry sand to enable you to space it out more easily. When you come to thinning, do this in several stages until you reach the required distance between plants. This is so the young plants can give each other protection while they are very small. You can eat a lot of thinnings, for example, brassicas (cabbage family), onions, lettuces, carrots and turnips.

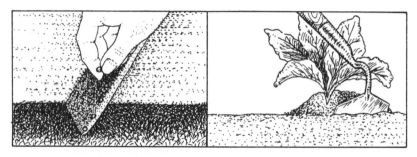

Growing vegetables in containers

Nearly all common vegetables can be grown in good soil-less compost in growing bags and containers which are large and deep enough to hold them adequately. The one thing you must be sure to do is to give them sufficient water – sometimes several times a day in summer if it is very hot, and to this you can add a liquid or soluble balanced feed once a week. Obviously it is going to be much more expensive to grow vegetables in this way than either to buy them or grow them in the open ground, but if you yearn for the taste of home-grown vegetables in season and you are short of space, all you need is a sunny corner.

Problems

While not being a truly organic gardener, I like the food I eat to be uncontaminated by chemicals, however environmentally friendly they are claimed to be. Vegetables will get attacked by pests and diseases, but if growing conditions are good, they should not be so badly affected that the entire crop is lost, especially if individual seriously attacked plants are removed.

This is a short list of the pests and diseases likely to be encountered when growing vegetables. There are many more associated with particular plants which are described in detail in the many excellent books specifically on vegetable gardening that are available today.

ROOTS AND TUBERS EATEN. Leatherjackets, millipedes, slugs, woodlice. Cover with crop-protection sheet and mulch soil with woven sheet mulching. Trap slugs in jam jars half full of stale beer.

Or, Cutworms, chafer grubs, vine weevil grubs, wireworms, cabbage root fly, carrot fly, onion fly, swift moth caterpillars. Treat soil with a soil insecticide and keep crops covered with crop protection sheeting.

HOLES AND NOTCHES IN LEAVES. Earwigs, pea and bean weevils, caterpillars, flea beetles, capsid bugs. Cover with crop-protection fleece. Remove large pests by hand.

Or, Slugs and snails. Trap as above.

Or, Pigeons and other birds. Cover the area.

BLACK, GREEN, GREY INSECTS IN CLUSTERS ON LEAVES, STEMS, ROOTS. Aphids. Spray with horticultural soft soap or hand pick; cover with crop-protection fleece.

WHITE, MOTH-LIKE INSECTS ON LEAVES. Brassica whitefly. Cover crop.

BASE OF STEMS BLACK, SHRUNKEN OR ROTTEN. One of a number of basal stem rots associated with poor growing conditions – wet, cold soil or compost and overcrowding. There is no cure, and affected plants should be removed. In young seedlings a similar condition is caused in the same way and is known as damping off or black leg.

BLISTERED OR TUNNELLED LEAVES. Leaf miner. Unlikely to be serious.

BROWN SPOTS ON LEAVES AND PODS. Leaf spots. Indicates poor growing conditions. Remove affected leaves or plants if infection serious. Try to improve conditions for subsequent crops.

YELLOWING BETWEEN VEINS. Magnesium or manganese deficiency. Can indicate a too high pH. Treat area with Epsom salts or sequestrene and check pH before resowing the area.

CROPPING PLAN FOR SMALL VEGETABLE GARDEN

Plan A: use on Year 1, on first part of your plot, in Year 2 on third part, and in Year 3 on second part (see below).

Treatment	Main Crop	When to sow	Recommended Varieties	Succession Crops	Recommended Varieties
Bulky Organic Manure	Peas	Early March–late June	'Feltham First' (early) 'Hurst Green Shaft' (main crop)		
	Broad Beans	November, or Feb–April	'The Sutton' (short) 'Jubilee Hysor'	Carrots, sow July. Beetroot, sow July.	'Autumn King' 'Vita Longa' 'Detroit' 'New Globe'
	Runner Beans	May–July	'Red Knight' 'Prizewinner'	Cabbages, plant Sept.	'Spring Hero' (round-headed)
	French Beans	End April–June	'The Prince' 'Cropper Tepee'	As above	As above
	Onions*	March	F1 'Albion' 'Rijnsburger Wijbo' 'Santé'	Cabbages, plant Sept.	'Durham Early' 'Harbinger'
	Shallots	February	Plant from sets	As above.	As above.
	Leeks†	March	'Lyon Prizetaker' 'Winter Crop'		
	Lettuce**	March–June	'Action' (butterhead) 'Great Lakes' (crisp) 'Little Gem' (cos) 'Red Salad Bowl' (looseleaf)	Sow lettuces for succession.	
	Tomatoes‡	March (under glass) plant out May	'Outdoor Girl' 'Sweet 100'		
	Spinach	Feb–May	'Monarch Long Standing'	Lettuce	'All the Year Round' (butterhead).
	Spinach Beet Chard	Spring for summer. Autumn for winter and spring.	Perpetual Spinach Rhubarb Chard		
	Celery	Sow under glass in March. Prick out into Frame April. Plant out June.	'Golden Self-Blanching' 'American Green' (no earthing up required).		
	Marrows Courgettes	Under glass March–April. Outdoors May.	F1 'Raven' 'Gold Rush' (yellow)		
	Cucumbers	As for tomatoes.	F1 'Burpless Tasty Green'		
	Peppers‡ Aubergines‡	As for tomatoes.	F1 'Redskin' (pepper) 'Carape' (pepper) 'Slice-Rite No. 23' (aubergine) F1 'Moneymaker' (aubergine)		

* Onions can be grown from sets – plants can be started under glass.
† Leeks can be started earlier in a cold frame.
** Lettuce can be sown in February in cold frame.
‡ Tomatoes, peppers and aubergines are not suitable outdoors in north.

	Year 1	Year 2	Year 3
First Part	A	B	C
Second Part	B	C	A
Third Part	C	A	B

CROPPING PLAN FOR SMALL VEGETABLE GARDEN

Plan B: use in Year 1 on second part of your plot, in Year 2 on first part, and in Year 3 on third part.

Treatment	Main Crop	When to sow	Recommended Varieties	Succession Crops	Recommended Varieties
Fertilizers and Lime (Check pH first before applying lime – do not lime if pH is above 6.5–7.0)	Brassicas* Cabbages	April–May for winter crops. March–April for summer cutting. July–Aug for following spring	'January King' (winter savoy type) 'Hispi' (summer, pointed, early) 'Minicole' (summer, compact, stands well) 'First Early Market No. 218' (spring)	Onions as ground is cleared in spring or autumn.	'Ailsa Craig' (can be sown in spring or autumn) 'Senshyu Semi-Globe' Japanese onion sets
	Sprouts	Sow March/April, plant out May/June	F1 'Rampart (early)' F1 'Fortress (late)'		
	Cauliflower	Summer under glass Jan–March. Main crop March/May	'Snow King' (early) 'Thanet' (winter) 'Dok Elgon' (autumn) 'All the Year Round'		
	Kales	March/April transplant June–Sept	'Dwarf Green Curled'		
	Broccoli	March–May. Transplant when large enough	'Early Purple Sprouting' 'Red Arrow'		
	Calabrese	As above	'Romanesco' 'El Centro' F' 'Eusebio'		
	Seed bed for greens	March onwards			

* Brassicas and other green crops require high nitrogen levels for healthy leafing and therefore are suitable for following peas and beans which fix nitrogen in the soil. All brassicas require a high pH in order to be less likely to be troubled by club root disease. Brassicas need firm planting so the ground should be well firmed around the plants.

Plan C: use in Year 1 on third part of your plot, in Year 2 on second part and in Year 3 on first part.

Treatment	Main Crop	When to sow	Recommended Varieties	Succession Crops	Recommended Varieties
Fertilizers only	Potatoes*	Early–late April	'Ulster Sceptre' (early) 'Estyma' (early) 'Désirée' (red-skinned, main crop, heavy yield)	Winter spinach, cabbages, turnips, spinach beet.	'Norvak' (spinach) 'Offenham' 'Flower of Spring' (cabbage) 'Golden Ball' (turnip)
	Carrots†	March, successionally	'Kundulus' (round, early) F1 'Navarre' (main crop)		
	Beetroot	Apr successionally	'Boltardy' (round, good for early sowings) 'Monopoly' (one seed produces one plant only; easier to thin out)		
	Parsnips	Feb–April	'New White Skin' (canker resistant)		
	Swedes	May–June	'Marian'		
	Turnips	March–July	'Green Top Stone' 'Purple Top Milan'		

* Potatoes do not want a lot of organic matter in the soil as it encourages slugs.

† Root vegetables tend to fork and become misshapen if they come into contact with fresh manure, therefore 2nd year after manuring suits them best.

DISTORTED OR SWOLLEN ROOTS.

1. *Club root disease.* Serious disease of cabbage family. There is no cure so pull up and burn plants. Do not grow brassicas on that land for several years. Raise young plants in individual containers and plant deeply.

2. *Gall weevil.* In this case there will be a maggot inside the swelling. Not serious. No treatment necessary.

3. *Eelworm.* No cure. Do not grow crop affected on that land for at least 6 years.

SPLIT, DISTORTED OR FANGED ROOTS IN ROOT CROPS. Irregular watering. Try to ensure consistent water supply.

Or, Fresh manure in the soil. Do not plant on newly manured ground.

Or, Stones. Remove as many large ones as possible from the ground.

ROOT ROTS. Several different diseases cause rots in vegetable fibrous roots, root crops, and bulbs such as onions. There is no cure and crops so affected should not be grown on the same land for several years. Rotting can also occur in heavy, cold, waterlogged soils so try to improve such soils before using for vegetables.

WHITE POWDERY COATING ON LEAVES, SOME DISTORTION. Powdery mildew. Remove badly affected plants.

YELLOWING LEAVES WITH WHITE FURRY FUNGUS BENEATH. Downy mildew. Remove affected plants.

MOTTLED LEAVES. Possibly virus. Remove affected plants and burn. Protect against aphids which spread viruses from plant to plant.

POOR BRASSICA CROPS – heartless cabbages, sprouts with loose, 'blown' rosettes instead of tight buttons, cauliflowers with loose, small or missing 'curd' (the white part). This is usually caused by insufficient firming and the plants blowing about in the wind. Brassicas should always be planted in firm soil and in windy districts sprouts should be individually staked. Drought, shade and impoverished soils can also cause these conditions so always plant in a sunny spot, fertilize well with a balanced feed, and give plenty of water in dry spells.

22

FRUIT

You need space to grow a lot of fruit but even the smallest garden should be able to accommodate the new, narrow-growing apples like 'Ballerinas' and 'Minarettes', or plums, peaches, apples and pears in containers on dwarf root stocks. Strawberries can be cultivated in growing bags and cane fruit trained on the house wall. Espalier and fan-trained forms also make good wall plants. There is nothing quite like the satisfaction of picking and eating something you have grown yourself.

What to grow

Soft fruits. Into this category come strawberries, and also raspberries, blackberries and hybrid berries such as loganberries, boysenberries and tayberries, which are also known as cane fruits because of their growth habit.

Bush fruits. These are soft fruits which grow on a low woody bush, e.g., blackcurrants and gooseberries.

Top fruits – those which produce their fruits on a tree-like form, e.g., apples and pears, and also stone fruits.

Stone fruits – those having a hard stone in the centre, e.g., plums, cherries, peaches and apricots.

Vine fruits – grapes.

Miscellaneous – e.g. figs.

SOFT FRUITS (INCLUDING BUSH FRUITS) can be grown in most parts of Britain. Strawberries do not have to be strawed down but it keeps the fruit cleaner and healthier and makes picking easier. Black polythene or tarred strawberry mats can be used instead if straw is unavailable. Strawberries also make excellent container plants.

Raspberries require the support of posts and wires. A similar system can be used for blackberries and their relatives, or these can be grown against a wall or fence, again trained on to wires at intervals.

Bush fruits must be given adequate space to develop – 6 feet (2 m) is not unreasonable. Their flowers are easily caught by late frosts, so choose a site which is not a known frost pocket.

All fruit in these categories prefer an open position in full sun, though blackberries will tolerate some shade. The soil should be in good condition, with plenty of organic matter added, and a slow-release, high-phosphate fertilizer or quick-release, balanced food incorporated at planting time, depending on whether this is autumn and early winter, or late winter and early spring. In subsequent years a balanced fertilizer can be given in spring.

The traditional planting time for soft and bush fruits is autumn, with spring (March, usually) a good second choice. Most strawberries and raspberries are still obtained as bare-root plants, but there is an increasing tendency towards containerization, which means that in theory you can plant at any time of the year providing weather and soil conditions are favourable. If you are planting strawberries in the spring, do not be tempted to take a crop off them the first year. Strawberries are technically herbaceous perennials, cane and bush fruits are shrubby plants, and so the general rules of planting for these types should be followed (see pages 177–8, 211–12). They will all require plenty of water to give good fruit. Conserve the moisture around strawberries with straw or black polythene; other soft fruits benefit from mulching, which also helps to keep the weeds down.

Propagation

Soft fruit plants do not last indefinitely and should be replaced when they begin to lose their vigour – three years in the case of strawberries, about five for raspberries, and nine or ten years for bush fruits. Blackberries can be allowed to continue for many more years than this, however, providing they are growing well, appear healthy and have been adequately pruned.

Soft fruits are very susceptible to virus diseases. This is generally the cause of a decline in cropping and you should never propagate from any but the very healthiest plants. It is usually better not to propagate from your own or anybody else's stock, but buy new Ministry of Agriculture certified plants from a reputable nursery. However, if you are absolutely certain your plants are healthy you can try producing a few of your own.

STRAWBERRIES can be propagated by rooting the young runners produced into individual pots, which are then grown on and planted out when they have become established plants of a decent size. 'Sweetheart' and Alpine strawberries can be grown from seed.

RASPBERRIES produce many new canes and these can be dug up and replanted. The same applies to all other cane fruits, but *blackberries* and *hybrid berries* will also root if the tips of new canes are pulled down and buried in the soil. Once rooted, they can be severed from the parent and replanted.

BUSH FRUITS such as *currants* and *gooseberries* can be propagated by hardwood cuttings (see page 216) taken in the autumn.

BLACKBERRIES AND BUSH FRUITS will produce new plants from seed with gay abandon. It can be an interesting exercise to grow these on to fruiting size, but you will not know what you are getting until they settle down into some sort of fruiting routine – you might be lucky, you might not. Otherwise, propagate from suckers or cuttings.

Obtaining soft fruit plants

Plants are available from specialist and general nurserymen (by mail order or collection), also from most garden centres, some supermarkets and general mail-order catalogues. If plants for sale are produced from virus-free stock, Ministry of

Agriculture certified stock, the vendor will usually say so, and if possible you should always look for this, even if it costs a bit more. Strawberry seed is available from seed merchants.

Recommended varieties

> *Strawberries*: Honeoye – good flavour and appearance.
> Hapil – High yield and quite good flavour.
> *Raspberries*: Glen Moy – early, high yield.
> Autumn Bliss – autumn-fruiting variety.
> *Blackberries and hybrid berries*: Ashton Cross – good flavour, like wild blackberry but less rampant.
> Thornless Loganberry L654 – fruits look like raspberries but flavour is more acid. Less vigorous than some varieties.
> Tayberry – purple fruits, good flavour, heavy cropper.
> Boysenberry. Resembles a dark raspberry but the flavour is like that of a blackberry.
> *Gooseberries*: Jubilee – good culinary and dessert variety.
> Invicta – high yielding and immune to American gooseberry mildew.
> *Blackcurrants*: Malling Jet – late flowering so not as easily frosted – large, long-standing fruits on long stalks.
> Ben More – heavy crops and good flavour.
> *Red and white currants*: Laxton's No. 1 is the most popular early.
> Red Lake – good mid-season variety.
> White Versailles – white berries.

Pruning, training and maintenance

STRAWBERRIES. After fruiting, remove mulching material and runners not required for propagation, then cut all the leaves off so just the crown is left.

RASPBERRIES (SUMMMER FRUITING). Remove all canes which have borne fruit when they have finished, and restrict number of new canes to 6–8 per stool, removing the rest. Tie in to wire framework, and in spring prune back canes to about 6 ft (1.8 m).

RASPBERRIES (AUTUMN FRUITING, AND NEW CANES). Cut all canes down to ground level in spring.

BLACKBERRIES AND HYBRID BERRIES. Remove fruited canes and train those required to fruit the following year into a fan-shape. As new canes grow up in the summer, tie together in the middle of the fan. Then, in the autumn, cut out the old canes in the fan, and train in the new ones, thinning out and shortening back if necessary.

GOOSEBERRIES, RED CURRANTS AND WHITE CURRANTS. These should initially be trained to grow on a short, single leg to facilitate picking. In winter cut back the growing point of each branch by half and shorten back side shoots to a node about 3 in. (75 mm) from the main branch. Remove weak, diseased, badly placed and crossing branches and those growing into the centre.

On bushes more than three years old reduce all side and main shoots to five leaves in autumn.

Gooseberries and red and white currants can be trained as single, double or triple cordons if space is short. These are supported by wires, a fence or a wall. They are best bought trained, and pruning will then consist of reducing all the side shoots to 5 leaves in June, then reducing them to two buds the following winter. Shorten back the leader in winter by one-third until it reaches the required height, then treat it in the same way as a side shoot.

BLACKCURRANTS. These are grown as a multi-stemmed 'stool'. After planting, prune the whole bush down to ground level. Many new shoots will come up from the base. The first winter following, it is not necessary to prune except to remove weak, crossing, dead and overcrowded wood. In subsequent years, remove all fruited wood, leaving only strong, unfruited stems. If there are not many of these coming up from the bottom, prune to a new shoot down the stem of the fruited branch.

Spacing distances for newly planted soft fruit plants

Strawberries: 15–18 in. (375–450 mm) between plants, 30 in. (750 mm) between rows.
Raspberries: 18 in. (450 mm) apart, 6 ft (1.8 m) between rows.
Blackberries, loganberries, etc. 6–12 ft (1.8–3.5 m) apart depending on variety, 6–7 ft (1.8–2 m) between rows.
Blackcurrants, red and white currants, gooseberries, 5–6 ft (1.5–1.8 m) between bushes, 6 ft (1.8 m) between rows.

Top fruit (including stone fruit)

The nice thing about apples, pears, plums, cherries and the like is that not only do they fulfil a useful function but they look decorative, too. However, before you rush out and buy one for the centre of your lawn, there are a few things to bear in mind.

SIZE. Top fruit grown on its own roots has a very vigorous habit in general, and so those trees you buy are grafted on to a different rootstock which slows down vegetative growth and brings them into bearing earlier.

APPLES are nowadays grafted on to M27 (very dwarf, suitable for tub cultivation), M9 (dwarf) and the semi-dwarf MM106. Choose a very dwarf type if you are extremely short of space – these will require staking all their lives – or a fairly dwarf-growing form if you have more room. Young apple trees can be obtained in a variety of free-standing forms – pyramids and bush trees are again useful in comparatively small spaces but can make mowing difficult underneath as the branches come so low down. For this reason a half-standard on a 4 ft stem might be a better choice, though it may be grafted on to a less dwarfing rootstock so could grow into quite a big tree in time. Standard fruit trees are not often seen now as they grow into such large trees that picking is very difficult.

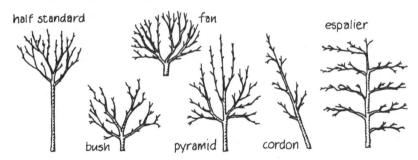

half standard   fan   espalier

bush   pyramid   cordon

In addition to the free-standing forms, cordons and espaliers (and occasionally fan-trained forms) are available, suitable for planting against walls and fences or training on post and wire supports.

FAMILY TREES are apple and pear trees where several varieties, which pollinate each other, have been grafted on to the same rootstock. This enables you to grow several varieties in a small space.

'Ballerina' trees are special varieties which produce no side branches, all the fruit being formed on spurs off the main trunk.

'Minarette' trees are specially trained forms of normal apple and pear varieties. They are somewhat like an upright cordon and are treated as such.

PEARS are usually grafted on to Quince C rootstock, which is semi-dwarfing, or sometimes on to Quince A which is less dwarfing, but more suitable for weaker-growing varieties, not-so-good growing conditions, and poor soils. They are obtainable in the same forms as apples.

PLUMS (including damsons and gages, which are similar) used to be grafted on to a number of rootstocks, most of them vigorous, except for St Julien A, which is semi-dwarfing. Now a more satisfactory dwarfing rootstock, known as Pixy, has been developed, resulting in the production of trees with a much smaller habit and which come into regular fruiting quicker. If you have only limited space, choose this type. Plums are available as half-standards (which make quite size-able trees eventually), bush, pyramid and fan-trained forms for walls and fences. Wall-trained plums fruit very well because of the additional warmth of the wall or fence.

PEACHES, NECTARINES AND APRICOTS. These are taken together as they are very similar in many respects. In most parts of the country the only practical form, particularly for apricots, is the fan, planted against a warm wall. Fan-trained trees are usually grafted on to St Julien A or Brompton rootstock so become quite large in time, but in certain cases Pixy is now being used. This makes a good small bush for a confined space or tub culture, but is really too small for fan-training, although stock grafted on to Pixy will start to bear fruit considerably sooner.

CHERRIES. At one time, cherries were not practical for any but larger gardens as there were no dwarfing stocks known, but there is now a semi-dwarfing stock called Colt, which makes cherries a more viable proposition for the small garden. Bush and half-standard forms are available, but the easiest to look after is the fan.

Planting distances for top fruit

Half standards, 18–20 ft (5.5–6 m).
Bush, 10–15 ft (3–4.5 m) depending on rootstock.
Espaliers and fans, 16–18 ft (4.8–5.5 m).
Cordons, 2 ft (600 mm).
'Ballerinas' and 'Minarettes', 2 ft (600 mm).

POLLINATION. Apples and pears, some plums and most cherries
will not in general set a proper crop unless they are cross-
pollinated with another suitable variety. The variety chosen
must be compatible as a pollinator, so before you dash round
to the nearest garden centre and fill the car boot up with
young fruit trees, make sure they are all of some use to each
other. The book *The Fruit Garden Displayed*, published by the
Royal Horticultural Society, gives a comprehensive list of
varieties and their compatibilities. Better garden centres will
also advise you on compatibility.

*Some recommended varieties, with pollination compatibilities where
appropriate*

Apples. Early: Discovery (dessert) – pollinates Arthur
Turner.
Mid-season ripening: Arthur Turner (cooker) – pollinates
Discovery.
Laxton's Fortune (dessert) – pollinates and is pollinated
by above varieties.
Early winter ripening: Spartan (dessert) – pollinates
Arthur Turner.
Late winter ripening: Laxton's Superb (dessert) – self-
fertile, pollinated by and pollinates Newton Wonder.
Newton Wonder (cooker) – pollinates and is pollinated
by Laxton's Superb.
Pears. Conference – self-fertile, also pollinates and is
pollinated by Williams' Bon Chrétien.
Williams' Bon Chrétien – early ripening, see above for
pollination.
Plums. Victoria (culinary and dessert) – self-fertile.
Early Rivers – very early, black fruit with golden flesh.
Pollinated by Victoria.
Peaches (self-fertile) Amsden June. Peregrine. Rochester.
Nectarines (self-fertile) Early Rivers. Lord Napier.
Apricots (self-fertile) Moor Park.

Cherries (sweet) Early Rivers. Governor Wood (these two pollinate each other). Stella (self-fertile).
Cherries (acid). Morello. Self-fertile and pollinates Governor Wood.

Buying fruit trees

Top fruit trees will usually be sold as two or three-year-olds. Maidens are trees in their first year after grafting and although cheaper, require training from scratch so you will not get fruit as quickly. Ideally you should look for a nicely balanced head of evenly spaced, healthy branches, or, in the case of a fan or espalier, well trained, correctly spaced branches according to the form the training has taken. Many fruit trees are now sold in containers for planting in full leaf, so make sure there are no evident signs of disease and that the tree has been properly maintained in its container (see page 210).

FRUIT TREES MAY BE BOUGHT FROM general and specialist nurseries by mail order or collection. If possible, try to obtain those covered by the Ministry of Agriculture's certification scheme to ensure you are buying healthy stock. Fruit trees can also be obtained from some supermarkets and general mail order catalogues.

Planting

APPLES AND PEARS need an open position, well prepared, well drained soil (pears will stand slightly wetter ground) and a slightly acid soil (pH 5.5–6.5). *Plums* like similar conditions, but do not appreciate a very acid soil.

PEACHES, NECTARINES AND APRICOTS prefer a slightly alkaline, but not chalky position. Bushes should be planted in the warmest, most sheltered part of the garden, but the best position in most places in Britain is against a warm, south or west-facing wall.

CHERRIES do not like heavy clays, but do well in a soil with plenty of substance, deep and well drained.

The method of planting all fruit trees is similar to that for ornamental trees and bushes (see pages 211–12) and timings are the same. Do be careful not to plant the union between the rootstock and scion (seen as a kink or knob at the base of the trunk) below soil level, as the top part will root and you will lose the dwarfing effect of the rootstock.

Bushes and trees require firm staking and tying, at least in the early years. Fans, cordons and espaliers must be tied to strong galvanized or plastic-covered wire spaced about 18 in. (450 mm) apart or to fit the trained branches. This wire can either be attached to the wall or fence or to stout posts in the ground. Cordons are usually planted and tied in at an angle of 45°. This angle can be reduced as the bushes grow, to enable you to reach the tops more easily.

If you are growing fruit trees and bushes in grass, leave a square of bare earth around the base of the trunks for a year or two until the trees become established.

After-care

Pruning is the main regular job, and the trees should be sprayed as a matter of course against pests and diseases. Check stakes and ties when you prune and at intervals in between.

Young trees require a lot of water in the early stages and moisture can be conserved by giving a mulch of grass clippings in the summer.

Try not to let the trees carry any fruit the first year after planting. It seems hard, but it is kinder to the plants and beneficial in the long run.

Do not grow grass right up to the trunk for the first few years after planting.

Feeding

You cannot go far wrong if you give a balanced feed, according to the manufacturers' recommendations, in spring, providing your trees are growing well, and a regular mulch of organic material if you can. If you overfeed them, especially with a fertilizer containing a good proportion of nitrogen, you will find they make too much growth at the expense of fruiting. While good strong growth is necessary to build up a healthy framework, at some stage you want your labours to bear fruit, so to speak. If your fruit trees seem reluctant to oblige, switch to a high-potash fertilizer. If this still does not have the desired effect, try grassing down the bare earth around the trunk. The additional competition should slow down growth and force the trees into thinking about what they are really there for.

In acid soil, rhododendrons and azaleas are unrivalled for spring display.

The impressive bracts of pieris (flame of the forest), an excellent plant for lime free soil.

A well trained Espalier pear tree. *(Tim Sandall)*

Red currants are a much under-rated soft fruit. *(Tim Sandall)*

Bedding plants combine well with permanent subjects for extra summer colour.

Bedding plants used to create a colourful informal summer border.

A mass planting of petunias makes a breathtaking formal display.

Spring bulbs are invaluable for early colour.

A rock garden enables many plants to be grown in a confined space.

A herbaceous border should be as colourful in spring as summer.

Amelanchier lamarckii (snowy mespilus) – a superb shrub or small tree for all seasons.

Mesembryanthemum (Livingstone daisy) will survive long periods without water.

'Silver Jubilee' – one of the best hybrid tea roses of modern times.

The dark red flowers of *Rosa moyesil* are followed by striking flagon-shaped hips.

A well clothed pergola can look as good from a first floor window as it does from the ground.

Clematis 'Madame le Coultre' and climbing rose 'Danse du Feu' are ideal plants for a pergola.

A well designed wooden fence can be used to advantage to divide a large open stretch of garden.

A hanging basket of mixed bedding plants blends well with the dark summer foliage of *Clematis montana* 'Rubens'.

A prizewinning container display is a joy to customers of this tea room.

An eye-catching array of containerized plants enhances the lines of a modern garage – but watch the weight!

Even a very small front garden can accommodate a selection of colourful containers.

The site for the Anglian Water Conservation Garden, autumn 1991.

The completed garden, early spring 1993.

Propagation

As has already been said, young fruit trees are produced commercially by grafting and this is not a worthwhile exercise for the weekend gardener.

Young apples, pears, plums and cherries can easily be raised from pips and stones, but you're unlikely to get new stock bearing more than a passing resemblance to the parent. It is interesting to do this, providing you are not disappointed if your swans turn out to be geese, but you must remember that as these plants are growing on their own roots, they will not have the dwarfing and earlier fruiting influence of the rootstock, so your babies could end up very big, and take a long time to bear fruit, which may or may not be worth eating anyway. However, if you cannot resist planting pips and stones to see what comes up, it is worth remembering that perhaps that most famous apple variety of all, the Bramley Seedling, originated by chance in just this way. Peaches, on the other hand, can produce quite reputable progeny from stones, as long as you do not mind waiting a few years till they are old enough to fruit.

Pruning

The golden rule is *never* to prune more than is necessary to form a well shaped tree and encourage the production of fruiting spurs. Under-pruning is better than over-pruning.

Apples and pears

HALF-STANDARDS AND BUSHES. *Young trees.* Cut the maiden tree to a bud at the height required in autumn and winter. The following summer several shoots will result; choose the three or four best-placed and healthiest (this is the stage at which you may buy a bush from the nursery), and remove the rest. These shoots should be shortened back at the end of the year by half or a third to a bud pointing in the direction you wish the shoots to grow. In subsequent winters shorten the leaders by a third, or by half, and remove all branches not in the correct position to give you an open cup-shaped bush.

Established trees (about four years old). Remove all dead, dying, badly placed and crossing branches in winter. Shorten the laterals produced the previous summer by about one-third if you find that only the buds near the tips tend to break in the

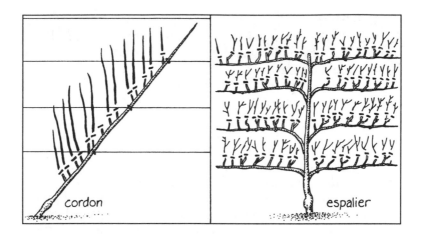

cordon   espalier

spring. You may leave the leaders unpruned if the tree is growing well. Fruit buds should then form on two-year-old wood.

PYRAMIDS. Treat *maidens* as above. Cut back the resulting main shoot the following winter to a bud on the opposite side. Repeat this every winter until the desired height is reached – this method keeps the main stem upright. Prune back the laterals at the same time by a third or a half. Shorten laterals from these to 3–4 buds and their sub-laterals to 1 bud.

Prune *established dwarf* pyramids in summer (July–August). Prune back the new lateral growth to about 4 buds and also any side growths from these buds, prune any sub-laterals from these to 1 bud. Prune new branches arising from the main stem back to 4 buds. Tie back short laterals. Cut back the main leader on the stem by about a third or a half in winter.

CORDONS. Plant a maiden and immediately prune any side-shoots back to about 3 buds, to a downward-pointing bud. In late July–August cut back all shoots arising from the main stem to 3–4 buds, and any shoots arising from these to 1 bud. Fruit buds will form at the base after about 2 years, and until this happens the arising laterals you should prune back to 1 bud.

ESPALIERS. You will usually buy these ready-trained with 3 to 5 branches which are trained on to strong wires in appropriate positions as already described. To form extra tiers, choose 2 well positioned laterals arising from the leader, which you

298

treat in the same way as that of a pyramid, and train them out on to further strands of wire. Prune each main branch of the espalier in summer like a cordon.

FANS. Again, it is as well to start with a well trained young tree with two arms, though you can cut back a maiden to form your own. Prune these arms back the following winter by a third or to a half, and allow 3 evenly spaced shoots to grow out on the topside of the branch in the summer. Rub all others out. The next winter, treat these branches in the same way until the whole of the available space is covered, then you can summer-prune the tree in a similar way to an espalier.

Plums and cherries

BUSHES AND HALF-STANDARDS require as little pruning as possible. Do this in April to avoid infection by silver leaf disease. Cut out dead, diseased, badly placed and crossing branches completely. the more you cut back, the more unproductive regrowth will follow.

DWARF PYRAMIDS AND FANS are trained in a similar way to apples and pears but you should delay the winter pruning until April. Pinch back shoots which are not needed to 6 leaves. When other shoots have reached the required length pinch these out as well. Then in late summer, after fruiting, shorten all pinched-out shoots by a half.

Peaches, nectarines and apricots

These are best trained as a fan against a warm wall. Pruning is time consuming and rather complicated, but the object is to encourage the production of new wood to fruit the following year. Peaches bear fruit on year-old wood, so the aim is to replace the wood that has fruited with new growths. Once you have built up a framework of branches by cutting back new growth by half in winter and tying in suitable resultant shoots in summer, you then pinch them out at 4–6 leaves in summer. There will be a new shoot or shoots growing out at the base. The fruit is borne on the pinched shoot the following season, remove this shoot in winter and tie in one of the new basal growths to take its place. Repeat the procedure each year. Treat nectarines similarly.

Apricots bear fruit on spurs as well as on one- and two-year-old wood, so do not remove unwanted laterals, as with peaches, but cut them back to 2 buds to encourage the formation of spurs.

Other fruit

The two most often encountered fruits which do not fit the above categories are figs and grapes.

FIGS are hardy but need shelter and warmth if the fruit is to ripen. They are best trained fanwise against a wall, and pruning consists of removing unwanted, badly placed, diseased and dying wood in March. The embryo fruit is produced at the tips of well ripened growths made the previous summer, and it helps to swell the fruits if you pinch out the tips of the shoots bearing them. The soil should not be too rich and the roots must be restricted by enclosing them with corrugated iron, brick or concrete and a rubble base. A cubic yard (or metre) of soil in the enclosure around the roots is ample. Alternatively, figs grow well in a big tub. Brown Turkey is the best and most flavoursome for outside planting.

GRAPES. Grapes will ripen only on a very warm wall. They require similar growing conditions to those of figs, except the roots need not be enclosed. The easiest way to train them is informally by removing the fruited canes in winter and tying new growths to wires, trellis or similar as they are formed. Suitable outdoor varieties such as 'Brandt', which is also a very ornamental plant, should always be chosen. In favourable parts of Britain, you should be able to grow wine-making grapes on posts and wires in the open ground. Producing good wine-making grapes from these is a specialist subject beyond the scope of this book.

Pests and diseases

A whole book could be written on this subject alone. The problems that plague all types of fruit are so numerous and so likely to occur that it is better to take regular action before the trouble starts. If you use approved and recommended chemicals, according to the manufacturer's instructions, the fruit should be quite safe to eat. Apart from viruses, which generally show up as distorted or mottled leaves and a general loss of vigour, and for which there is no cure, most pests and diseases can be prevented by spraying at the right time, so it is as well to get into the habit, but you may also encounter the following:

SILVER LEAF DISEASE is caused by a fungus which enters through a wound in the bark made in winter and causes a silvering of the leaves and die-back. The affected branches should be removed below the staining you will find in affected wood, and the wounds painted with a wound sealant. It usually affects members of the plum and cherry family, so to avoid the risk prune only during the summer.

FIREBLIGHT has become more common in recent years, especially in the southern half of England, and affects members of the family Rosaceae, of which most top fruits are members. The leaves wilt and hang down as though they have been scorched, they soon turn brown and the branch dies. It is a very infectious disease, so cut out and burn all affected parts immediately.

CRACKED BARK. Usually caused by poor growing conditions or bacterial canker, sometimes a fungal infection is also involved. Dead and dying branches should be removed. Do not expect fruit trees to do well in bad conditions. Mulch and feed regularly. Plant new trees in the best position you can provide.

NUTRIENT DEFICIENCY SYMPTOMS are a yellowing or reddening of the leaves, browning between the veins and leaf-edge scorch. They can be relieved by giving a quick-acting balanced feed or, if practical, a foliar feed of a soluble fertilizer.

BIRDS can cause havoc to both soft and top fruit, eating buds, flowers and the fruit itself. If practical, net the plant or enclose all soft fruit in a properly constructed fruit cage.

NO FRUIT. The general cause of this, apart from birds, especially if the bushes have flowered normally and, in the case of top fruit, suitable pollinators have been provided where necessary, is frost, and you can tell if your flowers have been frosted if the petals remain normal but the centres turn dark brown or black. If a frost is forecast and it is practical to do so, cover the plants overnight with fine netting, such as old net curtains, or protect strawberries with cloches. Otherwise you'll just have to put up with no crop or a greatly reduced one for that season. Some apples have a tendency anyway towards biennial cropping – having a large crop one year and next to nothing the following.

Healthy fruit is rarely so badly affected with pests and diseases that it becomes a serious problem.

APPLE AND PEAR SCAB can cause trouble in certain seasons. Clean up all leaves and affected fruit and dispose of hygienically to prevent the disease being carried on from year to year.

PLUM APHID may be a nuisance on the young growths of members of the plum family, causing distortion and disfigurement with honeydew and sooty mould. It will not generally affect the crop and, as the shoots mature, the aphids will disappear. Trees netted against birds can be worse infested as birds will pick off and eat many pests.

AMERICAN GOOSEBERRY MILDEW will spoil a crop by covering the fruit with a whitish or yellowish deposit. This is the only time I would suggest spraying with a fungicide – *before* the disease appears.

PEACH LEAF CURL. Spray twice at fortnightly intervals in March with Bordeaux mixture. This fungal disease is spread through rainwater, so protecting outdoor peaches and nectarines at this time of year from rain falling on the branches will eliminate much of the problem.

CODLING MOTH CATERPILLARS can cause serious damage to the centres of apples. Trap the males with a pheromone codling moth trap in June to prevent the females being fertilized.

OVERWINTERING PESTS AND DISEASES can be controlled by greasebanding the trunks of top fruit to trap flightless insects, and by washing dormant trees and bushes with a tar-oil solution in winter.

23

GARDENING UNDER GLASS

Of course, an attractive garden does not *need* glass. You can grow suitable vegetables at the right time, plant subjects which are hardy in our climate, and buy in plants which need a warm start, all without providing protection of any kind. All glass is expensive, both in its initial provision and in upkeep, and especially to heat, so if your only intention is to raise a few bedding plants or grow your own tomatoes, do not bother with it. If you long to grow exotic vegetables, choose varieties that will grow outdoors. It is often argued that you can save a lot of money for the outlay of a greenhouse but this is true only if you are prepared to go into the matter scientifically, and produce enough plants or crops to be able to sell your surplus economically. Otherwise greenhouse gardening is an interesting but expensive hobby.

The same applies to cloches and cold frames. If you can knock something up out of a roll of polythene and some wire, or some old glazed windows and second-hand timber, then you are on to a winner, but if you intend to equip yourself with one or more of the very good but comparatively pricey items now available, you must want early or late vegetables very badly or have a strong urge to propagate masses of plants, to justify the cost.

Conservatories are a rather different matter, however. Their popularity has rocketed in recent years and they are no longer glorified lean-to greenhouses but aesthetic and functional additional rooms. While these are in an even higher price bracket than the ordinary free-standing greenhouse, not only do they enable you to indulge whichever aspects of indoor gardening take your fancy, they bring the outdoors inside the home.

Gardening under glass is a whole science in itself, and it is beyond the scope of this book to do more than scrape the surface of the subject, but included here is a list of what you could consider if you feel the urge to experiment, and suggestions for how they can be used.

Cloches

These come in many shapes and sizes.

GLASS PANES AND CLIPS are simple and can be dismantled for storage, but the glass is easily broken. Rigid plastic sheeting may be used instead but must be handled carefully, as it can scratch, which will eventually reduce light transmission.

POLYTHENE SHEET AND WIRE HOOPS (tunnel cloches) are the most useful for covering long stretches. The materials are inexpensive but the polythene soon deteriorates and should be renewed annually.

PLASTIC CLOCHES are obtainable in a variety of shapes and sizes based on a rigid curved or square section frame and rigid or flexible horticultural-grade PVC. Many have tops which can be slid open without having to remove the whole structure to gain access to the crops growing underneath. Make sure that these have adequate anchorages – most of them have prongs on the bottom which can be pushed firmly into the ground – otherwise they can blow away in a strong wind.

Uses

1. To warm the soil in spring before making early sowings.
2. To give protection to early-sown crops.

3. To protect overwintering crops from conditions of extreme wet and cold.

(Note: If you only want the cloches for warming the soil, you can achieve just as good results by covering the dug and broken-down soil with sheets of polythene weighted down with bricks for a week or two before sowing. A refinement of this is to cover the ground after sowing with slitted plastic film, through which the young plants grow. The film warms the soil and acts as a mulch to the crops.)

Cold frames

These are usually low structures, about 30 in. (750 mm) tall at the highest, covered with glass, horticultural plastic or polythene, but vertical ones which can be converted to tomato houses are also available. The walls can either be of transparent material, in the case of a low frame, or solid. The clear top of the frame (or front of a vertical one) is removable or openable and solid walls can be made of brick, wood, concrete, or other similar material, even straw bales or turves if you only want a temporary structure, or alternatively of glass or horticultural rigid plastic. There are many good self-assembly and ready-assembled models available, or you can make your own quite simply by obtaining an old window, complete with glass (these are often advertised in the small ads in local papers by people who have had replacement windows installed) and fitting it over a large, strong, wooden box.

Although 'cold' frames are so called because they are unheated, they can have soil-warming cables installed if required.

PROPAGATING FRAMES work on the same principle but are smaller and tighter fitting in order to provide the necessary humid atmosphere. These can be home-made and unheated, or have soil-warming cables incorporated, but there are scores of very good electrically and paraffin-heated ready-made models on the market. They are generally used to provide a warm environment in a larger glass structure, or can be placed on a light window-sill.

Uses

1. To speed up germination of seeds by giving them a warm atmosphere.

2. To raise early crops which would not be hardy in the open ground (e.g., salads).

3. To protect slightly tender plants and newly rooted cuttings over winter.

4. For striking cuttings – the added protection facilitates rooting.

5. For hardening off greenhouse-raised plants before planting out in summer. In this case the young plants are removed from the greenhouse and placed in the frame, the top of which is left open during the day and replaced at night in case of late frosts. Eventually the top can be left off all the time, and when all risk of frost is past the plants can be put out in their final positions.

Greenhouses and conservatories

Generally speaking, greenhouses and conservatories can supply the same sort of facilities as each other, the main difference being that conservatories have a wider range of building materials in their construction, and often, if they have been added to a property as a sun-room extension, they may have a solid roof, which cuts down the available light. Modern conservatories are also double-glazed.

Although you may not need planning permission or building consent to erect a free-standing or conservatory-type structure if it does not exceed a certain area, it is advisable to check first.

Greenhouses are usually purchased these days as ready-to-assemble units, which can either be bought for do-it-yourself erection, or in many cases, an erection service is available as an optional extra from the stockist.

They are mostly made nowadays from either aluminium, which is by far the most popular, or timber, but occasionally iron-framed ones are seen. One or two firms are now selling PVC-U greenhouses, which combine the low maintenance attributes of aluminium with the good looks of painted timber. Aluminium greenhouses are light and easy to assemble and require no further maintenance to the constructional materials once erected but they tend to look a little austere in the surroundings of traditional architecture. Timber greenhouses are usually made of cedar wood. They blend considerably better into the garden scene but the timber requires periodic treatment with a cedarwood preservative. They also

306

require slightly more skill in their erection.

Sometimes softwood greenhouses are available – these also have to be treated, or preferably painted, which increases the time required for regular maintenance considerably.

Galvanized iron-framed greenhouses are less common and are generally used in connection with semi-rigid plastic sheeting or polythene. These are much cheaper but also much less permanent and can have problems associated with the polythene or plastic deteriorating and also with ventilation. They tend not to look as attractive, either.

Conservatories are usually made from PVC-U, aluminium or timber, often incorporating other building materials, such as brick and stone. Timber has a better appearance than aluminium and plastic, but requires more maintenance.

Greenhouses are obtainable in a variety of shapes: *Rectangular* ones are the most common and perhaps the most useful for the majority of gardeners. Some firms make extension modules which can be added to a smaller greenhouse. Mini-green-houses, similar in all respects except for the size, are also available. In very tight spots, they can be useful, but it is better perhaps to look on them more as a large, vertical garden frame.

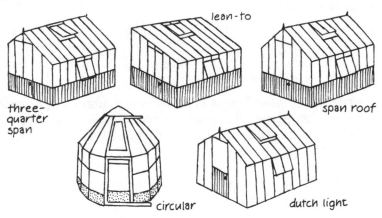

three-quarter span

lean-to

span roof

circular

dutch light

LEAN-TO GREENHOUSES are next to the rectangular ones in the popularity stakes. They can be attached to a house wall, high garden wall, or over a door. They are almost as satisfactory as the free-standing ones and much warmer. Sometimes plants can be drawn towards the light and away from the solid walls so the plants should be turned regularly. They are slightly cheaper as you only have to purchase three sides. A modification of this is the mini-lean-to which is only as wide as the 2 ft (600 mm) staging it can accommodate. It is invaluable for very small areas, but heating and ventilation can be a problem.

DUTCH-LIGHT GREENHOUSES have sides of large glass panels which slope outwards. They are very light and make good cropping units but it is expensive to replace the large panes should one be accidentally broken.

THREE-QUARTER SPAN GREENHOUSES have an asymmetrical roof span which means that one side wall is much shorter than the other. This can have its uses in specific cases but they are hard to come by.

CIRCULAR GREENHOUSES are really comprised of many narrow side and roof panels arranged to give a rounded shape. They are quite decorative in appearance but the working space is very limited. They are also much more expensive than the equivalent growing area of a rectangular glasshouse.

MANSARD-ROOFED GREENHOUSES have two sloping roof surfaces at each side. They are very attractive but expensive and not really practical as a small unit.

DOMED GLASSHOUSES are really more of a novelty than anything else, with their space-age shape, although a large one can make good cover for a small swimming pool, and they can look quite nice as free-standing conservatories.

TUNNEL HOUSES comprise a series of metal hoops supporting heavy-duty, clear polythene. They are an economical alternative to glass for a large area, but the polythene has to be renewed frequently.

In addition to the basic shapes, there are also other factors to take into consideration.

CURVED EAVES are attractive, especially if the construction is attached to your main property, but expensive, and by no means essential.

GLASS TO GROUND greenhouses have all sides fully glazed. They admit most light but require most heating as the heat loss is greater. The useful growing area is bigger because there are no solid panels to obscure the light.

308

PARTIALLY GLAZED greenhouses have a solid wall of aluminium, plastic, wood or brick for part of the way up the sides. They are much warmer than glass-to-ground houses but all crops requiring light have to be grown on staging above the solid part, and only shade-loving plants or equipment can be accommodated underneath the staging. This type of glasshouse is much safer where young children are involved as they cannot run straight into the glass. In high-risk areas, glass can be replaced by toughened, clear plastic sheeting.

SHED/GREENHOUSE COMBINATIONS. These have glazed sides and a shed section at the back. They can be useful if only a few plants are to be grown, otherwise you are far better with a small shed and a vertical cold frame.

Choosing a greenhouse

Greenhouses can be obtained from glasshouse stockists, some garden centres, direct from the manufacturer in certain cases, from DIY outlets and general mail-order catalogues, though here the choice is limited.

You will have to decide what shape and of what construction you want your greenhouse. In addition, before you buy it is as well to look round to see what you get for your money. Many greenhouses are offered as 'package deals', but prices, and the 'package' they contain, vary considerably. For example, you will probably need *staging* on which to work and place trays and pots. *Ventilation* is very important, so does the greenhouse have sufficient, both as opening roof lights, and panels lower down, to ensure an adequate circulation of air, or do these have to be provided as an optional extra? A *gutter and downpipe* are not essential, but certainly it is useful to have a tub of rainwater near the greenhouse and the side glass stays clean longer if rainwater is not running down it all the time. Some greenhouse prices include all these, some do not.

Accessories

DOUBLE GLAZING AND OTHER INSULATION. With the high cost of heating a greenhouse, insulation in winter is essential. Some glasshouses are supplied with double glazing as standard, but they are pricey. Some have glazing bars capable of taking a secondary pane of glass or acrylic and these might be a good buy. Even if you cannot afford it now, you might want double

309

glazing later. There are methods of attaching a second pane, such as magnetic strip or special clips, so if you intend to insulate in this way, make sure it is feasible for the model you mean to buy. With cedarwood or other timber it is easy to fit secondary glazing, but with some aluminium frames you can run into all kinds of problems.

An alternative is bubble insulation, where bubbles of air have been trapped between two flexible layers of polythene. This works very well apart from the reduction in light transmission and the condensation which forms between the glass and the bubble polythene. This type of insulation usually lasts about three years before becoming so opaque through sunlight and algae as to require replacing. Bubble polythene need not be removed in summer and will provide some protection against excessive heat and light. It is easily fitted to most glasshouses with special clips. Thermal screens of insulating materials and netting can also be installed to cut down the roof height and heat loss through the upper glass and there are special insulating nettings also available. There are constant developments in this field being introduced on to the amateur market, so if you intend to heat your greenhouse in winter, consult the supplier at the time you buy it about the most suitable for the particular model you have in mind.

SHADING. In summer, you have a temperature problem in reverse, for as the sun gets stronger, heat soon builds up under the glass. You can obtain roller blinds from greenhouse accessory stockists, but much cheaper are the proprietary white paints which you can brush on to the inside of the glass to filter the hottest of the sun's rays. There is an even better one which you paint on to the outside and which becomes transparent and therefore lets in more light again, when it rains. Shading nets are also available.

AUTOMATIC OPENING VENTS. These work either by a lever mechanism controlled by the contraction and expansion of fluid inside the piston cylinder, or by a small electric motor operated by a thermostat. If you are out or away a lot, they are a useful accessory, but are no replacement for regular supervision.

MAXIMUM AND MINIMUM THERMOMETERS are essential for checking how high the temperature inside the greenhouse has risen, or how low it has fallen, over a period of 24 hours. The highest and lowest temperatures are recorded either by markers pushed up and down by the liquid in the thermometer tubes, or electronically.

Heating

If you decide to have heat in the greenhouse itself, and not just in propagating frames inside, you have several choices available. *Natural gas, domestic fuel oil, and solid fuel heating* are really only suitable for larger structures and work with water pipes in a similar way to central heating in the home.

PARAFFIN STOVES are perhaps the easiest and cheapest forms of free-standing heaters and can vary from the very simple to the highly sophisticated but they have a common problem in that they must be well maintained or they will emit fumes harmful to plants and because of this, and also because they give off water vapour as they burn, ventilation must be watched carefully.

NATURAL GAS AND PROPANE GAS can also be used in flueless heaters but again there is a problem of fumes so adequate ventilation must be provided.

ELECTRICITY is possibly the most expensive but the most efficient form of heating (though if you are on the Economy 7 tariff your night costs are considerably reduced). It can be used to power fan, convector, panel or tubular heaters, soil-warming cables or prefabricated electric blankets. It gives off no fumes and can be accurately regulated by thermostat. In addition, an electric fan heater can be used as an extra means of ventilation and air circulation in summer by blowing cold air around the greenhouse.

Watering

If you are away a lot, you may like to consider some aids to help the watering situation.

CAPILLARY MATTING can be placed under the pots on the staging and kept constantly damp by dipping one end into a reservoir. The plants absorb what they need through the compost behind the holes in the base of the pots (or through a wick up the central hole of a clay pot).

311

MICROBORE IRRIGATION is a more controllable method, in which each plant or group of plants is watered by drip-ends fed by thin plastic pipes. Some drip-ends are capable of being regulated for rate of flow, and the whole system can be connected to an electric timer for complete automation.

MIST UNITS are devices for keeping the air humidity high and surrounding conditions very damp and are especially useful for striking cuttings under glass. A fine spray of water is turned on and off automatically as necessary, usually by an 'electronic leaf' of 2 electrodes which turn on the water when the film of water between them dries out. They should be used with care in greenhouses also containing established plants as they can cause leaf rotting and disease.

Siting the greenhouse

Greenhouses are usually supplied with a plinth of the same material they are constructed with and this can be placed straight on to the earth or concrete where the house is to be erected, or, preferably, put on to a foundation and dwarf wall of bricks or concrete.

It is really a matter of personal preference whether you decide to concrete or pave the whole floor or leave borders down one or either side. The soil in borders can eventually become disease ridden and will require sterilizing, or preferably changing if you are growing the same crops year after year, but if you are growing conservatory-type permanent ornamental plants, these can be planted safely into the border soil. The alternative is to use pots or growing bags, replacing the compost annually.

It is often recommended that the best position for siting a greenhouse is running east–west, which admits most light and provides both a sunny and a shady side, but in many gardens the ideal aspect is not possible, so aim for an open, sheltered, level position away from objects which cast a heavy shade, and especially not under trees. Having said this, even a north-facing lean-to can be put to good use if no other aspect is available, though the choice of plants is more limited. If possible, the greenhouse should be accessible to the nearest water supply and preferably the electricity mains as well

If you are erecting your own greenhouse, do take notice of the instructions supplied with it and follow the manufacturer's recommendations and the sequence of construction – this is usually done for a reason; not only does it make the assembly easier, but if you try to short-cut or use your own methods you can often end up with a bent frame and a pile of broken glass.

Plants to grow

You can grow just about everything in a greenhouse, providing you can give the conditions that suit the plants.

THE COLD (UNHEATED) GREENHOUSE. This has no heat as a matter of course, though some temporary heating may have to be provided in exceptionally cold weather. The simplest uses to which it can be put are those of a cold frame, but there is a lot more besides that you can do. In winter a display of hardy plants in pots can cheer up the dullest months – you can use any early flowering shrubs – they will come into flower much earlier and not be spoiled by bad weather. You can also grow early perennials – hellebores, polyanthus, lilies of the valley, doronicums and the like, hardy annuals, which will come into flower in early spring from an autumn sowing protected through the winter in the greenhouse and bulbs in pots. In all but the coldest winter you can overwinter your pelargoniums, fuchsias and other perennial bedding plants in a cold house.

Winter lettuce sown in October will be ready for cutting in April. Slightly tender peaches and vines can be grown indoors without heat. Once the temperature has reached around 45°– 50°F (8°–10°C) in *spring*, you can make early sowings of most vegetables for planting out in pots.

You can continue to grow ornamentals throughout *summer* – hydrangeas, fuchsias, pelargoniums, begonias, and many more, or you may prefer to turn to vegetables like peppers, tomatoes, aubergines, cucumbers, melons, etc.

What you must bear in mind, however, is that you may not be able to grow all these things *together* successfully. If you have a large vine blocking most of the sunlight, you won't be able to ripen tomatoes as well, and flowering plants needing a lot of light will suffer. The fun is experimenting to see what you can get away with.

THE COOL HOUSE. If you can maintain a temperature of 45°–50°F (8°–10°C) in winter by one of the methods of heating and insulation already described, you can, in addition to the plants suitable for a cold house, grow a wide range of slightly tender plants, shrubs such as *Rhododendron simsii*, datura, abutilon, *boronia*, *acacia*, and plumbago, bulbs like hippeastrums, Scarborough lilies, and arum lilies, perennials such as carnations and chrysanthemums, and pot plants like cyclamen, *Primula malacoides* and calceolarias.

In *spring* you can germinate the seed of tender summer vegetables and summer outdoor bedding plants, once a temperature of 60°F (15°C) can be maintained, usually from mid-March.

In *summer* all the plants suitable for the cold house can be grown as conditions will be identical.

In *autumn* you can take cuttings of half hardy perennials such as pelargoniums (geraniums) and sow seed of cyclamen and schizanthus, the poor man's orchid. If you sow suitable varieties of lettuce in October, you should be able to cut from February, and you can also grow mustard and cress and radishes.

THE INTERMEDIATE HOUSE. If you want to maintain a temperature of 55°F (13°C) or more, night and day, even in the coldest days of winter, it is going to cost you money, but if you can afford it, it is worth it, because many of the houseplants which struggle to survive in difficult conditions in the home will do very well with the increased light, regular temperature, and higher humidity of this kind of environment. Dracaenas, poinsettias, marantas, ferns, coleus, the choice is endless, and also tender vegetables will appreciate this temperature. You can force strawberries, and figs grown in this heat will fruit in late spring. Bedding plants for outdoor summer display can be raised in spring.

THE WARM ('HOT' OR 'STOVE') HOUSE. A temperature of over 64°F (18°C) in winter and 70°–81°F (21–27°C) in summer, will give you your own touch of the tropics, because those plants which can normally survive only in a warm, light room – crotons, kalanchoes, peperomias, caladiums, etc., together with most of those suitable for the intermediate house – begonias (ornamental-leaved forms), swiss cheese plants, etc., can be grown. The increased humidity will compensate for the higher temperature.

From a practical point of view, intermediate and warm greenhouses are not feasible as they are far too costly to heat.

314

However, this type of environment can be created in a conservatory or sun-lounge attached to the house and used as an extra room, where you can enjoy the warmth as well as your plants.

Do not forget that an enclosed heated propagator or horticultural electric blanket will enable you to raise young plants at higher temperatures than those of the greenhouse in which it is placed, if necessary. You can also, if necessary, section off an area of a larger greenhouse to provide a different environment.

Looking after the greenhouse

What you do regarding the cultivation of individual plants will largely depend on type and variety, but there are general rules of maintenance which will apply in most cases.

1. If the greenhouse is constructed of timber, make sure it is regularly treated or painted.

2. Always keep the glass clean outside and in, especially in winter when light is at a premium. Dirty glass can considerably reduce the amount of light reaching the plants, particularly if it is dirty on both sides. Thorough washing with detergent and water, to which has been added some weak bleach, is usually adequate, though greenhouse glass cleaners containing a disinfectant and algicide and cleaning agents to make the glass sparkle are available. Unlike bleach and many disinfectants, they can be used without taking the plants out of the greenhouse as they are harmless and can be hosed off if necessary rather than being removed with a cloth or sponge. Do not forget to get as much of the algicide as you can down the cracks where the panes of glass overlap each other, or the glazing bars.

3. Keep your eye on the thermometer, especially in very cold or very hot periods. Forgetting to use shading or to increase the ventilation in summer, or to close the vents and turn up the heating in winter, can be fatal to plants.

4. One way of making conditions more tolerable in sunny summer weather is to 'damp down' the floor and staging with water during the day when the heat builds up. Do not do this during the evening as it can encourage moulds, rotting and other diseases when the temperature drops.

5. If you do not have any automatic watering aids, keep a

315

watchful eye on the watering. In winter, spring and autumn you will have to observe your plants carefully to see if and when water is needed, but in summer, especially if you are growing plants in pots and bags, you may have to water several times a day. It is best not to water late in the day when the greenhouse is cooling off.

6. At least once a year, try to give your greenhouse a thorough clean-out. Remove the plants and all debris, and scrub down the benches, staging, timbers, glazing bars, structural members, the floor, and anything else you can lay your hands on, with a disinfectant. At the same time you can wash the glass thoroughly and paint or treat anything that needs it. Late summer is the best time, especially if you have to move out tender plants, unless you have tomatoes or other crops which are not movable, when you should do the job in autumn or spring.

In order to reduce pests and diseases hiding in the nooks and crannies, as you do this you can treat the greenhouse with pest and disease smoke cones to fumigate it. It is especially important, however, to ensure that any chemicals used are safe in the confined atmosphere of the greenhouse.

7. Inspect the greenhouse regularly, but more often in winter, and remove all dead bits that have dropped off on to the pot tops, staging, floor, etc., before they can start to rot and start diseases. Check plants over as a matter of routine as well and take off all dead parts, dying leaves, spent flowers and the like, for the same reason. You will also notice any signs of pests and diseases, which can be dealt with accordingly.

Pests and diseases

Most of the trials and tribulations affecting other garden plants (see pages 168–73, 215–16) also affect those under glass, only worse, because the increased warmth and close atmosphere will encourage them. There are, however, many which are especially annoying in the greenhouse, the most common of which are listed in the table opposite.

Note: Most common insects are attracted to yellow colouring. Many insect pests can be trapped successfully by suspending the yellow sticky cards readily available from garden centres amongst the foliage of glasshouse plants. These should be positioned *before* signs of infestation, and removed when the surfaced becomes thickly covered with trapped insects.

316

COMMON GREENHOUSE PROBLEMS

Symptoms	Cause	Remedy
Rotting flowers and buds, grey mould or discoloured blotches on leaves, stems and sometimes fruit	Botrytis	Spray with Benlate. Remove affected parts. Reduce watering and watch humidity in cold weather.
Powdery dust on leaves, new shoots distorted	Powdery mildew	Spray with Benlate.
Web-like covering on leaves which look dry and discoloured, red dust-like deposit	Red spider mite	Mist regularly and increase humidity.
Stems rotted off at base	Basal stem rot	No cure – pull up affected plants. Do not overwater.
Red pustules on leaves	Geranium or carnation rust	Spray with propiconazole. Do not use on edible crops.
Yellow mottling or discoloration	Virus	Non. Pull up and burn.
Papery patches on leaves	Sun-scald	Increase shading in sunny weather.
Tiny, white, moth-like insects	Glasshouse white fly	Spray regularly with an insecticide suitable for use under glass.
Yellowing leaves which drop	Overwatering	Reduce water, especially in winter.
Woolly-looking insects	Mealy bug	Spray with an insecticide suitable for use under glass.
Clusters of green or brownish insects on shoots	Aphids	As above.
Patches of scale on stems	Scale insects	As above.
Plants or seedlings drawn up	Insufficient light	Try to improve conditions if possible.
Roots eaten off	Leatherjackets, millipedes, vine weevil grubs, wireworms, chafer grubs, cutworms	Usually occurs in greenhouse soil but can happen in pots if they are in contact with soil. Treat soil or compost with a soil insecticide. Vine weevil grubs can be controlled with beneficial nematodes.
Petals eaten	Earwigs	Trap in pots filled with hay or finely shredded newspaper.

24

SHEDS AND SUMMERHOUSES

These two pieces of garden equipment can be taken together, because they have many things in common, though one is a near essential for many people, and the other is a definite luxury.

A *shed* is a necessity if you have no garage or anywhere else you can store garden tools and other paraphernalia. Sheds are usually made of timber, though all-metal ones can be purchased. Sometimes cheap plywood models are seen but these should only be chosen where cost is the prime consideration.

When choosing a shed, you should examine it carefully for construction defects. Sheds can either have a ridged roof, or a pent roof which slopes in one direction only – which you choose does not matter as long as it is well covered with roofing felt, but some people think a ridged roof looks better. You should check the timber parts for quality and workmanship – avoid sheds with gaps between the boarding, knotholes or warping.

Sheds are expensive, but you will notice as you look around

318

that prices vary considerably. Apart from the quality of the timber, there are many other ways in which a shed can appear reasonably priced, but not be all it seems. For example, does it have a *floor*? Many do not, except as an extra, so check this point, even if it does not bother you because you intend to erect it on a concrete base. What about *preservative treatment*? Most wooden sheds are made of softwood and, without adequate preservative, will eventually rot, especially those parts near and in contact with the ground. Sometimes you have to pay extra for this, or you may have to do it yourself, but large firms often have facilities for immersion treatment before assembly, so choose this if you can.

Then there are the *windows*. Most wooden sheds are given one window, but not all, so enquire if this is included as standard. A lot of windows, however, do not open, and you will find the heat builds up most uncomfortably in summer if you cannot have a through circulation of air between the window and the door. And is the window really big enough to enable you to work inside if necessary?

How about *delivery and assembly*? Some prices include delivery, but is this to anywhere, or just within a certain radius of the factory? Other firms, usually small local ones, offer a free erection service, but many more provide this only as an optional extra.

There are other considerations when choosing a shed which will be of a more personal nature. First, you must decide what you want it for. *Storing tools*, of course, but what kind? Hand tools are best hung up from nails, clips and racks, so you must have a free run of wall where you can do this. Seed trays, garden chemicals, paint pots, nails, screws and all the rest of the clutter you soon begin to accumulate will need shelves, so there must be adequate space for enough of these to make it easy to find what you're looking for. If you have a mower, mechanical raker, fertilizer distributor, cultivator, wheelbarrow or anything else requiring free-standing floor space – summer garden furniture, bags of compost, fertilizers and the like – you will have to buy one with a fairly large floor area and a door big enough to get the stuff through. You may also find you have to equip yourself with a ramp, or ramps, in order to get machinery over the threshold.

You may want your shed as a *workshop*, so you will need a work bench and possibly something to sit on as well. The golden rule is, always buy at the outset a shed large enough for all your requirements. One big shed is cheaper than a lot of little ones, and there is nothing worse to look at than a back garden full of assorted and often decrepit storage places. Of course, even a small shed is better than none at all, and these days many firms are making mini-sheds which really amount to a waterproof cupboard. If you are very pushed for space, these will take small garden tools and perhaps a mower, but little more.

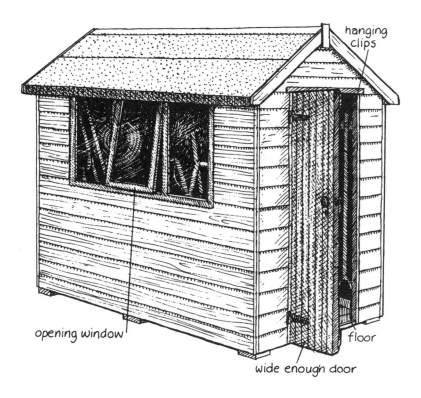

hanging clips

opening window

floor

wide enough door

METAL SHEDS are very tough and long lasting, and if properly treated at the factory, require little maintenance. Prices in general seem to compare favourably with timber, but they are cold, so using them as a workshop can be a freezing experience in winter, though you can use a temporary heater inside with a higher degree of safety. You may find condensation is a problem on the walls, so tools should be well coated with oil or silicone for storage.

SHEDS CAN BE PURCHASED FROM shed retailers, garden centres, some builders merchants and DIY stores, direct from the manufacturers in certain cases, some hypermarkets, by mail order from advertisements in newspapers and the popular gardening press, and from many general mail-order catalogues.

Sheds for storing produce

Sheds, whether of timber or metal, are really not suitable for storing bulbs, potatoes, apples, and the like, because their poor insulation allows too great a fluctuation in temperature and they are not always frost-proof at very low temperatures. If you have only an odd box or sack of something to store over winter, you can give additional protection by covering the containers with plenty of old sacking, discarded blankets, etc., but if you are going into self-sufficiency in a big way, it might pay you to line the shed with hardboard, which is much easier if the shed is made of timber, and then fill the cavity between the inner and outer skin with fibreglass quilt.

Siting the shed

The same regulations apply for sheds as for greenhouses. Usually you do not need permission unless the structure is very large, but it is as well to check. It is also wise to consult your landlord if you are in rented accommodation (or the freeholder if you do not own the freehold), especially if your property is owned by the local authority, as some are not too keen on sheds unless of an approved design (and rightly so – you've only to view many allotment sites from the train to see just how dreadful badly constructed storage places can look!).

A shed is not a pretty sight at the best of times, so, if possible, try to place it out of view, but choose a place where it is not a chore to fetch things out of it and put them away. An alternative to hiding it is to disguise it with a screen of plants – be careful, however, if you grow things right against it, as you will want to get at it for maintenance, and if you want a good light through the window, do not obscure it with tall things. Do not forget that even if you cannot see it, your neighbour might be able to see nothing else, so consider others before you put it up.

If possible, try not to place it under the heavy drip of trees, as it does not do the timbers or the roofing felt a lot of good.

Where you have mowers, and other heavy machinery

stored in it, you will have to make an easy path to and from the door – not grass, which usually gets trodden off.

A shed can be erected directly on to the ground, but will last longer if you can give it a concrete or brick foundation, and it is not a bad idea to leave air-holes to allow the underside of the timber floor (if you have one) to be ventilated. Alternatively, you can place it, with or without a wooden floor as well, on a concrete base.

SUBSEQUENT MAINTENANCE. All timber sheds will require regular treatment with a wood preservative. All of those now available are suitable – if cost is your prime consideration creosote can be used – there is still nothing to beat it for efficacy but only if it is well away from plants as the fumes given off for a long time afterwards are very harmful, and if you do not intend to store crops or tubers, bulbs, etc. inside as the smell can cause taint.

Good-quality roofing felt should last many years, but some people recommend painting it regularly with a bituminized waterproofing compound.

Metal sheds require nothing for a long time, then a thorough painting inside and out will keep them in good heart for many more years.

Note: With the present rise in crime and thefts from sheds and gardens, make sure the shed is fitted with a strong lock.

Summerhouses

Summerhouses are really like up-market sheds, unless you want to go to town and erect a permanent stone or brick structure, in which case you must check with the relevant authorities first. In their most basic form they are only sheds with an open front, but in recent years a whole new industry has sprung up, and you can now get summerhouses with fancy shapes, French doors, Georgian bows, leaded lights, decorative shutters, window boxes, balconies, internal partitions, roof shingles, and even facilities for lining the walls with insulating materials. Some are nearly as large and well appointed as small bungalows and are often made of cedarwood, which looks most attractive. They are also very expensive.

It is my opinion that unless you have a very large garden and desire to get the most out of a part of it that you cannot see, or unless you have a young family keen to spend summer nights under the stars, the amount of use you get out of one in your average English garden does not justify either the cost or the space it occupies. It is either too cold, in which case you do not want to go out of the house, or too hot, when you would rather be sitting under a shady tree. Even when the sun is just right, you are best out under it on a lounger with a long drink than cabined up in a glorified shed. Of course, the better-class ones *look* very nice, but it is a lot of money to lay out on looks if you are not going to get the benefit in other ways. Of course, many people will argue that they get a lot of use from theirs – which is why, I suppose, there are so many about. If you do have the money, and the size of garden to warrant one, then it does open up another aspect.

Choosing a summerhouse

Inspect your prospective purchase for workmanship. If you are satisfied on all counts in that respect, the choice is up to you. Again, you will find a larger one of more use, as you will wish to furnish it with garden chairs, a table, and other items to make outdoor living more comfortable.

USES. Many people buy a summerhouse intending it to double up as a shed, but if you want to use it properly, i.e. as a leisure extension to the home, this really is not practical, as who wants to take afternoon tea surrounded by all the junk, machinery and equipment you shove into your garden shed? It looks terrible from the outside, too, as summerhouses in general have much more glazing than ordinary sheds, so everything is on view. Some inexpensive summerhouses are often open-fronted anyway, so you could not use them for the permanent storage of anything that mattered. Most summerhouses are more expensive than the equivalent cubic capacity in a garden shed, so it is a dear way of buying storage space.

Do have a paved area outside the summerhouse so you can spill out on to this without damaging the surrounding garden. This is a good place to construct some form of barbecue.

SUMMERHOUSES ARE USUALLY OBTAINED FROM specialist stockists and manufacturers, and some garden and leisure centres.

Siting the summerhouse

Because of the nature and design of many of them, and especially the larger ones, do check that there are no building restrictions before you commit yourself.

Choosing the position is mainly a matter of personal preference and the places that are suitable and available within the garden, but if you can find a sunny spot, it is likely to be of greater use to you throughout the year.

If you really want to splash out, you can invest in a revolving base so you can follow the sun or shade around, otherwise a summerhouse is erected in a similar way to a shed.

As most summerhouses are quite attractive, if possible it should be placed where you can get a pleasant view of it across the garden. There is certainly no need to hide it away, as you would a shed.

SUBSEQUENT MAINTENANCE. As for sheds.

Hybrids

Some smaller firms will produce buildings to order which are a combination of, say, a summerhouse with an enclosed compartment for storing tools and other belongings, or a structure which is part shed and part lean-to greenhouse. While these are not widely available, if your space is limited, it is worth making enquiries to see what's going. You may find someone locally who will make one for you as a custom-built job, so explore the possibilities if you think this type of building is what you need.

25

THE INVISIBLE GARDEN

Unless you are an obsessive plantsman, or want to spend every waking minute in an intimate relationship with the soil – and if you are, you would not have needed this book in the first place – there is no need to feel deprived if you have, or intend to have, a home with no garden in the accepted sense.

As living space in the twentieth century has become increasingly at a premium, many kinds of property now have no real gardens. However, just about everyone has some form of outdoor place where plants of one type or another may be grown quite successfully. In any case, far better to be able to indulge what little growing space you have than to be over-whelmed with a large neglected garden that you have not time, strength, money and/or inclination to care for properly.

The ideas suggested here for no-garden gardens can equally apply to patios and paved areas, walls and window-ledges, even if you have a conventional garden as well.

Flats, flatlets and maisonettes

Many of these have some area of garden in the vicinity allocated to each resident, but there are a lot more which do not. Often there is a balcony attached to the flat, though, and some enterprising developers may have even included a planting area in the top of the wall surrounding this. Otherwise the floor area can accommodate a wide variety of plants in tubs and other containers and the wall inside the balcony could have hanging pots and baskets on it. If there is no balcony, the window-ledge is usually wide enough to take some kind of trough, or the area immediately under it could have a window box attached to the wall where it is accessible by leaning out of the window. (But do be careful! This activity is only for the comparatively young and fit.)

Do ensure before you embark on this enterprise that there are no restrictions on growing plants on the walls written into the deeds, or the agreement with the landlord, if you are a tenant. Owners of rented accommodation often do not like their tenants interfering with the structure of the property by drilling the wall for hooks, brackets, trellis, etc., so regulations relating to this must be firmly investigated before you start.

Assuming there is nothing standing in your way, it is then up to you to make sure that anything that you do put on the wall which overhangs the street or area accessible to other residents or the general public is more than firmly attached, bearing in mind the amount of buffeting it is likely to receive if the flat or whatever is at first-floor height or above. Very high flats receive tremendous amounts of wind, and what would be normal at ground level becomes more and more of a howling gale the higher up you go. Pots, boxes, baskets, etc. becoming detached and falling off could at the least make you very unpopular or land you in court, and at the worst they could kill someone.

The wind factor greatly affects the type of plant suitable for high-rise gardening, of which more anon, but do not let this put you off, because there are still plenty of things you can grow successfully.

Mobile homes

Some sites allocate a small amount of garden per unit, but if the site owner or local authority prefers the public open-plan approach to the overall landscaping, there is usually still enough space around the home – on the paths, sitting-out areas, etc., to grow a wide range of plants in containers. Some mobile home manufacturers actually incorporate window boxes or other planting areas into their designs. The walls of mobile homes are not suitable for supporting climbing plants.

Town properties and village cottages

Many small, older houses in towns, and some cottages in rural areas, have virtually no land attached to them. At the front you step straight out on to the street, at the back there is often just a tiny concreted yard, frequently heavily shaded with your own or neighbouring buildings all around it. The concrete area is generally too small to be worth digging up and replacing with a conventional garden, but it can be made quite attractive with an assortment of pots, tubs, troughs and other containers standing on it, window boxes and baskets, and it may be possible to pick out some of the concrete where it adjoins the walls in order to grow climbers in the soil beneath (it may be necessary to improve or replace the soil for this purpose). If it is practical, the existing concrete may be taken up and decorative paving laid instead, or the paving could be laid on top of the concrete if it is level and reasonably sound, but many such areas have no rear or side access and the hassle of carting everything through the house to the front door may not be worth the bother, especially if plenty of containers are used to cover it up.

A further consideration is that paving should not cover up an existing damp course, or it will be totally useless and you will start to get all kinds of damp problems.

You must be sure that the walls are sound before containers are attached to them. There are few sorrier sights than a large basket smashed to pieces on the ground beneath because its weight was just too much for the crumbling brick-work or defective mortar it was screwed to.

Non-existent front gardens can be dealt with in much the same way, but it may be wiser not to use free-standing tubs because of the risk of vandalism, theft or of causing an obstruction to the public highway, and, as in the case of flat-dwellers, wall containers have to be more than firmly anchored – it might not be just the contents that get damaged if they fall off. Just how much gardening you can do at the front of a property which adjoins the highway (including the footpath) depends largely on the attitude of the highways department of the relevant local authority.

Flat roofs

Many properties have a flat roof even if they do not have a garden. Roofs can make quite good areas on which to place containers of plants, but bear in mind the following:

1. Unless you have an easy access on to the roof from inside the property, it can be quite a nuisance getting out ladders to heave containers and compost up there, and plant, water and maintain your elevated garden, and there is also the risk of your falling!

2. Do not put anything heavier on the roof than the timbers are capable of supporting. The containers themselves have to be fairly weighty, otherwise they can blow right off in a strong wind, and when they are full of moist compost they are even heavier. If in doubt about how much load the timbers can bear, place them towards the edge of the flat roof, where the walls can take some of the stress.

3. Choose plants which will not object to strong winds. Those all right for the window boxes of flats would be suitable.

Free-standing containers

In theory, as long as a thing is capable of holding a reasonable amount of compost, you can grow something in it, and you do not have to spend a lot of money on something specifically designed for the purpose. Here are a few ideas for improvised containers:

PLASTIC AND METAL ICE CREAM AND OTHER LARGE CATERING CONTAINERS. These are not suitable for using outside in winter because frost can penetrate easily, freeze the compost, and kill the plant, but they can look quite decorative in summer, especially if the sides are concealed with trailing plants and they are, of course, free of charge. They are only temporary as the plastic eventually becomes brittle and breaks, and the metal ones usually rust. They need drainage holes in the bottom, otherwise they become waterlogged. They may look a bit austere but can be painted in pastel or gay colours –

328

quite effective in the right place, and it prolongs the life a little.

PLASTIC AND GALVANIZED BUCKETS, BOWLS, BATHS, ETC. The same remarks apply as for the previous items.

LARGE, HEAVY WOODEN BOXES. These can blend in quite nicely, especially if treated with a coloured spirit wood preservative (*not* creosote). The timber of which the box is made should be fairly thick. The box should be slightly raised from the ground it stands on with bricks or similar to prevent the bottom rotting quickly.

STONE AND EARTHENWARE SINKS AND TROUGHS, OLD BAKING BOWLS AND SIMILAR KITCHEN EQUIPMENT. These are certainly not cheap to buy – if you can find any – but look very attractive. Sinks can contain dwarf shrubs or bedding plants, or can be planted as 'sink gardens'. Sometimes you can pick up old white glazed sinks and other obsolete sanitary equipment at a nominal cost from plumbers and builders. These can be coated with a PVA adhesive and then covered with a mixture of equal parts cement, sand and peat to make them look like stone, but it is fiddly. A quicker method is to paint them with car undersealing compound and then shot-blast them with coarse sand and pea gravel while the bitumen is still wet.

Earthenware containers are not really suitable for outdoors in winter as the frost can sometimes crack them.

They should have drainage holes in the bottom or they will become waterlogged.

OLD CHIMNEY POTS. Again, these are not cheap, but can sometimes be found in antique shops. They are an awkward shape to plant successfully, but trailing plants like ivies look nice.

BRICKS. Laid un-mortared, these make good plant holders up to 18 in. (450 mm) high and if they are not permanently bonded, they have the advantage of being movable if you want to change their position.

If troughs are constructed of brick, mortared or otherwise, and placed against a wall, the wall should be thoroughly damp-proofed with polythene, felt or similar before filling the container with compost.

LOG-ROLL EDGING. This comprises split logs, wired together along the flat side and is usually used for edging beds and paths, but can be made into a circle to form a well insulated and attractive planter.

Containers from garden centres

RECONSTITUTED STONE TUBS AND TROUGHS. These look lovely, and are a 'must' if you are going to town on a containerized garden. Very expensive and heavy, but they do not freeze through as quickly in winter, hence plants have a greater chance of survival in very cold weather.

CONCRETE TUBS, TROUGHS AND PLANTERS. Some look a bit basic, but can be suitable for a very plain scheme. Others are a good imitation of stone or reconstituted stone and once planted up and weathered, look quite all right. Can be quite heavy.

CLAY POTS, TERRACOTTA URNS AND OTHER CLAY CONTAINERS – STRAWBERRY POTS, ETC. These are quite expensive but blend well with either brick or stone. They are very easily broken by impact, and can also crack in frosty weather. Lighter than stone if weight is a consideration.

WOODEN TUBS AND TROUGHS. These are usually constructed of oak, elm or other hardwood and can be purpose-made, or empty beer barrels sawn in half. They should have been treated with some form of preservative and should be stood on bricks when planted up. Given the proper treatment, they can last many years. But remember that large ones can be pretty heavy to move around.

PLASTIC TUBS, TROUGHS, PLANTERS, LARGE PLASTIC POTS, ETC. These come in a variety of forms, shapes, sizes, colours, from the tasteful to the frankly hideous. They are a useful low-priced alternative to stone, concrete and wood containers, especially for summer bedding, but break down with constant exposure to sunlight and become brittle. They can also freeze through quickly in winter so compost and roots can freeze solid in winter, which can be severely detrimental to many plants, especially bulbs. They are very lightweight, especially when filled with a soil-less compost, which may or may not be a good thing, depending on where you want to place them.

There are also firms which make low-cost, lightweight containers out of recycled materials, such as paper and wood pulp. They are comparatively temporary as they disintegrate eventually but blend well with most surroundings as they are of a neutral colour and texture.

GROWING BAGS. These plastic bags filled with a growing medium have revolutionized container and no-garden gardening techniques. There is virtually no end to the temporary plantings you can achieve with them – annuals and bedding plants, vegetables, strawberries, herbs, etc., but because of their design construction and the type of compost used they are not suitable for permanent plantings.

POTATO BARRELS, STRAWBERRY BARRELS AND HERB POTS. Potato barrels are large plastic containers with drainage holes and the theory is you place three or four seed potatoes in a little peat or compost at the bottom in spring and as the tops grow, you earth them up with more compost or peat, through which the tops keep growing. Eventually you reach the top of the barrel, and when the plants have matured sufficiently (the length of time this varies according to the potato variety), you should have new potatoes growing from all the length of underground stem which you earthed up. This can be quite successful if done properly, and can be impressive when you have harvested your own spuds from the balcony of your high-rise!

Strawberry barrels are somewhat similar, but have staggered holes all the way up the sides in which you plant young strawberry plants, with a few more at the top. As the plants grow and root into the compost in the barrel, they will begin to flower, fruit and make runners which hang down the side and look quite attractive. I have never found you get as big a crop with strawberries grown this way, but as with the potatoes, it is nice to show off with home-grown strawberries grown in the most unlikely situations.

Herb pots are like a small version of a strawberry barrel. They are generally made of terracotta and enable you to grow a satisfyingly large number of fresh herbs in a small space. It is advisable to overwinter them indoors in a cool, light place to prevent damage to the container and the herbs.

Wall containers

Again, there is a wide choice available and while it is possible to improvise by screwing or suspending plastic food containers and the like on the wall, much more of the receptacle can be seen than in the case of those which stand on the ground, and improvised ones can look rather shoddy so it is perhaps better not to spoil the ship for a ha'porth of tar.

Containers suitable for walls can broadly be divided into four categories:

WINDOW BOXES. Originally, these were made of wood and if expertly made could be quite expensive unless you were the handy sort of do-it-yourself person who could knock one up. Sometimes ready-made ones are available at garden centres. An easy alternative is to use a substantial plastic trough. These can be found in a range of sizes and colours to suit more or less any window. Wrought-iron supporting brackets are also obtainable, which screw to the wall under the window, the top anchoring the front of the trough when fitted on to it. Another method of fixing is to screw strong gallows brackets to the wall and then firmly screw the box to the top arms of these brackets. This method would also be suitable for a wooden box.

Window boxes should never be placed on the window-ledge without securing them, either to the window frame, or to the window-ledge through the bottom of the box, or by running a strong piece of wood or metal across the window-opening directly in front of the box. If this is not done, when the box is fully planted and growing strongly, it will topple over and off the sill.

HANGING BASKETS. The most widely recognized basket is made of wire mesh, once galvanized, now more commonly plastic-coated, or all plastic, attached to chains which suspend it from a gallows or wrought-iron bracket. The baskets come in several sizes and, if possible, the bigger the better as plants grow more successfully in them and do not dry out as fast.

A modern version of this is the solid, all-plastic basket with a built-in drip tray which prevents it from dribbling after it has been watered – a consideration if it is placed at first-floor level, and a further advantage is that the solid sides stop it drying out as fast as the open-sided ones, but the container is more difficult to conceal than the mesh type which can have suitable plants growing through it.

Mesh and solid plastic baskets can also be obtained as half-forms, with a flat-sided back. These are designed for screwing against the wall through 'eyes' at the top. Obviously

332

they cannot take as many plants as they are only half the size, but plants do quite well in them in their relatively more sheltered position against a wall.

If you want a hanging basket at a height which you cannot reach easily without a ladder, consider buying a bracket incorporating a pulley mechanism, or place a separate lowering device between the bracket and the basket, so it can easily be brought down to a convenient height for watering and servicing.

MANGERS. These are like a giant version of the half-basket and were originally used for feeding horses, cattle, etc., with hay in a barn or stable. Until recently only second-hand ones were available, but several firms, realizing their horticultural potential, are now making new ones for garden purposes. They are used against the wall in the same way as a half-basket, although because they are much bigger and deeper, a more spectacular planting can be achieved. It is advisable to cover the wall against which the manger is placed with water-proofing material (polythene, etc.) before filling it with compost.

HANGING POTS. Recently, a whole new breed of pots suitable for hanging from a hook has appeared. Basically, these resemble a slightly up-market plastic flower pot with a built-in drip tray, and an incorporated plastic hanger to suspend it by. They come in several sizes, colours, and variations of design, but the principle is the same. They are intended to contain one plant only, the larger ones suitable for, say, a good-sized fuchsia, and the smaller ones capable of holding perhaps an ivy-leaved geranium.

Some shops sell inexpensive clip-on 'suspenders' for converting ordinary plastic plant pots into hanging pots. These are made to clip over the narrow plastic rim around the top of the pot, while at the other end of the arms leading from these clips is a hook by which to hang the newly converted pot.

Some manufacturers are even producing clip-on drip trays as well, which makes it more convenient for hanging in a conservatory.

Devices are also available to clip a ring of plastic plant pots around a drainpipe to conceal it, and to clip a small pot onto a fence or wall. These are eye-catching, especially in quantity, but the pots dry out quickly if they do not receive diligent maintenance.

Terracotta and ceramic pots are obtainable in hanging form, usually suspended by means of non-rotting thick string, and in half-pot form, for screwing to the wall.

Other hanging ornamental containers can be obtained in the form of black (plastic) cauldrons, and similar. You either like these or . . .!

How to plant up tubs, troughs and other containers (including solid hanging baskets and pots)

If you are only using your container for a temporary display – for example, summer bedding and winter/spring bedding (not hanging pots for the latter), a good soil-less compost will be quite adequate. In a reasonably large tub, or whatever, you can usually get two consecutive plantings from one fill-up of compost – say, a spring bedding scheme of wallflowers and bulbs followed by a summer one of geraniums, French marigolds, lobelia, etc. After this the compost becomes rather 'played out' and full of old roots, so it is better changed. Small pots, baskets, tubs, etc., need new compost every time they are replanted.

Tubs, troughs, large window boxes and the like intended to be used for permanent plantings are best filled with a John Innes-type, soil-based compost. It is not necessary to put drainage crocks at the bottom of containers if they have adequate drainage holes.

Always remember to fill the container, if it is a large one, *after* you have positioned it in its final place!

It is difficult to lay down hard and fast rules about how the tub or whatever should be stocked, and a list of suitable plants for particular types of container is given at the end of the chapter, but generally speaking, taller ones look better with taller plants in them, although shorter ones, and trailing things, can be used around the edge. The tallest subjects should be in the centre of a container designed to be viewed from all sides, or at the back if it is placed against a wall. Flat planters look best with plants that are not too tall. In the case of a window box, dwarf varieties should always be used if there is any chance of taller ones obscuring the window. Trailing plants hanging down the front of the box or trough are most effective.

In the case of a permanent planting, it is not necessary to keep repotting but the appearance and wellbeing of the plants

334

is improved if the top 2 or 3 in. (say 75 mm) of compost is removed annually and replaced with fresh.

Maintenance of containers

In winter, very little need be done if suitable containers were used in the first place and the planting done properly. Large, heavy stone troughs, tubs, etc., should not freeze solid except under very extreme conditions. Cheaper, thin concrete and plastic containers can freeze through in certain circumstances and therefore if the plants in them are somewhat choice and if it is at all possible, they should be placed in a cool, light place – perhaps a greenhouse, light shed, or unheated room, until the cold snap is over, or the container wrapped in bubble polythene insulation material. Many very hardy subjects would not be adversely affected by some freezing, especially if the compost is kept on the dry side.

In summer, containers, even thick stone ones, can dry out very rapidly, particularly in sunny spots. Once a soil-less compost dries out it is very difficult to wet it again – the water just runs straight through, so you should always try to keep the containers adequately watered so they do not ever reach this state. Sometimes this means watering a small tub or window box in a hot or windy position two or three times a day, especially when the plants are well grown. Nothing looks worse than a half-dead tub of plants. This is why it is very important that containers placed on flat roofs should be easily accessible without a lot of palaver.

In a short time, the nutrients contained originally in the compost will become exhausted so a weekly liquid food should be given during watering between the months of April and August inclusive.

It certainly pays to instal one of the automatic watering systems now available, which save hours of maintenance time and heavy lifting. A timer can be installed so the watering is done as and when you want it, without your having to worry.

How to plant up and maintain a mesh hanging basket

The time for this is between mid–April and June.

The problem with containers with open sides – mesh baskets and mangers – is keeping the compost in the basket, and also the rapidity with which they dry out. For the sake of appearance and to keep the compost in, you can line the basket with sphagnum moss. In the case of a very large one, or a manger, hay is more economical. For moisture conservation, you can add a layer of polythene perforated to allow surplus water to drain through and place an old saucer or cereal bowl in the bottom. Water-retaining polymer granules are also available which absorb many times their own volume of water. They are added to the compost before planting. Various manufactured liners are also sold. These are made of foam, bituminized paper, coir, wood and paper pulp. These products are not as natural-looking as moss but if the basket is well filled, they will not be noticed eventually and will conserve water better. Add compost gradually, and about every two inches (50 mm) work small bedding or trailing plants (e.g. ivy) through the mesh holes so their roots are in the basket but their stems are outside the mesh. These will eventually grow to cover the outside of the basket and trail down around it. Repeat this process until about 2–3 in. (50–65 mm) from the top of the basket, when you add the plants intended to grow at the top. These are usually geraniums, fuchsias or other substantial bedders, filled in around the edge with smaller bedding plants. Work in compost around them until they are firmly planted. Leave a small depression in the top to make it easier for watering.

After planting, allow the basket to settle down and start to grow without disturbance for a week or so before hanging it up where it is intended to go. Ideally, this interim stage should be in a cool, shaded greenhouse, but the basket will re-establish itself just as well placed on a flat surface away from wind and hot sun. Modern mesh baskets have flat bottoms to make it easier to stand them on a surface: if you have an older type with a round bottom it can be stood upright in the neck of a small bucket or similar.

Feeding and watering is essential from the start if a hanging basket is to be kept in top condition. Never allow it to dry out, even if it means watering one in a hot or windy position several times a day. Give a weak liquid feed twice a week. If a basket should become too dry, give it a thorough watering by submerging it to just under the rim for an hour or so in a bucket or other container of water. Even if you have used a polythene inner lining the water will seep through the drainage holes. If you automize your watering, this is much less likely to happen.

It is wise to hang a basket in a position you can easily reach for watering, to avoid the temptation to skimp the job if it is inconveniently placed. Otherwise, use a lowering device as previously described.

Suitable plants for container planting

Shrubs for permanent planting in medium and large tubs

Top fruit on dwarfing rootstocks. Not very windy sites.
Small acer (maple) species. Not very windy sites.
Aucuba (spotted laurel).
Bay (Laurus nobilis).
Berberis (barberry).
Camellias. Cool sites, ericaceous compost and lime-free water needed, not for exposed positions.
Ceanothus (Californian lilac). Not very windy sites.
Choisya ternata (Mexican orange blossom). Not very windy sites.
Cistus (sun rose). Not very windy sites.
Cotoneaster.
Daphne. Not cold or windy sites.
Elaeagnus (oleaster).
Escallonia. Not cold sites.
Euonymus japonica varieties (evergreen spindle bush).
Heathers. Ericaceous compost and lime-free water needed.
Hydrangea. Not windy sites.
Hypericum. Not cold windy sites.
Holly.
Kalmia. Not cold sites, needs ericaceous compost and lime-free water.
Laurel.
Ligustrum (privet).
Magnolia. Not exposed sites.
Mahonia.
Olearia. Not cold, frosty sites.
Osmanthus. Not cold, windy sites.
Pernettya. Ericaceous compost and lime-free water needed.
Pieris. Cool sheltered site, ericaceous compost and lime-free water needed.
Rhododendrons and azaleas. Conditions as for pieris, above.

Roses. Bush, shrub and standard roses do quite well in large tubs in some sun but look uninteresting in winter. Not suitable for very exposed sites.

Skimmia.

Syringa (lilac).

Viburnum.

Yucca. Not very exposed sites.

Also group plantings of the shrubs below.

Small and trailing shrubs suitable for window boxes, small and medium tubs and troughs and large hanging baskets

Berberis (barberry). Dwarf varieties.

Cistus (sun rose). Dwarf varieties. Not cold windy sites.

Daphne. Dwarf varieties. Not cold or windy sites.

Euonymus. Dwarf evergreen varieties.

Heathers. Ericaceous compost and lime-free water needed.

Hebe (shrubby veronica). Dwarf hardy varieties.

Hypericum. Dwarf varieties.

Ivies.

Japanese azaleas. Provide some shelter in cold windy sites. They need ericaceous compost and lime-free water.

Miniature roses. Not exposed sites.

Vinca (periwinkle).

Shrubby and herbaceous herbs. Will require splitting and replanting regularly.

Temporary ornamental plants for tubs, troughs, window boxes, hanging baskets and growing bags

Hardy annuals. Low-growing ones for exposed sites, window boxes, small tubs and hanging baskets.

Half-hardy annuals (summer bedding plants).

Half-hardy foliage plants (cineraria, helichrysum, etc.).

Trailing nepeta (catmint).

Spring bedding plants (wallflowers, winter pansies, forget-me-nots, etc.).

Dwarf spring flowering bulbs (snowdrops, crocuses, miniature daffodils, species tulips, dwarf irises, scillas, etc.) – not small pots and hanging baskets.

Summer bulbs (star of Bethlehem, dwarf gladioli, chincherinchees, ixias, tuberous begonias, etc.).

Bedding perennials (pelargoniums, fuchsias, pansies, begonias, marguerites, lantana, verbena, heliotrope, etc.).

Other subjects for container planting

Salads and many other vegetables.

Soft fruit and strawberries.

Water plants and miniature water lilies.

Herbaceous perennials but these are not very exciting when they are out of flower.

Conifers (dwarf ones for small containers, taller and stronger-growing ones for big ones).

Most alpines and rock plants (a sharp, gritty compost is required and very good drainage). These are especially attractive in sinks and small troughs either on their own or with one or two miniature shrubs and conifers. For best results give bright light and an open position.

Some plants suitable for growing on walls in large containers

Camellia. Not cold exposed sites.

Ceanothus. Not cold exposed sites.

Chimonanthus (winter sweet).

Clematis. Container must be placed out of full summer sun.

Cotoneaster.

Escallonia. For warm walls.

Figs. For warm walls.

Hebe. Warm walls only.

Ivies.

Jasmines.

Lonicera (honeysuckle).

Passiflora (passion flower).

Pyrancantha (firethorn).

Climbing roses (less rampant varieties).

Viburnum burkwoodii.

26

IN DUE SEASON

What To Do When

Because gardening has many aspects which are not hard and fast, it is not easy to say specifically when is or is not the correct time for doing a certain job. In fact, many tasks can be done absolutely in the wrong season, and the fortunate gardener often still gets away with it.

However, it is true to say that because of the make-up of plants, or owing to other factors beyond our control, there is often an optimum time for doing a job, and conversely, certain times when some things should not be attempted – for example, moving a deciduous plant at the peak of its growing season, and in full leaf, because it would lose more water through its abundance of leaf pores than its disturbed roots could take up, so death is likely to occur. Or sowing certain seeds in cold wet soil at the wrong time of year, as they are almost certain to rot.

The following guide is intended to help you plan what you should be doing at a particular time of year. Even this is not categorical, however, as it is intended for the garden-owner living in an area of average temperatures and climate – those lucky enough to live in warmer places, e.g. the south-west of Britain, could bring the suggested times forward up to 3 or 4 weeks, those in the colder north and north-east would be well advised to let things mark time for perhaps another 2 or 3 weeks.

Above all, once you have done things a few times, you are likely to find experience is your best guide. You will soon know what works best for your plot – it may not even be the same as for the chap next door. No two gardens can ever be the same.

January

BY THE FIRESIDE. A lot of your gardening can be done, and probably is even best done, in this position in the first month of the year. Read seed catalogues, and send off orders, for both flower and vegetable seeds. It is not too late to order dormant ornamental plants and fruit trees and bushes either.

Have a critical look at the garden through the window and see if there are any alterations, either structural or to the growing plants you think you ought to make, and keep these in mind.

IN THE SHED. There will be a lot of days when you cannot work outside this month, but you can go through your tools and make sure that they are clean and well oiled and sharp, where appropriate. It is a good time to get the mower serviced and any electrical equipment checked over for faults. Seed trays and plant pots should always be clean before they are re-used. so you could give these a quick bath. Check stored summer crops, bulbs and tubers periodically to make sure they are not rotting. If any of them are, throw them out immediately, and examine those next to them to make sure the infection is not starting to spread.

Put early new potatoes 'rose' end upwards (the end with most 'eyes') in a wooden box, to sprout.

IN THE GREENHOUSE. If you have a heated greenhouse, you can sow sweet peas, begonias, gloxinias, freesias, aubergines, tomatoes, cucumbers, leeks, large onions and summer cauliflowers. Do not be tempted to sow bedding plants too soon, they will be ready before the weather has warmed up sufficiently to plant them outside. This applies particularly to seeds sown on kitchen window-ledges. Light levels are still comparatively low at this time of year, especially in the house, and seedlings soon become drawn-up and unhealthy.

Pick off and remove dead leaves on overwintering tender plants before they begin to rot and encourage disease in the greenhouse. Do this regularly all through the year with plants under glass.

OUTSIDE. The maxim for this month is: when in doubt, leave well alone. Do not walk on frosty ground or dig it if you can help it, and do not walk on frozen lawns or you will damage the grass and encourage diseases. Do not prune or plant in frosty weather. If plants arrive that you cannot deal with, immediately put them in the shed or garage and cover with straw, sacking or similar insulating material to prevent them drying out.

Assuming the weather is open, you can:

Plant roses, fruit trees and bushes, deciduous shrubs, trees and hedges. Also Jerusalem artichokes in the vegetable garden. Prune apples and pears, wall climbers and shrubs, soft fruits, outdoor vines.

Do not prune stone fruits (cherries, plums, etc.) because of the risk of infection with silver leaf disease.

Spray dormant fruit trees with tar oil to control overwintering larvae and aphids.

Move shrubs around the garden if you are doing a bit of re-design work.

Check stakes and ties, especially after high winds, to make sure they are firm and not chafing the plants.

Construct and remake paths, walls and other structures during non-frosty periods. Check paths and other walkways for slippery algae, mosses and lichens and if necessary treat with moss killer.

Dig any undug empty parts of the garden, adding manure or compost if you have it, and lime, but leave a month between applications of each if you are applying both lime and manure or compost.

Fork over lightly any compacted soil between ornamental plants. Do not dig deeply or you will damage the roots.

Protect the crowns of slightly tender herbaceous plants with bark or leaf mould, and shrubs with a screen of polythene or netting on the windward side. Check plants, especially trees

342

and roses, for holes in the soil around the base – this is caused by wind-rock and if left, they will fill with water and the roots will rot. Frost will also loosen the soil around plants, which should be gently firmed down.

Turf new lawns in suitable weather. January can often be a mild month and established lawns may grow quite long. Lightly trim with a sharp mower, but only in open weather when no frost or cold winds are forecast for some time. If you are not sure, it is better to leave well alone.

Force rhubarb by covering the crowns with old buckets or other light-excluding material.

In snowy weather, shake the snow off evergreens, especially conifers, as it can pull the branches down and even break them, permanently spoiling the shape.

Make a hole in the ice on fishponds by placing a tin can of hot water on the surface for a few minutes.

Harvest winter vegetable crops. *Cover* winter brassicas with fine mesh against bud damage.

February

All the jobs for January can continue to be done in February, and also the following –

IN THE GREENHOUSE. *Sow* in a warm greenhouse, or heated propagator, *Begonia semperflorens*, pelargoniums, aubergines, French beans and celery.

Start into growth dahlia tubers and chrysanthemum stools from which cuttings can be taken later in the month.

OUTSIDE. Sow early vegetables and sweet peas in mild areas *only* and protect with cloches.

Plant Jerusalem artichokes, chives, horseradish, summer flowering bulbs. Start planting hardy herbaceous plants later in the month.

Prick out seedlings sown under glass last winter.

Top dress soft fruit with a high-potassium fertilizer such as sulphate of potash to encourage healthy flower and fruit production.

Prune back and re-pot fuchsias and other half-hardy shrubs overwintered in a cool place indoors in their pots. Start giving warmth and moisture to waken them into growth, and take cuttings towards the end of the month.

Prune winter jasmine after flowering and cut back large-

343

flowered clematis and shrubs flowering after July on growth made in the current season (e.g., *Buddleia davidii*).

Cut down autumn fruiting raspberries to ground level.

Spray (twice at 3-weekly intervals) peaches etc., with Bordeaux mixture against peach leaf curl.

March

Things are really beginning to move now. All the jobs for January and February should be completed as soon as possible.

IN THE GREENHOUSE. Sow half-hardy annuals.

Sow runner and French beans, celery, tomatoes, cucumbers, melons and aubergines.

Start into growth tuberous begonias.

Take cuttings of coleus, fuchsias, begonias, chrysanthemums, pelargoniums and dahlias.

Prick out pelargoniums, *Begonia semperflorens* and seedlings sown earlier.

Hang up yellow fly traps.

OUTSIDE. *Start sowing* hardy annuals where they are to flower. In cold areas, wait a bit.

Cover vacant ground in the vegetable garden to warm up.

Sow peas, broad beans, lettuces, radishes, carrots, leeks, parsley, parsnips and spring onions. Cabbages, turnips, beetroot and French beans can be sown in cold greenhouses, frames and under cloches. (Cold areas will need some cloche protection for all early March sowings.)

Plant early potato seed tubers.

Spray with Bordeaux mixture against peach leaf curl.

Trap slugs.

Prune roses and spray with a fungicide against black spot. Also prune figs.

Lift leeks not required for immediate use and heel in to prevent continued growth and leave ground free for new crops.

Start fertilizing vegetables with quick-acting fertilizers according to type of crop. Also roses and ornamentals with a balanced feed.

Plant hardy herbaceous plants, summer flowering biennials, alpines and other plants in containers. Also conifers, but make sure they are kept well watered and misted all the subsequent season.

Apply total weedkillers to paths and drives.

Cut hard back ('stool') shrubs grown for their ornamental bark (cornus, some willows, rubus, etc.).

Begin cutting the lawn, setting the blades high, if it is starting to grow. Old lawns benefit from a scarifying with a lawnraker or spring-tined rake to remove dead bits and 'thatch'. Kill moss. Aerate lawns on heavy ground. Apply spring fertilizer towards the end of the month. Prepare new sites for seeding later.

April

UNDER GLASS. *Sow* seeds of outdoor tomatoes, cucumbers, melons, marrows, sweet corn.

Prick out or pot up earlier sowings of flowers and vegetables.

Complete sowing of half-hardy annuals.

OUTSIDE. *Continue planting,* or transplanting, evergreens and conifers, but see warning about keeping them watered under 'March'. Continue planting containerized plants. Finish *dividing* and planting or replanting herbaceous plants. Plant dahlia tubers towards the end of the month and also gladioli corms.

Sow seeds of hardy perennials and some biennials for next season. Continue sowing hardy annuals. Also sow herb seeds.

Plant aquatic plants from the middle of the month.

Stakes and other *supports* will be needed for herbaceous plants and taller annuals as they grow. Stake *before* the plants fall over!

Prune spring-flowering shrubs like forsythia after flowering.

In the vegetable garden successional crops may be sown and also seed beds for brassicas (members of the cabbage family) and leeks. Early peas may need staking, also broad beans may need support in windy areas. Plant out vegetables sown early under cloches and glass towards the end of the month. Plant main-crop potatoes and onion sets.

Thin out rows of seedlings as necessary.

Mulch ornamentals and fruit with compost, cocoa shell, bark, manure, etc. – do not use grass clippings unless your lawn is first class, annual meadow grass seeds will begin to grow in all the least desirable places.

Spray for pests and diseases but only if necessary trap slugs in all parts of the garden.

Make compost with all garden and kitchen waste.

Continue to mow lawns lowering the blades a little as the month progresses. Continue to give high-nitrogen fertilizer. Reseed patches. Sow new lawns when the soil has warmed up enough to encourage quick germination.

Keep the hoe moving between crops and ornamentals to control weeds and aerate the soil.

Dead-head spring bulbs when the flowers have faded. Do not tie together daffodil foliage, but it can be cut off if 6 weeks have elapsed since the flowers died.

May

The bulk of the work will be outside from now onwards as the days are considerably longer and warmer (with luck!).

IN THE ORNAMENTAL GARDEN. *Sow* hardy annuals for successional flowering and also half-hardy annuals in situ in warm sunny borders. Continue sowing biennials and some perennials.

Harden off bedding plants.

Divide and replant Christmas roses (hellebores), some spring-flowering alpines, and polyanthus.

Continue dead-heading bulbs. If space is required for summer bedding, lift bulbs and heel in elsewhere until the foliage has died. Tidy up foliage as it withers.

Plant dahlia tubers and chrysanthemums. At the end of the month, plant out half-hardy bedding plants which have been thoroughly hardened off in their summer flowering position.

Continue to plant containerized stock, but do make sure you give it plenty of water in hot dry spells. Slightly tender shrubs in containers are best planted now. Make sure all herbaceous plants and tall annuals are now adequately *staked*.

Plant up tubs, troughs, window boxes and hanging baskets for summer display.

Prune evergreen and spring-flowering shrubs as soon as flowering is over.

Clip quick-growing hedges like privet and lonicera.

Tidy up rockeries and cut back plants threatening to out-grow their positions.

Dead-head lilac, rhododendrons.

Keep an eye on tubs, troughs and other containerized plantings so they do not dry out. Give them a weekly liquid feed from now onwards.

346

Take cuttings of herbs and many alpines.

Mow lawns regularly and feed if necessary. Apply a selective weedkiller if required.

This is a good time to construct and stock a new *pond* or *water garden*, or clear out and divide the plants in an established one.

IN THE VEGETABLE PLOT. You will be starting to *harvest* the first of your early sown crops, especially salads. Successional vegetable and salad crops can still be sown. Continue to apply quick-acting appropriate *fertilizers*.

Sow winter brassicas, French and runner beans, marrows in frames and ridge cucumbers under cloches.

Keep staking peas and beans.

Pinch out the tops of broad beans to discourage black fly. (These make a tasty vegetable if boiled for a minute or two.)

Plant out brassicas, celery, sweet corn, leeks and tomatoes, cucumbers and aubergines if they are thoroughly hardened off, also melons in frames.

Earth up early potatoes.

Dig ground as it is vacated by harvested crops.

In the fruit garden do some light *thinning* to the shoots and branches of stone fruits which would be at risk from silver leaf disease if pruned in winter.

Lay straw between the plants in strawberry beds.

Net soft fruit to keep the birds off.

GENERALLY. *Water* thoroughly fruit, flowers and vegetables in dry weather. Apply a *foliar feed* from time to time to give plants a boost.

Hoe to keep down weeds.

UNDER GLASS. *Plant* tomatoes, aubergines, peppers, melons and cucumbers in their cropping positions. Give some *shade* from very hot bright sunshine. *Maintain humidity* by damping down the floor but make sure there is plenty of *ventilation*.

June

Now you are beginning to see the fruits of your labours, but there is still plenty to be done.

IN THE ORNAMENTAL GARDEN. Plant out all the rest of the half-hardy and tender bedding plants.

Divide spring-flowering perennials, including irises.

Cut back early-flowering perennials to give a second flush later in the season.

Continue sowing seeds of biennials, and transplant those already sown to nursery beds.

Dead-head all ornamental flowering plants regularly.

Train and tie in climbing and wall plants regularly from now onwards.

Prune late spring-flowering shrubs as soon as the flowers have faded.

Take cuttings of pinks and helianthemums.

Check stakes amongst tall plants.

Water tubs, boxes, pots and hanging baskets regularly – daily if necessary. Feed weekly.

Keep mowing the lawn regularly, watching for signs of drought, and leave clippings on in hot weather.

Continue trimming hedges.

AMONG THE VEGETABLES. You can still *sow* crops for succession, also endives and winter turnips and swedes, and *thin out* where necessary.

Plant out runner beans and tomatoes, also courgettes, marrows, cucumbers, peppers, aubergines, brassicas and leeks.

Stake runner beans and tomatoes.

Pinch out side shoots on tomatoes (leave these if they are the bush varieties).

Keep top dressing with suitable fertilizers.

Harvest early potatoes, peas and beans and other early crops.

Finish earthing up main crop potatoes and spray with Bordeaux mixture against blight.

Hand pollinate melons and marrows.

THE FRUIT GARDEN. *Mulch* soft fruit to conserve moisture in the soil and swell ripening fruit.

Hang codling moth traps in apple trees.

Summer prune gooseberries.

UNDER GLASS. *Make sure* greenhouses do not overheat in hot weather.

Shade crops, especially cucumbers, and *damp down* to increase humidity. *Ventilate* fully on hot days.

Continue removing side-shoots from tomatoes.

GENERALLY. Keep *watering* in dry weather, and *hoe* regularly. Give liquid or foliar *feeds* if necessary. Continue making *compost*.

348

Now and again, on a warm day, *take time off* to sit in your garden and enjoy it.

July

This is traditionally the month when the average gardener has his or her mind less on doing the garden than on getting the most out of what summer weather we get. There are still jobs to be done which cannot be avoided – dead-heading, weeding, hoeing, feeding, watering in drought periods, and making sure all stakes, ties and other supports are provided where necessary and are in order – this is the month when thunderstorms usually start in earnest, and gardens where plant supports have been skimped can be laid flat in an hour. However, a lot of July gardening is more what you *want* to do, if you are keen, than what you have to do.

As far as the *ornamental garden* is concerned you can *take cuttings* of pelargoniums, either in the glasshouse, or in warm gardens, outside, and border carnations and pinks. Also cuttings of many perennials including pansies, and semi–ripe cuttings of most hardwood shrubs which will strike from cuttings, outside in pots in sheltered spots, or in a cold frame or greenhouse. Propagate roses also by budding. Propagate carnations, pinks and some shrubs by *layering*.

Prune early summer–flowering shrubs (philadelphus, weigela, etc.) as they finish flowering.

Dry herbs for storage.

Cut slow–growing and conifer hedges – beech, Leyland cypress, etc.

Cut the lawn but raise the blades again if the weather is very dry, and leave the clippings on.

IN THE VEGETABLE GARDEN make the last successional *sowings* of quick-maturing varieties of peas, lettuces, radishes, carrots, etc., and thin out earlier sown crops.

Plant leeks and winter brassicas.

Pick and *harvest* crops as they become ready. Lift shallots and dry off thoroughly before storage. Harvest and dry off onions. Sow Japanese onions in northern areas.

Spray main-crop potatoes at 3-weekly intervals with Bordeaux mixture against potato blight.

Earth up celery.

FRUIT. *Summer pruning* of trained forms of top fruit may be done now.

Tidy up strawberries that have finished fruiting and make new plants by layering runners.

Finish pruning plums and cherries.

Prune blackcurrants.

Train wall peaches and nectarines, new blackberry and hybrid berry canes.

Cut out old raspberry canes and thin out and tie in new ones.

Support heavily laden branches of apples, pears and plums to make sure that they don't split from the trunk with the weight.

Pick soft fruits as they ripen.

UNDER GLASS. *Sow* cyclamen and any annuals required for autumn and winter flowering.

Gather tomatoes and other glasshouse vegetable crops as they become ready.

Remove yellowing leaves from tomatoes, cucumbers, etc.

Watch temperature, watering and humidity. Give regular *liquid* feeds.

Spray against pests and diseases.

Finally, be generous. If you take your holiday this month and are likely to be away for some time, let the neighbours have some of your peas and beans. They will not last indefinitely without getting too old to be really tasty, and you will be popular with your friends! Also, tell them they *must* pick your sweet peas – if they are not picked regularly, they will stop flowering. Do not forget cucumbers and courgettes, either, the plants will not make any more if they are not regularly picked.

August

This is another month when you will probably not want to do any more than you have to. If you are feeling well off, it might be an idea to treat yourself to some garden furniture, then you can get as much out of the garden by relaxing in it as you put into it with days of honest toil.

Bulb and other catalogues are usually available from now onwards, so arm yourself with a pile of these and a long cold drink (or hot soup, and watch the rain pouring down) and get your orders in early – first come, first served.

Another leisure activity you might like to try during the summer months is visiting gardens which are open to the public. They are not all attached to stately homes, many are small private ones open for charity under local or national schemes. Some of these sell off their surplus plants and you can often pick up a bargain. You can also get a lot of good ideas which you could adapt for your own purposes. Also many major seed companies open their trial grounds to the public in August. This is a marvellous opportunity to see how particular varieties have stood up to rigorous trial conditions and make some notes on things you might like to try yourself next year.

However, if you feel like doing something rather more strenuous, *most of the jobs suggested for July can still be done this month*, except it is rather late for successional vegetable sowings, but if you use really quick-maturing varieties, and you do not want the space for anything else, it is worth a try. It is also rather late for budding roses but given the best conditions, this should still be successful. You could also be doing the following:

IN THE ORNAMENTAL GARDEN. Keep hoeing, dead-heading, watering and hand weeding. Stop feeding or apply an autumn, high-phosphate feed.

Prune rambler roses by removing the oldest flowered wood. Train the new growths to fit the space available.

Clip lavender and other quick-growing hedges.

Sow hardy annuals for early flowering next year, but if your garden is cold and wet, it is better to wait until next spring.

Plant autumn-flowering bulbs such as colchicums (naked ladies) and *Crocus speciosus* (the true autumn-flowering crocus). Some lilies and other summer bulbs can be planted now, and towards the end of the month, winter bulbs, daffodils especially, will be available.

Order bulbs and ornamental plants from catalogues.

Start planting out biennials for spring and summer bedding.

Prepare lawn areas for seeding next month.

THE VEGETABLE GARDEN. *Sow* spring cabbage, spinach, beet and endive. Also winter lettuce, Japanese onions, winter radishes.

Lift onions and ripen off for storing. Also lift second early potatoes.

Continue *picking* and *harvesting* crops when ready. Runner

351

and French beans especially should be picked regularly to prevent them going out of flower. Make sure runner beans have plenty of water.

Earth up leeks, celery and the stems of winter brassicas to prevent windrock. Provide Brussels sprouts with stakes if it is likely they will get blown about, otherwise the sprouts will not be firm and hard but will 'blow' and be loose and open.

Plant winter brassicas.

Dig ground as it becomes vacant.

Stop outdoor tomatoes after five trusses.

FRUIT. In addition to the jobs described for last month, this is the best time of the year for *planting* new strawberries.

IN THE GREENHOUSE. Continue *sowing* annuals for winter flowering. *Feed and water* growing crops and *watch* temperature, humidity and ventilation.

Remove lower leaves from tomato plants, and dead and yellowing leaves on all crops under glass.

Pot up prepared bulbs for indoor display and place in a cool, dark place to start into growth.

GENERALLY. Continue composting all green waste except diseased material, which is best burnt.

September

The arrival of the season of mists and mellow fruitfulness means that if you've been taking a bit of time off to enjoy yourself, you really ought to be easing yourself back into something of a gardening routine.

THE ORNAMENTAL GARDEN. Continue to *plant* bulbs, biennial bedding plants and start planting lilies, peonies and red hot pokers. Many other herbaceous subjects can be planted this month, and early-flowering ones divided and generally tidied up in the herbaceous border. Plant rock plants, conifers and other evergreens, as the sun is much cooler and the mists often found at this time of year will help to re-establish them before the really hard weather comes.

Continue to *sow* hardy annuals for next year in favourable positions.

Take hardwood cuttings of all types of deciduous woody plants this month.

Towards the end of the month, *lift* tender perennial bedding

352

plants such as geraniums, begonias and fuchsias and bring into the greenhouse or frost-free light shed to overwinter.

Clear other annuals and bedding plants as they pass their best so prepare the ground for spring bedding. *Rough-dig* ground not needed for bedding and leave to weather over winter.

Finish *pruning* ramblers and summer-flowering shrubs.

THE LAWN. This is a busy month for the lawn, getting it in trim after the rigours of the summer. Give a good *raking* to get rid of dead moss, thatch, clippings and other rubbish, a thorough *spiking*, and a *top dressing* with a mixture of fine soil, peat and coarse sand. *Overseed* thin lawns and bare patches and give a high-phosphate autumn food. *Sweep off* or scatter worm casts when they appear.

Raise the mower blades from now onwards when cutting the grass.

Sow new lawns – they will grow rapidly before winter in the warm soil.

THE WATER GARDEN. Plants will be starting to grow less quickly now, so it is getting too late to stock new pools satisfactorily. Any dead bits you can see in the pond ought to be removed. Fish will not be feeding as much either, so give food less often. Remove any early fallen leaves from the pool or they will decay and pollute the water. If your pond is very small, you could consider making a timber frame and attach to it some small mesh wire or plastic netting to keep out leaves.

IN THE VEGETABLE GARDEN. *Plant out* spring cabbages.

Sow winter spinach, Japanese onions, and lettuces in frames.

Protect winter lettuce and endives with cloches.

Dig land as it becomes empty.

Clear haulms and garden rubbish. Green stuff can still be composted although it will take longer to break down. Burn diseased material if it is safe and convenient to do so. *Shred* woody prunings.

Finish picking outdoor tomatoes, cucumbers, marrows, courgettes, peppers, aubergines, etc., before the frosts.

Earth up celery, leeks and brassicas.

Harvest and store root vegetables.

Lift main crop potatoes.

FRUIT. Plums, peaches, and nectarines will be ready for *picking* early in the month, as will the very earliest apples and pears.

Finish summer pruning of top fruit as soon as possible, also pruning of soft fruit. Raspberries can still have their old wood cut out and new canes thinned.

Pick blackberries and autumn-fruiting raspberries. Do not prune autumn-fruiting raspberries till the spring, then they should be cut right down to ground level.

Under glass. Continue caring for and picking greenhouse crops. *Sow* cauliflowers for growing under glass. Watch the ventilation on cool nights. Take late-flowering chrysanthemums inside.

GENERALLY. September is a good month to undertake any form of constructional work – concreting, paving, walling, etc. It is still warm enough for the job to be comfortable, and it will have settled down well before the hard frosts start. Also fences and other timber can be treated with suitable preservatives.

October

THE ORNAMENTAL GARDEN. This is mainly a month to continue those jobs started last month – *dividing and replanting* herbaceous perennials, *taking up* old bedding plants and replacing with biennials and spring bedding plants, and removing tender perennials to the protection of the greenhouse.

Lift dahlias and gladioli corms – hang upside down to dry before cleaning them, dip in fungicide: dry off thoroughly and store in a cool, dry place.

Continue *planting* evergreen shrubs and conifers. Plant bare-root deciduous stock, including most shrubs and roses, from the end of the month (containerized plants can be set at any time of the month). Also continue planting bulbs.

Hardwood cuttings can still be taken.

Sow sweet peas, in frames.

Clear up fallen leaves regularly or they will pollute pond water, block drains, and kill the lawn and small perennials including alpines. Stack in a heap to form leaf mould, which is a valuable source of humus.

Mulch with leaf mould, compost or manure while the soil is still warm.

Continue *to mow* lawns in dry weather with the blades set high. *Seed* new lawns until about the third week in the month. Continue raking, spiking, top dressing and feeding as

354

described for September, if necessary. Keep a watch out for dead and dying patches and take action.

Start *turfing* from now onwards. Continue throughout winter and spring in favourable weather.

THE VEGETABLE GARDEN. *Harvest* root crops before they become coarse and are attacked by soil-borne pests. Store in shed or freeze.

Clear up spent crops and consign to the compost heap.

Sow lettuce in frames. Also over-wintering broad beans in mild areas.

Plant lettuce and spring cabbage, also Japanese onion sets.

Cover winter crops with cloches.

Trap slugs and snails.

Spray against late pests and diseases.

Earth up celery and leeks.

Cover the curd of late cauliflowers by bending a leaf over it.

Dig ground, manuring if necessary.

FRUIT. Most apples and pears will be ready for *gathering* this month and should be stored if absolutely sound, individually wrapped in newspaper, in a cool room. *Plant* containerized fruit bushes throughout the month, leave bare-root stock until after leaf-fall. Finish planting strawberries by mid–October.

Spray peaches with Bordeaux mixture against peach leaf curl. Put greasebands round the trunks of top fruit trees. Continue *pruning* currants and gooseberries. *Prune* figs in mild districts.

Take cuttings of gooseberries and currants.

IN THE GREENHOUSE. Most summer vegetable crops will be over by now, so give the greenhouse a good clean-out on a warm day (see page 316, point 6). Let everywhere dry off properly and then rearrange all the overwintering plants to get the best light they can.

Give the same treatment to garden frames. It is essential in winter to allow as much light as possible into the greenhouse and frame and it is surprising how much is lost through dirty glass, especially overlapping panes, during the shortest months of the year. *Pot up* some mint and parsley and take in for winter use. Provide heat for tender subjects.

355

November

This is the month of clearing and planting. In all parts of the garden, move spent plantings and crops and compost or burn. Cut-down dead perennials and shred the prunings. Sweep up and collect leaves.

Many gardeners prefer to do the bulk of their *rose pruning* this month and in all but the very coldest parts of the country, if you want to leave the garden as tidy as possible for the winter, it is quite safe to do this. Otherwise shorten back all long growths by at least a half to prevent the bushes rocking in the wind. Also prune thorn hedges.

Fork over lightly flower and shrub beds which you have tidied up.

Dig thoroughly all vacant ground, manuring if necessary.

Remove and clean up canes and stakes from summer flowers and vegetable crops.

Check tree stakes and ties to make sure they are sound and not damaging the trunk in any way.

Take off yellowing leaves from winter brassica crops as they occur.

Keep off slugs and snails from susceptible herbaceous plants by covering lightly with ashes or cinders.

Winter prune apples and pears, also prune bush and cane fruits and vines.

Burn all prunings immediately to prevent infection by coral spot disease. Otherwise remove to a waste disposal site.

Erect temporary shelter for less hardy shrubs.

Protect slightly tender perennials with bark or leaf mould. Also alpines not liking wet conditions with a supported pane of glass or clear plastic.

Continue constructional work in frost-free weather.

Inspect stored crops, especially fruit, dahlia tubers and gladioli corms and remove any diseased ones.

Treat canker in apples and pears – cut out diseased tissue down to clean wood and paint with a canker paint.

Spray dormant fruit trees and bushes, deciduous trees and shrubs and rose trees with tar oil.

Net fruit trees and bushes, also spring-flowering trees and shrubs against damage by bullfinches.

Lift winter vegetables as required or use from store.

Sow hardy broad beans and round-seeded peas in mild

areas. Protect with cloches.

Make sure the crops already protected by cloches are all right. Trap slugs if the weather is mild.

Take hardwood cuttings of hardy evergreen plants (e.g., holly, laurel); put in a cold frame or greenhouse to root.

UNDER GLASS. With tender plants, keep a close watch on the thermometer and increase the heating if necessary. With plants being overwintered in a cool or cold greenhouse make sure the temperature does not drop below freezing.

Even pelargoniums are hardier than one imagines, but will not stand being frosted.

Put up temporary or permanent double glazing or transparent insulating material if possible to prevent much heat loss through greenhouse glass.

Remove dead and yellow leaves on greenhouse plants.

Plant all kinds of deciduous trees and shrubs, roses, climbers, and fruit trees and bushes. Continue to plant herbaceous plants and evergreens in open, mild weather. Do not plant in very wet, sticky weather or severe frost. Complete planting bulbs and replanting biennials.

Lawns are best left alone unless the weather is very open and mild, when you can top lightly – leave them alone if they are wet, though.

December

Most of the work suggested for November can continue through December as long as the weather does not deteriorate.

Otherwise start the indoor maintenance jobs listed under January (tools, mowers, cleaning pots, etc.).

Seed catalogues will usually arrive this month, so you can sort out next year's orders.

Cover any plants arriving in bad weather with sacking in a shed or garage till conditions improve.

Do not forget to knock the snow off evergreens and make a hole in the ice on the fish pond to enable the fish to breathe.

Last but not least, pick some holly and other greenery, bring a few pots of flowering plants in from the greenhouse, put some bowls of bulbs about the place, enjoy eating your store of fruit and vegetables and winter greens, have a happy Christmas and remember the days get longer from 21 December!

27

WATER, WATER EVERYWHERE

Before embarking on this chapter, I will apologize in advance to everyone in those parts of Britain, such as the north-west of England, north Wales and many areas of Scotland, where lack of water has, so far, not been a problem, as it can be frustrating in the extreme to read of heat-seared landscapes when all you are praying for is for the rain to hold off for an hour. However, even with no shortage, water conservation is likely to become a big issue for the rest of this decade, so please do not dismiss out of hand what follows.

The major revolution in gardening in the Nineties is likely to be the way the average household in the United Kingdom pays for its domestic water. And allied to this is the fact that over the last thirty years weather trends have been towards alternating periods of very wet weather and droughts.

Most of us have been accustomed all our lives to turning on the taps in our homes and, for a fixed price, we have been able to have as much water as we have wanted, whenever we liked, and for whatever purpose. We may have complained about its taste, or its colour, or the number of chemicals added to it or supposedly inadequately removed from it, but the fact remains that wherever we travel in Britain, providing a mains water supply is available, we can be reasonably sure that we can obtain a tumbler of water which is fit to drink.

However, for various political and economic reasons, which it is not necessary to go into in a gardening book, the probable policy in the near future is that we pay for the actual amount of water we individually consume, rather than spread the cost comparatively evenly across the whole population. The most likely way that this will be achieved is by metering.

Although generally an unpopular prospect as far as gardeners are concerned, it has to be admitted it is a fair one. It is ridiculous to use for irrigation purposes water that has been expensively treated to make it fit to drink straight from the main. In fact, mains water is far from ideal for plants. It is frequently very cold, much more alkaline than many species like, and can contain elements such as chlorine which many plants do not tolerate well in regular doses. Unfortunately, over the years it has become so much easier to attach a hosepipe to the mains supply to water newly planted subjects and to supplement rainfall during dry spells that the practice of collecting and storing rainwater has largely died out. Downspouts of homes built since the Second World War channel roof water, not to a butt or tank to be used when necessary on plants or individual areas of the garden which require a good wetting, but straight underground to a soakaway.

As more and more of us have water meters compulsorily installed, unless we are so rich we can pour money down the drain, we will need to examine our consumption very carefully, and nowhere more so than in the garden.

Of course, having to conserve water is not new. Many of us will remember the drought summer of 1976 which, following a warm, dry summer in 1973, a poor but largely dry summer in 1974, and another pleasantly warm, dry summer in 1975, ran many reservoirs perilously low. Hosepipe bans were enforced in many areas, but just as we began to think we would have to readjust our lifestyles completely, the rains came, and there were no further serious worries until the mid to late Eighties.

The difference this time was not only that we began to experience hot, dry summers, but rainfall at other times of the year was also lower than average, giving no opportunity for either reservoirs or underground natural water holding areas to be adequately replenished. Added to this problem was the fact that the way of life for most families had become so much more sophisticated, with automatic washing machines the norm, dishwashers growing in popularity, the daily bath or shower now considered essential, and the increasing use of other little luxuries such as private swimming pools, jacuzzis, pressure washers and the like, all consuming massive amounts of treated water.

The prophets of doom feared a shift in climate, with summers becoming hotter each year, warm, dry winters, and a desert situation settling over our green and pleasant land.

This, fortunately, did not turn out to be the case and, after mid-1992, widespread flooding made the news rather than dried-up reservoirs, but it is still essential to examine our use of water and make savings wherever necessary, and the garden is one place where some change in attitude towards watering and some modifications in design can bring about great benefits.

The water-saving garden

Most gardens can be modified to use much less water than they already do. There are many ways to make a garden much more thrifty where supplementary watering is concerned. How many of these ideas are necessary depends very much on geographical location and temporary climatic conditions, but there are few gardens which would not benefit in some way from at least one of these ideas. Remember, too, that cutting down on watering also cuts down on the time spent in looking after the garden – time which you might find more usefully employed in sitting in the garden and enjoying it!

SAVING RAINFALL. Although conserved rainwater is not likely to be sufficient to see you through a prolonged dry spell, it will certainly help to save tap water. In general, plants prefer soft rainwater to tap water anyway, so it is always worth having a supply. Most rainwater is saved in butts or tanks filled from downspouts off the roof – if yours runs directly into a soakaway, there are several products available to divert the water into a container until this is full, when the rainwater will automatically start running into the soakaway again. Devices are available to connect several butts in series. Rainwater butts should always be covered with a lid to prevent green algae growing in the water and mosquito and other water-borne harmful larvae becoming a problem. For anyone with a large garden with an open, unplanted piece of ground near the property, or someone contemplating building a new home, it is worth considering installing a large underground water storage tank from which water can be pumped when necessary.

WALLS, FENCES AND HEDGES. Hedges will require plenty of water to get them established, and strong-growing, tall hedges will remove much moisture from the soil. Consider replacing some hedges with walls and fences, especially openwork ones like pierced screenwork and trellis, which will not cause the same quirky down-draughts as solid structures. Remember that in a very sunny garden, a wall or fence with a hot, sunny face will also have a cool, shady one, so if you want to grow shade-loving species in an unsuitable area, this kind of structure can be useful. If you feel nothing else but a hedge will fulfil the purpose, choose one capable of withstanding drought, such as potentillia for a low hedge or sea buckthorn (*Hippophae rhamnoides*) for a taller one. (See also Chapter 7, page 122.)

PATHS, PAVING AND OTHER HARD FINISHES. In a really problematical situation, much of the cultivatable area can, as a last resort, be covered with paving. As this is to be more than merely functional, choose finishes which are as attractive and com-plementary to the landscape and surrounding architecture as possible, and if large areas are involved, try to incorporate more than one type of finish for additional interest. (See also Chapter 8, page 131.)

THE LAWN. If seeing your lawn turn straw-like every time the temperature rises and rainfall drops off worries you, you may be happier replacing it with gravel or paving. Paving a sunny spot will make the area even hotter, and this will have an effect on the plants you choose in the vicinity. If you cannot live without a lawn, a very high-grade mix will usually recover better after drought than an all-purpose one. If you intend to lawn a large area where water shortage could be a problem, some seed companies will supply you with a special

361

drought-resistant mix not available 'over the counter'.
Raise the mower blades during a prolonged dry spell, and leave the clippings on to prevent excess moisture loss. Do not fertilize or apply weedkillers, especially in dry form, if a period without rain is forecast.

SOIL CONDITION. A humus-rich soil will retain moisture much longer than one containing no organic matter. Keep your soil in good heart by incorporating manure, compost, or any of the other bulky soil additives listed on pages 94–9.

MULCHING. A 1½–2 in. (40–50 mm) mulch of bulky organic material, such as chipped or pulverized bark, farmyard manure, well rotted garden compost, shredded garden refuse or cocoa-shell or, alternatively, a covering of pea gravel, black polythene or porous mulching sheet will help to retain moisture in the soil. Polythene and other mulching sheets can be disguised by covering with a thin layer of soil or gravel.

SUITABLE PLANTS. Moisture-loving plants are nearly always likely to need additional watering in dry spells. With the aid of soil conditioners and mulches, it is possible to grow a reasonably wide range of popular plants, but unless you have a naturally wet area fed by springs, you may have to forget about water gardens and bogs requiring regular 'topping up'.

Plants with grey foliage are generally very drought-tolerant. The grey colour is due to millions of tiny hairs over the leaf surface which cut down transpiration, thus preventing undue moisture loss. Plants with succulent or semi-succulent leaves, such as ivy-leaved pelargoniums, mesembryanthemums and portulaca, will also survive long spells without water successfully, as they store large quantities within their tissue. However, these drought-adapted plants, most of which have originated in warmer climates than our own, are ill-equipped to deal with severe wet and cold. Hairy-leaved plants will often rot during a long wet period, and if the wet leaves are frosted as well, severe damage occurs. Succulent plants can also rot in excessively wet conditions, and will usually die in frost as the stored moisture in the leaves can freeze and burst the leaf cells. Such plants should be used with caution in most parts of Britain, or treated as half hardy and given cool glasshouse protection in winter.

ROCK GARDENS. Many alpines, especially those with succulent

cold-tolerant leaves, like sempervivums, sedums and some saxifrages, are naturally geared up to tolerate conditions receiving very little water. Some rockery plants sold as 'alpines' are, however, merely dwarf forms of shrubs or herbaceous plants requiring normal quantities of water in order to survive. If you wish to grow the widest range of these plants, you may find it better not to construct a raised rock garden as such, but instead create a modified 'scree' level with the ground and mulched with granite chippings or pea gravel. This will dry out less quickly, while providing a cooler root run.

CONTAINERS. Generally speaking, container growing is a water-extravagant form of gardening as most plants grown in containers dry out much faster than if they were planted direct into the garden soil. On the other hand, ornamental tubs and the like can be a very attractive feature of a garden. If for one reason or another containers are essential, use as large ones as possible, fill with soil-based compost, and incorporate water-retaining polymer granules into the compost before planting.

'HARD' LANDSCAPING FEATURES. In a really difficult situation, where it is impossible to grow attractive plants without regular watering, it is sometimes advisable to fall back on features other than living plants. Suitable items would be a well placed and well designed piece of statuary, an attractive seat or even a piece of ornamental low walling. Such features can be used to complement other pieces of hard landscaping, such as paving, walling or fencing.

PLANTING UP. Because most plants are now available from the nursery or garden centre in containers of one sort or another, it has become physically possible to replant them in their permanent positions at almost any time of the year. In the days before containerization, it was virtually impossible to dig up and replant at any other time than when the plant was dormant – that is, in most parts of the United Kingdom, during the period between the end of October and the beginning of April. As far as water conservation is concerned, however, there is a lot to commend continuing to plant only during this time, as this is when the soil is generally at its most moist and when plant roots are in active growth, re-establishing quickly in their new surroundings. It is obvious, therefore, that the amount of artificial watering needed during the period following the move is likely to be much less than if replanting takes place during warmer, drier periods of the year.

AUTOMATIC WATERING AND TIMING DEVICES. As yet these are not approved of by most water companies, as their attitude is that any automated watering device encourages the consumer to use more water. My personal feelings are that a contrivance which enables one to deliver water accurately and for a set period has to be less profligate than wantonly pouring a watering can over a container, when most of it runs off the surface and is wasted, or splashing a hose about indiscriminately.

Automatic watering really comes into its own for container gardening which, if the plants are to receive enough water, is a tiring and time-consuming occupation and can, as I have already said, be extremely wasteful of water. It consists of a framework of ½ in. (15 mm) plastic pipe to which are connected microbore pipe spurs leading to the various items to receive regular watering. Water is delivered accurately to the surface of the soil or compost by means of drip or spray ends. To be fully automated, a battery-operated timing device and pressure-reducing valve should be connected to the tap before the main pipework; the most sophisticated of these timers can now be programmed to deliver water for a desired length of time for one or several periods during the day, every day or on specified days of the week only. Once one has used one of these gadgets for a little while, it becomes possible to judge fairly accurately when and for how long to water, setting the controls to do it all automatically.

Various other appliances are available to run off the main pipework system, such as pop-up lawn sprinklers or a porous hose which is buried in the ground and seeps along its length for the time water is running through it, the theory being that it provides water where it is most needed – at the roots. But whilst it could be argued that to deposit water exactly where it is required rather than distributing it all over the garden regardless of which plants need it and which do not is in itself a saving, my sentiments are that if the garden is properly designed and stocked to take account of the need for a reduction in artificial watering, this kind of apparatus should not be necessary.

THE ANGLIAN WATER CONSERVATION GARDEN

The following list of genera refers to the plan on pages 366-7

1 Drought resistant hedge
Potentilla

2 Hebes and Junipers

3 Semi-shaded borders
Euonymus
Mahonia
Aucuba
Polygonatum
Hedera
Bergenia
Hosta
Chaenomeles
Epimedium
Brunnera
Lonicera

4 Climbers for pergola
Eccremocarpus
Celastrus
Passiflora
Solanum
Wistaria

5 Herbaceous border
Catanache
Geum
Sedum maximum
Agapanthus
Anemone hybrida
Verbascum
Helenium
Ceratostigma
Nerine
Kniphofia
Gypsophylla
Stipa
Bearded iris
Solidago
Potentilla
Crocosmia
Acanthus
Helianthemum
Chrysanthemum maximum
Heliopsis

Ecinops
Erigeron
Hardy geranium

6 Tall shrubbery
Lavatera
Choisya
Hypericum
Berberis
Hibiscus
Kolkwitzia
Eucalyptus
Elaeagnus
Buddleia
Euonymus
Cytisus
Olearia
Tamarix
Philadelphus
Cotoneaster
Escallonia
Cortaderia

7 Low shrubbery
Ceanothus
Genista
Cistus
Rosmarinus
Spartium
Weigela
Berberis (low-growing forms)
Pyracantha 'Red Cushion'
Hedisarum
Olearia x scillionensis
Yucca
Santolina
Cytisus
Spiraea
Elsholtzia
Potentilla
Ulex
Hypericum

8 Scree garden
Arenaria
Geranium (alpine varieties)
Dianthus (alpine varieties)

Sedum
Veronica (alpine varieties)
Campanula carpatica
Leucanthemum
Zauschneria
Sempervivum
Saxifraga
Thymus (dwarf forms)
Phlox (alpine varieties)
Lewisia
Armeria
Cotyledon
Acaena

9 Silver/grey/glaucous beds
(Note: silver/glaucous leafed varieties of the following genera)
Potentilla
Phlomis
Perowskia
Lavendula
Santolina
Eryngium
Artemesia
Ruta
Nepeta
Alyssum
Convolvulus cneorum
Caryopteris
Cistus
Dianthus
Thymus
Asphodeline
Artemesia
Stachys
Achillea
Salvia
Teucrium
Senecio
Ballota
Anaphalis
Helichrysum
Cineraria
Festuca

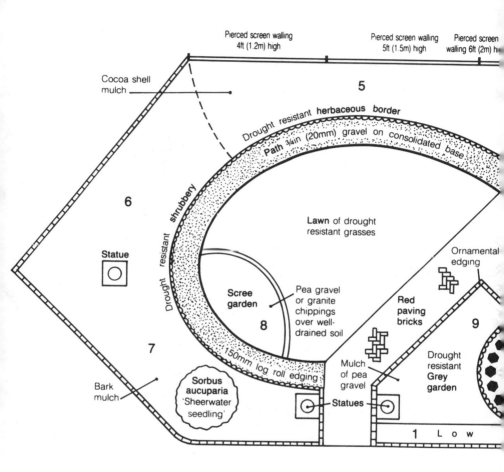

Pierced screen walling
4ft (1.2m) high

Pierced screen walling
5ft (1.5m) high

Pierced screen
walling 6ft (2m) hi⟩

Cocoa shell
mulch

5

Drought resistant herbaceous border

Path ¾in (20mm) gravel on consolidated base

6

Drought resistant shrubbery

Lawn of drought
resistant grasses

Statue

Scree
garden

Pea gravel
or granite
chippings
over well-
drained soil

Ornamental
edging

Red
paving
bricks

9

8

150mm log roll edging

7

Bark
mulch

Sorbus
aucuparia
'Sheerwater
seedling'

Mulch
of pea
gravel

Drought
resistant
Grey
garden

Statues

1   L o w

The Anglian Water Conservation Garden

During a prolonged period of drought in 1991, Anglian Water Services,
aware of a rift between the recently privatized water companies and the
numerous gardeners in the country, decided to set up a demonstration
garden in the east of England, an area of low rainfall even in years of
average rain, to prove that it is possible to have an attractive garden without
the unlimited use of artificial watering, where ideas for economizing on
water and using it sensibly in the garden could be seen in an actual garden
situation.

366

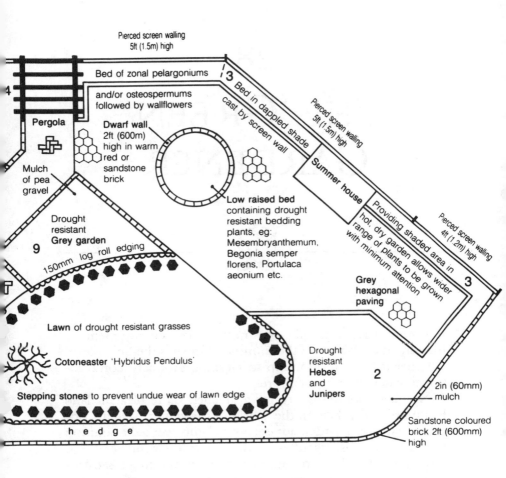

Pierced screen walling
5ft (1.5m) high

Bed of zonal pelargoniums
and/or osteospermums
followed by wallflowers

Bed in dappled shade
cast by screen wall

Pierced screen walling
5ft (1.5m) high

4

Pergola

Dwarf wall
2ft (600m)
high in warm
red or
sandstone
brick

Summer house

Pierced screen walling
4ft (1.2m) high

Mulch
of pea
gravel

Low raised bed
containing drought
resistant bedding
plants, eg:
Mesembryanthemum,
Begonia semper
florens, Portulaca
aeonium etc.

Providing shaded area in
hot, dry garden allows wider
range of plants to be grown
with minimum attention

Drought
resistant
Grey garden

9

150mm log roll edging

3

Grey
hexagonal
paving

Lawn of drought resistant grasses

Cotoneaster 'Hybridus Pendulus'

Stepping stones to prevent undue wear of lawn edge

Drought
resistant
Hebes
and
Junipers

2

2in (60mm)
mulch

h e d g e

Sandstone coloured
brick 2ft (600mm)
high

A 600-sq. yd (500-sq. m) plot was made available at Springfields Gardens in Spalding, Lincolnshire, and I was invited to design a garden which, although fitting into the setting of a public park–like display garden, could be adapted for an average plot attached to a modern house or bungalow. The completed garden was officially opened to the public on 10 July 1992 and, although it has hardly stopped raining ever since, it has nevertheless established itself as a useful source of reference to the many gardeners who have been or are soon to be affected by the compulsory installation of water meters.

28

THE 'GREEN' GARDENER

It cannot have escaped your notice that 'environmentally friendly' is the phrase of the moment. Green is the 'in' colour, whether it be in relationship to cleaning products, constructional materials or horticulture.

Nowhere has this desire for a greener, more pleasant land had more effect than on the world of gardening. When I first began work as a garden adviser, my clients wanted a solution to their problems, regardless of the cost to their surroundings. Now most people who consult me, while wanting a satisfactory answer to their questions, are more aware of potential damage to the environment and are anxious for remedies causing as little harm as possible.

This is a promising trend. In the past, gardeners have received a great deal of criticism for some of the methods they employed to achieve their aims. Much pressure has been brought to bear in recent years for the introduction of more 'natural' forms of cultivation and theoretically this should herald a new beginning for ecology.

The problem is, gardening is anything but 'natural'. Manipulating plants for our own aims is a highly artificial exercise. Left to its own devices, nature would shape the planet very differently from one which is primarily convenient to mankind.

In an overpopulated world, unless action is taken to tackle the problem of providing for the needs and/or wants of a proliferating population at its roots, then any other moves towards protecting the environment of a particular moment have to be a series of compromises. And the ecological situation itself is not a static thing, but alters and adapts as circumstances change through time.

Some points affect the modern gardener very seriously. Through broadcasting and print, he or she is bombarded with conflicting opinions and advice from different lobbies with their own particular axes to grind. Unfortunately, the true picture is often obscured by stentorian propaganda, and the ordinary gardener who just wants to do the right thing is left in utter confusion.

Most issues are not just black or white and, to form the best opinions, it helps to stand back and view the arguments from all sides, especially where they concern the following subjects especially dear to the modern gardener's heart and which are guaranteed to generate more hot air during discussion than the sun itself.

NATIVE PLANTS. It is probably because so much countryside, along with its particular flora and fauna, is being lost to the developers every year that there is a sudden wave of nostalgia for indigenous trees and shrubs and native British wildflowers. This is an excellent concept on the large scale. Enlightened local authorities and appropriate ministries are transforming roadside verges and motorway embankments with copses of young trees and special seed mixes of native grasses blended with wildflowers, creating habitat and in time, one hopes, putting right some of the damage to the environment that has been done particularly in this century.

It is natural to want to carry this concept into our own patch of earth, but the modern compact enclosure which serves the majority of us as a garden is a far from easy place in which to recreate a tiny piece of rural landscape.

For instance, most native British tree species grow much

369

too large in time for all but the largest gardens. Many planning authorities make the mistake of specifying beech, wild white cherry, mountain ash, alder and birch as screening trees around new, small properties, but this is the type of landscaping scheme which can only lead to future problems when the trees have grown so large they obscure light inside and out, their roots have lifted drives and penetrated drains, and their leaves have clogged gutters and downspouts. Modern houses are not 'natural', and with the wealth of ornamental garden trees available, albeit originating outside Britain, it seems misguided sentimentality to insist on only those species which, through one accident of nature or another, were around in this country a thousand or so years ago. Habitat can be created far more successfully in large, open spaces where it can be allowed to develop without hindrance. Pressure should be brought to bear on public bodies, especially county and district councils and other landowning local authorities, to make sure this is the case.

A similar argument applies to native shrubs. Modestly attractive as they are in a garden setting, and excellent for providing a whole host of wildlife with food and shelter, well, so are many non-native species and cultivars. The pyracantha outside my kitchen window which gives the local blackbirds so much pleasure in winter as they strip it bare of its red berries may have its origins in China rather than northern Europe, but it is no less an admirable garden shrub because of this, and the blackbirds do not seem in the least concerned whether it is Chinese or British.

Indigenous wildflowers are vital to the ecology of an area, not just for their attractive appearance, but because they are host plants to many species of butterfly and moth. It is not easy to give over all or part of your garden to their cultivation though, as you will often see recommended. There is much more to growing wildflowers than scattering a few packets of seed or allowing the weeds to grow in your lawn. Particular wildflowers occur in a certain locality because growing conditions are just right for them – the right soil, right light, right control of neighbouring plants by other flora and animal wildlife. In a garden situation, unless these conditions are reproduced fairly accurately, they frequently struggle to survive, looking unsightly and providing little habitat for butterflies and beneficial insects. A wildlife garden, although not impossible to establish both aesthetically and functionally, is not an easy option for the lazy gardener, often under the impression that for 'wild' read 'neglected'. It is, in fact, far harder to achieve successfully than a conventional garden, and requires a great deal of study and understanding of why a specific habitat occurs naturally before ever the first native plant is introduced.

PRESERVATION OF TREES. Britain has suffered very much in the past from the indiscriminate felling of mature trees. Today, having largely seen the error of its ways, it is in danger of suffering from not felling enough.

It is an excellent thing that in the United Kingdom many specimen trees and built-up areas containing mature trees are now protected by Tree Preservation Orders, making it illegal to fell or otherwise interfere with a tree so as to affect its appearance or its chance of survival. However, certain elements of the 'green movement' are tending to become carried away with the preservation of every dying stump or self-sown sapling at all costs, resulting in many suburban areas becoming overgrown with badly sited large trees to the extent that the quality of life of both residents and gardens can be affected. One garden I know is situated in an area with a 'blanket' TPO in force. Between this garden and the one next door was a line of ugly, mutilated poplars, well past their best and beginning to cause great structural problems as they were within feet of house walls on either side. The owners of both houses felt that removal was the only future, and yet it took months of applications, site discussions, council meetings and letter writing before consent was finally obtained. It was interesting to see that because the trees had been regularly lopped to reduce their height, and they were growing in such a confined space anyway, the only place in the district where it was noticeable that they had been removed was from the kitchen windows of the two affected properties!

Many planning authorities go to great lengths to preserve unsuitable trees, often past their best, in unsuitable situations when freely granting planning permission for the land on which they are growing, so the development is forever affected by having to take account of these trees. Far better, if in their wisdom these planning gurus feel building development is the best use for the land in question, to encourage a scheme in which young, appropriate trees and new houses are planned together to mature alongside each other to overall good effect in years to come. Trees are not immortal, they grow old as the rest of us do, and it is not necessarily a sin to make way for the young.

THE PEAT ISSUE. A decade ago, if you wanted to use peat in the garden, you did so with a clear conscience. Then some of our best-known media gardening pundits suddenly became aware that a lot of the peat being used in this country was being dug from environmentally sensitive moorland sites, destroying habitat and rare plant and animal wildlife which it would be almost impossible to re-establish.

Gardeners and horticulturalists, of course, got the blame, because it was well known that they used peat on the garden and in potting composts. It was not as well publicized that much more peat than they would ever be able to use was, and still is, being burned as fuel.

It was also kept somewhat quieter than it ought to have been that much peat used for horticultural purposes is actually dug from lowland sites of little agricultural value and even less environmental significance, but of great economic importance to the area as many local lives depend on the industry. This kind of fact does not have the same sensational 'green' ring about it.

The situation is now that one cannot own up to using peat for any purpose whatsoever without being branded a destroyer of the world. It is useless to suggest that the vociferous anti-peat brigade visit the restored peat workings in parts of Somerset, where what was once low-grade pasture-land has been transformed into wetland habitat supporting many more species of wildlife that it did previously, or to remind them that the Norfolk Broads, so valuable both for habitat, recreation and landscape, were themselves originally created by digging for peat. They will not be satisfied until all gardeners abandon all use of peat for good.

These are fine ideals, and because of the pressure they have brought to bear on compost manufacturers and other inter-ested parties, no doubt there will come a time when this is possible, but at the time of writing this book, it seems they have a long way to go.

There are several alternatives to peat. The first to be

introduced was processed bark, followed by treated and composted wood waste and paper waste, then coir, the husk off the coconut, which was until a few years ago used mainly for matting.

The problem with composts based on wood waste and by-products is that, whereas the composition of peat, and therefore compost made from it, tends to be fairly stable and predictable, these are inclined to vary in composition and texture depending on the raw materials used, and situations have occurred when one batch of a proprietary product had been an excellent growing medium, whereas the next one was, frankly, rubbish. This, no doubt, is a problem which should be overcome eventually, given enough research.

Coir-based composts have a problem of a different nature, in that they do not retain plant nutrients and to keep plants growing strongly in coir compost necessitates much more regular feeding than in peat-based ones. This itself raises another environmental issue, in that fertilizers washed out so readily are likely to find their way into watercourses – in recent years a growing worry has arisen about the amount of nitrates found in drinking water and other salts ending up in streams and rivers. A further environmental argument heard against the use of coir is that all the raw material has to be imported into this country, using vital and irreplaceable fuel resources to transport it here. Moreover, many people feel that the Third World countries exporting coir would probably be able to put it to better use in their own agricultural systems.

Non-peat composts are considerably more expensive than peat-based ones, and it is hard to imagine that more than a handful of environmentally concerned individuals will pay twice as much for a product that works only half as well.

The peat issue is really about an environment changing as the balance of nature alters. As an increasing human population develops an increasing interest in gardening, with its sophisticated techniques and the expectation of first-class results, some aspect of the world around us is almost bound to change to accommodate it.

SHREDDING AND COMPOSTING V. BURNING. Most gardeners enjoy a good burn-up. There is something very satisfying about seeing a pile of rubbish reduced to a pile of ashes which can then be spread on the garden as a useful source of potash. Unfortunately, bonfires in recent years have become very unpopular, with smoke and smuts dirtying property and gases polluting the upper atmosphere.

The alternative to this is composting. Garden compost is a useful soil conditioner and it seems only right that the plants which have derived so much benefit from the soil during their lifetime should give a little back at the end of it.

Unfortunately, composting is not without its own drawbacks. In breaking down, the rotting material releases methane gas, one of those which contribute to the so-called 'greenhouse effect', when the heat produced at the surface of the earth cannot escape through the layer of pollution above. In a balanced eco-system, no one substance should be produced so excessively as to threaten the environment, but with a system dominated by any one species, such as ours is, excesses and imbalances are bound to occur, and the production of methane – from composting garden rubbish, rotting farmyard manure, and even the intestines of domestic food animals – is one of them.

The other shortcoming of composting is that much garden refuse is too large or too woody to break down well. The laborious way round this is to cut everything into small pieces with secateurs before adding it to the heap. The easier method is to use a shredder.

This, too, has its opponents. Most shredders, although they can efficiently reduce a large heap of woody rubbish to a small pile of ready-to-spread or compost material, are either powered by electricity or petrol, therefore both consuming vital and dwindling energy resources. They are also incredibly noisy, so adding to the already out-of-hand noise pollution of our so-called civilized society to which modern gardeners sadly contribute a great deal, with their power mowers, spin-trimmers, hedge clippers, chain saws, cultivators and all the other buzzing, whining paraphernalia that it now seems hard to live without.

As bonfires are becoming more and more anti-social, it is increasingly difficult to dispose of badly diseased or heavily infested material hygienically. All pests and diseases are destroyed in a hot fire, but they are unlikely to be in even a well made compost heap which heats up well in the centre. As it is inadvisable to leave such rubbish lying about in the

374

garden, the only answer is to take it to the local tip, to become somebody else's problem.

CHEMICALS. Next to the peat issue, chemicals are probably the most emotive topic on the gardening front at the present time.

Garden chemicals are basically either organic (derived from natural sources) or inorganic, though some compound fertilizers and insecticide mixtures can be a combination of both.

Those gardeners who prefer only to use chemicals of natural origin often shun those from any other source. It is quite possible to control most common pests and diseases using organic chemicals alone, and it is not necessary to use artificial fertilizers to produce bountiful crops. However, the mistake is often made that all organic chemicals are empathetic to the environment and non-injurious to an eco-structure, whereas all artificial ones are harmful. For instance, one of the most efficient insecticides is derived from the pyrethrum plant, yet its range is so wide that it can wipe out many beneficial insects along with the 'nasties' causing the problem. On the other hand, pirimicarb, a man-made product, is specific to aphids and will leave other insects untouched. It is possible to make up a whole range of home-grown 'brews' to wage war on the little beasties which deface your plants, and yet, because concentrations of chemicals in them tend to vary, none of them is theoretically as safe, or as regularly efficient, as those manufactured under strict laboratory conditions and quality control. And whether a fertilizer is derived from organic or inorganic materials, it is still capable of being over-applied, causing it to build up in the soil to undesirable levels, or seep away into adjacent watercourses.

In an ideal world, where all plants and animals were in perfect balance, there would be no need for supplementary treatments of any sort. Pests would have their own predators, and even diseases would have sufficient parasitic controls to keep them in check. The Nitrogen Cycle would work efficiently, those plants and animals removing nutrients from the planet in order to live returning the same elements to the earth on death.

However, this system has never worked particularly efficiently, even before the world became overpopulated, resulting in plagues and pestilences. Over the long term, everything would either return to normal or evolve accordingly, but we are here *now*, we do not generally see things in the long term, and to augment our synthetic lifestyle, it becomes necessary to take action against the things that pose a threat.

When it comes to pest – and even, to some extent, disease – control, probably the most efficient and ecologically sound method is to use artificial barriers. Cabbage root fly can be prevented by putting a collar of old carpet or similar on the soil around the stem at planting time, for example, but better still is to cover whole areas to be kept free from pests with crop-protection sheeting. Growing fruit in a cage will also do away with the need for spraying, but even this method of defence has its disadvantages, the main one being that in excluding the plants from harmful insects you also exclude beneficial ones and wildlife as well, so those pests which are impossible to keep out, such as slugs and snails, are able to run rife. And in an ornamental situation, there is little point in having a pretty border if it is covered up so you cannot see it.

To be truly 'environmentally friendly' really requires a change of attitude in gardening. In the flower garden, we should not be so worried about the odd blemish, but work at the overall effect rather than the detail. Most pests and diseases are temporary anyway, and disappear after a time. If they do not, then maybe we should examine whether in fact they have a place in the modern garden anyway. New plant varieties are being bred all the time, which eventually should cut down the necessity for controls of this kind. Do not worry too much if your vegetable and fruit crops do not look like those on the supermarket shelves – it will have taken a lot of chemicals to get them looking like that. The domestic garden of the future should be one where people, wildlife and plants can exist side by side to the detriment of nothing or nobody. In the meantime, help in moderation and with caution may be necessary.

THE USE OF RAW MATERIALS IN THE GARDEN. Every time I or one of my colleagues recommends the use of certain raw building materials in the garden, especially gravel or sand, we are swamped with letters from people asking us if we realize how much we are destroying the environment by their mention. They have to be quarried, causing damage to the landscape, and the nuisance created by the lorries which transport them around should not be encouraged.

Admittedly this is true, but the short-term upheaval can in the long term be beneficial. In my part of the country – eastern England – some of the best wetland beauty spots were man-made during the extraction of sand and gravel. The fact that many worked-out gravel pits are used for land-fill is not so much the fault of the removal of the raw materials, but the fact that we have not yet got our act together properly regarding the disposal and recycling of domestic and industrial waste.

And I am always curious to know how these grumblers manage to survive long enough to complain. Presumably they do not live in houses of brick, stone or tile, as the raw materials for these had also to be removed from the ground. Timber shelters would entail chopping down trees and straw is the by-product of environmentally unfriendly monoculture. Apart from living in a hedge bottom, all that remains is grass huts, and mighty uncomfortable they must be in our unpredictable British climate!

Gardeners are unlikely to please all parties, however thinking, caring, and conscientious they might be. At best, all they can do is consider the world they share and not knowingly cause unnecessary nuisance or harm. Then on balance, the pleasure and benefits they provide should far outweigh all other issues.

INDEX

*Page references for charts and illustrations are shown in **bold** figures*

(HT, large flowered), 187, 188, 191, 194, 200; miniature, 187, 188, 191–2, 194, 195, 196, 200, 225; rambling, 187, 192, 195, 196, 201; shrub, 185, 187, 188, 192–3, 195, 196, 200; standard, 187, 195, 196

rotary cultivators, 54–5, 63

rubbish, disposal of, 61, 65–9, 77, 373; *see also* bonfires, compost and composting

rubble, use and disposal of, 76

sand, 26, 30, 85, 91, 93, 376–7; *see also* soil types

saws, 47–8

screens (boundaries), 110, 128

secateurs, 46–7

seed, 12, 13, 15, 17, 27, 30, 31; *see also* propagation

seed trays, 13, 27, 30

seedlings, 19, 28, 30, 93

shade-tolerant plants, 225

shears, 46

sheds, 318–22, 341; choosing and materials, 318–19, 321; hybrid (with greenhouse or summerhouse), 324; maintenance, 322; obtaining, 321; siting, 321–2

shredders, garden, 57

shredding, 374

shrub roses, *see* roses

shrubberies, 208–9

shrubs, 205–19, 236; acid-loving, 271; for acid gardens, 274–5; advantages and disadvantages, 205–7; after-care, 212–13; choosing, 210–11; dwarf, 225; in herbaceous borders, 176; obtaining,

209–10; pests and diseases, 215–16; planting, 211–12; propagation, 216–17; pruning, 213–14; removal of, 73–4, 128; suggested plants, 218–19; uses, 207–9

silt, 31, 85; *see also* soil

soil, 11–12, 15, 16, 26, 30, 31, 32, 33, 62, 63, 82–101, 361; acidity of, *see* acidity, pH, sour soil (below); aerating, 62, 85, 91, 93; assessment, 87–8; colour, 87; composition, 82–4; nutrients, 85; pH, 84–5, 86, 89; subsoil, 32, 83–4, 86; topsoil, 33, 83

soil additives and conditioners, 88–91, **98–9**; *see also* fertilizers, lime, manure, perlite, potash

soil types (and how to improve): assessment, 87–8; chalk, 86–7; clay, 85; loam, 84–5; marl, 87; peaty, 86; sandy, 86; silt, 85–6; sour, 13, 16, 30, 85; stony, 87

sowing, 31, 44, 159, 162

spades, 41–3

sphagnum moss, 31; peat, 269, 270

spin trimmers, 55

strawberries, *see* fruit, soft; strawberry barrels, 331

suckers, 32

summerhouses, 322–4, choosing, 323; obtaining, 323; siting, 324; *see also* sheds

surfacing, 131–41; concrete, 134–5; grass, 139; gravel, 132–3; paving slabs, sets, etc., 135–8; tarmacadam and asphalt, 133–4; timber, 138–9; *see also* drives, paths, patios